CROSSING BORDERS,

CLAIMING A NATION

CROSSING BORDERS,

CLAIMING A NATION

A History of Argentine Jewish Women, 1880–1955

SANDRA MCGEE DEUTSCH

DUKE UNIVERSITY PRESS

Durham and London

2010

Printed in the United States
of America on acid-free paper ∞
Designed by Amy Ruth Buchanan
Typeset in Dante by Achorn International
Library of Congress Cataloging-in-
Publication Data appear on the last
printed page of this book.

Duke University Press
gratefully acknowledges support
from the Dr. and Mrs. W. H. Timmons
Professorship of Borderlands History,
University of Texas, El Paso,
which provided funds toward
the production of this book.

CONTENTS

List of Illustrations and Tables vii
Acknowledgments ix
List of Women xi

Introduction 1

1. "If the Water Is Sweet" 13
Jewish Women in the Countryside
2. "I Worked, I Struggled" 42
Jewish Women in Buenos Aires
3. "A Point of Connection" 73
Pathways into the Professions
4. "Not a Novice" 105
Prostitutes
5. "A Bad Reputation" 123
Family and Sexuality
6. "What Surrounds Us Dissatisfies Us" 148
Leftists and Union Members through the 1930s
7. "A Dike Against Reaction" 172
Contesting Anti-Semitism, Fascism, and Peronism
8. "We the Women Have to Do Something" 205
Philanthropies and Zionism

Conclusion 236

Appendix 249
Notes 257
Bibliography 319
Index 363

LIST OF ILLUSTRATIONS AND TABLES

MAPS

1. Argentina xiii

2. North and Central Argentina xiv

3. Jewish Colonization Association Agricultural Settlements xv

4. Greater Buenos Aires xvi

FIGURES

1. German Jews in Colonia Avigdor, Entre Ríos, wait for their furniture 18

2. Sephardi foods 33

3. Jews dressed to dance the *pericón* 39

4. A *conventillo* (tenement), Buenos Aires 49

5. An overcrowded public school, Villa Crespo, 1935 58

6. A party for Matilde Israel, a bride from the Izmir community, 1938 65

7. Dr. Sara Satanowsky, 1918 90

8. Cipe Lincovsky 95

9. Berta Singerman 97

10. Algarrobos Cemetery, Colonia Mauricio 109

11. A dance in Colonia Avigdor, 1938 131

12. Fenia Chertkoff 155

13. A *recreo infantil* (after-school center) 158

14. Victoria Gucovsky 160

15. Isa Kremer 188

16. Relatives of political prisoners in Villa Devoto prison, 1941 194

17. Fanny Edelman 202

18. Leaders of the of Moisesville OSFA (Organización Sionista Femenina Argentina) center, 1939 210

19. Women selling flowers and candies for the Asilo Argentino de Huérfanas Israelitas, 1925 213

20. Berta de Gerchunoff at the Villa Crespo OSFA center, 1939 230

APPENDIX TABLES

1. Jewish Agricultural Population 250

2. Literacy Rates for Women over Six Years Old, by Origin, 1914 250

3. Origins of Families Registered in Mediterranean Jewish Communities in Buenos Aires, 1960 251

4. Foreign-Born Jewish Population in Buenos Aires by Birthplace, 1936 251

5. Jewish Population in Argentina, by Province and Territory 252

6. Percent of Women in the Labor Force by Age, in Greater Buenos Aires, 1960 253

7. Percent of Jewish Women Age Fourteen and Older in the Labor Force by Birthplace, in Greater Buenos Aires, 1960 254

8. Literacy Rates for Women by Age and Origin, in Buenos Aires, 1936 254

9. Literacy Rates for Women Age Fifteen and Older, in Buenos Aires, 1936 255

10. Occupational Distribution of Women in the Labor Force Age Fourteen and Older, 1960 255

ACKNOWLEDGMENTS

Numerous individuals and groups assisted me with this project. Ana Weinstein and Hélène Gutkowski supplied sources, interviewees, expertise, and *cariño*. The Centro de Documentación e Información sobre Judaísmo Argentino Marc Turkow, directed by Weinstein, and the Instituto Científico Judío (IWO), under Abraham Lichtenboim, were indispensable. Mónica Szurmuk and Richard Walter read the entire manuscript; Judith Elkin, Donna Guy, and Margaret Power read large portions of it; and Jeanne Delaney, Judith Friedenberg, Nicolás Iñigo Carrera, Marion Kaplan, Daniel Lvovich, Cheryl Martin, Pamela Nadell, and Jorge Nállim read chapters. Patricia Flier, Noemí Girbal, and Dora Schwarzstein, whose death I mourn, provided university bases and much more. All of the aforementioned gave warm and invaluable assistance. I give special thanks to AMILAT, Haim Avni, Dora Barrancos, Margalit Bejarano, Luis Blacha, Adriana Brodsky, Susana Carioli, Thomas Cohen, Irene and Rosa Cusien, Mabel Damián, Torcuato di Tella, John Fahey, Federico Finchelstein, Nora Fistein, Jorge Gilbert, Silvia Hansman, Adela Harispuru, Mieke Izjermans, Elizabeth Jelín, Robin Judd, Esther and Salo Koval, Asunción Lavrin, Jeffrey Lesser, Fanny Mandelbaum, Enrique Martínez, John Moore, José Moya, Kristine Navarro, Raanan Rein, Fernando Rocchi, Eva de Rosenthal, Mariela Rubinzal, Leo Senkman, Robert Singerman, Lila Sintes, Rosalie Sitman, José and Ilse Smilg, Kathleen Staudt, Lynn Stoner, Graciela Tevah de Ryba, Lili Trumper, Alejandra Vitale, Docha and Osías Wainer, Paloma Wainstein, Mark Wasserman, Barbara Weinstein, Rosa Woscoboinik de Levin, and Ruth and Robin Young. I am deeply grateful to Valerie Millholland, senior editor of Duke University Press, for her advice and support. I thank Leigh Barnwell, also of the Press, for her painstaking help.

The following facilitated my research in many ways: Simone Abadi, Esther Abourachit, Vicky Aguirre, Nora Alvarez, Ann Ankowski, Bernardo Armus, Lois Baer Barr, Daniel Bargman, Lawrence Bell, Graciela Ben Dror, Elena Berflein, Alicia Bernasconi, Julio and Celia Bernator, Andrés Bisso, Scarlet Bowen, Berta Braslavsky, Julia Schiavone Camacho, James Cane, Donald Castro, Etel Chromoy, Vanda Ciporin, Marcela Crocce, Golde Culperstein, Maceo Dailey, Marcelo Dimenstein, Bruria and David Elnecavé, Myriam

Escliar, Rosita Faingold, Norberto Ferreras, Matis Finkel, Lea Fletcher, Alicia Frohman, Raúl García Heras, Florinda Goldberg, Marta Goldberg, Nancy González, Norma González, Oscar González, Angel Grushka, Sofía Gutman, Will Guzmán, Joel Horowitz, Juana Hülze, Liz Hutchison, Steve Hyland, Sherry Hyman, Marta Jurkowicz, Renata and Pedro Kanof, Ilse Kaufman, Natalia Kohen, Alfredo Kohn Loncarica, Clotilde Lainscek, Julia Levi, Carolina Koss, Yolanda Leyva, Mirta Lobato, David Maldavsky, Lola de Marcoff, María Gabriela Mizraje, Ana Monín, Judit Moskovitch, María Silvia Ospital, Helena Pardo, Margarita Pierini, Amalia Polak, Beth Pollack, Mario Ranalletti, Rosa Rapaport, Rosa Perla Resnick, Brenda Risch, José Roffé, Graciela Roitman, Rachelle Rubenstein, Mina Ruetter, Rita Saccal, Basil and Linda Samuel, Edgar Samuel, Catalina Saugy, Hernán Scandizzo, Silvia Schenkolewski-Kroll, David Sheinin, Ana María Shua, Heather Sinclair, Ruth Sommer, Nora Strejilevich, Elena Sujoy, Judy Sweeney, Horacio Tarcus, Fabiana Tolcachier, Liliana Tuccio, Pablo Vila, Carlos Waisman, Tea Wolf, Efraím Zadoff, and Alicia Zarranz.

Institutions and foundations backed this project. Charles Ambler, Sam Brunk, Howard Daudistel, Steve Riter, and Michael Topp facilitated financial support from the University of Texas, El Paso (UTEP). I thank the UTEP Oral History Institute, UTEP University Research Institute and Faculty Development Leave programs, library grant program of the University of Florida Center for Latin American Studies, Council for International Exchange of Scholars (CIES)-Fulbright; Littauer Foundation, and National Endowment for the Humanities.

Directors and employees of archives, libraries, and other organizations gave me enormous assistance. In addition to those cited in the bibliography, I thank the Asociación Comunidad Israelita Latina de Buenos Aires, Biblioteca Juan B. Justo, Biblioteca Nacional, Biblioteca Nacional del Maestro, Centro de Investigaciones y Difusión de la Cultura Sefaradí, Federación de Entidades Culturales Judías (ICUF), Federación Libertaria Argentina, Mundo Israelita, Seminario Rabínico Latinoamericano Marshall T. Meyer, Unión de Mujeres Argentinas, and Universidad Di Tella library, all in Argentina. I appreciate the aid I received from the Institute of Contemporary Jewry of Hebrew University and the Israeli National Library, in Israel; the British Library Newspaper Reading Room, in London; and, in the United States, the UTEP Library and Special Collections, and the libraries of the University of New Mexico, University of Texas, Austin, and University of Florida.

I wish I could describe how each person and institution helped me, but I will have to confine myself to describing the contributions of one individual. A fellow dreamer and true partner, William Durrer helped and supported me throughout this project.

LIST OF WOMEN

Absatz, Flora: A Polish immigrant, textile worker, and union leader

Aslán, Hélène R. de: A philanthropist and president of Ezras Noschim and Consejo de Mujeres Israelitas

Attach, Regina: Raised in Argentina and Damascus, she was abandoned by her father until adolescence and became a seamstress.

Braslavsky, Berta Perelstein de: An educator and member of the Communist Party, Junta de la Victoria, and Communist-aligned intellectual groups

Chertkoff, Fenia: An educator, Socialist leader, and advocate of women's rights

Edelman, Fanny: A leader of the Communist Party and Unión de Mujeres Argentinas who joined the Spanish Republican cause

Efron, Paloma ("Blackie"): A jazz singer and radio and television host

Elnecavé, Bruria: A Zionist leader who moved from Bulgaria to Palestine to Buenos Aires

Felman, Mika: An anarchist turned Communist turned Trotskyist, she fought in the Spanish Civil War.

Flami, Golde: A stage and screen actress who performed in Yiddish and Spanish

Furman, Luisa: A teacher and volunteer in Villa Domínguez, fired under the military dictatorship of 1943–45

Fux, María: A pioneer of modern dance

Genkin, Dora: A Polish immigrant, Communist, and textile-union leader

Gerchunoff, Berta Wainstein de: A Socialist feminist who became a Zionist leader

Gilenberg, Teresa: A Polish worker active in the Communist Party and Liga Argentina por los Derechos del Hombre

Gucovsky, Victoria: A leading Socialist writer and orator, and a member of a distinguished Socialist family

Hassid de Treves, Catherine: From Izmir, she settled in the province and later the city of Buenos Aires.

Isaharoff, Judith Cohen de: A Sephardi Zionist leader from Samarkand

Kanutsky, Guitl: A Polish tailor, union leader, Bund member, and Communist

Katz, Ilse: A German immigrant who moved from Entre Ríos to Buenos Aires

Langer, Marie Glas de: A physician and psychoanalyst from Vienna

Lincovsky, Cipe: An actress in the Yiddish theater and in Spanish-language plays and movies

Liniado, Elena: A Damascene woman abandoned by her husband who raised her children in a tenement

Mayo, Luna de: She moved from Izmir to Posadas, where she and her husband ran a store and she participated in philanthropy.

Mesulam de Levy, Estela: A member of a family from Istanbul, her education was curtailed.

Nissensohn, Sofía Rabinovich de: She grew up in Carlos Casares, studied in Buenos Aires, and became a Zionist leader.

Scheiner, Rosa: A dental surgeon who moved from the Socialists to the Socialist Worker Party and probably became a Communist

Schliapnik, Clara: A physician, activist in Villa Domínguez, member of the Junta de la Victoria, and socialist Zionist

Schnitman, Sara: A physician and researcher who experienced discrimination

Simsolo, Victoria: A pioneering Sephardi physician

Singerman, Berta: A Russian immigrant who became a famous reciter in Spanish

Tawil de Ini, Chola: Of Aleppine and Palestinian descent, she became a Zionist.

Woscoboinik de Levin, Rosa: A physician, pioneer oncologist, and Communist

Yadid, Farida: An Aleppine immigrant and resourceful mother

Yadid de Chami, Matilde: Farida's daughter, a factory worker and journalism student

Ziperovich, Rosa Weinschelbaum de: An educator, union leader, and Communist in Santa Fe Province

MAP 1. Argentina. Maps 1–4 prepared by Raed Aldouri, director, Regional Geospacial Service Center, UTEP, and William Nelson.

MAP 2. North and Central Argentina.

MAP 3. Jewish Colonization Association Agricultural Settlements.

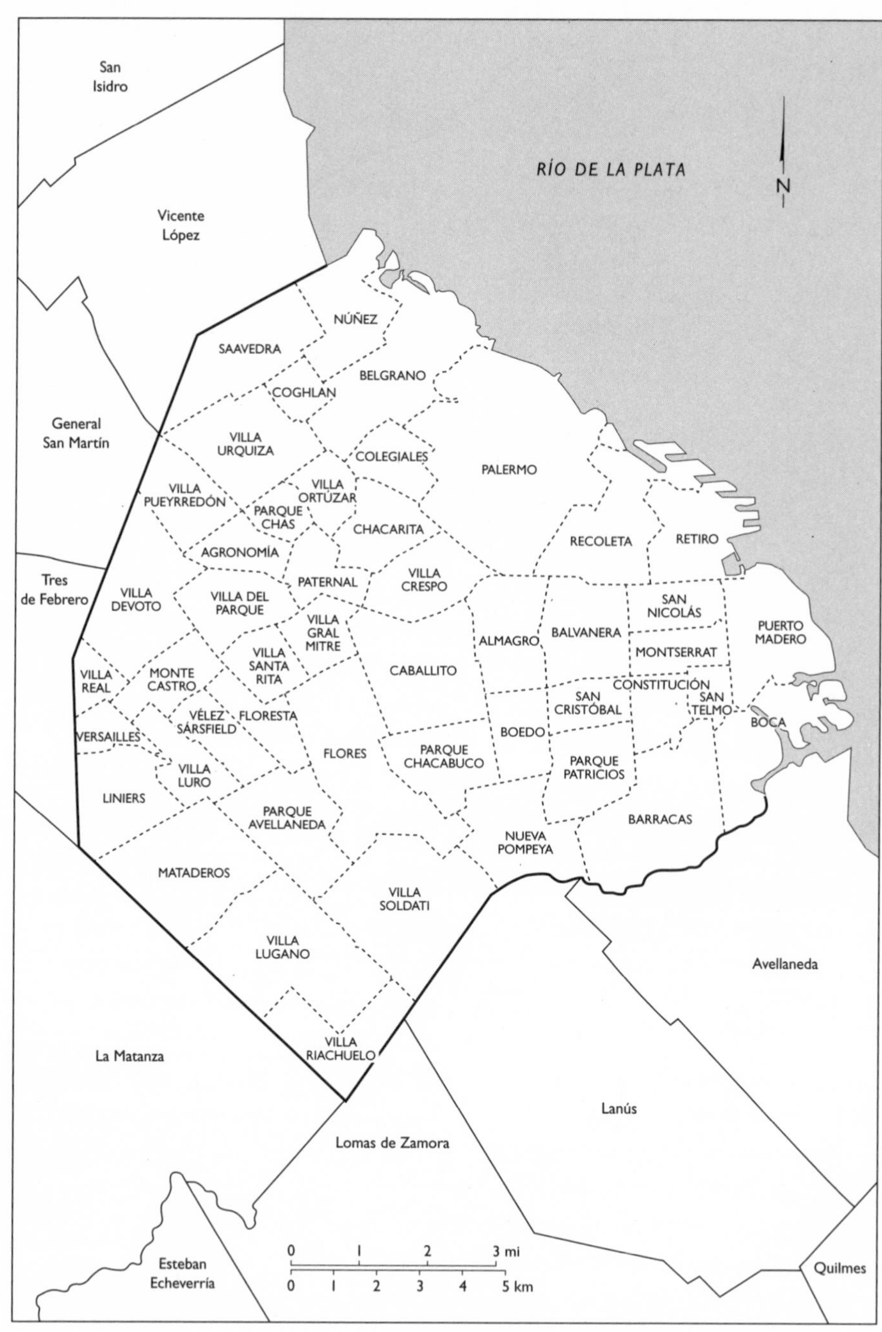

MAP 4. Greater Buenos Aires.

INTRODUCTION

Specialists who study borders note that national identities are often forged at the edge of society. This project began as an inquiry into how a group doubly situated on the margins, as Jewish and female, helped build the larger imagined community of Argentina. However, I found that Argentine Jewish women were not always marginal. The tension between their centrality and marginality helped determine their fates along with the history of this nation.[1]

As they journeyed toward the center, Jewish women played crucial roles in Argentina and its Jewish community, the largest in Latin America and the third largest in the hemisphere. They created institutions that tightened communal bonds and identities, and they helped establish farms, unions, the Communist Party, and the national cinema, activities critical to Argentine development. This study explores the contributions of immigrant and first-generation women to their communities and nation in the face of discrimination from both quarters. It addresses the following questions: How did Jewish women partake in the Argentine dreams of pluralism and upward mobility and negotiate cultural, political, class, and gender borders? Were these women insiders or outsiders? How did transnationalism influence their activities? Through what means did they claim spaces in the nation and engage with national projects? How does putting them at the center revise Argentine history?

Studies of immigration to Latin America typically focus on the experiences of men. Concentrating on women instead reveals issues vital for Jews and other groups that have been ignored in the literature, such as sexual norms, teacher training, and sociability. Thus, this work provides a more rounded portrait of immigrants' lives.

This is the first broad, book-length examination of the history of immigrant women of any background and their descendants in Latin America.[2] It is also the first such treatment of Jewish women in the region. Myriam Escliar's short book, *Mujeres en la literatura*, analyzes aspects of Argentine Jewish women's lives but does not focus exclusively on their history. Gloria

Rut Lerner's thesis, "La historia del Asilo Argentino," examines the Jewish girls' orphanage in Buenos Aires, and Beatriz Kushnir's *Baile de mascara* studies Jewish prostitutes in Brazil. There are several collections of Latin American Jewish women's reminiscences, but they are not scholarly studies.[3]

Historical works on Latin American Jews rarely mention women, and when they do, it is usually as prostitutes.[4] While prostitution is a significant topic, one wonders why researchers and observers have ignored other aspects of Jewish women's lives.[5] They have blotted out equally compelling images of Jewish women as agricultural pioneers, film stars, and human-rights activists. One reason for this concentration on sex workers is that Argentines have tended to see Jewish women as the sensual others. Another is that Argentine Jews were preoccupied with Jewish prostitution because they thought it hurt their reputation.

We know little about Latin American women's sexuality in the 1900s, except for prostitution.[6] Even the studies of this practice, however, focus on attempts to curtail or control it. This book instead treats the intimate experiences of a wide range of Jewish women, particularly the vast majority who were outside the sex trade.

One must place this study within the context of Argentine Jewry, which is not a monolithic group. Argentine Jews represent a set of Eastern, Central, and Western European and Mediterranean communities that in turn fragmented by language and region. Jews from around the Mediterranean began to arrive in this immigrant society about 1880, which is the starting date for my study. Some traced their ancestry back to the expulsion of Jews from Iberia in 1492, and their families had communicated in forms of Spanish for centuries. Others, lacking this connection, spoke Arabic. Today the first and sometimes both groups are commonly known as Sephardim, yet throughout most of the period under examination here, such Jews instead identified themselves as Damascenes, Moroccans, and the like. Since the category of Sephardim did not truly exist in Argentina until the 1940s, when Jewish women helped construct it, I prefer to refer to the people who had lived under Muslim rule as Mediterranean.[7] Jews from Russia and other Eastern European locations began to come en masse in the late 1880s, after the earliest Mediterranean arrivals. The descendants of Eastern European immigrants form the majority of Argentine Jews. A few Central and Western Europeans reached Argentina before the 1930s, but the era of fascism witnessed a large-scale migration of German speakers, and a tiny one of Italian speakers. A small number of Holocaust survivors and North Africans arrived after the Second World War, completing the Jewish communities. The book concludes at this juncture, in 1955. Class and residence patterns as well as place of origin divided Argentine Jews. And just as there is no single Argentine Jew, there is no single representative Argentine Jewish woman.

Most experts in Jewish studies have recognized that one cannot cast all Jews in the same mold. In general, scholars have chosen to specialize in one particular group, such as the Sephardim or Ashkenazim (Europeans of Yiddish-speaking descent). Instead I study Argentine Jewish women in all their diversity, to understand the similarities and differences among them.

How does one define a Jewish woman? The usual answer is that the daughter of a Jewish mother is Jewish, whether or not she declares herself as such, practices the Jewish religion, or belongs to Jewish organizations.[8] Sander Gilman, however, points to other possible definitions of Jews.[9] Focusing on religious observance and communal involvement as the key indicators of Jewishness, Argentine constructions leave many people outside the category.[10] Some Argentines of leftist backgrounds tend to privilege class and political affiliations and repudiate ethnic sources of identity. They would not consider as Jewish a revolutionary unconnected to Jewish groups or an atheist, no matter what the person's ancestry, cultural preferences, or evolving self-definition.

One must consider these views, for they suggest how some Argentines see themselves and others.[11] Nevertheless, they rest on fixed, monistic notions that contrast with scholarly perceptions of identities as fluid, contingent, and multifaceted.[12] Furthermore, it is unclear how some of the women in question identified themselves, and many Jewish Argentines would claim them as Jewish. I include these persons in the study, but out of respect for Argentine opinions, I describe the women as being of Jewish origin.

This study examines how Argentine Jewish women created identities; forged relationships; worked inside and outside the home; and helped build labor, political, and communal groups. It does not treat their religious, child-rearing, or consumption practices, or their production of art, music, or fiction. Neither does it systematically analyze how Jewish men or non-Jewish Argentines constructed these women as subjects. The book focuses on women's lives, not on comparing women's experiences with those of men, although it shows how relations with men affected women.

Recently the history of gender, defined as constructions of male and female and the power relations they symbolize, has eclipsed the history of women in Latin America.[13] While I have contributed to this trend,[14] in this book I return to women's history, which may buck the historiographical tide. I do so because many aspects of women's experiences remain unknown, and Jewish women offer a useful lens through which to view the history of Argentine women and of Argentina. This is not a compensatory exercise. Without basic knowledge of women's familial, political, professional, and associational roles, it is difficult to write gender history, or indeed any kind of history. Putting women at the center brings overlooked issues to the forefront and provides fresh insights into broad phenomena. As Kathryn Kish Sklar noted, women's history offers "a new perspective on worlds jointly inhabited by women and men,"[15] suggesting that one cannot isolate women from the gender context. This, then, is a history of Jewish women within the context of gender relations in Argentine Jewish communities and the larger society.

Put another way, this is a history of women and borders. Borrowing from research on how the U.S.-Mexico border shapes identities in this region, scholars have utilized this conceptual tool to illuminate metaphorical as well as physical boundaries. Borders are a compelling paradigm for understanding the choices people make in their everyday lives. I use the word in several ways. It refers to spaces where Jewish women encountered people of other backgrounds: on territorial boundaries or within neighborhoods, towns, movements, professions, and kitchens. Borders also separated customary from new styles of deportment. The immigrant generation brought languages, practices, and experiences from the home to the host society. In their daily routines, women navigated cultural boundaries, choosing from the local and the foreign and utilizing what I call the border skills of flexibility, adaptation, and reinvention. Indeed, borders offer opportunities for creative change. Straddling several worlds, Jewish female immigrants, along with many of their daughters and granddaughters, inhabited what George Sánchez calls a "cultural borderland." Finally, borders represented limits imposed on Jewish women, such as those that bounded the home and community of origin, as well as gender norms and prejudice. Jewish women reacted to these lines in different ways, contesting, crossing and crisscrossing, avoiding, reinforcing, and reproducing them.[16]

Kathleen Staudt and David Spener found that "the lines themselves create special kinds of spaces that often differ from the core, the mainstream, or the heartlands. Borders also imply margins."[17] For example, Jewish women who settled in the countryside inhabited a frontier zone. Margins and center, however, refer to power relations as well as physical locations. The well-off and accepted women, the insiders, occupied the metaphorical center; women who suffered from poverty and discrimination were outsiders, the ones who lived on the edges. Their sex and minority-group status seemingly made all Jewish women outsiders. Throughout the period under study, Argentina denied women citizenship rights. Women could not freely choose their occupations until 1926, vote at the national level until 1947, or exercise full authority over their children until after 1955.[18] Nor could women participate fully in the most important Jewish institutions. Anti-Semitism also hurt Jewish women, especially in the 1930s and 1940s. Jewish women were not completely marginalized, however. Their stories reveal how the Jewish communities and national society excluded and included them, and how Jewish women pushed toward the center, complicating our understanding of patriarchy and anti-Semitism.[19]

Considerations of borders are intertwined with transnationalism, another theme of this book. Members of immigrant communities who "take actions, make decisions, and feel concerns within a field of social relations that links together their country of origin and their country or countries of settlement" engage in transnationalism. So do persons involved in organizations and cultural exchanges that operate across national boundaries.[20] Jewish women did not completely leave Europe and the Mediterranean behind: from Argentina, they followed the Russian revolution and other events overseas. By participating in antifascist and leftist movements, some sought to create a more just Argentina and Europe. Circulating through countries, Jewish prostitutes participated in transnational sexual commerce. A few truly transnational women influenced countries beyond those of their birth or residence by transforming their art and ideas and constructing global organizations. Zionist women laid claim to both Israel and Argentina.

When Jewish women claimed Argentina as their own, they were participating in state formation. "State" means a pact of rule; "state formation" denotes how those in power effectuate their rule by engaging the popular classes. The ruling class maintains dominance by alternately coercing, regulating, and convincing the rest of society to accept or submit to its projects, which specify who belongs to the nation and who does not. Therefore state and nation are interconnected. Inequalities notwithstanding, the interaction between those above and those below goes both ways. The people below accept, rework, or contest projects imposed from above. Not only elites and armies build states; so do commoners, as they help shape the imagined community of the nation and tie their dreams and identities to it.[21]

Largely missing from the literature on state formation in Latin America is work on women's participation.[22] This book sheds light on that understudied dimension. By creating hybrid identities, Jewish women linked themselves to Argentina. They also did so in ways as prosaic as seeking government favors, celebrating national holidays, and marrying for love rather than by parental dictate.[23]

Choosing one's husband related to the sense of freedom that many Jewish women associated with their adopted country. Through this connection, they engaged with the liberal project that was consolidating in Argentina when Jewish immigration began and that was hegemonic until the 1930s. Jews everywhere have gravitated toward this ideology, which promoted their emancipation.[24] Argentine liberalism stressed universal secular education, individual mobility, immigration, and freedom of thought, religion, and association, all of which Jewish women embraced. Many Jewish women appreciated liberal approval of voluntarism, as well as the endorsement by Domingo Faustino Sarmiento, Argentina's president from 1868 to 1874, of women's expanded roles. Other liberal tenets, such as free-market economics and a democratic political model that was autocratic in practice, did not appeal to all Jewish women. Nor did liberal disparagement of some ethnic groups, including Jews. Some liberals expressed ambivalence about Jews, although generally accepting them as long as they joined the melting pot.[25]

Despite its problematic nature, many Jewish women appropriated and reworked liberalism. Fighting to include themselves and other outsiders, they felt entitled to share in the liberal promise of opportunity and liberty. Jewish women's organizations fostered networks, community involvement, and representative governance, practices known as social capital. Creating social capital meant engaging with the liberal state to make it more pluralistic and democratic.[26]

Jewish women's reshaping of the liberal project demonstrates that it was not static, as some historians think. Indeed, in the 1930s and 1940s, Argentine leftists, including some Jewish women, adapted and defended aspects of liberalism.[27] Here is one example of how putting Jewish women at the center illustrates larger historical processes.

New projects became hegemonic by the 1940s: right-wing nationalism, or Nacionalismo; and its successor, Peronism, which eventually incorporated liberal and reformist elements. Both, however, were authoritarian.[28] Juan Perón's first administration (1946–55) had a complex impact on Jews, which is another reason for extending this study until 1955, when he left power. Peronist policies uplifted Jews economically, repressed Jewish and other leftists, and obstructed yet also aided some Jewish groups.[29] Nacionalismo sought to exclude Jews from the nation; Peronism largely kept Jews from entering the country, yet it included many already there. Some Jewish women contested both projects. They combated Nacionalismo and negotiated with Peronism, advancing their own notions about who belonged to the nation and how they should share its benefits.

This study, then, reassesses twentieth-century Argentine nationalism. Most scholars, including myself, have painted it as authoritarian and exclusionary.[30] If many Jewish women fashioned their own nationalisms, other Argentines must have, too, and their efforts await examination. Again, inserting Jewish women illuminates broader currents in Argentine history.

One of these broader currents is the emerging debate over whiteness. People in the United States constructed Jews as nonwhite, a lesser shade of white, or an in-between racial group until the 1930s or 1940s.[31] In Brazil, with its large population of African descent, Jews were seen as both nonwhite and nonblack, threatening and privileged at the same time.[32] Specialists generally equate Argentina with whiteness, regarding the immigrants (except those from East Asia and neighboring countries) and native-born elite as indistinguishably white. According to such views, the upper class considered some immigrants better than others but apparently saw all as of the same race. At the same time, Argentina erased many people of color; its armies killed Indians, and folklorists, census takers, and other government officials obscured black and indigenous identities.[33] José Moya asserts that since immigration resulted in an overwhelmingly European population, whiteness was unimportant,[34] but this depends on how Argentines defined whiteness. The history of Argentine Jewish women complicates the notion that Argentines regarded all European and Mediterranean immigrants as equally white. Sometimes locals questioned Jewish claims to whiteness, and some Jewish women wondered if they fit in this category.

I depict these themes through the experiences and thoughts of Argentine Jewish women. Their detailed stories reveal their varied and complex encounters with the state, borders, transnationalism, inclusion and exclusion, and race. The stories go beyond dry facts to show how women felt about these processes and to inject life into history.

Social, cultural, and political in nature, these themes are primarily explored qualitatively. I use available statistics on Argentine Jewish women, but they are inadequate in some respects.[35] Therefore, to discern patterns I examine multiple cases and perspectives drawn from the surviving sources. I rely on many voices to establish these patterns and highlight the diversity of Argentine Jewish women, whose experiences cannot be distilled into those of a few individuals. To keep these voices straight, I ask the reader to consult the list of recurring characters. While I make some comparisons with women of other origins, firm conclusions about the specificity of Jewish women's experiences must await similar studies on other groups of women.

The women's narratives come primarily from oral histories, autobiographical writings, and the files of the Argentine branch of the antiprostitution Jewish Association for the Protection of Young Girls and Women. The historian who uses such sources faces a gender-related problem, among others. The main Argentine Jewish oral history archive, the Archivo de la Palabra of the Centro de Documentación e Información sobre Judaísmo Argentino Marc Turkow, largely contains interviews with men, and men have penned many of the memoirs. Argentines often recommended that I speak with men, although these authoritative persons often could not answer my questions about women. Even some women focused in their writings on the men in their lives, partly because exploring their relationships to men helped women reflect on their identities and aspirations. I read these sources from the margins, paying close attention to "offhand remarks and casual biographical details" on women, as well as the gaps and silences so revealing of female marginalization.[36] I also supplemented these works by interviewing women and collecting women's memoirs that had been privately printed or had received little notice.

I conducted about eighty interviews, mostly with women. I looked for individuals who had reached maturity well before 1955 and represented the diversity of Jewish women. Two specialists on Argentine Jewry, Ana Weinstein and Hélène Gutkowski, gave me invaluable assistance in locating interviewees. Recommendations from activists and scholars, as well as word of mouth, helped me find others. I also met likely candidates at communal, cultural, and political gatherings.

Memory and purpose affect oral testimonies and autobiographical writings. Remembrances change and can reflect the interviewee's or author's aims of the moment. A subject places her narrative within the context of an individual or collective identity that may not reflect identities held in the past. To justify her life and communicate its importance to others, she may downplay or highlight certain facets in accord with her current views and intended audience.[37] For example, some women emphasized their Jewishness because that is how they identify themselves today, because asserting such identities is more acceptable now than before in Argentina, or because interviewees thought that was what I wanted to hear. One must take these elements of storytelling into account when analyzing oral histories and memoirs.

Other dilemmas of oral history concern the relations between interviewer and interviewee. While I respected the women and thought they respected me, both sides asserted power in the relationship. I prepared a list of questions to ask each woman, and initially I stuck to my agenda. Yet interviewees had their own agendas and often preferred to stress what was important to them, sometimes avoiding my questions to return to points they considered critical. They wanted to focus on what they were proud of having accomplished, and these parts of the dialogue usually were the most fruitful. For example, they revealed women's activism in solidarity and antifascist movements overlooked by scholars and unknown to me. Over time I learned to ask open-ended questions, listen to what the women chose to discuss, and not overly direct them. If they brought up intriguing issues, I followed up with questions. Respect for the speaker, however, does not entail blind acceptance of her story.[38]

The subjectivity inherent in personal storytelling can be useful. As Ann Farnsworth-Alvear observes, "the inaccuracies and exaggerations of people's own descriptions of their lives" reveal their "interpersonal, emotional world."[39] Impressions of anti-Semitism fit into this category. Whether Jewish women genuinely experienced discrimination may be difficult to judge; what counts is how they perceived their relations with other Argentines.

These considerations indicate the limits of using oral history and autobiographical writings to locate facts. Since relatively few documents recorded Jewish women's deeds or thoughts, however, one must use these sources to find information not available elsewhere. They are vital for grasping the texture of daily life, women's construction of identities and ties to the nation, and what women consider significant.[40] One must compare the documents to other works and evaluate them carefully, but this also is true for other sources. All have biases, gaps, purposes, and intended audiences, and all are partial.

To a lesser extent than oral history and memoirs, I use literary works as sources, and one should interrogate these as well. Blurring the distinction between literature and history, postmodernists claim that all texts are constructed and all writings are historical artifacts. I agree with Lynn Hunt's observation that novels and police reports are not the same, although the difference is difficult to explain.[41] I prefer to mine historical documents for specific information and fiction for sensibility and customs. Yet there may be overlap, for some novelists report on situations they have researched firsthand, choosing a fictional genre to develop their characters or advance theories that seem credible but cannot be proven. Several novels on Argentine Jewish prostitution fit these characteristics.[42] Fiction sheds light on contemporary debates and people's thoughts, feelings, and intimate experiences. It describes emblematic situations, sentiments, and characters that resonate among readers. I also found it useful to compare fictional depictions with other sources.[43]

Utilizing interviews, memoirs, fiction, and other materials, the chapters in this book explore the themes of state formation, borders, inclusion and exclusion, transnationalism, and race through the lives and perceptions of diverse Jewish women. To highlight these intersections between themes and women's lives, the book's organization is primarily thematic rather than chronological. Chapters 1 and 2 offer the context essential for understanding the discussion. The first chapter focuses on women farmers and residents of the interior of Argentina, and the second on women in Buenos Aires. Work, education, leisure, and adjustment to Argentine life are the primary topics. In kitchens, clubs, streets, and workplaces, women navigated cultural, ethnic, and gender borders, in general observing the lines that separated Jews of distinct origins. Patriarchy and economic hardship relegated many women to the fringes. Others, marginalized intellectually, managed to move toward the center by studying and promoting learning. Jewish women claimed spaces in Argentina through reading local authors,[44] voluntarism, and participation in patriotic events. Except at certain moments, they experienced relatively little anti-Semitism until the 1930s, although their status and race were ambiguous.

Chapter 3 represents a pioneering look at how Latin American women experienced the professions, examining Jewish educators, medical personnel, and entertainers. Although poverty, opposition by family members or males in general, antileftism, and anti-Semitism created barriers, numerous women experienced acceptance in their fields. Skills acquired abroad helped these professionals move to the center of their disciplines, even as the whiteness of some of the entertainers was debated. Some transnational figures altered cultural developments outside Argentina. Many Jewish women linked their careers to the construction of a sense of nationhood more inclusive than the prevailing model.

The transnational sex trade brought Jewish sex workers to Argentina and prompted the view of Jewish women as the sensual other. To track prostitution and keep women out of brothels, the global Jewish Association for the Protection of Young Girls and Women established a branch in Buenos Aires. Chapter 4 studies the entry of some Ashkenazi women into prostitution and their experiences as laborers and members of social networks. Contesting domination by reformers, pimps, and madams, the women sometimes earned more than other female workers, controlled their labor, and achieved upward mobility.

Chapter 5 discusses courtship, marriage, and sexuality among other Jewish women, charting crossings from foreign to local norms, which did not necessarily evolve toward permissiveness. Fearing that Catholics would label Jews as promiscuous, Jewish groups supervised lower-class women's sexuality. Thus, prominent Jews marginalized these Jewish women on sexual grounds to claim spaces for Jews as a whole in the nation as respectable citizens. Nevertheless, some women transgressed borders through extramarital sex and marriage to Catholics. Many others asserted their choices less visibly and resisted the authority of parents, husbands, and communal leaders.

A vital part of Central and especially Eastern European identities was political, as the next chapters show. Chapter 6 discusses anarchists, Socialists, Communists, and union members, largely before the mid-1930s. Chapter 7 continues the story, adding antifascists. Battling fear, repression, and notions of women's place, some Jewish women crossed borders to join leftist groups, where they helped construct alternatives to liberal and right-wing projects. Through transnational campaigns against fascism, anti-Semitism, and the Axis, they resisted local and foreign authoritarianism. Their struggles for a more inclusive nation aroused hostility from powerful sectors, including the military government (1943–45) and Juan Perón's administration (1946–55), which shunted Jewish and other militants to the sidelines.

Chapter 8 treats women's participation in Zionism and philanthropy.

While most charities strengthened the boundaries enclosing the Jewish communities, female Zionists weakened these borders as they helped unite many Jews behind support for a Jewish nation. In the process, Mediterranean women participants helped forge a broad new sense of Sephardi identity that superseded narrow particularisms. Even as many Jewish women aided their communities and Israel, they highlighted their *argentinidad* by linking their festivities to patriotic holidays and imitating Catholic foundations. Some activists fostered transnational exchange through their participation in global networks. Their demands for a greater voice in Jewish affairs met male opposition. Yet various governments, including Perón's, accorded favors to women's groups, suggesting they were closer to the center of Argentine society than that of their own communities.

The conclusion revisits the themes discussed earlier and situates Argentine Jewish women in historiography. It shows how they fit within and revise the literature on social and political currents, women, Jews, and immigrants. Focusing on Jewish women highlights popular constructions of nationalism and democracy, the fluidity of liberalism, and the racial hierarchy, among other topics.

The book demonstrates that Jewish women were both included and excluded. Anti-Semites and some members of the political and professional elites did not accept them, and Jewish men excluded them from leadership. Many non-Jewish neighbors, colleagues, and political actors, however, included them. Their origins notwithstanding, Jewish women helped build a pluralist nationalism and spread it in schools and other arenas. Argentine Jewish women were foreigners as well as disseminators of national culture, insiders as well as outsiders.

CHAPTER ONE

"If the Water Is Sweet"

Jewish Women in the Countryside

If the water is sweet, we will have a good future.
—Bela Trumper de Kaller, interview

The miracle takes place: they have become Argentines.
—Violeta Nardo de Aguirre, "Canto a la Colonización Judía"

Some Ashkenazi women pioneers in Argentina were known for their optimism and determination. When Bela Trumper de Kaller and her family reached their plot near Moisesville, Santa Fe, she tasted the water from the well. Although the land was barren and parched, she claimed that the sweetness of the water heralded a good future.[1] Desolate huts surrounded by tall weeds and cattle trails greeted the first Eastern European Jews who disembarked from the train at Carlos Casares, Buenos Aires, en route to Colonia Mauricio. Yet nothing flattened the women's spirits, observed Marcos Alpersohn, one of the settlers: "When I remember those dignified and valiant women of the colonization I see them wrapped in a brilliant luminosity . . . In their imagination they painted the future with the most beautiful colors and transmitted these to their husbands, believing firmly in an easy future, free and happy in the new home, sweetening with this image the sorrows of a gloomy present."[2]

Rural experiences have been studied and celebrated more than any other aspect of Jewish life in Argentina.[3] Many Ashkenazim remember the agricultural colonies nostalgically. "All our life was simple, clear and transparent, with the blue color of goodness and honesty," recalled one woman.[4]

Despite these memories, most Jewish immigrants did not stay long on farms or in small towns. Starting in 1889, many Jews from the Russian empire settled in the countryside. Around the same time, Moroccans established themselves in small towns, followed by migrants from the Ottoman empire. Eastern Europeans and Germans joined the agriculturalists between the wars. But today only a tiny percentage of Jews remains in those settings. Like other Argentines, most Jews found better opportunities in cities.

While short-lived, their rural sojourn was significant. In 1895 a majority of Jews were living in the agricultural colonies, and by 1914 about a quarter lived on these lands and another quarter in nearby towns.[5] Thus, a considerable percentage of the early immigrants became Argentines in the countryside. By proving themselves in arduous pioneer conditions, they demonstrated that they belonged in this land. Their pride in their achievements contrasted with the frustration experienced by Jews and other Argentines during the turbulent times after 1930. These factors help explain why many Jews remembered rural life as a golden era.

The positive perceptions of women reflected these achievements and their crucial roles in them, which intersect with the themes of this study. Regarding state formation, they became Argentines alongside their male relatives, imagining and constructing the nationality. Jewish women helped create the farms and stores that cemented them to their new homeland, as did the children they raised there. Contrasting the sweetness of liberty with czarist and Nazi persecutions, they linked their destinies to the nation that had accepted them. The social capital that many Jews built promoted democratic engagement and a sense of belonging. Many Jewish women not only adopted liberal and progressive beliefs but participated in shaping them.

Jewish women in rural areas negotiated borders. They lived in border spaces, where they met people of different backgrounds who acquainted them with local customs. Jewish women alternated between the new and the old, inhabiting a cultural borderland. While some scaled barriers that had confined women to domestic chores, most reinforced gender, racial, and communal walls.

Poverty, illiteracy, and gender norms marginalized many Jewish women, as did sporadic anti-Semitism. Through education and voluntary associations they trudged toward the center. Their quest for higher status in their communities and the larger society met varying degrees of success.

Eastern and Central European and Mediterranean Jewish women settled in the hinterlands. Linguistic and cultural differences separated them, as did their times of arrival. Nevertheless, all faced borders, exclusion, and the challenges of state formation in the rural milieu. This chapter moves back and forth in time to treat their encounters with these themes.

Work and Settlement

Eastern and Central European Jews[6] became farmers and ranchers on peripheral lands in Entre Ríos, Santa Fe, Buenos Aires, La Pampa, Santiago del Estero, Río Negro, and Chaco, the first of which hosted the most settlements (see maps 1–3). The Jewish Colonization Association (JCA)—founded in 1891 by Baron Maurice de Hirsch, an Alsatian philanthropist—controlled most of these tracts and the accompanying colonization. The JCA provided families with steamship tickets, land, a primitive dwelling, livestock, seed, tools, and other necessities. The colonists had to pay the JCA for their farms and found themselves in onerous conditions. Never plowed, most of the land was of marginal quality. Allotments were often better suited for cattle than farming, but they were generally too small to make ranching feasible. Natural calamities such as droughts and locusts struck the colonies regularly. Many immigrants lacked farming experience, while others brought methods unsuited to the rough terrain. Conflicts with paternalistic and sometimes arbitrary JCA male administrators compounded the problems. It is unclear how many Jews passed through the colonies, but at their height in the mid-1920s, 33,000 Jews resided on the land and another 10,000 in nearby towns (see table 1 in the appendix). Those 43,000 people represented approximately a fourth of Argentina's Jewish inhabitants. About 300 German-speaking farm families settled in Entre Ríos, Santa Fe, Buenos Aires, and La Pampa in the 1930s, briefly replenishing the declining rural Jewish population.[7]

Moroccan and Ottoman Jews journeyed individually to the interior; any aid they received came from family members already in Argentina. Arriving from the 1870s on, the 802 Moroccans who lived outside the capital in 1914 mostly resided in railroad towns in Chaco, Entre Ríos, Santa Fe, and Córdoba. In these locations, including JCA colonies, they established fabric and general stores that often were branches of *porteño* (Buenos Aires) businesses owned by relatives or friends. Reaching Argentina by the turn of the century, a few Turkish and Syrian Jews became peddlers in the interior. Some saved enough money to establish urban businesses.[8]

Exceptions to the rule of individual settlement were the graduates of Alliance Israélite Universelle (AIU) academies whom the JCA sent as administrators and teachers to the colonies. A French philanthropic association, the AIU founded schools in Muslim Mediterranean and West Asian countries to educate and Europeanize Jewish children. The best students received scholarships to complete their studies in Paris. Since many spoke Ladino (Judeo-Spanish) or other forms of Spanish, the AIU hired its graduates, including a few women, to teach their coreligionists in Argentina.[9]

One must place Jewish women within the context of women's work in the interior. Long involved in cottage industries and farm labor, native-born women—often *mestizas*, or women of indigenous descent—over time were forced into low-paying service jobs or moved to cities. Women made up 17.1 percent of agricultural and livestock workers in 1895, but only 7.9 percent in 1914.[10] These figures probably did not include Jewish and other immigrant women farmers, who have received little attention from census takers or scholars.[11]

Eastern European and German Jewish women shared the burdens of country life. Mothers and daughters strung wire fences, planted trees, and plowed, sowed, weeded, and harvested the fields. Against the wishes of fastidious mothers, some girls cleared the land, chopped down trees, prepared wood for sale, and herded animals. Others obeyed their mothers and confined themselves to so-called women's work in the home. A JCA administrator praised one female colonist for taking excellent care of her orchard and vegetable garden, duties common among women. Women milked the cows, gave water to the animals, and made butter and cheese. Their tasks included raising poultry and preparing food for peons and harvest workers. Often they sold eggs, dairy products, and garden crops in nearby towns. If their families prospered to the point of keeping bank accounts and financial records, some women helped manage them. Women continued these chores after their husbands died, now as farm supervisors.[12]

Mothers and daughters also had domestic chores. They "adorned the poverty" of their homes, whitewashing and decorating walls and constantly cleaning. Women carried water from sometimes distant wells and gathered cow dung to make fires. In those days before electricity, washing and ironing were arduous tasks. Women also prepared meals, baked bread, and made jams and other conserved foods from their produce. After the evening meal, they made and repaired clothing by candle- or gaslight until late. While they worked, women and older daughters minded the often numerous younger children.[13]

The isolation and harsh conditions demoralized and marginalized many Eastern European women. Some wanted to return immediately to their homeland, despite the pogroms there. An elegantly clad resident of an Entre Ríos colony wept as she blamed her mother for sending her to a university in Europe instead of teaching her household skills. A female correspondent for *El Campo*, a periodical devoted to Jewish rural life, reproached farmers for not improving their wives' lot.[14] The monotony and seclusion of the colonies also drove some Moroccan teachers and their spouses to petition the JCA to let them leave their posts.[15]

Arriving forty-odd years after the first Eastern Europeans, Germans regarded their new surroundings with a mixture of dismay and hope. A twenty-year-old woman reached Entre Ríos after four months of rain had left mud everywhere. While she saw the difficulties as an adventure, they reduced her mother to tears, even though she had propelled the move to Argentina. It was hard for older women, who remembered the ease of life in Europe before Hitler, to adjust to poverty and backbreaking work. Relief over their escape from Nazism, however, tempered their grumbling. The newcomers Ilse Katz and her family thought they finally had their own place from which no one could expel them. Still, anxiety about loved ones who had been left behind added to fears of marginalization in an unknown land.[16]

After clearing the land and establishing a farm, German immigrants needed cash even more than women's unpaid labor in the fields. When disaster struck the Katz family—locusts devoured their grain, foot-and-mouth disease infected their cattle, the father became ill, and debts mounted—Ilse saw employment in the city as the only solution. She and other girls went to work in Buenos Aires and sent their wages home.[17]

Like other immigrant farming women in Argentina, Jewish women were excluded from landownership.[18] The JCA only accepted women as colonists if they were widows of men who had received land titles; those women were among the few who joined the cooperatives that played a major role in settlement life. Farmers' daughters and other women experienced in rural tasks unsuccessfully petitioned the JCA for land. Only one woman, head of a family, had received a plot by the early 1900s.[19] A handful of women, generally widows or Socialists, participated in cooperative meetings but were never leaders in the movement. As sometimes occurred elsewhere, widows had a greater voice and more property rights

1. Newly arrived German Jews in Colonia Avigdor, Entre Ríos, wait for their furniture. Centro de Documentación e Información sobre Judaísmo Argentino Marc Turkow.

than wives did. Although the Socialist-leaning *El Campo* favored their involvement in cooperatives, not until the 1970s did women assume greater roles.[20]

A few women fought to become insiders. Born in 1912 in Colonia Lucienville, Entre Ríos, Dora Schvartz shared farming duties with her father and rode horses with relish. Her readings led her to debate agricultural techniques, marketing, and cooperativism with fellow members of the Centro Juvenil Agrario, a social and intellectual group that she served as secretary, and with her fiancé. As a young single woman, she began to attend cooperative assemblies and provincial congresses of cooperatives, but she never became an officer.[21]

It was not necessarily easier to live in towns. Luna de Mayo left Izmir, Turkey, for a one-room shack without running water in a slum in Posadas, Misiones. She and her children waited there daily for her husband to bring her his earnings from peddling so she could buy food. Well-educated and clad in Parisian silks, Señora Hassid, also of Izmir, had trouble adjusting to San Pedro, Buenos Aires, where her husband established a business. As the town lacked sidewalks when she arrived in 1928, she wondered where to put her feet as she walked.[22]

As in Eastern Europe, Jewish women worked in family businesses and other enterprises in towns. One woman ran a lumber and charcoal business with her husband in Charata, Chaco. She was in charge of selling and often supervised the workshop; after her husband's death, she ran the entire establishment. Another widow took over her husband's peddling job in Carlos Casares, Buenos Aires. Such roles were not confined to Ashkenazim. Once her husband set up a general store, Luna de Mayo sold goods there. A fellow Izmiri, Regina Mendes de Salón, worked alongside her husband in their shop in Corrientes, tending to her babies between customers. Her husband's death and bankruptcy pauperized the illiterate Mendes, and she and her seven children found work taking care of a synagogue, moving to a house on its grounds. Mendes sewed for clients and sold home-cooked food to support her family.[23]

Ashkenazi women also needed to earn incomes. Like Mendes, they prepared food for weddings and other celebrations and labored as dressmakers and seamstresses. Some women ran rural commissaries, while others gave music lessons. A young woman who obtained an honors music degree in Rosario returned to Moisesville, the bustling center of Jewish rural life in Santa Fe province, to establish a small conservatory in 1923. Cooperatives hired female clerical workers, and a few women supported themselves through prostitution.[24]

Midwifery was a vital occupation. In the early years, few rural women who delivered babies had formal training. In one community in the early 1900s, the shoemaker's wife served as midwife. When called, she would stop repairing shoes, wash her hands with water, dry them on her dirty apron, and pronounce herself ready. As the lack of hygiene led to many infections and deaths, the pioneer doctor Noé Yarcho resolved to train a midwife for the colonies surrounding Basavilbaso, Entre Ríos. An opportunity arose when he met a woman from that town while treating her granddaughter. His instruction was brief, consisting of little more than showing her what to do and telling her to cut her nails and clean her hands with rock salt, as there were no disinfectants.[25]

Deborah Davidovich—who with her husband, Miguel Kipen, came to a colony near Villa Domínguez in 1912, when she was twenty-six—was an early Argentine-trained midwife. Socialist intellectuals who had escaped from Russia for political reasons, the couple knew little about farming and fared poorly. Davidovich had studied nursing and massage in Geneva and decided to learn midwifery. Leaving their son with her husband on the farm, she took their newly born daughter to Paraná, the provincial capital, where she pursued her education. When Davidovich received her degree, they returned to the countryside, where her impoverished patients, mostly other colonists, often paid her with food rather than money. She moved to nearby Villaguay to take a paying job; the children stayed with their father on the farm, and they visited each other when possible. Economic exigency, as well as the couple's belief in women's advancement, enabled Davidovich to cross gender borders by living and working apart from her family, which was highly unconventional.[26] Other Ashkenazi midwives studied in a less unusual manner at Russian and Argentine schools, some from Entre Ríos aided by provincial subsidies. Thus the government helped these Jewish women provide vital services and earn a living.[27]

Nurses trained in Europe labored alongside the first doctors in the colonies. Early in the 1900s, Ana Pikelín served as Dr. Yarcho's nurse for sixteen years, assisting him at the Hospital Clara in Villa Domínguez and in his visits to rural patients. After Yarcho's death, Olga Rogalsky, another nurse, joined her physician husband at the Hospital Clara, where they worked together for six years. One of the few professionals among the German women who arrived in the 1930s, a Frau Neumann served as a nurse in the hospital in Bovril, Entre Ríos.[28]

Locally educated Ashkenazi women slowly joined the small number of female professionals, challenging communal barriers that discouraged women from studying and entering the occupations. At first female and male dentists from large cities toured the colonies to treat patients, but eventually practitioners set up clinics: for example, a young woman graduate of the Universidad de Buenos Aires settled in Moisesville in 1928. Another woman returned to this town in 1936 as a notary. An early Argentine-born female university graduate from the colonies earned her degree in pharmacy in Córdoba in 1919.[29]

The first female physicians in the rural areas came from well-off, assimilated Russian families. Educated in Zurich, Dr. Paulina Weintraub settled with her engineer husband in Entre Ríos and began to assist Dr. Yarcho at the Hospital Clara in 1911. Weintraub served the colonies for ten years.[30] Dr. Clara Schliapnik emigrated with her family from Besarabia to Buenos Aires at the age of four. She married a fellow medical student and graduated in 1928 with a specialty in pediatrics, a field considered acceptable for women. The Hospital Clara hired the couple to head the facility from 1930 to 1945, essentially getting two doctors for the price of one. Because this arrangement was a bargain for the community and enabled both spouses to work in one place, there were several husband-and-wife medical teams in the colonies.[31] Such jobs helped women escape marginalization and work in their field.

As in the dentists' case, women locally born and trained eventually replaced European physicians. One woman who grew up in Lucienville, Entre Ríos, studied pharmacy and later medicine in Paraná. After graduating, she established an obstetrics clinic in Bernasconi, the town near Colonia Narcise Leven, La Pampa.[32]

A few AIU-trained teachers in the JCA colony schools were women, including Vida Malatón de Benzaquen of Tangier, who taught in Carlos Casares; a Señora Sabah of Algeria, who exercised her profession in Moisesville; and a Maestra Soussia, who worked in Rivera, Buenos Aires. All appear to have taught alongside their husbands, which rendered their work acceptable.[33]

The most privileged rural women were married to JCA teachers and administrators. A number saw themselves as queens of their small kingdoms, according to some of their resentful subjects. In the early years, these women taught culture and grooming to schoolgirls. Born in Palestine of Polish descent, Iona Makoff reluctantly followed her agronomist husband to Entre Ríos in the 1920s. Based in Basavilbaso, a tree-lined railroad hub and Jewish agricultural hub, she lectured the colonists on Zionism and Jewish tradition but socialized little with other women, whom she regarded as below her cultural level.[34]

A gulf separated insiders like Makoff from most female pioneers, the outsiders who cared for their families under precarious circumstances. A few immigrants brought skills, capital, and luxurious household goods, but most came with little. One's baggage, however, did not completely determine one's fate, for the wealthy Miguel Kipen could not sustain his farm, and the originally impoverished Señor Mayo established a successful business. A number of families prospered and paid off their mortgages, whereas others lost their land or never acquired any.[35] These class boundaries were apparent in the schools.

Education

Education offered Jewish girls the possibility of moving toward the center of society—if they could access it. Few schools graced the Argentine countryside, where illiteracy rates were high.[36] The JCA pledged to build a primary school for every hundred rural families, eventually establishing seventy-eight schools. Most offered three grades; some went up to six. The schools devoted half of each day to secular subjects and instruction in Spanish, and the other half to Jewish education. After the national government took over the schools between 1919 and 1923, JCA teachers offered the Jewish component on other premises. Intending to create modern, assimilated Jews, JCA schools were coeducational.[37]

However limited, these schools offered more learning to girls than most of their Eastern European and Mediterranean mothers had received. Of women over the age of six in 1914, 59.8 percent of those born in Argentina were literate, compared to 55.6 percent of those born abroad. Russian Jewish women had advanced in secular education by the turn of the century. Nevertheless, Russian women in Argentina—most of whom were Jews—were less likely to be literate than immigrant women as a whole, or than those of Italian and Spanish origin: only 48.2 percent could read and write (table 2). While some Mediterranean-born mothers had studied in AIU schools, a majority probably had received little if any instruction.[38]

The German speakers who came to Argentina in the 1930s reversed the pattern. Adult women in this group were relatively well educated, but their adolescent daughters generally worked in the fields, in the household, or in service positions in Buenos Aires. Few resumed the schooling that had been interrupted when they left Europe. The younger girls and those born in Argentina attended local primary schools, only a few continuing their studies elsewhere.[39]

Gender and economic concerns influenced the responses of Eastern European immigrants to their daughters' opportunities for schooling. At first, most parents were reluctant to send their daughters to school or did not realize the JCA expected girls to attend. Over twice as many boys as girls were pupils in Mauricio in 1898.[40] Many parents did not approve of coeducation or deemed reading and writing irrelevant for girls. Jews were among the many parents who could not afford to pay matriculation fees, or buy clothes and supplies for their children, or forgo their children's labor. A father in La Capilla, near Villa Domínguez, who could not buy smocks for his entire brood told his youngest daughter to learn from her older sisters, who attended school.[41]

Yet some adult women regretted their lack of learning and did not want these limits to constrict their daughters. They enrolled their children in schools and supervised their educations. Some mothers carried their children on horseback to the first school in Mauricio, founded in 1892, and complained when they thought the teacher neglected his duties.[42] Thanks to such parents and to educational opportunities, Jewish girls began to close the gap between Jewish and other women's literacy rates.

It was difficult to commute to schools that were often faraway and accessible only by dirt roads, which turned to mud when it rained. Ashkenazi neighbors took turns taking children to school by buggy, and some families paid for their children to ride in large, horse-drawn wagons. One girl commuted forty kilometers each way by sulky. More often, children walked several kilometers or rode horseback over longer distances.[43]

Girls often got to school late and disheveled. When one student tumbled off her horse, she waited for a passerby to lift her back on the saddle; for this reason, she was usually tardy. The jarring horseback rides wrinkled girls' clothing and broke their slates. This problem led one teacher to continually berate his students, who felt shamed and powerless. Satisfied when he had humiliated and marginalized them, the instructor repeatedly gave them new slates.[44] Other teachers, however, understood the obstacles their pupils faced.

Colony schools reflected the class structure. Depending on their economic status, mothers made their children's smocks from expensive materials or cheap sheets. Some students lunched on hard-boiled eggs, meatballs, or cheese and bread, while others ate little or nothing. Famished youngsters—or dogs—sometimes stole their classmates' lunch bags, which hung outside the school.[45]

Women sought to overcome hunger and other barriers to learning. Dr. Schliapnik headed a society in Villa Domínguez that oversaw the school and supported La Colmena, which, like other Argentine school cooperatives, provided food and supplies. Jewish women were the leading participants in these groups in the colonies. A conscientious member of La Colmena inspected the school daily for cleanliness and served the children a snack.[46]

Attended by all children of the area, schools were border spaces. Here young Jews interacted with other immigrants and *criollos* and absorbed Spanish. Since most children spoke Yiddish with their parents, however, some members of the early generation never mastered the local tongue.[47]

Schools also fostered a sense of argentinidad. A school inspector in Entre Ríos claimed in 1919 that Jewish colonists initially had "no other link to the nation that houses them other than the cent they harvest from it."

To tighten their bonds to the liberal fatherland, he wanted their progeny to grasp how the founding fathers had affected them personally. He emphasized Bernardino Rivadavia, who—as minister of government of Buenos Aires province (1821–24) and president of the United Provinces of Río de la Plata (1826–27)—had stimulated immigration, and President Domingo F. Sarmiento, who created the secular school system. The children should speak proper Spanish, divested of "the guttural pronunciation that so irritates the ear and produces such a bad effect in an Argentine school." Teachers should dictate works on liberal leaders and assign Argentine-authored texts. Their lessons should "constitute the nationality . . . [and] create of each Jewish offspring a child with markedly Argentine predilections."[48] These guidelines corresponded with the patriotic indoctrination that characterized Argentine public education after 1908.[49] While this nationalism was imposed from the top, some Jewish women soon would shape their versions from below.

Although access to schooling promoted literacy among Jewish girls, many, especially of the pioneer generation, studied no further than the few grades offered locally, or could not even complete them. Indeed, in the early 1900s, few Argentines went beyond the second grade.[50] Some Jewish girls repeated the last grade available, so they could maintain contact with learning. In newly settled areas outside JCA colonies that lacked primary schools, only prosperous families could afford tutors for their children. Like Jewish women in the United States, many sought inclusion through alternative forms of education. Those with means took correspondence courses or studied sewing, business, or music through Jewish organizations and private instructors and academies. Residents of larger towns took noncredit night courses. Teachers and the two Moisesville libraries sponsored a popular university that offered free classes in Spanish, mathematics, reading and writing, typing, and other subjects. Many young women, however, were too poor to seize such opportunities. One family could not spare two pesos a month for dressmaking lessons for their daughter. Embarrassed about their lack of instruction, some women hoped to absorb knowledge from their future husbands.[51]

Young women of Balkan, Turkish, and Moroccan descent entered school with fewer liabilities than their Ashkenazi counterparts: they already knew a form of Spanish, and the towns in which they resided sometimes offered more years of education than the colonies. Yet they, too, faced poverty, a paucity of schools, and Jewish norms excluding women from learning. Some mothers wanted their daughters to attain the skills they lacked, but others did not, and still others lacked the means to pay for schooling. Unable to educate her daughter, Sara, further than the seventh grade, Regina Mendes of Corrientes sent her to a dressmaker to learn the trade. Luna de Mayo let her daughters complete primary school in Posadas, but she permitted additional training only in the feminine arts of sewing, embroidery, and music.[52]

Further study at the primary, secondary, or tertiary level required going to another location. Initially parents could ill afford to send their sons away for education, and they assigned an even lower priority to their daughters. Even as some parents prospered, they did not change their minds. Moreover, they feared that outside a Jewish home and environment, their daughters would encounter predatory strangers or cross over to the Catholic world. Braving neighbors' criticism, other parents were more farsighted. They understood that depriving their daughters of further schooling could hurt them, particularly if they did not marry. Intellectuals like Davidovich promoted their daughters' education for its own sake.[53]

There were diverse strategies of financing schooling and maintaining familial and communal lines. Girls boarded with relatives or shared accommodations with siblings or friends. When families could not pay for their upkeep, girls worked in pensions or taught their owners' children. Well-off parents bought or rented houses in nearby towns where their children resided while they attended school, with older daughters overseeing the household and younger siblings. Separation from their children weighed heavily on mothers. If cities with schools were close to their farms, some mothers stayed with their children during the week and all returned home on weekends. Dora Schvartz accompanied her children to La Plata, Buenos Aires, for twelve years while they attended the university. One enterprising widow left the countryside for Córdoba, supporting her daughters' studies by opening a pension and knitting. Over time, education prompted entire families to move to neighboring towns, from which fathers commuted to the fields or permanently left the land.[54]

Transferring to a far-off school was not easy. One had to pass difficult examinations to enter, and to earn credit for entire grades often unavailable locally. Children prepared for these tests with parents and dedicated teachers, who tutored in their off hours, sometimes for free. A Señora de Plaza crammed knowledge into the first cohort of Carlos Casares that sought to attend porteño schools. The group included the future Zionist activist Sofía Rabinovich, who entered the prestigious Liceo de Señoritas in the capital. Friends and relatives introduced girls to school administrators or solicited aid from politicians to get them admitted. When such tactics were insufficient, some girls begged instructors for a chance.[55] Successful candidates formed part of what Benedict Anderson called an intellectual "pilgrimage" that bound together people of different regions and helped them imagine their nation.[56]

Most rural Jewish girls who pursued an education wanted to become teachers. As was true for many Latin American women at the turn of the century, teaching was the primary means of upward mobility; for Jews, it also meant entering the mainstream of Argentine society. Though teachers earned low salaries, they garnered prestige. Many returned to agrarian communities to practice their profession, serving as models for their pupils and playing other roles that transcended schoolhouse walls. Teachers organized libraries, alumni groups, and patriotic celebrations, making the school the axis of the community and tying the latter to the nation.[57]

Public-school teachers everywhere are expected to disseminate nationalism and national culture.[58] In the countryside, Jewish women often imparted these lessons to fellow immigrants and their progeny, as well as criollos. In the early 1900s, the adolescent instructor Sara Dachevsky gave her pupils in La Capilla their "first notion of . . . Fatherland" and the Sarmiento-style liberalism she and her colleagues had absorbed in their education. Drawing upon her leftism and the local milieu, however, she also reshaped this ideology. According to Dachevsky, the fatherland encompassed "even the *ranchito* [little shack] one could see through the schoolhouse window," a pluralistic view that included the dark-skinned criollos whom Sarmiento disdained. It is striking that on the frontier of settlement, Dachevsky and other women of marginal immigrant backgrounds occupied such central roles.[59]

Some Mediterranean women joined them or distinguished themselves in other professional realms. A young woman of Moroccan background graduated with honors from the normal school of Río Cuarto, Córdoba, in 1924. Another received an accounting certificate in Concordia, Entre Ríos, the following year. A family of Resistencia, Chaco, in 1928 boasted of five accomplished daughters: a teacher, three experts (*profesoras*) in embroidery, and one expert in tailoring. From Resistencia, in 1931, three young Mediterranean women set out for the villages where they would teach.[60]

Older Eastern European and German newcomers made efforts to learn Spanish. A few women enrolled in night classes offered by such cultural institutions as the Sociedad Kadima of Moisesville, founded by Jewish colonists in 1909. Distance and lack of time and money prevented most rural women from attending such schools. They absorbed Spanish from their children, criollo peons and servants, and their reading. Some, however, never mastered it because they remained within communal walls, or because their main contacts outside them were criollos who spoke rudimentary Yiddish or German, or German-speaking Russians.[61]

Eastern European and German colonists "found in the book the desired spiritual tranquility and vehicle for their enlightenment and self-improvement."[62] Some girls read until late at night, their parents at times complaining about the expense of lighting. One woman related, perhaps apocryphally, that her mother read the Yiddish newspaper with one hand while stirring soup with the other. At night family members read aloud to each other while they relaxed, sewed, or pursued other tasks. Eventually the younger generation read more and more in Spanish, joining other Argentine readers who, through their common texts, could envision a national community.[63] Yet fathers often continued to read periodicals and well-loved books in Yiddish to their children.[64]

Also preserving communal borders, young homemakers in the German colony of Avigdor, Entre Ríos, created a reading circle. They met every three weeks in private homes, discussing German books over coffee and *kuchen*.[65] Food reinforced the cultural continuity they sought through literature and made attendance enticing.

Families obtained reading material through various means. Better-off Eastern Europeans bought books and subscribed to porteño periodicals, such as the Socialist *La Vanguardia*, the labor-oriented *Di Presse*, and the mass-circulation *Di Idische Tzaitung*. Mediterranean residents perused *Israel*, published by Moroccan Jews. Neighbors shared reading materials, and peddlers rented books to farm families.[66] Yet the most important sources were libraries.

Cultural Activities

Ashkenazi women created and helped maintain libraries. Teachers established libraries in their schools, obtaining donated works as well as materials from the national public-library system. Pupils were no less active. Four young female graduates of the Moisesville primary school established a tiny collection in the house of one of these girls, Anita Witemberg, and in 1913 asked leading citizens to expand it into a true library. Over the next fifteen years, with local and government support, the Biblioteca Popular Barón Hirsch garnered 160 members, an impressive building, and a collection worth 60,000 pesos. Witemberg served as one of its presidents. A JCA administrator's wife donated 200 pesos for a library in Colonia Mauricio and convinced her husband to dedicate part of the JCA building to that purpose. The Socialist Fenia Chertkoff (see chapter 6) and Dr. Yarcho's wife founded libraries in Colonia Clara and La Capilla, Entre Ríos, respectively. Women raised funds for these institutions and became librarians—a well-respected profession—and library board members. A long-time officer of the Biblioteca Popular Domingo F. Sarmiento in Villa Domínguez, Dr. Schliapnik mentored young intellectuals.[67]

Female involvement in these voluntary associations was significant for several reasons. Through it, Ashkenazi and German women contested their historic exclusion from learning. While women of varied origins participated in libraries in porteño barrios, Jewish women may have been the only ones to do so in rural Argentina.[68] Through their activities in libraries, women helped create networks of civic engagement, interaction, and learning—or social capital—which in turn promoted democratic practices and links to democratic national projects. Furthermore, government backing gave library activists a sense of belonging to the nation.

A few women played similar roles in the German-speaking colony of Avigdor, known for its cultural life. Proud of her intellectual level, Frau Neumann established a small library in the hospital where she worked as a nurse and cofounded a newspaper, *El Pionero de Avigdor*, in 1946. Loni Riegner, who had emigrated to Argentina in a group led by her husband (see chapter 2), cosponsored teas where young women discussed ideas in Spanish. She also taught Jewish culture to preschool children and singing, dancing, table setting, and German notions of proper behavior to older students, thus strengthening gender and communal borders.[69]

Despite these activities, the Sociedad Kadima in Moisesville reported in the mid-1930s that twice as many men as women had consulted books in its reading room.[70] Lower literacy, time-consuming domestic chores, and lack of transportation were barriers to women. There are no statistics on how many women took books home, however.

By fostering schools, Bela Trumper de Kaller's daughter Frida challenged the limits on women's education. Born in a colony near Moisesville in 1898, Kaller attended school until she was ten and studied with a Hebrew teacher during vacations for several more years. When she was nineteen, Kaller married Isaac Gutman, who became a prosperous cattleman and Popular Democratic Party *caudillo*. In 1931, they moved to Moisesville because she wanted her daughters to continue their studies. Her wealth enabled her to sponsor causes and volunteer for the women's cooperative that aided the Hebrew primary school, Escuela Yahaduth.

As yet there was no secondary school in Moisesville, and few students could afford to study elsewhere. The only institute in the country that trained Hebrew teachers was in Buenos Aires, and its graduates rarely ventured to the provinces. To educate worthy but impoverished pupils, expand careers for women, and preserve Jewish culture, the principal Iosef Draznin wanted to add a secondary-level component to the Escuela Yahaduth. Kaller shared his dream. Spotting two girls who were milking cows, she asked their parents if this would be their daughters' future, convincing them to send them to the budding school. Kaller herself paid tuition and living expenses for these and other students. She recruited students and cajoled contributions throughout Argentina. Kaller and Draznin persuaded the Jewish education board in Buenos Aires to send examiners to test students. She became the treasurer and lone woman on the board of the new school, later called the Seminario de Maestros Hebreos Iosef Draznin. Over time, the Seminario added secular subjects to provide a well-rounded secondary education. At Kaller's insistence, graduates worked in the interior, prompting the creation of Hebrew schools in several provinces and also in other Latin American countries. Kaller's efforts to promote Judaism enshrined her as the mother of the Seminario, and she maintained bonds with its mostly female alumni for the rest of her life.[71]

Similarly reinforcing communal borders, women helped support other Jewish schools in the interior. They raised money for the Hebrew schools operated by Mediterranean and Ashkenazi synagogues in larger towns. Women also promoted the generally Communist-oriented Yiddish primary schools that arose in some colonies. Over time, most of these institutions included female pupils and teachers.[72]

Women colonists visited libraries and clubs to exchange thoughts and socialize. There, Eastern Europeans attended political lectures ranging from center to left perspectives, including Zionist variations. German men and women met weekly in the Avigdor library for cultural and musical evenings. On Saturdays, young Ashkenazi women exchanged books in colony libraries and spent hours discussing readings with young men. Libraries and clubs scheduled more formal literary debates, as well as so-called mailbox nights, in which youths wrote down topics, deposited them in a box, and discussed the one pulled out at random. During such evenings, many women met the men they later married.[73] Through these organizations, women strengthened communal walls yet also crossed them by discussing national politics.

Leisure, Cuisine, and Borders

Women's sponsorship of libraries and entertainment helped make small towns such as Moisesville, Villa Domínguez, and Basavilbaso beacons of sociability and culture. Their charities held benefit plays, concerts, and films. Women organized dances and other events, many featuring raffles or sales of donated goods to benefit philanthropies, political causes, and, in the case of Mediterranean women, synagogues and religious schools. Rites of passage offered occasions for celebration, as did religious holidays. Facilitating cultural exchange and civic engagement, Kaller, Schliapnik, Riegner, and other women housed lecturers, Zionists, and performers who toured the colonies.[74]

Women participated in amateur performances in local theaters. Starting at an early age, they sang, danced, played instruments, and recited. Love of acting and the desire to expand their horizons and socialize led young women to join theatrical groups. Schvartz copied and distributed the parts to her fellow actors in Basavilbaso, the men requesting roles that paired them with women they found attractive. Initially Eastern European thespians stuck to European works written in or translated into Yiddish, but over time they adopted Latin American plays. Spanish and Yiddish works favoring social justice were favorites, indicating ties to progressive national projects.

Works first performed by German amateurs, such as those written and directed by a woman residing near Moisesville, were in their native tongue. Eager to practice their new language and, in some cases, distance themselves from the country that had rejected them, German youth soon incorporated plays in Spanish into their repertoire. After premiering one such work in Avigdor, the local troupe performed it for audiences of Eastern European descent in Villa Domínguez and Basavilbaso.[75] Onstage, young women and men tightened bonds with Argentina and crossed over to other Jewish communities.

Jewish women generally mingled with *paisanas* (other Jews from their birthplace), yet they moved back and forth between foreign and Argentine habits. They met each other in cafes where, imitating local custom, they celebrated friends' departures and homecomings. On holidays and weekends, relatives and friends drank *mate*, an herbal tea that was the favored beverage of the Río de la Plata. During such visits, girls gathered on the porch, "to knit, embroider, dream" of their futures. Married women congregated in each other's homes to gossip, work for communal causes, and eat the characteristic foods of their group: Ashkenazim sipped tea and nibbled strudel; Germans enjoyed coffee and kuchen; and Mediterranean women savored Turkish coffee and baklava. Mendes and her guests sang Ladino songs and danced as she played the *dumbelek*, a bass drum. Female farmers welcomed new neighbors by presenting them with hens and eggs.[76]

By organizing festivities, Mediterranean women helped preserve their tiny communities from absorption by the rest of Argentine Jewry and the broader society. A widow helped unite fellow Sephardim of Bahía Blanca and neighboring towns by inviting them to her home to celebrate the Jewish New Year in 1919. Yet the scattered nature of the population hampered efforts to develop small-town Mediterranean communities. The lone Ladino speakers in their village, Catherine Hassid and her family cemented their identity by traveling to the capital. There they celebrated religious holidays with their relatives, as well as the festivities surrounding Catherine's wedding.[77]

Somewhat isolated from their compatriots, rural Mediterranean Jews could have reached out to Ashkenazim. Social activities and the marketplace occasionally brought them together. By the 1930s, Jews of Mediterranean and Eastern European descent attended the same Jewish institutions in several provincial cities, an amalgamating trend that proceeded in earnest after the 1950s. Yet most Sephardim and Ashkenazim did not cross the lines between the groups. While the Hassids were acquainted with the few Eastern European Jews who lived in San Pedro in the 1920s and 1930s, they preferred to socialize with non-Jews.[78] Preserving an Izmiri identity outweighed constructing a broader Jewish—or even Sephardi—identity. In 1945, *Israel* remarked in a tone of wonder that a Jewish ladies' philanthropic society in Rosario recruited not only Ashkenazi but also Turkish, Moroccan, and Syrian women.[79] This was the exception that proved the rule.

German contacts with other coreligionists also were limited. Occasionally German Jews visited and performed in Eastern European colonies.

German and Eastern European youths attended joint dances at times, yet language and cultural differences separated them. The sources do not mention German relations with Mediterranean Jews.[80]

Largely organized by women, weddings celebrated communal boundaries. The first nuptials in the colonies were frugal affairs; some of the stylized Ashkenazi weddings held in later years, however, were enormous, with 200 or 300 guests. The bride's family set up tables under large tents or an awning between the house and shed, and the bride's girlfriends bedecked the area with flowers, lights, and other decorations. The bride's mother and other female relatives, and perhaps hired cooks, spent days preparing such Ashkenazi delicacies as gefilte fish (stuffed fish), roast chicken with knishes (turnovers filled with potatos or onions), fruit compotes, and strudel and other pastries. The *novia*'s friends helped her with her hair, makeup, and gown. When the hour for the ceremony arrived, the groom and his party approached the midway point between the two houses, where they met the bride's party, accompanied by a band playing Eastern European Jewish music. The groups toasted each other and danced in the street. Then they headed to the wedding site, where the bride was waiting. Feasting, dancing, and gift-giving followed the ceremony, continuing until breakfast the next morning. Wealthier colonists subsidized nuptials of poorer neighbors.[81] Women's preparations ensured the success of these affairs, which symbolized the unity and reproduction of the Ashkenazi community, as well as its new roots in Argentine soil.

As the cooks for festive and daily occasions, women chose Argentine or Eastern European Jewish cuisine, or a combination of the two. Over time, criollo dishes predominated on many Ashkenazi tables, yet Eastern European Jewish fare usually appeared on religious holidays and other occasions that marked Jewish continuity. The lack of particular ingredients and increasing familiarity with local produce, however, led women to add Argentine touches to even the most Jewish of foods, such as the substitution of quince for apples in strudel fillings. As Hasia Diner notes for Italian women in the United States, as long as cooks experimented within certain limits, foods remained "traditional." European tastes may have led women to alter Argentine recipes they prepared. Women applied border skills of flexibility and innovation as they tested foods in their kitchens.[82]

German Jewish cooks also navigated cultural boundaries. They continued to prepare red cabbage, kuchen, filled doughnuts, and other recipes from their homeland when possible. Noting that butchers discarded beef tongues and livers, one impoverished housewife acquired them without

2. Sephardi foods. Centro de Documentación e Información sobre Judaísmo Argentino Marc Turkow.

charge and cooked them German-style. Over time, women adopted such Argentine foods as corn and grilled beef. A few drank mate, although some considered the usual practice of sharing a cup and straw unhygienic.[83]

Mediterranean Jewish fare differed markedly from Eastern European and German. Rice, stuffed vegetables, cheese-filled pastries, and delicate cookies and confections covered holiday tables. Lacking grape leaves, women wrapped cabbage or lettuce around ground beef and rice. Local influences, as well as the time-consuming nature of creating many pieces of food, led some women to emphasize criollo cuisine in their daily meals. Others, however, retained the dishes of their homeland—or Argentine renditions of them. Even Luna de Mayo, who served mostly Turkish fare, adopted criollo habits by breakfasting on grilled beef.[84]

The preparation of customary—albeit altered—foods indicated the desire to retain ancestral borders. So did keeping the Sabbath, reading Yiddish and German books, and singing Ladino songs. Yet Jews also relinquished some religious habits. Few wives, especially after the immigrant generation, took ritual baths after menstruation or wore wigs. Many women described themselves as observant but not "fanatical."[85]

Women observed dietary laws to varying degrees. Unable to acquire kosher meat, some gave up kashrut with few regrets. Other women, anguished by the problem, continued to separate dairy from meat products and avoid pork. A pious resident of Moisesville, who questioned the butcher's adherence to kashrut, restricted her diet to fruits and vegetables. When a girl studying away from home found that eating forbidden foods did not kill her, she became less religious.[86]

Some women strengthened their connection to Judaism in a novel manner. Following Jewish customs that restricted religious knowledge to men, conservative colonists originally did not want their daughters to attend religious classes in JCA schools; this opposition, however, faded over time. As in the United States and France, in Argentina Eastern and Central European women received more Hebrew and religious training than they had before immigrating, and they and their daughters took over the teaching of these subjects. Most students at the Seminario de Maestros Hebreos were women, as were its directors. Jewish women had absorbed the local norm of feminine spirituality. Moreover, delegating these matters to women allowed men to concentrate on farms and businesses, opportunities which had been less available to them in Europe.[87] These economic openings made women's border crossings acceptable.

Border Spaces

The Argentine frontier in general had long served as a cultural meeting place, and this was certainly true of the areas where Jews settled.[88] From criollo friends, servants, and schoolmates, Jewish women absorbed Spanish, local customs, foods, and herbal lore. The process of exchange worked both ways: non-Jews in some colonies learned fluent Yiddish or German, while Jews picked up an ungrammatical but colloquial Spanish. Criollo children watched services through synagogue windows and sang the liturgical melodies; eager for schooling and companionship, they sometimes attended Jewish culture classes in JCA schools.[89]

Jewish residents of both town and country interacted with a variety of people. Some colonists hired Russian, Volga German, and Polish workers, and gypsies begged at their doors. Italians, Spaniards, and other foreigners had farms nearby, and their children attended school with Jews. Traveling salesmen sold goods to farm women on their routes, while local workers fixed roofs and hung windows. When Loni Riegner contracted meningitis, policemen saved her life by bringing her penicillin from another town; she repaid the favor by ignoring their theft of her chickens. Another woman recalled that harvest laborers who arrived annually at her parents' farm in Entre Ríos "greeted us affectionately." At night she and other Jewish children watched criollos dance and listened to their scary tales. Criollo maids, cooks, and field hands hugged them and gave them candy bought with the workers' meager earnings. Teachers like Violeta Nardo de Aguirre of Moisesville, author of the poem quoted at the beginning of this chapter, served as role models for Jewish girls. Philanthropic Jewish women gave clothing and other items to criollo peons. Criollos may have had closer relations with Sephardim, who had few *paisanos* nearby and spoke Spanish, than with Ashkenazim.[90]

Cordial on the surface, relations between Ashkenazim and criollos were fraught with tension. They joined the same cultural, school, and sports associations in some towns. In municipalities within and near colonies, young non-Jewish men frequented parties sponsored by Jewish groups. Handsome criollos did not lack dance partners. Yet their customs, such as firing celebratory shots in the air, led some Jewish women to regard them as sinister.[91] For their part, poorer criollos resented their displacement by Jews and other latecomers, who took over lands the criollos had occupied without title and employed them as lowly peons and servants.[92]

Some locals regarded Jews with a mixture of fascination, greed, and ignorance. Criollos spied through the windows at women colonists, whom they viewed as exotic. A man pushed his head through the window of a shack near Carlos Casares in 1905, terrifying a woman who was breastfeeding her baby. To prevent peeping, girls in Colonia Clara in the 1920s and 1930s closed the shutters when they undressed. Local perceptions amused and exasperated Jewish women of diverse origins. When a dance partner informed Catherine Hassid that Jews had horns and tails, she showed him her backside and asked if she had a tail, too. The belief that Jews refused to eat pork because they revered pig heads shocked Regina Mendes and her daughter Sara Salón.[93]

Such attitudes sometimes verged on anti-Semitism. A few Catholic teachers in the colonies abused Ashkenazi pupils, leading a Jewish principal to force one to lecture on the positive aspects of Jewish immigration to Argentina. In this case, a Jewish man had the power to curb discrimination. Relatively rare before 1930, prejudice was more common in stuffy, stratified towns such as Corrientes, where everyone knew who was not

Catholic. Born there in 1922, Sara Salón felt her Jewish identity to be shameful. Absorbing local class as well as ethnic attitudes, she and her siblings lowered their eyes before wealthy Catholics. During Easter week, the family remained indoors, fearing attacks on so-called Christ killers, although such violence never happened. Only years later when she moved to Posadas, a border city whose diverse residents accepted ethnic difference, did Salón shed these feelings of exclusion.[94]

Anti-Semitism usually did not cause crimes against Jews. Jewish and non-Jewish thieves alike stole from Jews in colonies and towns. Impoverished criollos repeatedly tried to break into Mendes's shack in Posadas, where she lived before moving to Corrientes. Robberies could become bloody, as in Colonia Mauricio in 1897, when a horseman demanded money from a Jewish woman. When she said she had none, he smashed the butt of his gun into her head and face, causing serious injuries, and stole her prized silver heirlooms from Europe. In rural Entre Ríos the following year, burglars slashed the throat of a twelve-year-old Jewish girl as they ransacked a home. Occasionally criollos raped Jewish women and murdered Jewish men. Anger, cultural misunderstanding, and the desire for goods and women, rather than hatred of Jews, motivated these bloody encounters. In general, the countryside was violent, and knife battles among criollos were common. For this reason, when Dr. Paulina Weintraub visited her patients in the Entre Ríos backcountry during the 1910s, a chauffeur who doubled as bodyguard accompanied her.[95]

Some Jewish women, not free themselves from xenophobia and callousness, looked down on criollos. They judged the social lines separating Jews from impoverished peons as natural and inevitable. A store clerk in a small town cheated her non-Jewish customers, and others may have done the same. Like other Argentines, some used the pejorative *negro* to refer to poor people of color. Moreover, particularly in the early days, a number of Jewish women ostracized those who married non-Jews. When a Jewish woman in Montefiore, Santa Fe, married a Catholic, hostility from other Jewish girls forced her younger sisters to leave school.[96]

If for some criollos, Jewish women were the exotic other, the reverse was also true. Jewish women defined themselves partly in opposition to what they perceived as the others' ignorance, squalor, violence, and dark skin.[97] Claiming whiteness to distinguish themselves from criollos, these women, unlike the teacher Sara Dachevsky, accepted the racist premises of the liberal project. Yet they also identified with the courtesy, warmth, and generosity they attributed to criollos.

State Formation

As Ashkenazi farmers adopted local ways, they called themselves gauchos and regarded the word as praise. The term "Jewish gauchos" proudly highlighted several facets of their identity. The popularity of Alberto Gerchunoff's *Los gauchos judíos* (1910), signaled Argentine recognition of this phrase and Jewish claims to the nation. After the rise of anti-Semitism in the 1930s, however, the term suggested that not all Argentines accepted Jews; hence, they could not be gauchos, plain and simple.[98]

Yet before and after 1930, rural Jews reaped the benefits of political participation. A few Ashkenazi men won elections, mainly to local or provincial offices, and Ashkenazi caudillos like Frida Gutman's husband delivered votes to their party. Provincial leaders visited the colonies to mobilize support: for example, Eduardo Laurencena, the future Unión Cívica Radical governor of Entre Ríos (1926–30), spoke at Colonia Clara in 1918.[99] Although women could not vote until 1947, Jewish women utilized the political connections of their male relatives. Many acquired teaching jobs or government subsidies for libraries through Jewish and non-Jewish power brokers.[100] Their links to the political system demonstrate their acceptance in their new country.

Numerous Jewish women expressed their nationalism through patriotic celebrations. The May 25 independence day festivities assumed gigantic proportions in the colonies. Planned by school principals and teachers, official ceremonies venerated the nation and its liberal heroes and freedoms. Displays of the Argentine colors, flags, and pictures of founding fathers greeted colonists at the La Capilla school on May 24, 1917. The ceremony began around 8:00 p.m. with girls singing the national anthem, followed by female pupils reciting nationalistic statements, teachers delivering patriotic speeches, and students acting in vignettes. Girls arranged themselves to form the Argentine flag, the word "May," and the numerals 1917.

The program concluded at 1:30 a.m., but this did not end the celebration. Colonists danced until dawn, when all gathered in the schoolyard for the flag raising, national anthem, and cannon fire. Children then feasted on hot chocolate and oranges. After a well-deserved rest, townsfolk began to parade at 2:00 p.m. Flag-bearing girls led the procession to the plaza, where cannons roared and all sang the *himno nacional*. Teacher after teacher addressed the crowd, exhorting mothers to inculcate patriotism in their children. After recitations by female students, the people returned to the school, where sweets awaited the children. At sunset the national anthem and cannons proclaimed the end of the holiday.[101]

The organizers of this commemoration were Catholic, but Jewish girls participated in it as their mothers watched. From these standpoints, they could feel a bond with other Argentines engaging in similar activities at the same time.[102] Soon Ashkenazi women too planned such events, indicating how ordinary Argentines displayed nationalism. On the July 9 holiday (also a celebration of independence) in Moisesville in 1922, Jewish girls presented an Argentine flag they had made to their school, one of them giving a patriotic speech. Receiving the flag, their teacher, Clara Schragovich, described its glorious history that "inflamed the heart of all good Argentine women." Jewish women helped organize a May 25 celebration in this town in 1933 that included a play praising immigrants. Jewish ladies' philanthropical societies provided refreshments at such festivities.[103] All participants claimed a part in Argentina.

Female colonists prepared their children to dance the *pericón*, featured in patriotic celebrations in Entre Ríos. They dressed boys in gaucho-style outfits and girls in long, brightly colored dresses, white aprons, and white or blue scarves. One woman, too poor to buy a dress, made one for her daughter out of a curtain. Non-Jewish and Jewish teachers taught their pupils the intricate steps of the dance. Accompanied by a recitation of verses, the complicated and picturesque dance captivated audiences of mothers and fathers. Those who did not understand Spanish asked their children to translate.[104]

Many gatherings featured Argentine themes. Jewish female educators offered public lectures on Sarmiento and other liberal exemplars. The Asociación Cultural de Maestros of Moisesville, which included Jewish women, celebrated May 25, 1924, with a *fiesta campestre*, featuring a criollo-style barbeque. By evoking such "gaucho" customs, women solidified their Argentine identities.[105]

Many Jewish women openly embraced the Argentine nationality—or felt obligated to show they did. Immigrant mothers listened to their daughters read aloud the constitution and materials from their schools' civics courses. On their first May 25 at the Avigdor school, two German sisters recited verses in Spanish that they had memorized without comprehending a word. Demonstrating their argentinidad, Luna de Mayo and other women became citizens to share their children's nationality.[106]

Dancing the pericón, dressing their children in gaucho costumes, reciting flowery patriotic verses, and singing the national anthem with gusto

3. Jews dressed to dance the *pericón*. Centro de Documentación e Información sobre Judaísmo Argentino Marc Turkow.

were among the ways Jewish women, young and old, performed their allegiance to Argentina.[107] Schragovich claimed the flag and history of Argentina as her own and spoke for Argentine women as a whole. The acceptance of practices that women did not fully understand bespoke their spontaneous joy. Some Germans felt particular delight in celebrating the land that had offered them security from Nazism. Confections offered to children symbolized the sweetness of liberty and refuge; grown in Entre Ríos, oranges represented the bounty of local fields.

Imposed from above, however, some rituals also seemed oppressive. The regimentation of patriotic festivals like the one in La Capilla formed part of a response to immigration. As the number of foreigners increased, by the late 1800s, many Argentines deemed it necessary to unify the country. Influenced by older liberal ideas, some thought that immigrants would modify the nation, which they envisioned as a melting pot, whereas others defined argentinidad exclusively in terms of the pre-existing Spanish or criollo culture. Advocates of the first conception thought cultural change would go both ways, whereas proponents of the second wanted foreigners to adopt local habits. The increasing popularity of the second, more defensive notion prompted measures charging schools with a nationalizing mission, and the festivities described above reflected this focus. By the early 1900s, what Lilia Ana Bertoni called essentialist nationalism prevailed over liberal cosmopolitanism.[108] Still, this was not yet a nationalism that completely excluded Jews.

Newly arrived from despotic countries, some Jewish women may have felt compelled to participate; others abstained altogether. Yet many embraced nationalism and broadened the version imposed from the top. They put their stamp on patriotic rites by focusing on matters of special importance for them, such as Sarmiento's educational program and the beneficial aspects of immigration. In doing so, they disregarded this president's ambiguous views on Jews and other immigrants.[109] To essentialist nationalists, the sight of Jews dancing the pericón meant these immigrants had relinquished prior allegiances. That they, too, could dance the pericón or give patriotic speeches had a different meaning for Jewish female participants. It signified that they, with their distinct identities, belonged to the nation and shared in its rights, a privilege the Russian empire and Nazi Germany had denied them. The state imposed the dance on them, but they chose to perform it because it illustrated freedom and acceptance. Rather than acquiesce to a monolithic, unchanging model of Argentine nationality, these Jewish women helped construct a pluralistic and evolving one.[110]

Conclusion

In 1936, the author Rebeca Mactas, Marcos Alpersohn's granddaughter, described a fictional colony, Las Acacias, solely inhabited by the elderly.[111] This vision of a dying settlement represented the migrations by Jews and others to cities, whose modern conveniences and business, educational, and social opportunities beckoned. Poor soil and the JCA's rigidity also prompted colonists to move, and Mediterranean migrants sought to end their isolation. The dearth of young women in German colonies, caused by the daughters' flight and the JCA's tendency to import families with sons, led young men to abandon farming.[112]

Arduous rural conditions honed Jewish resilience, recalled one woman: they prepared Jews for anything Argentina could bring them.[113] Shedding the image of outcasts and exiles, Jews became Argentines, the "miracle" that Nardo de Aguirre described. Even as they left for the cities, as described in the next chapter, the immigrants took with them firmly implanted Argentine Jewish identities.[114]

Colonies and towns were border spaces offering Jewish women ingredients for creating these hybrid identities. Using border skills of innovation and adaptability, the women combined the foreign and local in cuisine, language, celebrations, and other customs. They crossed boundaries by adopting new roles, such as teaching religion and entering the professions. Yet they also strengthened communal markers by supporting synagogues, organizing weddings, and socializing within their group. Uninterested in the broader society or unable to participate in it, some women reinforced borders.[115]

Jewish women assumed critical roles in state formation on the frontiers of Argentine society. By marrying and bearing children, they demonstrated faith in an Argentine future; through these means as well as reading and attending far-away schools, they also imagined an Argentine community and performed their membership in it. Many women appropriated Argentine history, culture, and civic awareness and imparted these notions to their children, other Jews, and criollos in homes, classrooms, and plazas. The social capital they built promoted democracy and, as in the case of school cooperatives, social justice. Through these practices, they helped refashion liberalism into a more egalitarian and pluralistic project than the one intended by its founders and many contemporaries. Claiming whiteness, however, not all Jewish rural women included criollos in this project.

Political leaders reciprocated by signaling that Jewish women belonged in the nation. Women received provincial subsidies to study midwifery and attained official recognition and funds for libraries. Through political connections, many found teaching jobs.

Jewish women were both included and excluded. Surmounting intellectual marginalization, some Ashkenazi and German women moved to the center of communal life as professionals, mentors, and promoters of reading and education. Yet the mainstream political system excluded them, while Jewish and Argentine customs prevented them from owning land or leading their communities. Many Jewish women remained mired in economic and educational deprivation. Nor was the rural milieu free of anti-Semitism.

Still, some Jewish women may have occupied more central roles in their communities and society than their criolla and immigrant counterparts. They tasted the water and found it at least bittersweet, if not sweet. Like their male relatives, most put deep roots into Argentine soil.

CHAPTER TWO

"I Worked, I Struggled"

Jewish Women in Buenos Aires

I worked, I struggled.
—Esther Furman, interview

Immigration does not only mean to move
from one country to another.
—Bruria Elnecavé, *Crisol de vivencias judías*

Buenos Aires seemed a "marvel," as one German immigrant recalled. When she arrived in the late 1930s, prices were low and gaiety reigned on the Costanera, the popular park along the river. But another immigrant, Esther Furman, a Polish seamstress who toiled in the family sweatshop, had little time for gaiety.[1] For her and many other newcomers, life was anything but easy.

Whatever their circumstances, newly arrived women had to make adjustments. They needed to find economic niches and affordable housing. Balancing the possible and the desirable, they set educational and professional goals for themselves and their daughters. Loss of status and burdensome memories afflicted many women. As Bruria Elnecavé, a Bulgarian who arrived in 1938, implied in the epigraph, immigration—and internal migration—entailed complex changes.

In this adjustment process, Jewish women picked up Spanish and local customs to varying degrees in neighborhoods, schools, and other border spaces. They also kept and reproduced some influences they brought with them. Crossing and retaining borders, Jewish women selected relatives and paisanos for their social networks, sometimes adding acquaintances outside their family and community. Gender norms confined many women and prevented them from leading their communities, yet some scaled these barriers to pursue novel opportunities.

Gender notions, poverty, and prejudice marginalized many Jewish women. Class affiliation affected access to education and leisure activities, and it as well as gender prescriptions created onerous double or triple days for working-class women like Furman. Yet some women had resources that cushioned their adaptation, and laborers made up for their lack of schooling by reading, taking courses, and making use of libraries. With some significant exceptions, extreme anti-Semitism rarely touched women before 1930; more common was the feeling that inclusion demanded muting one's Jewishness.

Establishing families, clubs, and hybrid identities, Jewish women claimed spaces in the new homeland. In Buenos Aires as in the countryside, they became Argentines through education and civic engagement. Cloaking themselves with the mantle of whiteness, some accepted the racist aspects of the reigning liberal project.

Settlement and Borders

Urban women were more heterogeneous than those in the interior. A few relatively well-off Western European Jews had settled in Buenos Aires by the 1860s, followed by handfuls of Moroccans.[2] Between 1889 and 1914, massive numbers of immigrants from the Russian empire overwhelmed the earlier arrivals. Beginning in the 1890s, Ottoman Jews entered the city; the Ottoman empire's collapse after the First World War spurred further immigration from its former dominions. By 1930, when their immigration had largely ended, the Mediterranean contingent accounted for 10 to 17 percent of the Jewish population.[3] Three decades later, over half of the Mediterranean Jews were of Syrian descent (table 3). The interwar period witnessed the arrival of a few Jews from Uzbekistan, as well as numerous working-class Poles and other Eastern Europeans. While German speakers had trickled into Argentina since the mid-1800s, Nazism forced an additional 40,000 to 50,000 Germans, Austrians, Hungarians, and Czechs to seek admission,[4] and the spread of anti-Semitic laws to their country convinced roughly 1,000 Italians to follow them.[5] Illustrating some of these trends, table 4 categorizes foreign-born Jewish porteños by nationality in the mid-1930s, during the Central European migration and before the Italian. It shows that Eastern Europeans formed the overwhelming majority, followed by, in descending order, Syrian-Lebanese, Turks, Germans, and

Austrians. Argentina accepted a few Holocaust survivors after 1945 and small numbers of Egyptians and Moroccans in the 1950s, completing the local Jewish communities. In 1947, about 249,000 Jews lived in Argentina, 166,000 of them in Buenos Aires (see table 5). Men and women of each nationality were further splintered by region and class.

The Jews settled in a diverse city. From the late 1800s until well into the 1900s, an enormous percentage of porteños were born abroad, particularly in Italy and Spain. Immigrants' offspring also accounted for a large segment of the population. In 1936, Jews 5.17 percent of this cosmopolitan mix, increasing slightly to 5.6 percent in 1947.[6]

Coming from the interior and abroad, Jews resided in distinct neighborhoods. Starting in the 1870s, Moroccans tended to establish their homes, fabric and clothing businesses, and synagogues in working-class San Telmo (see map 4). Several Moroccan women converted their homes into pensions for their male paisanos, who usually came alone and sent for their families or returned to the homeland to marry. A woman known as Doña Raquel used her San Telmo abode as a welcome center. Here Moroccans met and spoke in Jaquetía, a mixture of Spanish, Hebrew, and Arabic. The diminutive Raquel offered them lodging and a synagogue, known as El Templo Raquel, which occupied a room in the house. Each Passover, she prepared couscous, which she served to worshipers and distributed to friends. Bringing their countrymen into the fold, Raquel and other women strengthened communal borders.[7] For their part, in the 1890s Eastern Europeans congregated around Plaza Lavalle, site of the Congregación Israelita de la República Argentina synagogue.[8]

By 1900 Turkish, Aegean, Greek, and Syrian Jews, along with Turkish Christians and Muslims and other foreigners, had moved into the Bajo, abutting the port in lower San Nicolás. Contrasting with the neighboring financial and elegant shopping districts, this barrio was poor yet colorful. Its Jewish and non-Jewish inhabitants lived in inexpensive pensions and apartments and gathered alongside sailors in cafes. As a child in the 1920s, the future doctor Victoria Simsolo, daughter of a Cretan mother and an Izmiri father, played in *conventillos* (tenements) located next to brothels. Her family and relatives occupied apartments in the same building. Like their Moroccan coreligionists, young Turkish Jewish men migrated singly, sharing rooms while they saved money from their sales jobs and peddling to bring over their families or marry. Over time, some established fabric-importing businesses, which, along with their clubs and other institutions, dotted the area.[9]

In the early 1900s, Damascene Jewish men began to move into working-class Boca and Barracas along the Riachuelo River, neighborhoods harboring large Italian populations and polluting industries. They shared tenement rooms and hawked goods in the streets. Some sent back to Damascus for girls to wed, who were frequently escorted to Buenos Aires by their brothers. Unfamiliar with Spanish and often illiterate, many began their lives in Argentina in great poverty. Dressed in bright colors, their hair often adorned with flowers, the young women of the Damascene families who occupied an old building around 1910 laughed and chatted as they cleaned house together.[10]

From 1907 to the mid-1920s, the neighborhood with the largest Jewish presence was Once, in the Balvanera district. First to settle here were Aleppine men, followed by their families and Eastern Europeans. Jews lived in Once and worked there in peddling, small factories, and textile and retail businesses, helping to make the neighborhood the city's principal commercial zone. Kosher Syrian and Eastern European restaurants served Jewish customers. Ashkenazi housewives bought chopped liver and herring at Brusilovsky, while Arabic-speaking women purchased nuts, dried fruit, and sweets at Helueni. Synagogues, ritual baths, Yiddish theaters and newspaper offices, the Ashkenazi burial society, and a host of other Jewish institutions clustered in Once. It also contained bordellos run by the infamous Zwi Migdal, the Jewish society of pimps and madams.[11]

Jewish women in Once socialized with each other in their buildings, as well as in shops and institutions serving their communities. When Farida Yadid arrived with her two babies in 1920, her husband took them to their room in a tenement occupied by Aleppine families they had long known. At night Farida and several friends entertained the tenants, singing and playing the *derbeke* drum, improvising theatrical sketches, and organizing games. Friday nights were the most festive. Farida and other women returned from the ritual bath, perfumed in their Sabbath finery. After lighting the candles, each contributed a dish to the joint meal—bread, salad, hummus, and stuffed vegetables and grape leaves. The Aleppine peddlers and their wives performed their roots and momentarily forgot their poverty.[12]

By the 1920s, when cheap land became available in western Buenos Aires and public transportation expanded in that direction, Damascene and some Aleppine, Turkish, and Eastern European Jews moved to Flores, formerly the site of upper-class villas. In this and other outlying neighborhoods, humble families purchased land with small monthly payments and established homes. Quiet and tree lined, Flores became the seat of the largest Arabic-speaking Jewish community in Latin America, with synagogues, kosher restaurants, and groceries. Wealthier male residents commuted to their textile businesses in Once or the southern edge of downtown, while the majority peddled in the streets. Affluent Aleppine clans shared buildings in Flores. Each family had its own apartment, and children played in the patio while their mothers conversed.[13]

Bustling Villa Crespo was another multicultural neighborhood. Its first Jews came from Izmir in 1911, and Ladino speakers retained a significant minority presence in the barrio. Russian Jews started to arrive by 1920, and many Polish immigrants settled there in the 1920s and 1930s. Ashkenazim and Sephardim lived side by side, along with Italians, Spaniards, and native-born Argentines. Most Eastern European institutions remained in Once, which had a more religious character than the Ashkenazi sector of Villa Crespo; the latter, however, hosted Turkish and Aegean islanders' organizations. Bakeries and groceries catered to Ashkenazi and Sephardi tastes, and vendors hawked used garments, melons, and Mediterranean sweets. By 1936, 25 percent of Jewish porteños lived in Villa Crespo, compared to 22 percent in Once, and the Jewish population in the former area was growing more quickly than in the latter.[14]

Villa Crespo had a nonconformist flavor. It housed famous Sephardi and Ashkenazi cafes: in one of the former, Franco, Jews and bohemians drank Turkish coffee and listened to Mediterranean songs. Ashkenazi cafes and leftist clubs hummed with ideological debates, and a Jewish-owned bookstore featured lively literary discussions. Some Eastern European militants organized laborers in the weaving and tailoring workshops of this and neighboring barrios.

The impoverished Poles who arrived after the First World War accentuated Villa Crespo's proletarian quality. Mostly laborers and peddlers, Jewish residents lived in conventillos and shared apartments, their rooms doubling as sweatshops. Moving into one such abode in 1948, a Polish Holocaust survivor was disconcerted that its twelve residents shared a toilet that was simply a hole in the floor. After the filthy concentration camps, she could barely abide such conditions. Six months later, however, she and her husband were able to rent a tiny apartment nearby with a genuine bathroom. It took others longer to escape privation.[15]

In the 1930s and 1940s, Jewish entrepreneurs established textile factories in Villa Lynch, in suburban San Martín. This and other peripheral industrial areas housed Jews who worked in these enterprises. Two Polish sisters who had survived the Holocaust were among them. Moving in with a cousin in Villa Lynch, they were delighted to discover it specialized in textile production, as had their hometown, and to meet their paisanos there. Like Villa Crespo, Villa Lynch contained leftist Yiddish schools and institutions.[16]

Better-off Jews of varied backgrounds settled in affluent northern neighborhoods. Prosperous families from Rhodes, Salonika, and Cos left the Bajo for Colegiales, Belgrano, and Coghlan, where they joined other Jews of Balkan descent. They created a cultural center, Chalom, with its synagogue, youth group, and women's charity association, La Unión. Wealthy Syrians moved to Palermo, Belgrano, and the town of Olivos, in suburban Vicente López. The Central European Jewish migration to Belgrano in the 1930s and 1940s helped cement that middle-class neighborhood's German character. Here German-speaking Jews walked the same streets as their pro-Nazi compatriots. Women of the two groups, however, did not frequent the same tearooms, nor did their daughters attend the same schools.[17]

Not all Jews fleeing Fascism could afford to reside in bourgeois neighborhoods. The tea sandwiches they ate on shipboard had given Italian girls a festive preview of Argentina. When they and their families moved into pensions in drab outlying barrios, however, "the tea sandwiches and many other things ended."[18] One Austrian-born woman did not let her dingy rooming house depress her. Disembarking in 1943, Ilse Kaufman had endured the Nazi occupation of Prague, circumvented the Gestapo's threat to imprison her father, exhausted her funds sending her parents to Argentina, and survived a train trip across Europe in a compartment shared with an SS officer. The cramped quarters and uncertainties of life in Argentina were acceptable and even beautiful because they represented freedom.[19]

Jews were more segregated than other groups of immigrants: 3.5 times as segregated as Italians, and 2.7 times as Spaniards. Still, they were less so than were urban-dwelling Eastern and Southern Europeans in the United States. The desire to remain within their communities of origin and to get access to jobs and low rents partly determined this residential separation. So, too, did the fact that Jews were less like native-born Argentinians than were Italian or Spanish immigrants, and Jews tended to arrive later than most foreigners.[20] Nevertheless, ethnic residential borders were permeable. No neighborhood was exclusively or majority Jewish, not even Once, and by the 1930s and 1940s Jews had dispersed throughout the city and surrounding areas.

Despite their relative segregation, Jewish women absorbed local customs through their daily contact with non-Jews. A Holocaust survivor in Villa Crespo picked up Spanish from a neighbor and perfected her vocabulary by scrutinizing the blackboard that listed items and prices outside a grocery. The Italian shopkeeper feared she was a government inspector, seeking evidence of price increases.[21]

Work and Marginalization

No matter their origin, homemaking was the principal occupation of most urban Jewish women before 1955. The minority who were well off, especially those who had servants, concentrated on preferred domestic chores. A long-time resident of Egypt born in Rhodes migrated with her family to Buenos Aires in 1948. Although her hard-working husband soon provided a middle-class lifestyle, she made their children's clothing to save money. Focusing on cooking, she prepared tasty stews, stuffed grape leaves and vegetables, and Mediterranean-style pastries, transmitting love and customs through her cuisine.[22]

Many Central European and Italian refugees took on household tasks performed by their servants in Europe. Some could not comprehend their decline in status. A Hungarian daughter complained that her mother had brought from Europe a tray and other nonessential household items for which she had to pay custom duties she could ill afford. Her mother considered the tray a necessity: without it, she wondered, "how will the *shikse* [non-Jewish woman—in this case, a servant] serve you the meal?"[23]

Most Jewish homemakers, however, had never enjoyed the luxury of servants. Many among them, such as Elena Liniado of Damascus, faced the challenge of making a tenement habitable. "A superficial visit sufficed to wound one's eyes and turn one's stomach," recalled her son, who shared a bed with six siblings in a conventillo in Once in the 1920s. Liniado cleaned the room, with its moldy, grimy walls, and washed her brood and their clothing with water drawn from the building's lone faucet. Nor was it easy to fix meals in the shared kitchen or on a tiny brazier. After her husband abandoned them—a common occurrence among the Catholic and Jewish poor—the family survived on the four eldest boys' meager earnings and Liniado's stringent economizing.[24]

4. A *conventillo* (tenement), Buenos Aires. Archivo General de la Nación, Dpto. Doc. Fotográficos.

Women's management was essential for the domestic economy. Housewives like Liniado, who knew what to buy, where to buy it, and how to stretch ingredients, fed working-class families on limited budgets. Reliable customers convinced grocers to add free vegetables to their purchases. Farida Yadid made jellies, compotes, perfumes, and cosmetics out of rotting produce she acquired by the case at little or no cost. Many mothers stayed up late, mending clothes or altering hand-me-downs to fit their children. With little money to spare, even if there were several income earners in the family, women worried about covering emergencies. Since poverty-stricken parents commonly died young, taking in orphaned relatives often added to women's burdens.[25]

Many Eastern European and Mediterranean families could not take adequate care of their daughters and wives. A woman in 1914 noted an "infinity of Israelite children, abandoned" on the streets. There also were semiabandoned children whose fathers were unemployed or jailed and whose mothers were indisposed, institutionalized, or at work. Some children had parents who were prostitutes. Large numbers of widows and women forsaken or abused by their husbands were also in need. Jewish women were among the many destitute Argentines.[26]

Poverty led to agonizing separations. Regina Attach, her parents, and her brother, Selim, migrated from Damascus to Buenos Aires around 1908. When her mother died, her father José, a peddler, could not care for his children. He took Selim and Regina, then three years old, back to Damascus and asked his in-laws for another daughter to marry. Claiming that he had already killed one of their daughters, they refused to give him another. José returned to Buenos Aires, leaving the children with their grandparents, who died a few years later. Regina and Selim lived on the streets, sickly and starving, until they entered a Jewish orphanage. During this time, there was no communication between the children and their illiterate father. Later, living in Córdoba, José spotted a photograph of the Damascus orphanage and recognized his son among the inmates. He slowly accumulated money and sent for the children in 1922. To escape José's harsh control, Regina, who had acquired some education and independence during her struggles, took the unconventional step of moving alone to Buenos Aires when she was in her early twenties.[27]

Impoverished homemakers made painful choices. Farida Yadid spoiled her spouse, reserving the best food for him while her children went hungry. One day, when her father finished eating the soup his wife had prepared for him, he gave their daughter Matilde the soup bone so she could chew the little meat left on it. A neighbor shocked by this exchange shamed Farida into splitting the scarce meat among the entire family.[28]

To provide for their families and support their husbands' religious studies, Jewish women in Eastern Europe had long earned incomes. Peddling, sewing, and washing clothes were common pursuits, as was working alongside husbands in businesses and workshops. Industrialization and the accompanying social disruptions pauperized many Jewish families, particularly in Poland, and pushed women into textile mills, sewing, prostitution, and other trades.[29]

In the early 1900s, female employment rose among Jews in the Ottoman Empire. Urban women and girls knitted and sewed at home, receiving supplies and handing over the finished garments to male entrepreneurs. Other women were domestic servants or tobacco workers, like Farida Yadid. After the First World War, growing numbers of Jewish women—particularly in the Balkans—worked outside the home. Sewing and dressmaking were common occupations.[30]

Influenced by these experiences, Jewish women of varied classes and origins engaged in income-producing activities in Argentina. Women "helped out" in furniture, clothing, shoe, and tailoring shops; newspaper and market stands; bookbinding, printing, and furrier businesses; and other family enterprises. They also ran businesses out of their homes, taking in boarders, sewing, and laundry; making dresses; and managing pensions and the buildings in which they lived. Regina Attach learned sewing from an aunt who did piecework for an underwear factory. With her savings, Attach bought a sewing machine, rented a room, and worked for a bridal clothing establishment. Some women peddled homemade foods, lottery tickets, and other goods in the streets. Better-educated Mediterranean and Ashkenazi women found work in accounting and business administration and taught primary school, languages, music, sewing, and garment making. Some of these occupations could be lucrative; a piano teacher with forty or fifty students earned good wages.[31]

Working at home or in family businesses allowed women to oversee their children and move between domestic duties and paid work as needed. It also met other goals. In Argentina, Jewish women constructed their identities largely around marriage and motherhood, and a privileged status entailed domesticity. Working at home or calling their labor "helping out" enabled women to support families discreetly. This was more genteel and proper than placing women under the control of male strangers. Decorum was vital, for many Jews held women responsible for maintaining communal respectability.[32]

The interwar period brought an "avalanche" of impoverished Polish, Romanian, and Lithuanian Jews to Buenos Aires, and the women among them often were the sole wage earners in their families. Some Poles became sex workers, as had earlier Russian immigrants (see chapter 4), but most newcomers became domestic or manual laborers. From July 1929 to July 1930, the Jewish Sociedad de Protección a los Inmigrantes found jobs for 246 immigrant women: 165 seamstresses, 21 servants, 15 cooks, 2 darners, 1 dental technician, and 42 factory workers.[33]

In the mid-1930s, women and children constituted 70 percent of the textile workers, and over 75 percent of garment workers were women.[34] Some of these women were Jews. Having worked as weavers, seamstresses, tailors, and pressers in their homeland, many Poles took up the same positions in factories and workshops (*talleres*)—some owned by Jews—in Villa Crespo, Villa Lynch, and other neighborhoods. In the apparel industry, women were salaried workers, collaborators with their *tallerista* or tailor husbands, and pieceworkers at home. Often they alternated between wage labor during the three-month peak season and piecework and unemployment during the rest of the year. Custom assigned technology to men and painstaking and onerous manual labor to women. This was true for Esther Furman, who was nineteen when she arrived from Poland in 1933. She and her husband established a household and workshop in a series of small apartments. Her spouse operated the sewing machine, leaving the stitching by hand to Furman, as well as ironing the finished garments. Furman also carried heavy packets of clothing to the retailers. Female pieceworkers transported weighty bundles of cloth to their tenement homes, sewed twelve to fourteen hours a day, and carried bundles back to the business they worked for.[35]

A larger, mechanized form of production characterized most textile manufacturing, although some male workers purchased and set up a loom or two in a space shared with other aspiring entrepreneurs. Women worked in the mills, alongside their husbands on family-owned looms, or in their homes. The future labor activist Flora Absatz went to work in a mill in Villa Crespo at the age of thirteen in 1930, when she arrived with her destitute family from Poland. Her first job was to separate the silk skein into individual threads and put them on a spool; later she learned to connect the threads of one spool with those of another, so that the loom operator could continue work without interruption when a spool ran out.[36]

Whether in the factory or sweatshop, the textile or garment industry, women suffered from poor working conditions, long hours, exploitation, and their bosses' whims. They earned less than their male coworkers, and managers threatened them with fines and dismissal to avoid giving them raises or to force them to work faster. Firms often disregarded labor laws, and sexual and other forms of abuse were common. This was even true when employers were relatives. Absatz pleaded with her cousin, who owned the mill in which she worked, to allow her to arrange her schedule so she could study. Insisting that she alternate shifts, her cousin prevented her from attending school. When business was slow—as was common—women lost their jobs. In other cases, managers ordered women to wait at the mill for hours to see if any work turned up; if it did not, the women were sent home without pay. As employers preferred to hire young, unmarried women, it was difficult for older women to find work. The dark interiors in the plants only partially hid rats and insects from view. In the damp winters, the premises were cold; in the torrid summers, they were unbearably hot. As bad as these conditions were, the situation for women who worked at home was even worse, since they did not have set salaries, hours, or benefits.[37]

Occasionally, cruel bosses received their comeuppance. When her father died in the early 1930s, leaving the family penniless, a twelve-year-old Romanian girl abandoned school for work. While learning how to make women's hats, she cleaned the *taller*, sewed, and carried large containers of hats to other locations, working eleven hours a day for a total of ten centavos, or one-tenth of a peso. When her employer denied her a raise, she left for a prestigious shop downtown, where eventually she received sixty pesos per month. Her new boss, however, threatened to lower her salary if she refused to inform on fellow employees' transgressions. Having heard of her proficiency, her old *patrón* wanted to hire her to design and prepare patterns. She returned triumphantly after bargaining for a hundred pesos a month. Although that was an excellent salary for an eighteen-year-old girl in 1937, it would not have supported a family. This episode illustrates workplace subjugation and an employee's successful fight against it, yet it also shows how little even well-regarded female workers earned.[38]

Customers as well as bosses exploited female workers. Communist militant Teresa Gílenberg arrived in Buenos Aires in the early 1930s, having mastered the craft of lingerie making in Poland. Working independently, she visited potential brides to solicit orders and expected to receive payment after completing the alterations. As her customers were often as poor as she, she had to return many times to their homes to be paid. Independent dressmakers, seamstresses, and laundresses faced similar difficulties.[39]

Wives who worked outside the home faced a double or triple day. This was the case for Guitl Kanutsky, a Polish tailor and labor activist who came to Argentina with her carpenter husband in 1924, when she was twenty-five. She rose at 5:00 a.m. to perform domestic chores and purchased food when the shops opened an hour later. Kanutsky entered the garment workshop at 7:00 a.m., came home at midday to fix lunch, and spent the afternoon on labor organizing. Her son accompanied her to union and political gatherings. At night she made clothes for her family, and during weekends she cleaned, planned the household for the week, rested, and read. Her spouse, who worked a nine-hour day, left household duties to his wife, as did most of his male contemporaries. Whether his behavior angered Kanutsky is unclear. As she dryly observed, "I did everything, arranged everything."[40]

Kanutsky's compatriot Esther Furman faced a similar triple day. After the workday, Furman cared for the household and her two daughters, one of them emotionally disturbed; waited on her husband; and participated in some union activities. She loved reciting literature and longed for an education, but poverty and the gender code prevented her from getting one. In hindsight her dreams appeared "foolish": as she summed up her life, "I worked, I struggled."[41]

Refugees from fascist Europe also found it difficult to fulfill their dreams. While most adult women had been housewives, at least initially in Argentina, many had to work outside the home. Wives commonly collaborated with their husbands: one couple worked as domestics in the same household, and others managed businesses together. After such firms were on solid footing, the wives often returned to their homes. The time-consuming and demeaning task of revalidating foreign degrees kept the few female professionals from pursuing their careers in the wider society. A handful of medical personnel, however, ministered quietly to fellow exiles, while others occupied posts in communal institutions. Some felt frustrated that they could not return to the careers they enjoyed in pre-Nazi Europe.[42]

Although the uprooting had interrupted their lives, ironically it also continued trends under way in Nazi Germany. Nazis struck hardest at Jewish men, destroying their livelihoods and humiliating, arresting, and assaulting them. They weakened but did not destroy patriarchy among Jews. Defending their men from authorities; entering the work force, usually for the first time; and coping with crowded dwellings and privation, women showed a degree of adaptability often lacking in their spouses.[43] This behavior persisted in Buenos Aires, where German-speaking men insisted on sticking to their professions; partly for this reason, they were less likely than women to find jobs. Applying the border skills of flexibility and reinvention, former homemakers and their daughters engaged in diverse pursuits. They rented out rooms and served as translators. Tending to regard Central Europeans as highly cultured, Argentines sought these women's services as governesses, nannies, servants, dressmakers, milliners, hairdressers, manicurists, salesladies, and photographers. Central European and Italian women also became kindergarten and language teachers. Several eventually created their own retail businesses, while others, with additional training, became multilingual secretaries, business administrators, and designers. "Through sheer grit," noted one observer, the former head of a music conservatory secured a post as stenographer. Sympathizing with the exiles' plight, the Italian publisher Cesare Civita employed a number of young female compatriots in his Editorial Abril. These successes, however, were costly. According to a community leader, stress and unaccustomed labor promoted a relatively high incidence of disease among German women.[44]

Holocaust survivors also had to be flexible to find work. Pela Szechter, a Polish opera singer who had spent the German occupation in hiding, learned Yiddish after the war to earn a living by singing Jewish songs. This served her well in Argentina, where she sang for Jewish institutions before she married and gave up her career. Another Polish speaker, Lena Gartenstein-Faigenblat, had studied humanities at Warsaw University before the war. On the ship to Argentina, she befriended the head of the Argentine branches of Instituto Científice Judío (IWO) and Cultur Congres, institutions that preserved Yiddish culture. Overlooking her minimal knowledge of Yiddish, he hired her to manage Cultur Congres. In this capacity, Gartenstein-Faigenblat eventually became proficient in that language.[45]

How Jewish women's participation in wage labor compared to that of other Argentine women in the early 1900s is unclear, but the U.S. context provides some clues. In New York, Jewish women were much less likely to work for wages than other women during the period of mass immigration, according to surveys that, however, ignored the home industries that employed many Jews. Similarly, Argentine official figures on women wage workers in the 1940s excluded those who worked in this sector, where Jewish women were concentrated.[46] By 1960, the only year for which statistics specifically on Jews are available, 20 percent of Jewish women were in the labor force, compared to 23 percent of all women; in greater Buenos Aires, the percentages were 19.9 for Jews and 26.4 for all. At every age level, Jewish women were less likely to participate in the labor force than Argentine women in their totality. The Argentine-born Jewish *porteñas*, however, had the same rate as porteñas as a whole, while immigrants, especially from Asia and Africa, had considerably lower rates (see tables 6 and 7). Scholars have attributed the lower rates among foreign-born and older Jewish women to marriage and large families, and those among younger women to the pursuit of education.[47] Official statistics may have continued to mask Jewish women's participation in family businesses and income-earning household activities, although the latter had declined by 1960. By this year, the occupational profile of Jewish working women had also changed, as discussed in the next chapter.

Education

The literacy gap between Jewish and other women persisted into the 1930s, although it was shrinking. In 1936, 90 percent of all female inhabitants of Buenos Aires could read and write, compared to 84 percent of Jewish women. However, native-born Jewish women up to the age of 44, as well as foreign-born Jewish women under the age of 30, enjoyed literacy rates higher than or close to the norm for Argentine women as a whole and other immigrant women, indicating their increased access to schooling in their homelands as well as Argentina. The rates went down as the women's age went up. Only 59 percent of foreign-born Jewish women aged 50 to 54, and 38 percent of those over 65, were literate, rates far lower even than those of Spanish and Italian women (see tables 8 and 9).

Not as marginalized as their older coreligionists, many girls of Eastern European and Mediterranean descent nevertheless had to abandon their studies for work. Sometimes, however, parental decisions involved considerations beyond the practical. Estela Mesulam could not study beyond primary school, even though her mother Rachel, denied an education in her native Istanbul, had eagerly enrolled her children in a Protestant missionary school when they arrived in Buenos Aires in 1910. When her older daughter married and left home, Rachel felt the loss of her presence and participation in domestic chores and expected Estela to fill her place. Rachel also had realized that going to school involved leaving the house, and this conflicted with her ingrained belief that women should stay at home. Resenting the mental and physical absence that education entailed, she reproached Estela for isolating herself by reading. Little by little, Estela felt herself cloistered. She did not receive support from her father, who saw no need for his children to study: his sons would enter the business, and his daughters would marry. Mediterranean girls were not the only ones to experience such constraints.[48]

However, other parents, even impoverished ones, supported their daughters' education. Around the 1920s, a Polish woman invited a young Hebrew teacher living in the same conventillo to tea so her children could see how he sacrificed himself for his studies. Her daughter already was attending the top-notch Liceo de Señoritas. Economic opportunities convinced some Jews to reverse typical gender expectations. For example, a Polish family that arrived in 1931 permitted only its daughters to study past the primary level; the sons instead entered the prosperous family tailoring business.[49]

The Jewish girls under the wing of the Sociedad de Socorros de Damas Israelitas (renamed the Sociedad de Damas Israelitas in 1927) also received an education. The Ashkenazi and Mediterranean inmates of the orphanage the Damas founded in 1919, the Asilo de Huérfanas Israelitas, came from troubled and impoverished backgrounds. They attended public primary school half the day, and took lessons in Jewish culture, French, and vocational skills in the Asilo. The brightest obtained additional schooling.[50]

Young girls of the urban exile communities did not face the educational hurdles that had stymied their elders or their counterparts in the colonies. Since they had no degrees to revalidate, they simply started where they had left off in Europe, or repeated a grade. A significant minority of the German speakers attended Germania, Cangallo, or Pestalozzi, the German anti-Nazi schools. Students could start in kindergarten and continue through secondary school at Pestalozzi; many, however, transferred to public *colegios*. The German institutions provided a haven for victims of extreme anti-Semitism in their homelands, but this sheltered environment may have retarded crossing into local society.[51]

Some Jewish students experienced prejudice. In the 1930s, one primary-school teacher yelled at her Ashkenazi pupils and locked a girl in the basement, where she remained until her anxious mother found her. Another instructor could not believe that one student was an Italian Jew; she thought it impossible to be both. This disbelief added to the trauma of exile: first Italy had demeaned the girl as a Jew, and now an Argentine denied her heritage. Assuming Italian girls were Catholic, fellow students warned them to be careful around the *rusos*, which literally meant Russians but was commonly used to refer to all Jews.[52]

Despite their own foreign ancestry, or perhaps because of it, some first-generation Catholic teachers and school administrators enforced assimilation and conformity. Like her students, many of them Jewish, who lived in nearby tenements, the principal of a school in Villa Crespo in the early 1920s came from an immigrant working-class home. On her first day at work, she concluded that the pupils had lice. Determined to make them abide by her standards of cleanliness and order, she had the boys' heads shaved and ordered the girls to unbraid their hair and comb it thoroughly twice a day. The principal urged all students to wash their hair frequently. Fearful of authority, a few mothers nonetheless protested that their children might catch colds if they washed their hair often; however, they did not dispute the principal's control over their children's bodies. What most mothers or daughters thought about this incident is unknown. School

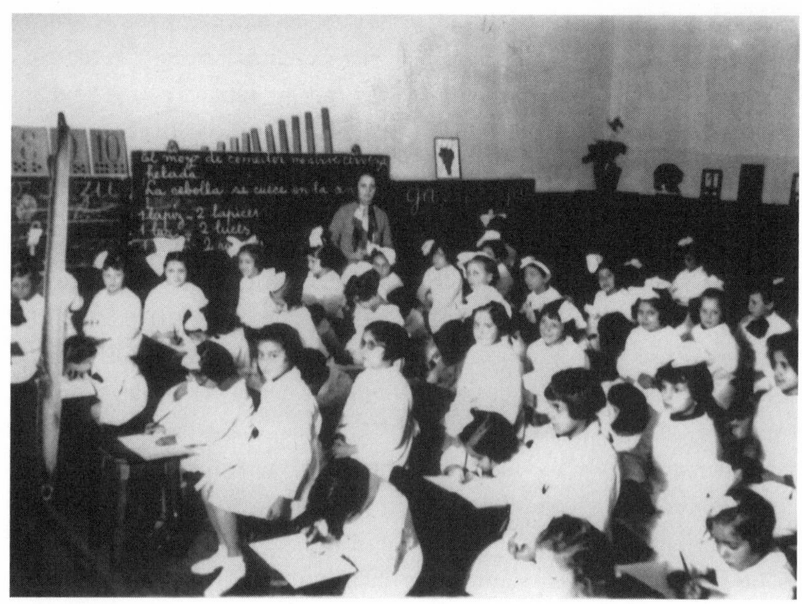

5. An overcrowded public school, Villa Crespo, 1935, attended by Ashkenazi and Sephardi children. Archivo General de la Nación, Dpto. Doc. Fotográficos.

authoritarianism may have compelled some Jewish girls to quietly blend in and even give up "external signs of being Jewish."[53]

Many teachers, however, welcomed Jewish pupils. Some *maestras* protested when parents removed girls from school to go to work. Teachers in La Plata treated a young Romanian immigrant kindly, one of them tutoring her in Spanish so she could pass the entrance exam. Classmates made fun of this *gringuita* until a sympathetic teacher reprimanded them and explained the difficulties of adapting to a new country. A Polish immigrant contrasted benevolent Argentine schools with those in her homeland, which often forced Jews to sit apart from other students.[54]

Even as teachers accepted them, Catholic Argentines frequently taunted their Jewish classmates as *rusas* or *gringas*. An instructor gave a text on José de San Martín to her class, which included a newly arrived Pole. Since she did not understand Spanish, the girl simply memorized the passage, and when the teacher called on her, she recited it in one breath. Impressed with the diligence and apparent patriotism of a pupil just off the boat, the instructor sent her to recite to the other classes and gave her a tiny Argentine flag. An envious classmate sneered, "Look at the *rusita*!"[55] Not always pejorative, such words at times were uttered neutrally or even fondly.[56] But they signaled that Jewish girls were outsiders.

The Jewish educational network also highlighted differences. To supplement schools in colonies and synagogues, the AIU and JCA began to establish ones in the major cities in 1911. The synagogue and AIU-JCA institutes emphasized instruction in religion, Jewish history, and Yiddish, Spanish, or Arabic, depending on the ethnic character of the school; they taught Hebrew only as a sacramental language until the rise of Israel. As of 1916, the AIU-JCA schools had taught 1,900 boys and 1,100 girls, including students at the girls' orphanage. The Yiddish schools, some of them secular, welcomed female pupils and kept tuition low to attract students from among the poor. Before the 1940s, all Ashkenazi schools, including leftist ones, fostered an attachment to Yiddish culture, thus excluding Central Europeans and Ladino and Arabic speakers.[57]

Mediterranean Jews lagged behind the Eastern Europeans in providing religious education for women. Some daughters of well-off families received private lessons from Hebrew teachers, but synagogue schools delayed accepting girls. While the Damascene Asociación Unión Israelita Sefaradí Or Torah admitted a few girls in 1921, the Aleppine Congregación Sefaradí Yesod Hadath created a separate school for girls in the late 1930s. Writing in *Israel*, the now adult Estela Mesulam, whose secular education had been cut short, protested this marginalization. She decried the fact that, unlike their Ashkenazi counterparts, Sephardi women could not study their history, religion, and traditions, predicting this would weaken Mediterranean communities.[58]

Regarded as an appropriate part of a lady's education, the arts did not provoke parental disapproval or communal opposition. Many young women, even the poor, took private lessons, while others studied at institutions. For a low fee, Ashkenazi women enrolled in the Asociación Musical Israelita Ioel Engel in Once, making up between a quarter and a third of its paid members. Mostly from the neighborhood, students, teachers, employees, dressmakers, and factory workers studied choral singing there, attended lectures, and listened to recordings.[59]

Women whose schooling ended with the primary level were not necessarily as deprived as one might think. They may not have studied for long, but primary schools in the capital offered a good basic education in the 1930s and 1940s, better than they did in later years. Moreover, the uneducated and dropouts often took advantage of libraries, inexpensive reading materials, and evening classes. In her expressive colloquial Spanish, the essentially illiterate Farida Yadid declared, "*burro acá, no* [an uneducated brute here, no]!" Yadid discovered that the neighborhood school would hold a night course for adults if she could gather at least ten students. She and Matilde, the daughter whom she had pulled out of school at age eleven to work, made two students, and Farida went door to door, recruiting the rest. When Matilde asked her if they were poor, Farida, boosted by her struggle for education, said, "Never say poor! Poor is he who has no knowledge. Poor is he who cannot think. We have no money. But not poor." Absorbing this insight, Matilde attended a secondary-level journalism school once she married and no longer needed to earn an income.[60]

Young Jewish women like Matilde enrolled in state and private vocational courses. The well-off *señoritas* who congregated in the Sociedad Femenina Israelita Pro-Enseñanza Profesional established a free school in 1912 to train Jewish girls in sewing and secretarial skills. In the 1930s, the Jewish-owned Instituto Comercial Rivadavia offered secretarial, accounting, and advertising classes and accelerated training to prospective white-collar and sales workers. In addition, Jewish girls enrolled in commercial courses at public secondary schools.[61]

Some Jewish women also pursued inexpensive educational opportunities provided by political parties and communal organizations. The Asociación Juventud Israelita Argentina established a free night school for workers, including university-level extension classes. Women attended the lecture series of the Colegio Libre de Estudios Superiores, linked to the Communist Party, in the 1930s, as well as the educational programs of the Socialist Universidad Popular La Luz between 1899 and 1930.[62]

Leisure, Inclusion, and Exclusion

Like their rural counterparts and other porteñas, urban Jewish women were active in libraries and cultural centers, many of leftist and Zionist orientation.[63] Whether women helped direct these political organizations is unclear. They played more visible roles in social groups that arose along lines of origin, neighborhood, and age. The Juventud Israelita de Barracas elected a woman to its leadership in 1914; in 1923, the Biblioteca Dr. David Wolfson of Belgrano had a female secretary. The Ateneo Juventud Hebraica Sefaradí, of the Turkish community in the Bajo, had a better record than these Ashkenazi groups: in 1929, six of its seventeen board members were women, among them Regina Sajón, the first woman of Mediterranean descent to graduate from dental school in Argentina. Not even the Turkish group, however, approached the gender equity of the commission of the Ashkenazi Ateneo Juventud Israelita of Rosario, which in 1935 was half female—suggesting that women may have exercised more power in the interior of the country. In both areas, however, women usually were relegated to the social and fund-raising committees.[64]

As in the colonies, in these urban voluntary associations, women sought insider status through learning and leadership positions. By creating social capital, women helped shape democratic practices and links to national democratic projects. At the same time, they solidified communal boundaries, since the membership reflected Jewish regionalism.

One association was ambivalent about women's involvement. Male students of prosperous Ashkenazi families founded the Centro (later the Asociación) Juventud Israelita Argentina (AJIA) in 1909. This reformist socialist group sponsored a library, magazine, and cultural and educational projects. The AJIA patronizingly wanted to "shake off . . . [women's] legendary apathy for all that relates to collective struggle." By late 1915, thirty young women, probably students, had joined AJIA, and half were active, submitting articles to its periodical, participating in governance, and teaching courses. Female members publicly contested male claims that women were inferior and intellectual activity impaired women's ability to have children. Yet women constituted only 11 percent of the total membership and 35 percent of the readers (not all of them members) who went to its library. By April 1916, the four women officers had disappeared from the leadership, two of them moving to the new female subcommittee.[65] This change shunted women to the sidelines.

Eager to discuss contemporary issues, female students joined male peers in creating the Ateneo Estudiantil Israelita in 1920. As one of its leaders, Clara Schliapnik (see chapter 1), then a medical student, recalled, "The world was ours, it was badly run, and we could change it." The Ateneo featured hot debates between Zionists and admirers of the Russian revolution like Schliapnik.[66] Not as comfortable or vocal in mixed company as Schliapnik, a number of secondary and university students, mostly Jewish, founded an all-female group in 1921 to encourage women to discuss intellectual matters. One meeting focused on suicide, another on revolution. This effort to prepare women to surmount gender barriers, however, lasted only two months.[67]

Clubs sometimes placed Jewish women in the spotlight. In 1929, a woman addressed the Asociación Juventud Cultural Sionista on "The Hebrew Woman through the Centuries." In 1925, the poet Raquel Adler discussed her work at AJIA, and the famous reciter Berta Singerman performed there. Female amateurs frequently recited in Spanish and Yiddish, acted in plays, sang, and played music. They also engaged each other in Ping-Pong, dominoes, and other games.[68] By displaying and refining these talents, women claimed inclusion in the Jewish communities. Whether they achieved it is another matter.

Founded in 1923, the Sociedad Hebraica Argentina hosted distinguished programs for its mostly Ashkenazi middle- and upper-class members. Although numerous women participated in Hebraica activities, they did not play significant roles in governance. By 1949, the lone woman on the board was a substitute representative. Women, generally young professionals, joined a feminine sub-commission, predictably also congregating in committees that organized parties, cultural evenings, and volunteering. Few women ran for internal offices in the early 1950s.[69] The more prestigious the association, the less likely it was that women figured among its leaders.

The Hebraica demonstrates the exclusion of Jewish women. They were absent from the leadership of key Jewish institutions—the boards of synagogues, burial and mutual-aid societies, credit associations, and banks—at a time when women were becoming more prominent in the Argentine polity. Jewish women's roles in civil society arguably were more important in rural areas and the interior than in Buenos Aires, which contained the most prominent Jewish associations.[70] Also, as the capital housed a greater number of alternative organizations and diversions, including non-Jewish ones, here Jewish women did not control sociability to the extent they did in the provinces.

Borders and Identities

Jewish women fortified their communities through clubs. Tightening bonds among Jews of Moroccan ancestry, women helped organize cultural events, dances, and benefits in the Club Social Alianza, founded in 1919. Women also helped bring German speakers together in the Jüdische Kulturgemeinschaft (JKG), established in 1937. In such groups, young women could meet their future husbands, a step toward perpetuating the community. For example, at the Centro Recreativo Israelita in Villa Crespo, created in 1922, Turkish girls danced with potential marriage partners. At the same time, club women adjusted to their new homeland. The

JKG offered Spanish lessons and, like other Jewish associations, celebrated Argentina's national holidays.[71]

Women also reinforced communal borders in their households. By speaking their native tongues, preparing customary dishes, and singing songs their mothers had sung to them, homemakers shared their heritage with their daughters. Many displayed cherished goods from their former homes overseas, such as Russian samovars. Such items assumed special importance for female exiles. Out of nostalgia and grief, they reconstructed small Central European and Italian enclaves in their homes, using the books, furniture, music, and pictures they brought with them and, in the German case, pride in a sense of order.[72]

Through the Centro Sionista N. Socolov of Parque Chacabuco, a working-class neighborhood, two girls helped nurture Ashkenazi laborers' identities. In a late 1930s broadcast of the *Hebrew Radio Matinee* on Radio Argentina, one girl reported that the Centro offered a warm and intimate "Hebrew Argentine home," providing personal connections through its cultural and social events. We offer rest and diversion to those who deserve it after a day of hard work, added the other.[73] These and other women helped foster the sense of togetherness and comfort in such organizations, firming up class and regional loyalties.

Both crossing and retaining ethnic lines, the Sociedad Hebraica Argentina stood out among the many cultural centers. The Hebraica offered art and book expositions, an extensive library, amateur theater, concerts, dances, courses, and sports activities. Prominent Jews and non-Jews such as Albert Einstein, Waldo Frank, Gabriela Mistral, Jacques Maritain, and Alfonso Reyes graced its podium. Ashkenazi women who participated in these events shared the intellectual sociability among Jews and the ties between Jews and the local cultural milieu that the Hebraica cultivated.[74]

Continuing a pattern from their homeland, where they largely integrated into the population, Italians did not join Jewish clubs or form their own. They tended to frequent non-Jewish groups, whose members often were unaware of their religious identity. One exception was the Leonardo da Vinci Society, created by young Jewish women and men to practice their native language and discuss its literature.[75]

As in the Da Vinci Society, women reinforced walls around their communities by socializing. Paisano neighbors conversed until the wee hours, and small groups of Italian refugees vacationed together. Immigrants from Kowel, Poland, sunbathed on the beach at Vicente López, as did

Sephardim on the shore in Quilmes. Farida Yadid welcomed friends and neighbors in her home by playing Arabic music and reading their fortunes in cards and coffee grounds. Some large immigrant families socialized almost exclusively among themselves, such as the Aleppine Tawils. Women of all backgrounds kept in contact with the paisanas they had met aboard ship—their ship sisters.[76]

Members of the Riegner group, named for Kurt Riegner, who led them out of Germany, tightened their German Jewish identities and soothed the wounds inflicted by Nazism and exile. These young women and men came in several installments to Buenos Aires and lived together in a rented house. There they observed religious customs and supported each other through the pain of knowing that they could not save their families from the Nazis.[77]

Food and hospitality reinforced communal borders. Immigrant women greeted visitors with refreshments from their homeland, supplemented over time with local treats. Regina Attach carefully served her guests in order of their age. They, in turn, thanked her by saying, in Arabic, "God bless your hands." Failure to observe the proper courtesies toward the host or guest could result in offense. The usual repast was anise liqueur and small plates of cheese, olives, and salads, or fruit, pastries, and Turkish coffee. The eventual addition of mate did not weaken the Damascene heritage.[78]

Women were at the center of the social occasions that represented the reproduction of the community. Well-off mothers organized parties to present their daughters to Jewish society, thus informing potential suitors of their eligibility, and to announce their daughters' engagements. Following a practice common in Argentina, friends of the bride organized parties celebrating the end of her unmarried life. Mediterranean women usually celebrated the bride's ritual bath. When she married in the 1940s, Chola Tawil, the daughter of a wealthy family from Aleppo and Jerusalem, received a large tray with soaps, perfumes, and stockings from her mother-in-law for this ritual. While sipping an almond beverage and eating pastries and candies, all prepared by female friends and relatives, women guests inspected the trousseau, comparing it to those of other brides. Tawil invited guests to a dinner at home after the civil ceremony, the religious ceremony at the Templo Libertad, the most prestigious marriage site for Jews of any origin, and a party at the Plaza Hotel. Most women, however, economized and celebrated their nuptials in private homes with close friends and relatives.[79]

6. A party for Matilde Israel, a bride from the Izmir community, Buenos Aires, 1938. Graciela Tevah de Ryba collection.

Women also were at the heart of religious holiday celebrations. They gathered their families for a meal, usually of foods reminiscent of their homelands. The substitution of local ingredients for those not available locally—beef for lamb, apricot or quince for tamarind—in Syrian cuisine did not make it less traditional. Before the High Holidays, homemakers purchased new clothing for husbands and children. Seated in the balcony of the synagogue and dressed in their finest garb, Mediterranean women gossiped and scrutinized each other's appearance. With all the chatter, displaying status and performing community outweighed praying.[80]

The religious festivities that Central European women helped arrange also defined their community. Commemorating Jews' liberation from oppression in Egypt, Passover had a special meaning for German speakers that set them apart from other Argentine Jews. In May 1935, forty-five recently arrived women and men attended the ritual meal and service at the Hilfsverein, the German immigrant aid society founded in 1933. A passage from the Haggadah, the Passover prayer book—"this is the bread of misfortune that our ancestors ate in Egypt"—led them to reflect on their persecution in Germany, painful exodus, and freedom in Argentina.[81]

Certain rituals took on added significance for these exiles. Ilse Kaufman had given birth to her son Carlos in German-occupied Czechoslovakia. Now enjoying a prosperous and secure life in Buenos Aires, she wanted her son to have a bar mitzvah, the male rite of passage, at the Templo Libertad. The rabbi refused because Carlos was not circumcised, a decision that outraged Kaufman, who claimed that the Nazis had prohibited this practice. The rabbi backed down when she vowed to have herself and her son baptized if he did not permit the bar mitzvah. The presence at the ceremony of the Argentine diplomat who had helped the family flee Europe represented their salvation. The gala reception at the exclusive Alvear Palace Hotel and the happiness surrounding the bar mitzvah symbolized the continuity of Central European Jewish existence, the family's rise from marginality, and its ties to its new homeland.[82]

Jewish girls of varied origins indulged in much the same leisure pastimes as their Catholic counterparts. They joined with boys to paddle boats and picnic in Tigre, the port at the River Plate delta; stroll, swim, and eat grilled sausages at the Costanera; or promenade through the rose gardens of Palermo Park. They went to friends' homes for parties, contributing food, drink, and records for dancing. In one such gathering in the 1930s, three sisters welcomed forty-six young men and women, who danced until dawn. Girls and their families dressed in costumes for carnival and joined merrymakers on the Avenida de Mayo. Rich women saw plays and operas, as did female workers who occupied cheap seats high up under the rafters. One proletarian girl and her family could afford to go to the movies only every two months, when they saw four films in a row. Girls from wealthier families saw movies weekly, met each other at respectable cafes, and ate out with their parents. Their mothers took them shopping on the fashionable Calle Florida downtown, which impoverished girls only saw if they worked there. While sometimes circumvented, class barriers to leisure activities proved more rigid than ethnic ones.[83]

In such pursuits, Jewish women crisscrossed the cultural divide. Privileged women could afford to dine at a pizza parlor, an Eastern European or Syrian Jewish restaurant in Once, or a German-Jewish *confitería* in Belgrano. Like other well-off Argentines, they vacationed at the beaches in Buenos Aires province and Uruguay; German Jews preferred the Córdoba highlands. The Ashkenazim patronized Spanish- and economical Yiddish-language theaters. During long afternoons in the 1930s, housewives selected from typical Argentine radio programs; the *Arab Voice*, which attracted Jewish and non-Jewish listeners; *Ashkenazi Hebrew Radio Matinee*; and *Sephardi Hour* from Uruguay.[84]

Buenos Aires offered many forms of entertainment, even for the poor, yet young women could not partake of them as freely as young men could. Growing up in the 1920s and 1930s, the daughter of prosperous Russian parents complained that her brothers could go out on their own, return home late, and engage in other activities forbidden to girls. She bitterly concluded that "to be a man signified freedom; to be a woman, imprisonment." Frustrated in her desire to study and explore the city, Estela Mesulam ironically became familiar with Buenos Aires only while chaperoning her sister and her fiancé. These young women dreamed of trespass.[85]

However, some women felt secure in their confinement and feared to trespass. Anxiety plagued a young bride of Persian and Syrian descent who had never been outside the household by herself. When she and her new husband drove to another city for their honeymoon in 1938, he left her briefly while he looked for a hotel. Unsettled, she worried about what to do if he did not return. Even female communal activists had difficulty finding their way around Buenos Aires, claimed an Ashkenazi woman writer in 1940, indicating their domestic seclusion.[86]

As some women breached the walls around their homes, others slowly scaled those separating Jewish communities. Living side by side, Jews of diverse backgrounds in Once, Villa Crespo, and other neighborhoods interacted daily. Some joined the same groups, such as the Club Israelita de Flores, whose ladies' board in 1933 included officers of Mediterranean and Eastern European descent. The Club Azul y Blanco, founded in late 1931, aimed at strengthening ties among young Jewish women of all origins. The Argentine national colors in its name underlined its desire to put aside regionalisms in the adopted homeland. Its overwhelmingly Sephardi membership suggested that this club may have brought Mediterranean groups together, but not Mediterranean and Ashkenazi Jews.[87]

Contact between Mediterranean and Ashkenazi women had increased by the 1940s. Before leaving Palestine for Argentina, the Bulgarian-born Bruria Elnecavé had lived with Polish Jews in a kibbutz. Finding little interest in Zionism among Sephardi peers in the 1930s and early 1940s, Elnecavé sought out Ashkenazi women who shared her vision. Indeed, Zionism prompted women's strongest efforts to cross communal borders (see chapter 8). The increasing entry of Sephardi women into universities also facilitated their acquaintance with Ashkenazim and cultural change. An Egyptian immigrant had little association with Ashkenazim until she went to Paris to study in the early 1960s. Her friendship there with an

Argentine Ashkenazi girl opened her mind to leftism, Zionism, and freedom from parental strictures.[88]

This is not to say that Jews of diverse origins—or even the same origins—necessarily embraced each other. Suspicions and resentments abounded, as in the case of German-speaking exiles. Central Europeans who arrived before 1933 aided refugees who came thereafter through such organizations as the Hilfsverein. Still, newcomers thought their wealthy predecessors looked down on them. One woman of the Riegner group had a letter of presentation to a family that had long resided in Buenos Aires. When she went there for tea, she felt her hosts treated her like a poor supplicant. She also believed that the Eastern European establishment rejected her and her fellow exiles, repaying them for the disdainful way that many German Jews had treated Eastern European coreligionists in Europe.[89]

The larger urban society usually accepted its Jewish inhabitants, especially before 1930. Other than vigilante attacks in 1910 and 1919 (see chapter 7), violence and blatant discrimination seemed infrequent. Calling Jewish women rusas and stereotyping them as Communists or prostitutes, however, were common. Perhaps prejudice was muted because few women asserted the Jewish component of their identities outside the communal arena. Generally they called themselves *israelitas* rather than *judías*, which did not obscure but softened their origin. Many Jewish women may have appreciated being able to meld with the crowd, while others may have resented submerging their backgrounds.

A beauty pageant illustrated the ambiguities of Jewish women's identities. In 1932, the tabloid *Noticias Gráficas* organized the selection of Miss Argentina, who would enter the Miss Universe contest. Each porteño neighborhood chose its candidate for Miss Capital, who would compete with the provincial Misses for this title. With a great deal of fanfare, Ana Rovner became Miss Once and then Miss Capital. The diligent eighteen-year-old studied at the Liceo de Señoritas, worked in the post office, and planned to be an attorney. Her beauty, however, overshadowed all other considerations. Described as tall, light-skinned, and blonde, Rovner was the epitome of porteña loveliness and "the melting pot of our race in formation," according to the sponsoring newspaper. It claimed she reflected "the Argentine sun, blue skies, modesty of the infinite plains and tall and elegant stature of the distant mountains." Apparently a black woman had represented South America in an earlier international pageant, and Rovner wanted to dispel this image. If the honor of representing Argentina fell to this woman of German descent born in Buenos Aires, no one could "speak of black South Americans," wrote *Noticias Gráficas*. Since Rovner did not become Miss Argentina, she lost the chance to change perceptions of the continent.[90]

The irony was that Rovner was Jewish, a fact the newspaper never mentioned. Given her last name and her residence in Once, many porteños may have guessed. Yet *Noticias Gráficas* overlooked or lied about details that would have clarified her identity, such as the fact that she and her mother were born in a Jewish colony in Entre Ríos. She probably was of Russian rather than German descent, but identifying her as Russian, which most Argentines linked with Jews, would have made her origins all too clear. These omissions indicated the limits of public acceptance of Jews. It was permissible to pick a Jew as beauty queen; indeed, it confirmed notions of Jewish women as sensual and attractive. A Jew could even symbolize Argentine womanhood and represent whiteness, and it is telling that Rovner portrayed herself in this light. By adopting local prejudices, tapping porteño fears of being perceived as nonwhite by foreigners, and linking herself with other Argentines of European ancestry, she deflected attention away from her problematic identity. Yet the accolades were possible only because neither Rovner nor the non-Jewish press acknowledged her Jewish roots. Instead, the media characterized her as the descendant of immigrants, nationalized over the course of time, although still German enough to be blonde. Cognizant of the deception, Jews took pride in the fact that Miss Capital and also Miss Palermo were Jewish, but the pride was bittersweet.[91]

Comparing Rovner and the first known Jewish beauty queen in the United States, Bess Myerson, exposes racial nuances of the two societies. Myerson overcame anti-Semitism among pageant leaders, business sponsors, and many viewers to win the Miss America contest in 1945. She resisted pressure to change her name and hide her origins. Aware that many did not see her as white, and allying herself with people of color, Myerson denounced racism and appeared on a panel with Miss Sepia America, despite opposition from Miss America organizers.[92] In contrast, Rovner apparently thought she could "pass." Perhaps Argentina offered Jewish women greater possibilities for doing so than did the United States.

If many Argentines betrayed ambivalence about Jewish women, Italian Jewish female exiles were ambivalent about their own identities. Commiserating with other antifascists, some anchored their identities to this association rather than to their birthplace or religion. While they were grateful for Argentine hospitality, many continued to identify with Italy, whose conversion to anti-Semitism was tardy and superficial, although lethal. The perception that the fascist government, not the people, had spurned them led a significant portion of the immigrants to return to Italy after the war. Older women who repatriated, however, recognized that their Argentine experience had changed them: they were less smugly bourgeois, more open to pursuits outside the home.[93]

In Argentina, unlike in their homeland, German Jewish women could truly be German. They prided themselves on being cultured, hard-working, and punctual, traits they associated with Germany but might not have emphasized when they lived there. Maintaining their language affirmed their claim to German nationality and reinforced distinctions between them and the Jewish majority of Yiddish origin. In Germany they had begun to see themselves as Jews rather than Germans of Jewish descent. This process continued in Argentina, where many women became more religiously observant. Rejected by their homeland, most German women remained in Argentina after the Second World War, but this did not mean that they felt integrated into local society. Some who had grown up in exile saw themselves as citizens of the world, prepared to live in many places if necessary. One woman's long residence in Córdoba, outside a narrow German Jewish orbit, set her apart. Her wide circle of Catholic and Ashkenazi acquaintances made her feel at home in Argentina.[94]

Apparent Nazi activity did not dispel such feelings. The fact that a priest denounced Nazi infiltration of Argentine schools in the tabloid *Crítica* in 1938 convinced one Jewish woman that her majority Catholic nation accepted and included her. Her parents had fled czarist oppression and brought her to Argentina when she was a baby. Staking her claim to the country, she wrote: "This is my fatherland, the one I love. Here I have completed my studies, and I have formed an Argentine family."[95]

Conclusion

The thousands of Jewish women who participated in state formation would have echoed her words. Firsthand experiences in schools and celebrations of national holidays, often taking place in Jewish institutions, reinforced their links to Argentina and its liberal project, as did mothers' secondhand experiences through their children. Through birth, redemption, patriotic feeling, and the creation of social capital, women asserted their Argentine status. They also did so simply by constructing hybrid identities or appropriating whiteness, like Rovner.

To some extent, their communities and the broader society relegated Jewish women to the fringes. Poverty marginalized large numbers of women and limited their access to resources and urban pleasures. The status of exiles declined at least temporarily upon arrival. Gender norms isolated many women in the home and excluded them from technology, education, and leadership in their communities. Jewish women seemed less prominent in Jewish urban life than in rural centers. Most neighbors, teachers, and coworkers accepted Jewish women, but toleration could hinge on submerging Jewishness, as in Rovner's case. Many Jewish women moved toward the mainstream by mastering their craft and pursuing educational alternatives, as well as claiming spaces in Jewish associations and seeking political change, as described in later chapters.

Moving from another country to Buenos Aires, as Elnecavé had done, inevitably meant crossing borders, both geographical and metaphorical. In neighborhoods, workplaces, and schools, Jewish women learned from Jews of other origins and from non-Jews. They crisscrossed cultures in their cooking, leisure pursuits, and other habits. Utilizing border skills, some immigrants reinvented themselves. Many scaled gender and communal barriers by attaining an education, imbibing Argentine culture at the Hebraica, or attending lectures at leftist libraries.

Breaching domestic or communal walls promised adventure, freedom, and enrichment; it could also promote insecurity and conflict. Many women found comfort in remaining at home, associating with their kind, cherishing old ways, and fulfilling expectations. Working within homes and helping out in family businesses increased income without overturning gender norms. These women avoided the anxieties of trespassing.

Even as they crossed the pampas or ocean for the cosmopolitan city, women strengthened communal borders. They helped integrate paisanos into their midst and socialized largely with them, celebrated the reproduction of community, maintained imported customs, and participated in schools and associations organized along regional lines. They fostered cordiality and diversions to help their peers forget their cares and adjust to Buenos Aires. United to a certain degree, Jewish communities, however, were stratified.

Migration and immigration were not always triumphalist narratives. Sadness and feelings of rootlessness could outweigh the upward mobility that some newcomers or, more typically, their offspring experienced. In the 1940s and 1950s, economic conditions improved for Jewish and non-Jewish Argentines alike. By this time, women increasingly were entering universities and professions, as described in the next chapter. Meanwhile, they worked and struggled to persevere.

CHAPTER THREE

"A Point of Connection"

Pathways into the Professions

I have genuine longings to be a teacher.
—Paulina Alianak, *Israel*, October 1925

For me dance has always been a need to give something, to express myself and find a point of connection with the life that surrounds me.
—María Fux, *Danza*

María Fux battled poverty, convention, and her family to become a pioneer of modern dance in Argentina. She performed in plazas and bars, making her art accessible to workers, and created a form of dance therapy for the handicapped and aged. Her therapy, venues, and medium were intertwined with aspirations of freedom and equality. For Fux and many other women, work served as "a point of connection" with society and the state.

This chapter documents Jewish women's entry into the professions, the factors that affected their prospects, and their perceptions of their trajectories. It follows the careers of educators, medical personnel, and entertainers. Women of other backgrounds were becoming professionals at the same time, but we know little about how they experienced this process.[1] This chapter, then, opens a window on Argentine women in occupational life.

There is no single narrative of Jewish women's professional achievement. Case studies reveal the nuances and patterns of women's engagement with borders, inclusion and exclusion, state formation, transnationalism, and whiteness. I privilege figures who crossed rather than stayed within boundaries, because they are better documented and better exemplify the themes of this book.

Jewish women's paths into professions were not always smooth. Class and gender borders were difficult to scale, particularly for Mediterranean women, and the exigencies of exile shut most Central European and Italian female immigrants out of careers. Many non-Ashkenazi women, however, entered professions after 1955. Some Jewish women were able to circumvent obstacles, often drawing upon foreign ties and experiences. At times, gender notions could facilitate as well as limit women's aspirations. As already described, women constructed hybrid identities by borrowing, adapting, and reinventing themselves, and they also utilized these border skills in their livelihoods.

A few prominent Jewish female entertainers were transnational figures who carried ideas and artistic genres from one setting to another. In the process, they transformed culture in Argentina and other countries. Political events on both sides of the Atlantic influenced their struggles to protect democratic expression.

Jewish women were both insiders and outsiders. Usually starting from the margins, a number managed to place their research and activities at the center of their fields. Encouragement, often from non-Jews, smoothed their way. The anti-Semitism confronted by Jewish women professionals rarely appeared obvious or overwhelming; discrimination based on gender and political affiliation seemed more common. Yet at times the motives for exclusion were so interwoven that it is difficult to discern which was primary.

Many Jewish women engaged with the state through their careers. Teachers imbibed liberalism in normal school and disseminated it in their classrooms. A sense of social justice led some professionals to at least implicitly transcend this hegemonic project and formulate more progressive ones. These women contested rightist and Catholic nationalists in the educational system and other arenas, and claimed space in an Argentina they defined more broadly than did these ideologues.

Their bodies and artistic preferences on display, stage and screen personalities were racially constructed. Critics and the public linked some with whiteness. Others, however, had more ambiguous racial identities.

The Professional World and Teaching

Argentine Jewish women differed strikingly from Argentine women as a whole by 1960. That year, almost half of all women in the labor force, but only about a quarter of Jewish women, worked in factories and services.

Jewish women were overrepresented in the clerical and commercial sectors, and in the latter as employers and self-employed.[2] Twenty percent of working Jewish women were professionals, compared to 16 percent of all Argentine women (see table 10).[3] In a study of female professionals in Buenos Aires in 1967, nearly a third of the sample was Jewish or of Jewish origin.[4] To utilize their skills, avoid anti-Semitism, and evade the control of men outside their families, Argentine Jewish women became disproportionately represented in jobs requiring education and fields that permitted some independence.

Jewish women transcended their humble beginnings upon arrival in Argentina largely through primary-school teaching. It was the first occupation for many Jewish and other Argentine women, and their springboard to other callings. This career promoted inclusion in learning outside the home, a world long denied to Jewish and other women.[5]

Teacher-training schools entrusted immigrants and daughters of immigrants—both Jewish and non-Jewish—with a nation-building mission. A prominent future educator, Berta Perelstein (known by her married name, Braslavsky) was born in 1913 on the edge of the colonies in Entre Ríos, where the first Jewish female teachers had appeared in classrooms a few years earlier. She and her family moved to Buenos Aires when she completed third grade. Her mother's dream was for one son to become a lawyer, another son a professor, and for Berta to become a teacher. The mother could not envision a career for Berta as grand as those she wanted for her sons; an older daughter had not gone beyond the third grade. Becoming a teacher seemed achievable for a girl of modest origins.[6] A passing grade on a difficult entrance exam and a letter her brother, a lawyer, obtained from one of President Marcelo T. de Alvear's (1922–28) cabinet ministers secured Braslavsky's admission into a normal school; even a girl of Jewish descent could gain access to a prominent politician. Among the first graduates of Sarmiento's teacher-training schools, her professors instilled in her his notions of liberalism, including universal, secular, and free education; the educator's duty to improve society; and women's vital roles in pedagogy. This daughter of immigrants felt privileged to receive such a good education. It also tied her to the liberal project and demonstrated her acceptance in Argentine society.[7]

Paulina Alianak, a normal-school student of Mediterranean origin in Buenos Aires writing in the mid-1920s, approached education with reverence. The one institution that stood for "Equality, Fraternity, and Liberty," school brought rich and poor together. Studying in this hallowed place,

Alianak followed in the footsteps of great men. Her first-grade teacher, who had comforted and taken pains to teach her, had inspired Alianak's "genuine longings to be a teacher," a mission that filled her with awe. Even the most powerful men respected women teachers, for they alone knew how "to place us on the threshold of the Temple of Science." Renowned educators like Sarmiento demonstrated the power of learning by defeating barbarism with a pen the way others killed their enemies with swords.[8]

Other women, however, saw teaching as confining. Born in 1905 in Córdoba, Ana Salzman wanted to study law. The rebelliousness of her father, who had rejected his family's religious orthodoxy, and her mother, who read feminist literature, inspired her. More conservative than their parents, Salzman's brothers shamed her into forsaking her dream, claiming that teaching was the only appropriate occupation for women. Salzman submitted to her brothers, although years later she defied them and received a degree as a notary, which she never used.[9]

Salzman might have agreed with scholars who argue that the school system did not truly emancipate women teachers, for it paid them little and employed popular notions of motherhood and caregiving to circumscribe their roles. Alianak contested these limits by identifying with prominent men and scientific prestige. Braslavsky and others contested them by using education to promote political change.[10]

Non-Jewish teachers ushered Jewish and other pupils into the profession and progressive politics. Rosa Weinschelbaum (better known by her married name, Ziperovich) valued her mentors Olga Cossettini and Amanda Arias in the normal school of Rafaela, Santa Fe, from which she graduated in 1930. They adapted modern educational techniques drawn from the worldwide Active School movement (described below). Arias welcomed pupils from poor and immigrant homes and helped them get housing, books, medical care, and provisions so they could remain in school, despite opposition from influential townspeople to these practices and the school's radical pedagogy.[11]

Jewish students confronted class lines in the normal schools that theoretically were dedicated to equality. Braslavsky transferred into the fourth grade, but some classmates, generally the daughters of professors and educational officials, had entered in the first grade. They were the ones expected to compete for the gold medal for the highest average in the last four years of study. One such girl and Braslavsky emerged as the candidates for this coveted award. The student body split into two factions, one supporting the sanctioned favorite, the less-privileged contingent favoring Braslavsky. The outsider won the medal.[12]

Such class divisions did not necessarily mean ethnic or religious divisions, and Jewish students rarely recalled anti-Semitism in the normal institutes. Some may have suppressed such memories. An exception was Ziperovich, who felt that her Jewish identity set her apart from most classmates, some of whom seemed to despise her difference. When her mentor Arias witnessed their behavior, rather than scold them individually, she discussed racial and religious discrimination with the student body and condemned it. Years later Ziperovich applied the same method when she faced students who discriminated against poor or dark-skinned classmates.[13] Like Sara Dachevsky, a teacher in Entre Ríos (see chapter 1), Ziperovich imagined the nation as one that included people of color.

Mediterranean Jewish women who sought to become educators were somewhat disadvantaged. They tended to enjoy less support at home and have fewer role models and companions of their background than their Ashkenazi counterparts had. As late as the 1960s, when an Egyptian immigrant studied French at the Universidad de Buenos Aires, she saw hardly any Sephardi women.[14]

Graduation from a normal school, even with a high ranking, did not guarantee a teaching position. There was much competition for the scarce jobs, and until 1958, there were no regulations governing the hiring of teachers. Even to get work in rural schools, women usually required political connections, which they accessed through their male relatives. The most dramatic example was Ana Salzman. When an unbalanced policeman of another political persuasion murdered her husband, a member of the Progressive Democratic party (PDP), Salzman persuaded the PDP government of Santa Fe to award her and her sister teaching posts in 1932 in remembrance of her slain husband.[15]

That year, Braslavsky graduated at the top of her class but could not find a job. Exalted status and clout were even more crucial in highly desirable Buenos Aires than in remote provinces, and positions may have been scarcer than usual during the Great Depression. The dearth of opportunities convinced her to enter the Instituto Nacional del Profesorado Secundario, where she worked on a college-level degree in physics education. The long-delayed ceremony to award her the gold medal took place in the Teatro Cervantes in 1936. Angered by the postponement and her unemployment, Braslavsky in her acceptance speech bravely criticized the educational establishment sitting before her. Shamed, the renowned education official Pablo Pizzurno found her a three-month substitute position.[16]

Braslavsky's political activism also put her on the fringe. Her leftist readings and her brothers' Socialist activism led the young student to reject the oppressive dictatorship installed by General José Félix Uriburu in 1930, as well as the government of his successor, the fraudulently elected President Agustín P. Justo. Despite official bans on student groups, Braslavsky participated in one affiliated with the left-of-center Federación Universitaria Argentina.[17] She was nearing graduation when Jorge de la Torre, the minister of justice and public instruction, expelled her, claiming she was a Communist. Braslavsky fought back, obtaining support from the Socialist deputy Juan Antonio Solari and the PDP representative Julio Noble, who demanded that de la Torre explain his actions. The congressional deliberations, however, did not restore Braslavsky to the Profesorado.[18]

Braslavsky chose other paths. Impressed by her strong convictions, the Communist Youth asked her to join them, and she did, despite parental opposition. Braslavsky drew closer to her boyfriend, who supported her and embraced her politics, and they planned to marry. An open leftist, she could not find a permanent job in a public school, but another possibility opened up. A year after her expulsion, in 1937, Braslavsky entered the new pedagogy program at the Universidad de Buenos Aires.

A more easily subdued woman would have fallen by the wayside, as depicted in a fictional story in *Israel* in 1925. Rebeca, a Jewish porteña, graduated from normal school with a distinguished record. Two years later, despite repeated visits to the education board, she was still unemployed. At this time, according to the author, 5,000 elementary teachers were out of work, and only positions in Chaco and La Pampa were available. Rebeca loved Buenos Aires and did not want to feel isolated, like her friends who had accepted jobs in distant locations. Deciding to teach high school, she, like Braslavsky, studied science at the Profesorado. Despite harassment by male students, who insisted that science was not for women, Rebeca graduated with a high ranking. Again mirroring Braslavsky, at the ceremony she addressed an audience including educational officials, yet she was still unemployed. Rebeca applied for an opening in a normal school headed by a friend and was assured that she would get the job. When an unqualified yet politically active man won the post instead, Rebeca gave up. In the ironic ending, she became the supposedly happy wife of a former classmate.[19]

While the account was purportedly fictional, its detailed description of conditions for educators lent it authenticity. It was emblematic of the experiences of many young women who were excluded from jobs and did not possess Braslavsky's strength or border skills of flexibility and reinvention. The piece provides insight into women stymied in their careers, whose lives have not been recorded.

Other potential teachers gave up their careers for marriage. One of the young intellectuals who defended women's rights in the Asociación Juventud Israelita Argentina (see chapter 2), Rosa Wernicke attained a teaching degree at an early age. This served as her springboard to the university, where she received excellent grades. When she married, like other women, she abandoned her studies and dedicated herself to her children.[20] Flexible teaching schedules and servants, however, enabled some privileged women to surmount these gender hurdles.[21]

Beginning her career in 1937 in the Villa Domínguez school where she had studied, Luisa Furman combined teaching with outreach. Her teachers and the school cooperative members who had fed her when she was young inspired her solidarity efforts. Furman took students with her to school in her sulky and visited peons to convince them to leave their children in school. After hours, she tutored her pupils without charge, a task she continued for twenty years after her retirement. When she stepped down from teaching, Furman volunteered in the school cooperative and founded a clothing service for needy children. A newspaper praised Furman for teaching with "a genuine Sarmientine passion," yet her belief in a nation that included poor criollos distinguished her from the schoolteacher president.[22]

This was also true of Ziperovich, who started teaching in her hometown of Moisesville in 1931. She then taught in country schools, served as assistant principal and principal in Rosario and, after 1955, supervisor of a school district north of Rosario. In this last capacity, Ziperovich became known for her efforts to retain disadvantaged students and improve the quality of instruction, which earned her the title of teacher of teachers. Her practices helped redefine the core of Argentine education.[23]

Before 1955, Ziperovich adapted and applied ideas from larger reform currents that later brought her fame. Starting in normal school, she absorbed the democratic impulses of the Active School movement that swept Western countries between the late 1800s and the 1930s. In that movement, John Dewey, Maria Montessori, and other pedagogues focused on the individual child, respected difference, emphasized freedom, and trusted in the power of schools to improve society. As part of this wave, Ziperovich defended the Argentine tradition of universal secular education, yet sought to convert the old positivistic style of teaching into one that sponsored free, active, enjoyable learning relevant to one's surroundings. Teachers needed to understand and accept their pupils' backgrounds, although this did not mean tolerating inequalities; educators should make schools more democratic, incorporating parents into their governance. Schools would then help catalyze broader social change.[24] Through her oppositional educational project, Ziperovich sought to make Argentina more egalitarian.

Authorities seized upon Ziperovich's politics to persecute her. In 1937, her principal accused her of using dangerous books, such as Raúl Scalabrini Ortiz's *Historia de los ferrocarriles argentinos*, which decried the handing over of local railroads to the British, and Jorge Icaza's *Huasipungo*, which exposed the exploitation of Ecuadorian Indians. Her activity in the Communist Party, which was illegal in the 1930s, and the teacher's union cost Ziperovich her job for a brief time. After she became principal in 1950, under Perón, she lost her job for six years. The military dictatorship that came to power in 1976 also fired her.

It is equally difficult to separate the intertwined threads of career and leftism in Braslavsky's life. She and Ziperovich were harassed primarily for political reasons, although their opponents may have seen their Jewish and Communist identities as interchangeable. Once Braslavsky entered the pedagogy program, rightists in the education ministry pressured the Universidad de Buenos Aires to expel her. Coriolano Alberini, her professor and dean of the college, planned to fail her because she was a Marxist. Braslavsky's student association rallied around her, as did the right-wing Catholic Centro de Estudiantes Santo Tomás de Aquino, with which she had maintained good relations. Had she not attended some of their masses, these rightists would have stigmatized this leftist woman of Jewish origin. The presence of well-wishers from across the political spectrum at the public examinations forced Alberini to give Braslavsky the highest score. When the university again threatened to expel her, the two student groups pressured the administration into allowing her to complete her honors degree in 1940. Her thesis discussed French Enlightenment influence on education in the Río de la Plata region before 1830. Braslavsky's training enabled her to explain these thinkers' rationalistic and scientific worldview and defend this liberal tradition against radical rightists who extolled Spanish colonialism. Although the thesis did not cite Marx, it was a leftist polemical text.[25]

Similar concerns inspired her first book, *Positivismo y antipositivismo en la Argentina* (1952). This materialist analysis demonstrated that both positivism and antipositivism contradicted a genuinely scientific mind-set. While Argentine positivists were less reactionary than those in other Latin American countries, they were linked to imperialism and the oligarchy. In place of these philosophies, Braslavsky favored Marxist thought and practice that built upon the progressive philosophical legacy of Argentine independence, thus claiming liberalism while modifying it. Published by a semiclandestine Communist press, the book initially sparked favorable reviews from Communist and other organs but then fell prey to shifts in party positions. Ironically, the party that had sheltered her made it difficult for Braslavsky, a loyal member, to sustain her voice.[26]

Her ideology precluded a position in a government institution, so Braslavsky and several colleagues set up the Instituto Argentino de Reeducación (IAR) in 1944. One of the few Argentine special-education facilities, IAR taught retarded and learning-disabled children and trained students and educators to instruct them. After studying with experts in France in 1948–49, Braslavsky pioneered the use of modern methods to educate dyslexic children in Argentina.[27]

What began as a peripheral activity put Braslavsky at the center of education. Indeed, she reconfigured the center to include special education, spreading the knowledge and bibliographic materials she had received in France. Her efforts in special education and research on reading brought her international recognition. Both Braslavsky and Ziperovich helped end male domination of educational research.[28] After Perón's fall from power, Braslavsky obtained a position at the Universidad de Buenos Aires in 1957, and in the mid-1960s she became full professor (*titular*) at this school and the Universidad de La Plata. Her militancy and distaste for the military that ruled intermittently after 1955 made her academic career a rocky one. Nevertheless, her visibility outside Argentina enabled her to survive expulsions and persecutions, as did her use of border skills to turn obstacles to her advantage.

Religion in the Schools

While education was a field open to Jews and others of immigrant origins, it was also historically subject to intervention by the Roman Catholic Church. Implemented in 1884, secular education in federal schools was part of the liberal program. Some provincial schools, however, retained Catholic education or adopted it in the 1930s, as happened in Santa Fe, where teachers forced some Jewish students to recite Catholic prayers. In this decade, national educational leaders seeking to spread the values of hierarchy and order embodied by the church permitted Catholic inroads. Asserting Argentina's Catholic nature, the military dictatorship of 1943–45 imposed Catholic education in all state schools. This measure, which became law in 1947 under Perón, made Catholic instruction obligatory, except for students whose parents opposed it because they practiced another religion. This minority had to attend morality classes. In the early 1950s, the spirit behind the law became more tolerant, and new textbooks accepted other faiths. The federal educational system returned to secularism in 1955, during the conflict between Perón and the church that preceded his ouster.[29]

Jewish women responded differently to religious education. Some parents did not remove their children from such classes because they did not want to isolate them or rouse the administrators' hostility, or because they did not care. Their daughters felt bored, suppressed, or indifferent—reactions they shared with many Catholic classmates. Some perceived the morality class as anti-Semitic because it ostracized Jews. Nor did morality classes always function properly: one woman recalled that often she had no teacher, or the instructors would impart Christian morality, the only kind they knew.[30]

Teachers were supposed to instruct their classes in the Catholic religion, but as Jewish women could not fulfill this requirement, they left the room while priests or other instructors taught the catechism. When Ana Salzman learned that a priest had injected anti-Semitism into his sessions, she remained in the classroom during religious instruction, which prevented future outbursts from him. A few enlightened principals saw Jewish faculty as the logical candidates to teach morality. While an Ashkenazi instructor enjoyed teaching one such class, she believed it represented discrimination.[31] Nevertheless, through such practices some Jewish teachers fought to include Jews in schools and a nation described as Catholic after 1943.

As Catholic education softened, the new civic religion of Peronism emerged. Instructors read aloud in class Eva Perón's autobiography, *La razón de mi vida*; displayed images of her and her husband; and assigned books and papers on Peronist topics. The cult of personality and spirit of conformity did not trouble some female teachers, both Jewish and non-

Jewish, but they repelled others. Educators particularly feared surveillance by progovernment faculty, administrators, and employees, who spied on teachers to insure their allegiance.[32] Some Jewish teachers battled marginalization, whether on religious or political grounds.

Teaching in Jewish Schools

Ashkenazi women also fought discrimination in Jewish education. The Instituto Superior de Estudios Religiosos Judaicos in Buenos Aires, intended to guide young men into university studies and teaching in Jewish schools, was established in 1943. To train enough teachers, it added a normal school for girls in 1950. Unlike the male section, the normal school did not prepare students for college. Instead, it offered scholarships and supervised living quarters in the Jewish girls' orphanage to attract young women, especially from the interior. Three years after the establishment of the female branch, female students outnumbered males.[33] By the late 1940s, most teachers in Jewish schools were female, yet it took twenty years for women to control the management of these institutions.[34]

Various factors helped feminize the Ashkenazi teaching corps. Men found better opportunities outside Jewish schools, which paid low salaries. The Holocaust, the creation of Israel, and immigration restrictions drastically cut the numbers of Jews entering Argentina, including the Eastern European men who had dominated the field of teaching. Nationalistic laws also promoted change. A 1938 regulation required private-school teachers to demonstrate proficiency in Spanish and Argentine studies. The military dictatorship of 1943–45 stipulated that such instructors should have local education degrees, revalidate their foreign degrees, or obtain a certificate from the national education board, and principals of foreign-language schools should be Argentine citizens. These rulings unintentionally expanded positions in Jewish schools for women, who composed the vast majority of Argentine normal school graduates.[35]

A gendered interpretation of communal needs also strengthened women's presence in Ashkenazi schools. By the mid-1950s, Jewish leaders urged female teachers to maintain religious customs in the interior by involving mothers in school activities and families in school holiday celebrations.[36] Mothers rather than fathers were now responsible for reinvigorating Jewish life, and female teachers became the nexus between mothers and the schools.

Ashkenazi women also predominated among faculty in secular Bund,

Jewish Communist, and Zionist schools, and Sara Fischer was prominent among them. Born in Poland in 1906, Fischer studied preschool education at a college-level Jewish normal institute in that country. She was an experienced teacher when she arrived in Moisesville in 1931, to work in one of the three existing Jewish kindergartens in Argentina. From there she transferred to Buenos Aires, found a base in the Zionist Bialik School, and attracted pupils to its kindergarten.[37]

Few Argentines, Jewish or not, valued preschool education, believing that it entertained rather than educated children. Utilizing her Polish expertise, Fischer converted kindergartens into genuine learning centers. Beginning in 1950 as inspector of Jewish kindergartens, and as director from 1958 on, she planned curricula, trained teachers, and fought to strengthen facilities and standards. Like Ziperovich, she was a teacher of teachers, observing classes, inviting experts to give seminars, and importing pedagogical writings. Fischer headed the Seminario de Maestras Jardineras, which grew into the Instituto del Profesorado para Jardines Sh. Y. Agnon in 1968. While this was a Jewish institution, its graduates received official degrees enabling them to work in any school. Fischer wrote materials for her courses and others at the Instituto, and she published a Spanish-Hebrew-Yiddish dictionary of kindergarten themes as well as journal articles.[38]

Under Fischer's influence, foreign and democratic ideas permeated Jewish education. Johann Heinrich Pestalozzi, who favored spontaneity and learning through doing, was among her models, as were Active School figures. Like Ziperovich, Fischer spread tolerance, solidarity with the poor, and a pluralistic national project. To promote diversity, she placed black dolls in classrooms in the 1950s. Fischer encouraged teachers to learn about their students' backgrounds and obtain free tuition for the needy.[39]

Fischer crossed over into the national arena. Many non-Jewish teachers attended her displays of educational materials and borrowed them from her. Fischer exchanged ideas with other teachers through national educational organizations and conferences. She quoted Sarmiento in her writings, and one of her admirers compared her to the North Americans this president had invited to create a teaching corps in Argentina. According to a colleague, she and her pedagogue husband became "the center and motor of Jewish education in Argentina."[40] Indeed, she redefined the center of both Jewish and Argentine education by incorporating in it a formerly peripheral field.

Medical Practice and Research

In her native Italy, Dr. Eugenia Sacerdote de Lustig had been on the fringe. Her mother had initially opposed a medical career for her, regarding the profession as unsuitable for women. Sacerdote was one of four women alongside 500 men in medical school, and many male classmates and professors never let her forget her minority status. Then, in 1938, the Italian Racial Laws stripped Sacerdote, her husband, and other Jews of their positions. Her spouse's employers transferred him to their new installation in Buenos Aires and helped secure visas for the family. They were safe, but she could not practice her profession because the Argentine government refused to recognize foreign degrees. Research was a possibility, but years had passed since her graduation, and she felt out of touch; furthermore, she feared making mistakes in Spanish. Nevertheless, she began to consult the medical school library. Sacerdote, her husband, and their three young children shared a household with her in-laws to save money, and dividing the child care with her sister-in-law left her afternoons free for such pursuits. Another Italian exile who had been her professor in Turin encouraged her to visit the histology department, since she had written her thesis in this area. The department head offered her a tiny space for a laboratory, in which she cultivated cells in vitro, a technique then unknown in Argentina. Dr. Bernardo Houssay, a physiology professor and a future Nobel laureate, invited her to join and present papers at the Sociedad de Biología.[41] When the military regime expelled Houssay from the university in 1943, however, his histology colleagues resigned in solidarity.[42] The director of the Instituto Oncológico, Dr. Angel Roffo, saved her by inviting her to set up a lab there for cultivating cancer cells—a new area of research for Argentina.

Situated between cultures and professions, Sacerdote ventured into unfamiliar territory. In the early 1950s, Dr. Armando Parodi asked her to cultivate cells in vitro in his virology department at the prestigious Instituto de Microbiología Malbrán. Shortly thereafter, Parodi accepted a position in Uruguay, leaving Sacerdote as department head, supervising research on a topic virtually unknown to her and Argentina. She learned virology while teaching it to her staff. She also began to cultivate and test human embryonic cells obtained from aborted fetuses that she secretly collected at maternity clinics. A polio epidemic hit Buenos Aires in the mid-1950s, and Sacerdote was at the heart of efforts to diagnose this disease. Each night after testing hundreds of suspected cases, she burned tissue samples to prevent contagion. The first person in Argentina to take the Salk vaccine, Sacerdote in turn vaccinated the first child recipient. Perched uneasily in her new and contentious country, this exile applied border skills to construct a career.

This was a particularly difficult period in her tumultuous life. She sent her children to Montevideo to escape the epidemic and visited them each weekend. At this time, in 1955, the many Peronist employees at Malbrán went on strike to protest the military's expulsion of Perón. Because Sacerdote disliked Perón—whom she saw as another Mussolini—and wanted to pursue her polio research, she continued to work. When strikers attacked and injured her, she resigned.

A democratic government finally recognized her. During Arturo Frondizi's presidency (1958–62), his brother Risieri Frondizi, rector of the Universidad de Buenos Aires, allowed foreign-degree holders to apply for positions. Sacerdote won the professorship of cellular biology in the Facultad de Ciencias Exactas y Naturales in 1959, and the rector formally accepted her Italian degree. When a new wave of military repression led her to resign in 1966, the Instituto Roffo hired her to head its research department.

Authoritarian politics repeatedly shunted her to the sidelines, and anti-Semitism sometimes lurked beneath the surface. Around 1950, when she was working at the Instituto Roffo, the Peronist government asked her to train a German doctor in her research techniques. The government revalidated his medical degree, yet it refused to do the same for her, which Sacerdote regarded as clear proof of anti-Semitism. Yet she did not experience gender bias in Argentina as she had in Italy. The many local women studying biochemistry, pharmacy, and medicine convinced her that Argentina was much more inclusive in this regard than her native land.

Persecution, exile, politics, and research difficulties in an underdeveloped country created immense barriers for Sacerdote, yet she found ways around them. She published over 180 papers and received numerous awards.[43] The circumstances of her life led her to adapt to constant change and develop varied talents. Like Braslavsky and Fischer, she introduced foreign techniques and inserted her research into the core of her discipline in Argentina.

Another refugee, Marie Glas de Langer, also arrived in Argentina when her skills were in short supply there. Born to a prosperous assimilated family in Vienna in 1910, Langer publicly renounced Judaism (although she never converted to Christianity), and her appearance and last name did not seem Jewish, yet she could not pass for a gentile. Her leftist schooling and encounters with anti-Semitism in her birthplace and Nazi Germany helped convince her to join the Communist Party. When Langer became a doctor in 1935, her Jewish background precluded a job or internship with the government medical service. Nor would the Jewish hospital hire this apostate. As an alternative, and in order to better understand herself and her female relatives, Langer, who had already taken psychiatry courses, studied for a year at the Viennese psychoanalytic institute with leaders in the field. Yet Freud had forbidden analysts to belong to illegal organizations, including the Communist Party. For Langer, the antifascist struggle assumed priority over psychoanalysis, and she and her future husband left for Spain in 1936, where they joined the International Brigade and treated the wounded. After the Loyalist defeat, they returned to Central Europe, then fled to Uruguay and settled in Argentina.[44]

Here Langer reversed her pattern and put her career above politics. Although she had not completed her training in Austria, few of her new analyst colleagues had more preparation than she. Together they founded the Asociación Psicoanalítica Argentina (APA) in 1942. In that decade she and a colleague translated the works of the Viennese-turned-British psychoanalyst Melanie Klein into Spanish. Like Klein, Langer disparaged Freud's phallocentrism. Langer's *Maternidad y sexo* (1951), a pioneering psychoanalytic work on female sexuality, contained insights from anthropology, other disciplines, and Klein. According to Mariano Plotkin, Langer "put women at the center of psychoanalytic discourse" in Argentina. While this might suggest a radical orientation, Langer's views were conventional, stressing motherhood and procreation.[45]

During her early years in Argentina, Langer feared exclusion. After the Second World War, she cut her ties to the Communist Party, reasoning that her identity as a leftist exile could put her at risk under Peronism. Langer did not see her ethnicity as a liability, since anti-Semitism was nowhere near as threatening in Argentina as in Austria. She became a citizen, although this was not enough to assure her professional future. Under Perón, only medical doctors could practice psychoanalysis, yet foreign-degree holders faced the revalidation hurdle. A Jewish Peronist medical professor helped certify her and other analysts with foreign diplomas, enabling her to practice until she revalidated her medical degree in 1959. Not long after that, she became president of the APA.[46] Thus Langer overcame her marginality.

Only in the 1960s did Langer renew her political allegiances. The Cuban revolution and its women's programs led her to question her earlier assumption that maternity was the essence of womanhood. The revolution also prompted her to inject Marxism into psychoanalysis. A target in the increasingly repressive 1970s, Langer fled to Mexico and worked in mental health in Sandinista Nicaragua.

Many of the early female physicians in Argentina were immigrants, and among them were Jews who, like Langer, were of immigrant backgrounds. In 1889, Ceçilia Grierson became the first woman to earn a medical degree in Argentina, followed by Elvira Rawson in 1892. Around this time, three women who had studied in other countries began to practice medicine, including Rosa Pavlovsky, a Russian Jew who revalidated her French degree in Argentina in 1893 and directed the pediatrics unit in the Hospital Francés for many years.[47] Margarita Zatzkin appears to have been the first Jewish woman to graduate from an Argentine medical school. She arrived in Argentina with her parents in 1891 at the age of seven. Poor yet determined, Zatzkin obtained degrees in pharmacy in 1905, only three years after the first woman graduated in this field in Argentina, and in medicine and surgery in 1909. She managed a pharmacy and never practiced medicine.[48]

Hobart Spalding notes that the sciences "often provide an entry for outsiders in developing countries."[49] This was true for Jewish women, who were disproportionately represented in medicine in Russia and Argentina. For a time Russia had a larger number of female physicians than any other country, and Jews composed a fifth of them in 1896.[50] Nevertheless, many more Jewish women sought admission into universities than government quotas permitted to enter. Russian Jewish women's raised expectations and belief in medicine as a means of upward mobility led them to this career in Argentina, where they were overrepresented. Between 1916 and 1920, women received 18 percent of the medical degrees awarded in the nation, a figure that oscillated in succeeding decades.[51] Between 1911 and 1920, a third of the women who graduated or arrived from abroad with medical diplomas were Jewish, most if not all of Russian origins.[52]

The most distinguished among these pioneers were the orthopedist Sara Satanowsky, who graduated in 1917; the internist Teresa Malamud, 1920; the pediatrician Perlina Winocur, 1920; and the ophthalmologist Paulina Satanowsky, 1921. All taught at the university level, although none attained a permanent full professorship (*cátedra*). Only a handful of women in any discipline at this time held this distinction.[53]

Female physicians found niches in women's, children's, or public health. Winocur served and taught in the public-school medical-inspection service. She published eighty articles, the most significant of which focused on children's diet and size, and school nutritional and health programs. Her book, *Desarrollo, alimentación y salud del niño*, guided generations of teachers, mothers, and school health officials. Perhaps assuming she could not win a full professorship, Winocur never applied for one.[54]

The Satanowsky sisters specialized in nontraditional fields for women. Paulina joined the ophthalmology faculty of the Universidad de Buenos Aires shortly after graduating, rising to an interim professorship in 1953. Her older sister, Sara, specialized in orthopedics, traumatology, and children's surgery; she published 130 articles. One of her colleagues considered her "a unique surgeon in the country, the most complete, the most agile." She, too, rose through university ranks, becoming the first woman interim professor in the Buenos Aires medical school in 1938, and extraordinary professor in 1940. She may have been the world's first female professor of orthopedics—traditionally a masculine specialty because it presumably requires strength. Small in stature, Satanowsky claimed that technique, not physical prowess, was the key. Of female physicians who graduated between 1911 and 1920, she alone directed doctoral dissertations, and she trained many well-known orthopedists. Head of her specialty in the Hospital Municipal Alvarez and president of the Sociedad Argentina de Ortopedia y Traumatología, the first woman to head this association, Satanowsky received many patients from the interior and neighboring countries.[55]

Satanowsky was both an insider and an outsider. Although prominent professors mentored her, she experienced discrimination on the basis of her sex and ethnicity. Many colleagues denigrated her as "la rusa." When she won the hospital post, a member of the selection board confessed she was so good that they could not reject her, suggesting this had been their intent. She again overcame prejudice by securing a professorship at a time of widespread anti-Semitism in medical circles. Her toughness helped her survive in a hostile arena.[56]

Argentine women composed a higher percentage of graduates in dentistry than in medicine, although the numbers were smaller. The same may be true for Jewish women. Fanny Blitz de Herschkovitz graduated in Buenos Aires in 1904, three years after the first women received dental

7. Dr. Sara Satanowsky, 1918. Archivo General de la Nación, Dpto. Doc. Fotográficos.

degrees; she was probably the first Jewish woman to graduate from an Argentine university.[57]

A few Mediterranean Jewish women became medical professionals. Regina Sajón, of Izmiri descent, was the first woman dentist of Mediterranean origin to practice in Argentina. Her community's acceptance of a female dentist helped smooth the way for Sajón's patient from the Bajo, Victoria Simsolo (see chapter 2), to become a doctor. So, too, did the encouragement Simsolo received from her mother, a devoted reader, and eventually her father. A cosmopolitan businessman, he initially gave priority to his son's aspirations, but when the latter abandoned his studies, the father switched his support to his daughter. Simsolo met no Mediterranean Jewish women in the *liceo* she attended or in medical school, although she befriended an Ashkenazi schoolmate with whom she interned at the Hospital Israelita, under the pediatrician Dr. Enrique Sujoy. Graduating in 1946, Simsolo accompanied Sujoy when he transferred to the Hospital de Niños as chief of the children's ward. It was a time when other Jewish doctors experienced prejudice in hospitals. Simsolo felt accepted, however, claiming that prejudice shifts affected Ashkenazim more than

Sephardim, who were less identifiably Jewish. She worked at the Hospital de Niños under Sujoy and assumed his post when he retired.[58]

The Ashkenazi doctor Sara Schnitman faced discrimination. A polio victim who graduated in Buenos Aires in 1936, Schnitman became known for her osteoporosis research, medical writings, and novels. Early in her career, she worked at the Hospital Rivadavia, where one day a flier on her desk advised readers to "Kill flies; the Mother's Club [mothers of patients] asks you to do so." A flier the next day said: "Kill Jewish women; the Mother's Club asks you to do so." Schnitman resigned in protest and transferred to the Hospital Israelita, where she and other Jewish physicians found refuge. In the 1930s and 1940s, Jewish male doctors reported even harsher experiences.[59]

Although the main obstacle that Dr. Rosa Woscoboinik de Levin encountered was political, it may have meshed with anti-Semitism. Woscoboinik entered medicine primarily to serve society, a mission that her leftist parents bequeathed her. Marrying when she was eighteen, Woscoboinik soon had a child and entered medical school in Córdoba, completing her degree at the Universidad de Buenos Aires in 1957. Her militancy cost her some positions, particularly during military rule. Being a Communist, a Jew, and a woman made her an outsider, Woscoboinik believed. Nevertheless, she became a pioneer oncologist, heading this department at the Hospital Alvarez, publishing over 100 articles, and receiving prestigious awards. Consistent with her progressive politics, she cofounded with her husband and, since 1992, has headed the nonprofit Fundación Oncológica Encuentro, which publicizes information on cancer and examines patients without charge.[60]

Spousal support helped Jewish women in medicine surmount barriers. Woscoboinik accompanied her husband, Emanuel, to Buenos Aires, where he wanted to study, although transferring to another school meant retaking exams and proving herself again. Yet the research partnership she formed with Emanuel, who specialized in a medically related field of biochemistry, helped Rosa survive troubled times. Clara Schliapnik and other female doctors found jobs in Jewish colonies as part of husband-and-wife medical teams (see chapter 1). Several dentists set up practices with their husbands.[61]

According to Carolyn Heilbrun, women's friendships also bolster the public lives of prominent women. Malamud and Winocur's acquaintance, dating from their births in Moisesville, nourished them; probably the sisterhood that bound Sara and Paulina Satanowsky did the same. Her sister-in-law's willingness to care for her children gave Sacerdote time for research. Female support helped counteract the stress of breaking into male-dominated professions.[62]

Entertainment

The experiences of female entertainers richly illustrate the themes of this book. Moreover, the images that formed around these women reflected popular constructions of race and of Jewish women as sensual others. For these reasons, I examine six entertainers in detail.

Unlike the situation in other professions, few if any gender, class, or ethnic constraints kept women out of acting. As in the United States, some Ashkenazi actresses started off in the Yiddish theater. Yiddish plays debuted in Buenos Aires in 1901, and thirty years later, the city was one of the four greatest Yiddish theater centers in the world.[63]

One of many actresses who catapulted from the Yiddish theater to the national stage was Golde Flami. Born in the Ukraine in 1918, she arrived in Buenos Aires at the age of five. Since her shoemaker father and dressmaker mother could barely feed their family of six, Flami went to work in a textile plant when she was twelve. The next year, she enrolled in night courses in secretarial skills, declamation, and dance. Her father took her to Yiddish plays, which she reenacted at home for her mother. Following a family tradition, Flami participated in an amateur theater group in Villa Crespo, and at fourteen she joined the troupe at the newly created Teatro Popular Israelita Argentino (IFT, for Idische Folks Theater), linked to the Communist Party.[64]

This was a natural place for a budding actress of Ashkenazi proletarian origins. The actors worked at their jobs during the day, rehearsed at night, and performed for free on weekends. The IFT "had great actors, who were carpenters . . . upholsterers, tailors: but each night they were actors."[65] The ensemble performed socially conscious plays for Yiddish-speaking workers, who paid little for their tickets. Flami labored eight hours a day in the factory and three hours each night at the theater. During ten years at the IFT, she perfected her Yiddish and her craft under David Licht and other foreign-born directors. By no means insular, Licht, who had studied with Konstantin Stanislavsky in Europe, taught this Russian director's method, described below, long before it caught on in Buenos Aires or New York. Benefiting from this foreign expertise, Flami's training differed from the local norm. When she won her first role in a film, she left the factory and IFT, yet in future years her career crisscrossed the Argentine screen and Jewish milieu. Her Ashkenazi leftist working-class identity remained constant.[66]

At the IFT, Flami had appeared in a variety of roles. Argentine directors, however, considered her looks exotic and preferred to cast her as a *femme fatale*. Her blonde beauty, which fit the sensual image of Jewish women, made her both an insider and outsider. By 1986, she had appeared in thirty-eight films—but never as a protagonist, perhaps because audiences identified her with the evil characters she portrayed.[67]

Possessing a similar Ashkenazi leftist identity, Cipe Lincovsky joined the IFT ensemble roughly when Flami left it, in the 1940s. Born in 1933, Cipe, as she is known, grew up in a Yiddish Communist and theatrical environment in Once. Her father, Ioel Lincovsky, was a leader of ICUF (Idischer Cultur Farband), the Yiddish cultural federation tied to the Communist Party. He produced Yiddish plays and helped found the IFT. As a baby, Cipe slept in a box that her mother carried to the theater. Cipe played her first role in Yiddish when she was four or five, learning Spanish only when she started school. The young actress trained at the Teatro Colón and IFT schools and participated in IFT productions and the Federación Juvenil Comunista.[68] For her, politics and theater were intertwined.

Throughout her life, Cipe sought to escape from gender confines. A neighbor in her building died in childbirth, teaching her to associate maternity with death. She also observed the circumscribed existence of the immigrant women around her. Years later, when asked why the great tragic characters were female, Cipe replied that women lacked outlets for their frustration. Lives confined to childbearing, housekeeping, and consuming led to neurosis and insanity. Women of previous generations cried even on happy occasions: "everything was a tragedy, menstruation, menopause, everything." As a veteran actress, Cipe contested this repression by inserting humor and eroticism into her solo shows.[69]

Cipe could not elude her gendered destiny, although she endured it on her own terms. She acquiesced to the joint decision of her father and her husband that she have a child, but she insisted on seeing Europe first, afraid she would die giving birth. In 1957, she joined a troupe heading for the First International Youth Festival in Moscow, where they performed in Stanislavsky's theater, hallowed ground for her. Once she fulfilled—and survived—her childbearing duty, Cipe took her month-old daughter to

West Berlin, where she performed in a play on the Warsaw ghetto uprising. By participating in an anti-Nazi theatrical work in early postwar Germany, she struck a blow against fascism and racism in the world.[70]

In doing so, Cipe became a transnational figure. Since childhood she had been well aware of anti-Semitism and right-wing nationalism, and she had fought them as a young militant. She advocated freedom, women's autonomy, and global radical change. These viewpoints and experiences nourished her German performance; in turn she brought back to Argentina lessons learned in Europe, including disillusionment with the Soviet Union. The Communist Youth expelled her for speaking frankly about what she had seen in Moscow, ending her IFT career, so she turned to the Spanish-language stage and screen. Nevertheless, Cipe remained a leftist and continued her exchanges across national boundaries as she performed in Latin America, Europe, and Israel.[71]

Her leftist sentiments marked many of her roles, such as in the 1974 film *Quebracho*, a sharp critique of a British company's exploitation of workers and manipulation of politicians. Playing the wife of a reformer assassinated for opposing the company, Cipe had a minor role. Nevertheless, hers was the face viewers remembered: quirky, poignant, full of suppressed emotion. Her transnational reputation helped her survive the military dictatorships of the 1960s through the 1980s, which blacklisted and threatened her, forcing her to work outside Argentina.[72]

Cipe kept her Argentine home in Once, and late in her career, like Flami, she returned to Ashkenazi themes. Celebrating the language of her upbringing, in the mid-1980s she starred in Scholem Aleijem's *Mama Loshn Idish* (Mother Tongue Yiddish), in Spanish, to acquaint a broad audience with "the great Jewish cultural values, forged in Yiddish." This, to her, was the Jewish heritage, and she criticized Israel for putting it aside.[73]

A leftist journalist asked Cipe why her shows demonstrated "a need to defend her Jewish condition." She insisted she was simply revealing herself: "I was born Argentine, Jewish and actress. Stop. I don't have to defend anything: this is what I am!" Like many other Argentines, she was a child of immigrants who contributed her background to the mix, she said.[74] Lincovsky's assertion of a Jewish space within a pluralistic Argentina rankled advocates of a monolithic nationality.

Yet they did not hesitate to separate her out as an exotic other. Reporters focused on her "typically Jewish face," passionate manner, and "strange attractiveness, difficult to forget, of a gypsy or sensual Jewess." Her sexual allure rested partly on "her strange, ugly and marvelous hair," dark, thick,

8. Cipe Lincovsky. Centro de Documentación e Información sobre Judaísmo Argentino Marc Turkow.

and frizzy—described in African-sounding terms that suggested Cipe was not quite white.[75] Racial perceptions, as well as ethnicity and politics, set her apart.

Another transnational leftist performer was Berta Singerman, born in a small Russian town around the end of the nineteenth century. Fleeing political persecution, her Socialist father Aaron installed his family in a room in Villa Crespo, where Berta listened to his nightly readings of Yiddish literature. Aaron was more interested in participating in the Yiddish theater, where he often took his young daughter, than in supporting his family. He stimulated Berta's love of acting and the arts and also inspired Berta's younger sister, Paulina, who became a comedic actress.[76]

Like Flami and Cipe, Berta Singerman moved easily from Yiddish to Spanish. When Berta began public school, she started acting in Yiddish companies during the winter and accompanying her father's theatrical tours of the colonies during the summer. She left the Yiddish theater when her father lost his money backing a tour and her mother insisted that she focus on school. She declaimed in the liceo and Jewish and Socialist settings, until poverty forced her to drop out of school in her fourth year. The minister of public education heard her recite, however, and recommended her to the elite Consejo Nacional de Mujeres, which funded her studies there in Spanish literature and declamation. Thus Argentine society accepted this impoverished girl of Yiddish background, who from now on recited in the national tongue.[77]

The Consejo recognized Berta as its best student and awarded her a diploma in declamation. However, she regarded the oratorical style taught there as formal and old-fashioned, and she used a more natural style in her recitations and the lessons she gave for pay. When she was fifteen, she met Rubén Enrique Stolek, a cultured Polish Jew almost twice her age who recognized her gifts. They married, Stolek replaced her father as her manager, and Stolek's literary friends spread word of her talents. In 1920, she had the lead role in a silent film, *The Saleswoman of Harrods*. Shortly afterward, a triumphant series of recitals in Montevideo launched her career.

Starting with her husband's circle, Singerman's ties with intellectuals ushered her into the worlds of literature and performance. Cultural luminaries sought out the woman with the distinctive voice and literary understanding, and poets wanted her to recite their verse. Some of these men fell in love with her, and she with them. Singerman was connected to the Grupo Anaconda, which included the writers Horacio Quiroga, Samuel Glusberg, and Alfonsina Storni. Its affiliates in other cities and countries invited her to perform. The poet Pablo Neruda and his compatriot, the writer and educator Gabriela Mistral, both future Nobel laureates, befriended her, as did the Mexican philosopher José Vasconcelos; the Cuban novelist Alejo Carpintier; the Brazilian modernists Osvaldo de Andrade, Tarsila do Amaral, and Lazar Segal; and the legendary Spanish writers Ramón del Valle Inclán, Federico García Lorca, Rafael Alberti, and Juan Ramón Jiménez, whom she deeply loved. Segal, Ismael Nery, and other Brazilian painters sketched her. Artists and authors inspired and stimulated her; they were also her promoters, sources of material, lovers, and political comrades.[78]

Singerman's fame knew no borders. She recited in the Americas and Europe and made a film in Spanish in Hollywood, *Nada más que una mujer*, in 1934. Combining a clichéd plot with poetry declamation, the movie nevertheless showcased Singerman's talent. Although she made another film and occasionally played stage roles, her fans clamored for recitals. President Justo attended her solo show at the Teatro Colón, the premier porteño theater, in the mid-1930s. Enamored of its literature, Singerman

9. Berta Singerman. Archivo General de la Nación, Dpto. Doc. Fotográficos.

was delighted to perform in Spain, where she captivated the royal family. When her audiences outgrew auditoriums, she recited in plazas and stadiums: to 18,000 people in the Plaza de Toros in Mexico City, and to 70,000 in Córdoba, Argentina. Addressing people outside the scheduled arena through loudspeakers became her practice, permitting larger numbers and the poor to hear her.[79]

A transnational sensation, Singerman added new works to her repertoire in each country and carried them to the next. She disseminated literature in Spanish throughout Spain and its former colonies. She also was a nexus between Spanish and Portuguese America, shuttling poetry back and forth.[80]

Singerman attracted huge audiences for several reasons. One was her innovative style as a performer. She studied her lines closely and memorized thousands of poems. Critics compared her voice to an instrument, but instead it was more like an orchestra. When she recited the folkloric "Pericón nacional," Singerman modified her voice to play male and female roles, at times crying out, at times laughing, alternating between singing and reciting the lyrics, always imitating criollo speech. She adapted her voice to each selection, reciting some poems softly and peacefully, others loudly and emphatically. She communicated the "musicality of the verse" and its soul through her body as well as her voice.[81]

The messages Singerman communicated also made her popular. She recited works whose main themes were mass suffering and liberation from injustice. She described her repertoire as "tied to the possibility of thinking and feeling, of being freer"; it was also tied to a transnational progressive project. Influenced by her father, Singerman identified with the left. A fervent supporter of the Spanish Republic, she denounced the Franco regime that overthrew it, and the Axis powers.[82] Her listeners around the world responded to her sympathy with the downtrodden and her aspirations for social and political change.

Neruda had predicted that "without Berta poetry would be silent," and indeed, as her career waned in the 1980s, and she died in 1998, no one replaced her. Hers was "an art that begins and ends with her," as a critic noted. She crossed many boundaries, carrying literature across national divides, shifting from a Yiddish to a Spanish-speaking orbit, and freeing poems from books and theaters and taking them to the streets.[83] In her career Singerman moved from the margins to the center of society, yet she transferred poetry from the center to the margins.

Although she, too, took her art to the streets, María Fux faced more impediments than Singerman. Born in 1922 of Russian parents, Fux began to dance spontaneously when she was tiny, becoming her lame "mother's leg that danced." Rather than rejoice over this feat, her parents discouraged Fux from dancing. Becoming a secretary when she was thirteen, she studied part time and finished secondary school seven years later, all the while reading and attending lectures. A talk on theosophy inspired Fux to rise and dance. A working-class woman in the audience told her she was Isadora Duncan incarnated and gave her a book on this famous modern dancer. Duncan came to symbolize Fux's path toward liberation, toward dancing freely rather than following set classical forms. Her new mentor paid for dance lessons, and avant-garde friends acquainted her with modern art, music, and poetry. The works of the musicians Maurice Ravel and Claude Debussy and the artists Salvador Dali, Pablo Picasso, and Henri Matisse awakened images that poured out of her as she danced. Jazz inspired her to improvise, to depart from the choreographed routine. She also found new forms of movement and self-understanding in silence.[84] Sharing a borderland with innovators like Sacerdote, Fux borrowed, extemporized, and took risks.

Fux's struggles continued. After four years of classes, in 1942, she began ten years of recitals at the leftist Teatro del Pueblo, which presented noncommercial works to the masses.[85] With little money or support, Fux perfected her craft in New York with Martha Graham. Malnourished, she fainted in class one day, convincing Graham to let her attend classes at no charge. After Fux had studied with Graham for nearly a year, the unapproachable master finally watched her dance to her scratchy Argentine records. Graham told her to cultivate her skills on her own: the teacher was within her, it was life.

Life in Argentina was no easier. Fux supported herself and her son by giving private lessons and training actors at the IFT, including Cipe Lincovsky. The government supplemented her meager earnings by sending her on tours of the interior, where she danced for people who had never seen a performance. In rural Chaco, she appeared in a dirty bar filled with drunks who whistled and shouted, seemingly expecting a stripper. A Victrola provided music, and torches illuminated the crude stage. Searching to connect with the unruly crowd, Fux said she needed quiet, just as one did to sense the moonlight and rustles in nearby *quebracho* groves. She danced to silence, classical and folkloric music, and García Lorca's poetry, carefully explaining each number. As the performance continued, the audience settled down and followed her movements. The final dance, accompanied by regional *chamamé* music, won loud applause. Fux also reached nontraditional audiences in the plazas and mines of the remote Jujuy province. These tours ended in 1955, however, when the government fired her for removing photos of the Peróns from a backdrop to mount a light show.

The IFT rescued Fux by sending her to the International Peace Congress in Warsaw in 1955. A Soviet official who saw her perform invited her to Moscow, where classic ballet reigned supreme. Fux's daring repertoire included modern, Argentine folkloric, and Ashkenazi music, the last segment challenging Soviet anti-Semitism. A silent number portraying pregnancy and birth was greeted at first by uncomprehending laughter, which subsided into a hushed understanding.

Fux's ties to the IFT and leftist circles and her artistic celebration of freedom contested the status quo and sometimes marginalized her, even after Perón's fall. Accusations of Communism and spying for the Soviets often kept her out of radio and television. Nevertheless, she gave two solo performances in the Teatro Colón, in the mid-1950s and 1960.[86]

Like Singerman, Fux transported ideas across national boundaries. She helped introduce modern dance in Argentina, teaching diverse audiences to understand and accept it.[87] When she retired from performing in 1999, she turned to teaching her own style of dance therapy for the elderly and disabled. Fux inserted notions of modern dance and insights gleaned from observing her mother's injury into her therapeutic craft. She authored several books on this technique and introduced it to Europe, establishing centers in Spain and Italy.

As Fux wrote, "for me dance always has been a need to give something, to express myself and find a point of connection with the life that surrounds me." She communicated a liberating message to a wide range of people, including the handicapped and disadvantaged.[88] Thus she embodied a progressive political project. Fux also took an unconventional dance style from the edges to the heart of the artistic milieu. At the same time, she moved dance from the center to the margins, freeing it from elite halls and performing it for the masses.

Hedwig Schlichter, or Hedy Crilla, found herself on the sidelines in Buenos Aires. Born in Vienna in 1898, she studied there and moved to Germany in 1920, where she acted on the stage and screen. When the Nazis came to power, Crilla migrated to Austria, France, and then Argentina, arriving around 1940 with her youth behind her and knowing little Spanish. Using the languages she knew well, she starred in and directed plays at the anti-Nazi German-language theater, the Freie Deutsche Bühne, and worked with French companies that did not want to return to occupied Europe. Her heavy accent largely excluded her from plays and films in Spanish until her later years.[89]

Disappointed yet determined, Crilla turned to writing and translating plays, directing, and especially teaching. Drawing upon her foreign expertise, in the 1940s she began coaching beginners and German- and French-speaking veteran actors. She established and supervised a children's theater between 1945 and 1973, and wrote plays for it. In 1947, Crilla opened a theatrical school in the Sociedad Hebraica Argentina, where she trained and directed Jewish and non-Jewish actors.[90] Prominent movie stars emerged from the film school she created in 1949.

Crilla's border skills were a unique strength. Migrating from one country to another had forced her to watch and listen intently to people, imitate them, and play with language. These habits enabled her to shape her students' delivery of their lines. As one who had adapted to frequent change, Crilla was open to new ideas. After discovering Konstantin Stanislavsky's books in 1942, she incorporated into her teaching his belief that the actor should deeply identify with the character and use a natural form of speaking and moving. These techniques contrasted with those used locally, where actors, trained in declamation, tended to recite their lines. By introducing method acting, she transformed Argentine theater.[91]

Born in a colony in Entre Ríos in 1912, Paloma Efron also was an innovator. Her formal schooling began when she was three, supplemented by guidance from her learned father, the Ashkenazi educator Jedidio Efron. Efron started to pursue music at the age of five in Buenos Aires, where the family had moved. A brilliant student, her secondary education ended at fourteen, when her mother became ill; the duty of nursing her for two years fell to her, as a daughter. Yet during that time she read voraciously, learned from the writers and musicians who frequented her home, and studied languages. After her mother's recovery, the sixteen-year-old girl found a job as librarian at the Instituto Cultural Argentino Norteamericano. She won her father's consent by citing his oft-expressed opinion: a woman could emancipate herself only through economic independence.[92]

Efron scaled musical as well as gender walls. In the Norteamericano, she found an album of black spirituals. Fascinated by the music, which was unknown in Argentina, Efron began to experiment with it on the piano. Soon this graduate of the national conservatory was singing spirituals, blues, and jazz. After listening to her rendition of a black spiritual at a party, the tango singer Carlos Gardel told her he did not understand her music, but it was beautiful and she should continue with it. Efron followed his advice, entering a 1934 radio contest by singing "Stormy Weather." Listeners chose her as the winner and picked her stage name, Blackie, launching her career.[93] Able to spot and ride the next wave, she pioneered jazz at a time when Argentines hungered for new melodies and rhythms.

Why did jazz captivate an Argentine woman steeped in Jewish and classical music, the daughter of an Ashkenazi communal leader? Blackie herself raised this question without answering it. Was it simply the music's quality and novelty that attracted her? A newspaper observed that "the music makes itself felt through her veins and the blood of the Jewish diaspora begins to mix with the taste for black culture," implying this was a natural blend. Perhaps her awareness of Jewish subordination permitted her, in her words, "to understand the pain of the Southern slaves, penetrate the mystery of African rites and the Harlem night." Efron identified with voices of suppressed black foreigners but not with local subaltern voices of the tango, which she enjoyed but could not sing. Her dark hair and eyes had earned her the nickname of *negrita* as a child, and the radio audience, linking her to her music, affectionately translated this into English. While *negra* is a common endearment for Spanish speakers, her nickname seemed to predispose Efron toward black culture.[94]

Efron became the first professional jazz singer in Argentina, singing on radio and in other venues and making records. Unimpressed, her father questioned her ability to interpret the music of a people unknown to her. He sent her to the United States for four years to live with her brother, who was studying at Columbia University.[95]

According to her memoir, Blackie truly crossed racial frontiers in the segregated United States of the late 1930s. She claimed to have studied musicology with the scholar George Herzog at Columbia, black literature with the author Langston Hughes, and African American singing with Rosamond Johnson, the sister of the poet James Weldon Johnson. Duke Ellington, Louis Armstrong, Ella Fitzgerald, and Marian Anderson were among the luminaries she befriended. At Herzog's suggestion, she studied folklore at the all-black Tuskegee University in Alabama. Her work at Columbia and Tuskegee must have been informal, for she did not enroll in either institution. In Harlem and the South, she walked through black neighborhoods, attended churches, and listened to the blues.[96]

In her memoir, Blackie rarely mentioned the racial discrimination she saw in the United States, perhaps because she saw no need "to repeat what everyone knows, the man of color was marginalized." She applauded President Franklin Roosevelt and his wife, Eleanor, for championing Marian Anderson, and Benny Goodman for hiring black musicians, while criticizing Al Jolson for blacking his face yet singing as a white man. These comments were few but revealing, and her experiences and friendships with blacks demonstrate her racial openness.[97]

Blackie returned to a busy life in Buenos Aires, where she sang and discussed African American music in theaters and on television. Leaving singing before her voice gave out, around 1953 Efron began her own television show, *Appointment with the Stars*, in which she described foreign celebrities she knew. This was the first of numerous radio and television programs over the next twenty years in which she discussed issues and personalities, and hosted politicians and entertainers from many countries. Efron invited Nat King Cole and other black U.S. entertainers to appear on her broadcasts and in shows she arranged for them. Her ability to sense new tastes, converse intelligently on many subjects, and oversee details helped her rise to the position of channel manager in the male-dominated field of television.[98]

Women were largely absent from television production and journalism in her era; to carve out a space for herself, Blackie relied on the perfectionism, strength, and directness she had long cultivated. She demanded that men accept her on the same level, often using swear words to drive home the point. Further violating proper feminine behavior, she donned slacks and *alpargatas*, the simple shoes worn by the poor, so that she could work comfortably and move silently behind the cameras.[99] Only a forceful and unconventional woman could have entered this male sphere.

Blackie never hid her ethnicity, but it did not play a major role in her work. She did, however, direct the choir and chamber orchestra of the Instituto Zimra, a Jewish music center founded by her father. She also was among the first media personalities in Argentina to invite rabbis and clergymen to converse with each other on the air.[100] This befitted an entertainer who inserted the music of a persecuted foreign group into the Argentine mainstream.

Conclusion

Unlike Blackie, some aspiring professionals faced walls they could not scale. Familial opposition, old-fashioned gender notions, and a lack of resources and contacts hampered many women. Sometimes, however, women turned barriers into advantages. Gender prescriptions helped women attain footholds in women's and children's medicine and Jewish education. The marginality of Sacerdote, Crilla, and Braslavsky inspired their creativity and experimentation.

Several factors enabled women to thrive professionally. Utilizing border skills, as well as importing techniques and information from other countries, seemed the most critical. The support of mentors, relatives, friends, and sponsors helped propel women into careers. The heightened expectations that accompanied many women's journeys from Russia also proved vital.

Through innovation and foreign links, some Jewish women moved from the margins to the centers of their fields. Moreover, by introducing their expertise, they redefined the center. Yet while Argentine society generally accepted these professionals, a number of them experienced discrimination, particularly on political grounds. Anti-Semitism, which permeated the measures governing religious education from 1943 on, stigmatized some Jews. Both being female and being Jewish hampered Sara Satanowsky, demonstrating the difficulty of untangling biases.

Constructions of Jewish women as sensual or racialized others marginalized and also benefited professionals. Flami's seductive, light-skinned beauty won her fame yet also confined her to unpleasant roles. Added to her open Jewishness, Cipe's exotic dark looks made her an outsider. Yet Blackie's interests and image provided her an entrée into a musical frontier.

The career women described here did not necessarily forsake their lower-class, immigrant roots. Flami and Cipe called attention to their backgrounds, and through their Communist activism, Ziperovich and Woscoboinik exalted their humble origins. The last two figures, like Furman, sought to help the poor.

A few Jewish women cross-pollinated ideas and practices transnationally. Berta Singerman carried poetry and messages of social justice across national borders, serving as an intermediary between Spanish and Portuguese America. Influenced by Argentine and European political struggles, Cipe used the stage and cinema to promote an antifascist world. Fux helped bring modern dance to Argentina and took her therapy to Spain and Italy.

Many Jewish women longed to become teachers, both to instruct the youth and build a nation. Alianak and Braslavsky expanded the liberal and egalitarian ideals they absorbed in normal school; Fischer and Furman instilled acceptance of people of color; and Ziperovich did both. In their hands, schools served as laboratories of democracy. Women also formulated progressive versions of the liberal national project and contested rightist doctrines in other arenas. Woscoboinik combined medicine with outreach, and Blackie championed the music of a persecuted minority. Aiming for a more democratic nation, Singerman and Fux brought art and messages of liberation to the masses, while Cipe and Flami claimed Jewish spaces in a pluralistic nationality. These professionals' struggles for social justice, freedom, and diversity demonstrated their points of connection with society.

CHAPTER FOUR

"Not a Novice"

Prostitutes

Their numbers [Jewish prostitutes] . . . are far too large for their presence not to be noticed, while many of them carry on their trade so ostentatiously that they would appear to the casual observer to be far larger in number than they really are.
—Samuel Cohen, Jewish Association, *Report 1913*

She was not a novice in the sad commerce, and having a practical sense she did not allow her "pimp" to exploit her.
—"Ezras Noschim,"
"Trata de blancas. Informe 1934–1935"

A British observer told a London audience in 1910 that "the traffic [in women in Argentina] is carried on by Jews and Jewesses, and to an extent which is far greater than many of you can possibly realize."[1] Until long after this date, many people in Argentina and Europe believed that a majority of prostitutes in that country were Jews, lured into the trade in Eastern Europe by Jewish procurers.[2] According to this view, these so-called white slaves were doomed to unwilling sexual servitude.[3] Whether Ashkenazi Jews predominated among prostitutes, or white slavery really existed, is another matter.

Argentine Jewish prostitution has fascinated writers and filmmakers; it is virtually the only aspect of Argentine Jewish women's lives covered in the historical literature.[4] While the topic is significant, one wonders why images of prostitutes have blotted out other Jewish women. The notion of Jewish women as sensual others[5] and the sensationalism surrounding prostitution are partly responsible. The notorious judicial exposé of a network of Jewish pimps, the Zwi Migdal, in 1930, also caught the attention of the public and scholars alike.

To restore balance to the historiography by focusing on the majority of Jewish women, I originally planned not to cover the minority, the prostitutes, in this book. I changed my mind for two reasons. First, studies have tended to concentrate on male procurers, regulation, Jewish opposition to prostitution, and Argentine views of the trade. We know little about the women themselves who sold their bodies. As Timothy Gilfoyle noted of sex workers in general, "one searches in vain for an exemplifying individual or narrative that personifies the complexity of the prostitute's world . . . Who exactly were some of these individuals?"[6] I sought to answer that question through a largely thematic approach, and to open a window on the lives of Argentine prostitutes, both Jewish and non-Jewish. Second, the specter of prostitution haunted Argentine Jews and foreign Jewish visitors, who thought the engagement of coreligionists in sex work stained the collectivity.[7] The Jews' reputation and claims to Argentine nationality thus hinged on women's honor. With so much at stake, Jewish prostitutes were indeed important.

Since prostitution and pimping threatened to exclude Jews from the nation, prominent Jews decided to eradicate these practices. Yet their assertion of control over prostitutes did not ensure the latter's conformity. Jewish women in the sex trade contested marginalization, whether imposed by communal groups, pimps, or madams.[8] Even in this despised livelihood, women struggled for dignity, upward mobility, and independence, and some succeeded to a degree.

Prostitutes crossed borders in diverse ways. They were involved in a transnational enterprise; capital, profits, entrepreneurs, and women's bodies circulated around the globe. Bordellos and streets were border spaces where Jewish prostitutes interacted with non-Jews and acquired local customs. Women who entered the field of sexual labor stepped over the line separating the permissible from the forbidden. Sometimes they crossed back to reputable lifestyles.

Notions of Jewish women as sensual and racialized other played out in prostitution. Men appreciated their vaunted beauty, but other foreign women had even higher market value. Some Jewish prostitutes appropriated the liberal national project's white ideal, setting themselves off from other sex workers they saw as nonwhite.

Documenting Jewish Prostitution

Sex workers formed part of the larger Jewish migration and the global movement of labor in the late nineteenth and early twentieth centuries. The same poverty that prompted Jews to leave Eastern Europe for Argentina pushed some women into this occupation. At times Jewish prostitutes stopped in France or other countries on the way to Argentina. Few, it seems, were born in the Mediterranean or Argentina.[9]

The history of Ashkenazi prostitutes is intertwined with that of several organizations. Created in 1885, the London-based Jewish Association for the Protection of Girls and Women attempted to keep Jewish immigrants out of commercial sex. Realizing that prostitution spanned national borders, it founded branches in and sent fact-finding missions to other countries. A kindred group, the Sociedad Israelita de Protección a Niñas y Mujeres "Ezras Noschim," was formed in Buenos Aires in the 1890s; in 1901, under Rabbi Henry Joseph and the administrator Alfred Gelpy, it became a branch of the Jewish Association. Gelpy boarded ships arriving in Buenos Aires to intercept potential prostitutes, interviewed women and family members, and tried to remove women from brothels and compromising situations.[10]

Rabbi Samuel Halphon succeeded Joseph in 1905 and headed the organization for twenty-five years. Its lack of resources, and perhaps the belief that women should be major players in a group concerned with women's issues, prompted a shift. Soliciting support, in 1926, Ezras Noschim asked representatives of Jewish philanthropies, including women's charities, to join the Jewish Association's board, and in 1930 Hélène R. de Aslán, a prominent philanthropist and wife of a communal leader, became president. This alteration at the top did not transform the group. Its views of sexuality changed little, and the male administrator, Selig Ganopol, who had assumed Gelpy's job in 1918, performed the same functions as his predecessor.[11]

These and other organizations opposed to white slavery are the main sources of documentation on the subject. Gelpy and Ganopol were the primary recipients and interpreters of sex workers' stories, which they transcribed and deposited in the Ezras Noschim archive, and summarized in communications with the London office. Delegates of the Jewish Association and other groups filed reports on their visits to Buenos Aires and delivered papers at international conferences. It is challenging to reconstruct prostitutes' lives from these sources, which tended to strain women's accounts and other data through the filter of the white-slavery narrative.[12] Furthermore, the stories are incomplete.

For their part, prostitutes or suspected prostitutes frequently lied about their histories and distorted their motives. They usually tried to present themselves in a manner appealing to Ezras Noschim and other investigators. Many wanted to protect their families from scrutiny or keep them in the dark. Some sought to deceive their listeners out of fear.

Numbers and History

Jewish prostitution accompanied mass migration to Argentina. In 1891, well-dressed Jewish madams and pimps stood outside the Hotel de Inmigrantes, where newcomers stayed upon arrival in Buenos Aires, to greet settlers destined for Colonia Mauricio. They chatted with female immigrants and gave children candy. Some aspiring colonists furtively handed them immigration certificates through the iron bars on the gate, enabling a number of women to enter. Warning the immigrants that rural life was onerous, the madams convinced a few observant Jewish men, along with their young wives and adolescent daughters, to accompany them. Those who remained learned that starvation had forced some earlier arrivals into the sex trade.[13]

Commercial sex followed Jews to several colonies. The JCA tried to expel prostitutes from Moisesville and Colonia Mauricio, but a few seem to have stayed or returned. A cemetery near Mauricio houses several graves separated from the others, probably containing prostitutes' remains.[14] We know where they are buried, but not how they lived during their brief sojourn in these communities. Almost all documents describe urban, rather than rural, prostitutes.

Were most prostitutes in Argentina indeed Jewish? The law of 1875 that legalized commercial sex in Buenos Aires required its female practitioners to register and receive regular medical examinations. According to government statistics, in 1909 nearly half of the registered prostitutes were Jews, who made up only 1 percent of the city's inhabitants. Yet women may have misrepresented their backgrounds, and, more importantly, the figures do not include the numerous unregistered prostitutes, many of whom were native-born Catholics.[15] By 1930, Jews accounted for perhaps 38 percent of the registered female sex workers in Buenos Aires (and 5 percent of the population), while French and Argentines composed 22 percent each.[16]

10. Algarrobos Cemetery, Colonia Mauricio, with what may be the graves of prostitutes separated from the rest. Author's photograph.

Although they may indicate trends, figures on prostitution are notoriously inaccurate, and those for 1930 are particularly questionable. As postwar political and economic chaos forced many Eastern European women, Jewish and non-Jewish, into sex work, they lost market value. In 1930, the British Jewish procuress Celina Dick reportedly shipped English girls to Buenos Aires for 120 to 150 pounds apiece, French for 110 to 130, Russians for 30 to 35, and Poles and Czechs for 25 to 30. Deemed less exotic, some *polacas* and rusitas may have claimed to be Frenchwomen, considered particularly desirable by many Argentines. That some women had passed through France, which was Dick's base of operations, and picked up the language there made it easier for them to pretend to be French.[17]

The 1930s witnessed sweeping changes. In 1934, the federal capital banned licensed brothels, and prostitutes no longer registered. Two years later, a national law declared bordellos illegal in most of the country.[18] Police estimated that the numbers of Jewish prostitutes fell sharply during this decade, and that the overwhelming majority of sex workers were Argentine-born. By the 1950s, Ganopol acknowledged that prosperity and declining immigration had virtually eliminated Jewish prostitution.[19]

As the earlier quote from Samuel Cohen, the secretary of the Jewish Association, makes clear, Ashkenazi prostitutes may have seemed more numerous than they were because of their conspicuous behavior. Jews never constituted a majority of prostitutes, although until the 1930s there were a disproportionate number of them relative to the tiny percentage of Jews in the population. This disparity, which was far greater than in Eastern European cities or New York, gave Argentina a bad reputation among Jews—and others. And even as Jewish participation in the sex trade declined, the association lingered.[20]

At least until the 1930s, disproportionate numbers of madams were Ashkenazi. Under the 1875 law, only women could manage bordellos. A law of 1913 prohibited parents, guardians, and pimps from corrupting women below the age of twenty-two; unless they knowingly employed minors, madams were exempt from the law. This gave women further incentive to procure sex workers and run houses of prostitution, even if the women were actually fronts for men. Ashkenazi women brothel keepers had appeared in municipal records as early as the 1870s, before the mass arrivals of Jews.[21] According to police data compiled in 1935–36, 22 percent of licensed brothel owners outside the capital, all women, were Russians and Poles, probably Jews—compared to 14 percent French and 41 percent Argentine. Jewish madams were concentrated in towns throughout Buenos Aires, with a few in other provinces.[22]

Entry into Prostitution

Did white slavers deceive Jewish women into prostitution, thus marginalizing and controlling them? Students of prostitution around the world debate whether white slavery existed.[23] Sources on Argentine Jews also disagree.

According to opponents of prostitution, criminal elements offered marriage to daughters of poor Eastern European families and money to their parents. Usually they promised a ceremony in Buenos Aires, or they married through *stille chuppe*, a practice in which men purchased *kesubahs*, religious marriage certificates without authorized signatures. The men took their supposed brides or fiancées to Buenos Aires, where they were forced into brothels, sometimes even sold to the proprietors.[24]

One apparent case involved a young Eastern European woman living in England with her family in 1911, who accepted a match arranged by a marriage broker. The groom proposed stille chuppe, while she held out for a religious ceremony. He maneuvered her onto a ship that headed for Buenos Aires. Fleeing from the bordello where he deposited her, she found her way to Ezras Noschim, which sent her back to England.[25] The woman's escape and desire to return to her family lent credence to her account.

Some women claimed that traffickers had offered them respectable employment. Seemingly fooled in this manner, a young woman in 1906 thought her ship was taking her to a promised job in New York, but she discovered her destination was a porteño brothel. When she complained to her escort, he beat her so badly that the ship's physician treated her. The doctor informed other Jewish passengers, who in turn notified Ezras Noschim, which met her at the port and had the man arrested.[26] The woman's resistance and the doctor's testimony gave her story weight.

What Samuel Cohen witnessed during his visit to Buenos Aires in 1913, however, made him question the white-slavery narrative. His conversations with licensed prostitutes led him to conclude that most had engaged in sex work in Europe and had gone willingly to Buenos Aires. Although he did not interview any unregistered prostitutes, he believed that many of them were the genuine white slaves, who had been fooled and coerced.[27] The Jewish Association continued to hold this divided opinion, adding in 1926 that those who had not been prostitutes before their arrival in Argentina had already "fallen" into promiscuity. Or, as Beatriz Kushnir pointed out, poverty and lack of dowries had demeaned them.[28]

Some thought white slavery diminished over time. Writing in 1924, Jacinto Fernández of the federal capital police claimed that before the First World War, many women had arrived not knowing their fate. The ones who now entered local bordellos, however, had been prostitutes in Europe, or their lovers had convinced them to take up this profession.[29] Largely accepting that women knew what awaited them, reformers switched their rhetoric and claimed that traffickers had "induced" or "enticed" their prey. They recognized that women exercised some will, although they still regarded them as innocent, immature, or foolhardy.[30]

Some entire families, often originating in Poland, were involved in prostitution.[31] One couple provided rooms and services for sex workers. Their teenage daughters, born in Argentina, had lived around prostitutes much of their lives. They started to have sexual relations very early and became professionals after their first menstruation.[32] Ezras Noschim also learned of several daughters who came from abroad or the interior to rejoin their prostitute mothers and probably enter their occupation.[33]

Sexual entrepreneurs tried to enlist or force their relatives into prostitution. A procurer's niece who lived in the Jewish girls' orphanage nervously confided to a teacher that her uncle planned to put her in a bordello when she got older. The orphanage forbade him from visiting her.[34] In another case, Ganopol spotted a newly arrived girl at the port with her suspicious looking aunt, who had sent for her and promised her a good future. He warned the girl to be careful and slipped her Ezras Noschim's address. When the immigrant found out that the promised job was prostitution, she refused it and fought off her uncle, who she claimed tried to rape her. Locked in a room, she dropped a letter to Ezras Noschim out the window to a passerby, who brought it to the group. The police raided the house, detained the man, and removed the girl.[35] Another young woman who came from Poland with her sister and brother-in-law let them introduce her to prostitution.[36]

Family ties may also have influenced Raquel Liberman, known for her role in destroying the Zwi Migdal. Although she originally asserted that traffickers had pushed her into a brothel after her arrival in Buenos Aires in 1924, in reality her husband sent for her and their two children in 1922 and died the following year. The only breadwinner in the family, Liberman left her children in Tapalqué, Buenos Aires, where they had lived, and sought employment in the capital. Her sister- and brother-in-law in Tapalqué belonged to the Zwi Migdal, then known as Varsovia, and the novelist Myrtha Schalom guessed that they forced Liberman into prostitution.[37] Yet perhaps the seamstress had asked her in-laws to usher her into this work, which offered better wages than sewing.

Husbands like Adolfo, who married fifteen-year-old Perla in 1918, were among the main instigators of women's turning to prostitution. Adolfo ordered Perla to earn money, so she worked outside the home until she had a baby. When the young mother turned eighteen, her husband beat her until she agreed to become a prostitute. Adolfo brought José over for dinner, told her to treat him nicely, and left them alone. José and another man, Aron, were her lovers for three years. When Adolfo ordered her to solicit men on the streets, Perla fled to her parents. Feeling vulnerable, she waited three years before approaching Ezras Noschim. She asked for a religious divorce, or *guet*; her child, whom her husband kept from her; and the opportunity to clean her life and build her self-esteem. Several witnesses corroborated her story, among them her former landlady, who had spotted José coming and going and the police dragging Adolfo off for beating Perla. She also knew that Perla had tried to commit suicide. Whether Perla escaped her husband's abuse and entered respectable society is unclear.[38]

Rather than find clients for their wives, some husbands sought to install them in brothels. Pesa emigrated from Poland, brought over her fiancé Yuda, and married him. The newlyweds lived off Yuda's earnings as a weaver. Swayed by his two sisters, who managed bordellos, Yuda soon tried to push his wife into one. Pesa obtained aid from Ezras Noschim and moved to her sister's home instead.[39]

One woman took revenge on her bigamous pimping husband. Already married to another through Jewish rites, Naftali wed Slawka in a civil ceremony in Poland. In the late 1920s, they arrived in Argentina, where Slawka claimed that Naftali beat her, forced her into sex work, and appropriated her earnings to buy liquor. In 1933, they returned to Poland, where they opened a gambling house. To end the abuse and control the profits, Slawka shot him in his sleep. The last notice Ezras Noschim received of her reported that she had been charged with murder.[40]

Some husbands and lovers persuaded women to enter the trade willingly. In one such case, a man brought his twenty-year-old bride from Poland in 1927, handing her over to a brothel in Tigre, north of the capital. Policemen also sighted her in a clandestine bordello in downtown Buenos Aires. When she was not working, she visited her husband,[41] suggesting she felt an attachment to him. One senses that she left Poland knowing her fate and did not resist it.

Impoverished and barely literate, Basia, a seamstress, left her daughter behind in Poland. Through her lover, she went to work in a brothel in Buenos Aires province in 1930. After receiving treatment for a venereal disease, she left prostitution and returned to sewing.[42] On her own and probably supporting her daughter, Basia most likely decided to sell herself to earn more money. The ease with which she moved back and forth from the needle trade indicates her boyfriend did not coerce her.

Not all married prostitutes entered the life at their husbands' insistence. A mother of two, Chaja frequented the shady *cafetines*, or bars, near the port. When licensed prostitution ended in the mid-1930s, many women practiced the trade in places like these. According to Ezras Noschim, Chaja did not sell herself out of economic necessity, for her husband Salomon, a barber, made a decent living; instead she sought a good time. Claiming that her example convinced Salomon to become a procurer, the group threatened to have the authorities expel him from the country or take away their children if the couple did not change their ways. Under this pressure, Chaja apparently returned to her home and Salomon to his former job.[43] Some U.S. reformers also blamed prostitution on poor

Jewish women's desires for luxury and entertainment.[44] Was Chaja's true motive diversion or profit? Did Salomon become a pimp or simply accept his wife's activity? What seems evident is that Salomon went along with Chaja's wishes.

Raquel's husband claimed she had left him to dance at a cabaret and support her lover with her earnings from prostitution. When Ganopol confronted her, she insisted that she was content and gave her daughter to her husband. Raquel did not live with her non-Jewish paramour, who had his own lodgings and respectable occupation.[45] Perhaps he paid Raquel, or they exchanged no money at all. Prostitutes had husbands and lovers unconnected to their profession. Maybe Raquel's work enabled her to leave an undesirable marriage, become financially autonomous, and enjoy sexual escapades. At a time when womanhood meant monogamy and maternity, by selling her body and giving up her child Raquel truly transgressed boundaries of respectable behavior.[46]

The main reason women decided to sell sexual services, however, was economic. Soon after arrival, poor Polish women learned they could earn more from prostitution than from sewing or factory work. Some adopted sex work as a practical means of achieving upward mobility, threatening to leave their husbands if they did not acquiesce. A Polish journalist noted that a number of families had made fortunes in this manner and then quietly sought admission into "normal" society.[47]

Ana arrived in Buenos Aires in 1928 with her husband, a street vendor, and their child. When she gave birth to a second child, the family became economically strapped. Ana took in boarders and had sex with them, perhaps for pay. She moved her business to another neighborhood, continuing to support her husband and children, now numbering three.[48]

Separated from her husband, Sura claimed that her earnings as a nurse and masseuse in the mid-1930s had not permitted her to support herself and the daughter who lived with her, or to bring another daughter from Poland. She earned 300 to 400 pesos a month in a cabaret near the port, where she danced, earned a commission on the drinks her customers ordered, and turned tricks.[49] This far outstripped the hat maker's salary of 100 pesos, described in chapter 2 as an excellent income for a young single woman at the time.

Sexual entrepreneurs may have deceived a few women into the trade, particularly before the First World War, but most women entered it knowingly, if not necessarily happily. Generally women became prostitutes to meet economic goals and support their families. Some entered sex work through their relatives and lovers, who at times forced them into prostitution.[50] Sexual experimentation also may have attracted a number of women.

Earnings

Prostitution could offer better earnings than other low-skill jobs earmarked for women. A fictional madam tried to convince a reluctant woman to accept her lot by arguing: "What difference does it make whether you work in this or that? . . . what you earn here in one month you will not earn in ten years as a servant. Look at my diamonds and the money I have in the bank. I was once like you."[51] Exemplifying this mobility, an impoverished woman transferred from a Polish to an Argentine brothel in the same transnational network, eventually rising to manage a house in Buenos Aires province. Convinced that prostitutes were captive victims, the police commissary Julio Alsogaray claimed that even wealthy madams had started out as "slaves."[52]

Brothel owners and procuresses could earn hefty profits. From her earnings as a prostitute in France, Taiba Pasternak de Rosenberg purchased two bordellos in Buenos Aires with a female friend. She continued to service clients in these houses while accumulating as much as 40,000 pesos from these ventures in two years. Her income soon enabled her to buy another brothel.[53] Brothel-keepers or prostitution rings purchased women from procurers, some of whom were female, such as the wealthy Celina Dick. By 1913, when the government began to prosecute male traffickers and pimps, it was easier for women than men to enter the country with their human cargos, or to convince local women to become prostitutes.[54]

A member of the Zwi Migdal prostitution ring, Sofia Schwartzman de Pasco owned brothels in suburban Buenos Aires. The judge investigating this criminal network found over 350,000 pesos in cash, mortgage certificates worth 310,000 pesos, and titles to twelve properties in her safety deposit box. Some of these assets, however, may have belonged to her lover, a trafficker. Another Zwi Migdal member was Esther Cohn, known as Ema the Millionaire. A madam, procuress, and moneylender, her net worth was over three million pesos.[55] Paying the Zwi Migdal's membership fee of 1,000 pesos had allowed these women to rise to the highest levels of sexual commerce.[56]

Far-sighted prostitutes provided for the future by shifting to other jobs in the sex trade. If they or their husbands belonged to the Zwi Migdal, aging prostitutes could become porteras in its houses. When one woman hit her forties, she started to cook in the bordello where she had serviced clients and her husband worked as a manual laborer. Eventually she opened a pension catering to prostitutes.[57]

Madams, procuresses, porteras, and pension owners were the female insiders in the sex business, with prostitutes below them. Nevertheless, hookers could earn a good deal of money, especially if they controlled their own labor. Brucha worked in a brothel for six years and saved her earnings, which were considerable, according to Ezras Noschim, because she had not had a pimp. She left prostitution and by the mid-1930s had lived off her savings for two years. Rajzla and her pimp left Lodz for better opportunities in Buenos Aires. She did not let the pimp exploit her, and eventually her savings allowed her to retire from prostitution and return to Poland.[58]

Raquel Liberman spent about four years prostituting herself, saving money, and paying a percentage to her pimp, Jaime Cissinger, for protection. Circuitously managing to buy her contract from Cissinger in 1928, she left prostitution and established a shop. Within a year, she claimed to have 90,000 pesos in several banks—and a suitor. José Salomón Korn courted and married her, but—unbeknownst to her—he, like Cissinger, belonged to the Zwi Migdal. Once they were wed, Korn robbed her of her savings and returned her to the bordello she had abandoned. Unwilling to engage in sex work and unable to retrieve her money, she filed a complaint with Julio Alsogaray in 1929 that exploded into a massive prosecution of the Zwi Migdal. In the end, the defendants were freed, but the criminal organization was shattered.[59]

Of particular interest are Liberman's finances. Myrtha Schalom theorized that Liberman had fabricated Korn's thievery to set his criminal associates against him, since he did not report this amount to the Zwi Migdal. It is difficult to imagine that she made 90,000 pesos in such a short time. If she did, how much money came from prostitution and how much from a single year of operating a store? Her income from sex work was at least sufficient to start a business. It is unclear whether she ever recovered her funds, if indeed they were stolen. The store failed after her marriage, and after she went to the police, she supported herself and her children by renting out properties she owned in the capital. Liberman had purchased real estate with her earnings from prostitution or her short-lived business and somehow hidden these assets from Korn.[60] One way or another,

Liberman did much better for herself as a prostitute than she would have done as a seamstress.

Not all prostitutes made large sums. A woman in a bordello could count on a lucrative stream of customers; her madam, however, pocketed as much as half of her wages. Payment to her pimp, who had installed her in the brothel, and any creditor, usually the madam, along with other expenses, came out of the other half. Brothel workers complained to Cohen in 1913 of high debts and lower earnings than anticipated.[61] A 1919 ordinance that prohibited large brothels in the capital strengthened the role of pimps, who advanced the money to place women in small residences, and in return took half of the profits.[62] The control wielded by pimps and madams meant less income for prostitutes.

Subjugation

Prostitutes faced multiple forms of exclusion. Those who solicited in the streets and nightclubs could be more selective than those in bordellos, but their livelihood was less secure. Since paid sex was legal only in licensed houses until the mid-1930s, policemen arrested and abused streetwalkers. Picking clients' pockets might also lead to arrest. If detained, women paid a fine and could wind up in jail, where they lost income and suffered from the humid cold and stench. Some evenings they could not find enough clients to cover their expenses; men sometimes wasted time flirting and trying to establish rapport. As one fictional prostitute told her erstwhile client, "I don't live off conversation. My name is ten pesos." Men haggled over the price, hurting women's pocketbooks and pride. Selling themselves cheaply threatened to cast them into the ranks of criollas.[63]

Themselves marginalized, Jewish pimps and prostitutes looked down upon their criollo counterparts. The Jews were complicit in the liberal project's racist pecking order that relegated native-born Argentine sex workers, often mestizos, to the bottom. In the Jews' view, criolla prostitutes dressed poorly, frequented dirty bars and hotels, and charged too little. Jews disdained criollo pimps for wearing flashy clothes, letting their emotions rule them, and coveting white women like Jews. Jewish sexual merchants saw Jewish sex workers who had criollo pimps as prostitutes of the lowest level. "Even among these bestial people there also are categories," noted a representative of Ezras Noschim.[64] Racism helped establish those categories.

A streetwalker lived with fear, starting with worries about how many clients she would find. Standing outside, half undressed in the dank porteño winter, she wondered if she could avoid illness and the accompanying loss of income. Expenses would not drop in sickness, even if earnings did. If she brought a brutal man back to her room, how would she protect herself from attack? Would he destroy her looks and livelihood?[65]

A brothel inmate also must have feared clients who might injure her, although she could call upon the madam or portera for aid. If she complained frequently about her customers, however, she might anger her superiors, who could assign her abusive men or find other ways to hurt her. She had other concerns as well. What if she caught a venereal disease and could not pass the medical exam? Skillful porteras knew how to conceal symptoms and fool doctors, which made it essential to get along with them. A woman working in a bordello also had to cope with exhaustion. Large sitting rooms were filled with men waiting their turn, insuring that each woman had ten to fourteen customers a night.[66] Madams, porteras, and clients overworked and maltreated prostitutes.

Lack of education also hurt them; indeed, it helped push women into prostitution. Unable to read or write, many prostitutes begged others to write their relatives for them. A young male teacher took pity on one prostitute and wrote her family that she was well paid and supposedly planning marriage. While he did this for free, others exploited prostitutes' illiteracy by becoming their paid scribes.[67]

Prostitutes displayed themselves and watched each other. Wearing revealing clothing, they walked the streets, sauntered through bars, and strolled among throngs of potential customers during intermission at naughty music-hall shows. Heavily made-up and dressed in clinging robes, women paraded through brothel waiting rooms.[68] Some wondered how long they could beat the competition.

Ganopol described with wonder a woman who was thirty-eight and had been a prostitute for six years: "[she is] relatively conserved, and, despite her degradation, does not lack a certain distinction and delicacy."[69] But inevitably women would age and lose their charms. Some worked as prostitutes until they were old, earning less and less each year. Unable to afford medical care, they relied on friends and relatives or municipal charity, some dying penniless.[70]

Nor did prostitutes benefit from the associations that offered burial, religious, and mutual-aid services to Jewish sexual entrepreneurs. Founded in 1906, the Varsovia society was forced by the Polish government to change its name to Zwi Migdal in 1928. Shortly thereafter it split into two: the larger segment, consisting of Poles, retained the title, while Russians and Romanians formed Ashkenazum. These male-ruled groups admitted only pimps, madams, porteras, and the like, as well as their spouses, some of whom were prostitutes. The Zwi Migdal had an estimated 424 members in 1930; of the 112 named or arrested in the case against it, only 35 were women. It excluded prostitutes (except as wives, as noted above), like the Ashkenazi community, which scorned the unclean.[71] Prostitutes not only suffered from exploitation, fear, and dependence on ephemeral beauty, but they faced possible destitution.

The question of marginality also hinges on the extent to which higher-ups brutalized sex workers. There are many accounts of Jewish pimps initiating Jewish women by beating and raping them, with madams joining in or more subtly convincing women to submit. Porteras and madams tried to keep women compliant and inside brothels.[72] This behavior may have particularly characterized clandestine houses or the minority of sex workers who indeed were slaves. Perhaps some entrepreneurs trained prostitutes in sexual techniques and obedience. It is also possible that women exaggerated the abuse they suffered, to win the sympathy of Ezras Noschim and public officials.[73]

Even after initiation, pimps had the reputation of subjugating and exploiting women. They could sell women to other men or rough bordellos, or threaten to do so. Some had gambling, drug, or alcohol habits. Their degree of inebriation, luck at cards or the racetrack, and women's earnings helped determine how pimps treated prostitutes. Pimps may have taken advantage of women's feelings for them, but women also may have manipulated pimps who fancied them. Nor could these men always guard their women. One prostitute moved to Brazil, lying to her pimp that she would return. Rajzla, described above, and other sex workers did not allow their pimps to exploit them; some, like Brucha, did not have a pimp. Women also switched pimps, as Liberman pretended to do when she arranged for a contact to purchase her from Cissinger. Thus men's power varied.[74]

Given this situation, why the Zwi Migdal punished Liberman by returning her to a brothel and stealing her money—if in fact it did so—is unclear. Some claimed it could not allow her to live independently, because her subterfuge might inspire other women to free themselves.[75] Yet some prostitutes openly left brothels and may have personally bought their contracts from their pimps.[76] Once Liberman denounced the prostitution ring to authorities, however, it repressed its women to prevent ruin. Prostitutes called as witnesses were loath to criticize the Zwi Migdal, fearing its revenge.[77] Others, however, contested subjugation.

Border Crossings

Some observers claimed that prostitution rendered women incapable of performing other work or resuming "normal" life. Unaccustomed to domestic chores and common routines, they reputedly slept during the day and stayed up at night. After seven years in prostitution, one woman abandoned it for marriage. She remained home for a year but became restless, quarreled with her husband, and went out with her former coworkers. Finally she left her spouse for another man, leading Ezras Noschim to suspect that she had returned to sex work.[78]

In fact, women left prostitution for other occupations. Separated from her husband after arriving from Poland in 1926, Paulina entered the life. Her employment in brothels for six to eight years, and her ability to fend off pimps, enabled her to save enough money to set up a successful corset-making business. For Paulina and others, sex work was but one episode in their lives, bounded by other jobs and marriage. They moved back and forth between respectable and disreputable behavior, the latter supporting them during financial emergencies and permitting them to accumulate capital for new ventures.[79]

In the underworld border space, Ashkenazi prostitutes encountered people of other backgrounds and constructed hybrid identities. They learned Spanish to communicate with their clients and surely mastered *lunfardo* more quickly than other Jewish female immigrants, as this porteño dialect originated and flourished in the criminal milieu. Combining foreign and local foods, Stanchina's characters dined on Eastern European roasted buckwheat groats, beet soup, and herring in their *pensión*, yet they also drank mate. In Jozami's novel about the fictional Cosia Zeilón, however, prostitutes in Jewish-run bordellos ate an Argentine lunch of soup, *puchero* (stew), and *bife a caballo* (steak and fried egg). Arrest and prison afforded unwelcome opportunities for interaction with police, non-Jewish prostitutes, and other Argentines.[80]

Prostitutes, madams, and porteras compartmentalized their lives, erecting walls between the professional and personal. On one side, they sold sex to clients. On the other side, they had intimate sex with and bore children to their husbands and paramours, who were not necessarily traffickers. They sent money to and maintained contact with family members in Europe and Argentina.[81]

Prostitutes crisscrossed the line separating professional from affectionate relations, relying on their coworkers for companionship, advice, and favors. A snapshot of Liberman shows her with two women friends, probably fellow prostitutes. "A remembrance of her friends Charne and Anchke" was carved on Dora's tomb; the two women who paid for this inscription presumably were prostitutes, too. Some friendships may have developed into lesbian relationships. Competitiveness, resentment, and the frequent transfer of women from one brothel to another, however, hampered ties between them.[82]

The borders between dishonorable and reputable society were permeable. Prostitutes were among the main patrons of the Yiddish stage until the Ashkenazi community prohibited their entry into many theaters. Hairdressers, landlords, the famous Brusilovsky delicatessen, and other stores accepted their money. Jewish and non-Jewish Argentines patronized the legitimate businesses some women established after leaving prostitution.[83]

Conclusion

Ashkenazi women never were a majority of prostitutes in Argentina, although disproportionate numbers were prostitutes until 1930 and madams after that date. Hardly novices, many had entered this occupation in Europe or at least knew the life that awaited them in Argentina. Few seem to have been slaves; that family members, poverty, and lack of alternatives pushed many into the trade, however, was as sordid as slavery. What one can piece together from the data, deficient as they are, is far more complex than the white-slavery narrative suggests, yet these women's lives remain elusive.

Prostitutes traversed many borders, starting with those that separated one country from another. In Argentina they lived in criminal border spaces, where they acquired new languages and foods. They negotiated boundaries separating private and professional lives and respectable and disreputable society.

Argentina, its Jews, and its criminal networks marginalized Jewish prostitutes. These women joined the working class that Jewish and non-Jewish Argentines variously hired, repressed, and tried to uplift. Sexual entrepreneurs exploited prostitutes, just like factory owners exploited their hired workers, although many would argue that prostitutes endured harsher working conditions and greater occupational hazards than other laborers. Already subjugated by poverty, illiteracy, and the lack of dowries before entering prostitution, the women were ostracized as unclean. Since they could not take advantage of services offered by the Zwi Migdal or Ashkenazi community, many sex workers lost their health and possibility of retirement. Ezras Noschim tried to remove them from prostitution, but it did not supply them with good economic alternatives.

However, to a surprising degree, Ashkenazi prostitutes achieved a degree of inclusion. Some experienced more autonomy and advancement than other female workers, and a number financed their reentry into society and new pursuits. A minority became wealthy insiders in the Zwi Migdal and ruled over the women who labored in bordellos. Moreover, businesses and prostitutes' families accepted them to a certain extent.

Jewish prostitutes in turn marginalized other women. Often of color, native-born sex workers were even poorer and more degraded than Jewish ones, who protected their superior ranking in the racialized sexual hierarchy and avoided being confused with their criolla counterparts. While considered white in this setting, Jewish prostitutes were not as highly valued as the French, and therefore some may have assumed French identities.

The presence of prostitutes in their midst shamed many Jews, who feared that these transgressors endangered Jewish spaces in Argentina. They deemed it insufficient to eradicate sexual commerce. To prevent further damage and prove Jews belonged in the nation, Ezras Noschim and other groups policed the behavior of nonprostitutes, as shown in chapter 5.

CHAPTER FIVE

"A Bad Reputation"

Family and Sexuality

Mama was very zealous of the family's honor.
—Estela Levy, *Crónica de una familia sefaradí*

Argentina "had a bad reputation."
—Benito Zak, interview

When one young Jewish woman left Poland in 1928 for Buenos Aires, her uncle wrote his brother in disbelief. Sending her there was akin to murdering her, he exclaimed. The rumors he heard about single Jewish girls in Argentina gave that country "a bad reputation."[1]

Sexual impropriety threatened to undermine Jewish claims to Argentina. Jews feared that Catholic Argentines associated them with the sex trade, even as Jewish participation in it declined. Apparently tied to prostitution, polacas and rusitas might be perceived as sensual creatures, easy prey for men. As Riv-Ellen Prell noted for the United States, if Jewish women displayed their sexuality, "Jews worried that their non-Jewish neighbors might more aggressively enforce their boundaries between insiders and outsiders."[2]

Ambivalent about Jews, who were not the desired immigrants, liberals had generally accepted their presence as long as they perceived that Jews worked hard, obeyed the law, and fused with the melting pot. By the 1930s, the radical right-wing, anti-Semitic Nacionalistas were competing for hegemony with liberals, as discussed in chapter 7. Nacionalistas asserted that Jews could never belong in Argentina, even if they submerged their identities. Carnal, materialistic, and symbols of modernity, Jews seemingly threatened the spiritual and heroic order that the Nacionalistas wanted to create. Jewish sex workers epitomized the sensuality that Nacionalistas despised.[3] Liberals and especially Nacionalistas would not accept into the nation Jews tainted by transgressive sex.

To dispel notions of promiscuity, Ezras Noschim tried to keep impoverished Jews respectable. The organization gradually redirected its primary focus from prostitution to family problems among the poor, which it believed pushed women into activities that tarnished Argentine Jewry. Jewish women were obliged to obey local standards of female comportment, such as premarital chastity, monogamous marriage, motherhood, and domesticity,[4] and Jewish men were supposed to marry, procreate, and rule over and support their families. By monitoring women and other family members, the organization's president, Hélène Aslán, hoped to forestall anti-Semitism.[5] Since Jewish inclusion hinged largely on women's reputations, they were expected to be as upright as other women—if not more so. Contesting their own perceived marginalization, Ashkenazi leaders further marginalized women in the process.

The preoccupation with women's behavior suggested fears that they were crossing borders to explore new personal and occupational possibilities.[6] Indeed, some made their own marital choices and questioned sexual and gender norms. Others, however, accepted or resigned themselves to familial and communal expectations. Guarding women's morality also maintained borders, in that it helped guarantee the reproduction of a minority group by insuring that Jews married among themselves and raised children within their community.

An understanding of women's intimate lives enhances our grasp of Argentine and Argentine Jewish history. Specialists in these fields emphasize women's roles in the household, yet they have only begun to explore what conjugality meant for women. The few studies that have appeared on women's sexuality in Argentina generally focus on the 1960s. Little is known about how ordinary women experienced sexual relations, courtship, and marriage before that decade.[7] Using a thematic approach while highlighting change over time, this chapter sheds light on these issues so integral to women's lives.

Communal Honor

At the beginning of the twentieth century, women observed caution on the streets of Buenos Aires. An English Jewish observer noted in 1913 that no respectable woman walked alone. As late as 1926, some Jewish women did not attend nightly meetings of philanthropical societies for lack of escorts. Surprised that well-off women rarely went out by themselves, Italian and Central European Jewish women who arrived in the 1930s felt stifled in their new surroundings.[8]

The immigrant generation of Mediterranean Jews tended to follow customs brought from abroad that prescribed careful supervision of daughters to ensure their virginity. Women symbolized the ideal of an inwardly focused family; rarely, if ever, were they supposed to leave the intimate domestic space. "Very zealous of the family's honor," Rachel Mesulam of Istanbul confined her daughter Estela (see chapter 2) within the home "in the oldest Oriental style," as Estela complained. These parents surpassed Catholic Argentines in their fervor to shelter their daughters.[9]

Young women of Mediterranean descent challenged this smothering protectiveness with varying success. Impoverished yet proud, Farida Yadid of Aleppo (see chapter 2) guarded her five daughters so they could make good matches. One afternoon in the early 1940s, they told her they were going to visit an aunt but instead headed to a dance. They returned home to find their mother, who had fastened a black rag to her clothes, accompanying herself on the drum as she sang in Arabic: "Badly behaved daughters have I! . . . Daughters who will become prostitutes if they lie this way!"[10] Like other Jews, Farida raised the specter of prostitution to insure her daughters' virginity and honor within the community. Freer than the Yadid sisters, the young Damascene seamstress Regina Attach fled her father's house in Córdoba to live alone in the capital in the 1920s (see chapter 2). Only her aunts' mild supervision and the eyes of the community checked her social life.[11]

Proper daughters—Jewish and non-Jewish—attended chaperoned events. The Turkish youths who founded the Centro Recreativo Israelí in Villa Crespo in 1922 wanted to maintain respectability. They went to girls' homes to invite them to dances at the Centro, picked them up, and brought them home, accompanied by the girls' parents and siblings.[12]

Jewish women had enjoyed greater freedom of movement in Eastern Europe than in the Mediterranean region. Nevertheless, Argentine convention and concerns about acceptance influenced middle-class Ashkenazi girls more heavily than foreign habits. In Carlos Casares in the 1920s, young women attended dances with their fiancés—and legions of relatives. Couples could not walk by themselves without inciting disapproval. In a Hebrew school in the same town around that time, boys sat on one side of the room and girls on the other. When a boy offered to share his book with a girl who lacked one, the teacher threw him out of class. Visiting Buenos Aires in the late 1930s, a young woman from Entre Ríos unknowingly violated social norms by giving her phone number to a youth she had just met. To prevent greater indiscretions, her parents did not let her remain in Buenos Aires once the two were betrothed. An Ashkenazi father in Paraná was considered permissive for allowing his daughter to go to the movies alone with her *novio* in the late 1930s—an exception that proved the rule. Some girls rebelled against these confines by keeping their private lives secret.[13]

Given such attitudes, it is remarkable that young women from the colonies left their homes to study. Perhaps upward mobility outweighed morality. And pension owners' careful scrutiny of the behavior of women boarders reassured their parents.[14]

Community leaders guarded female immigrants. Beginning in the 1880s, members of various Jewish organizations boarded ships to question unaccompanied women about their contacts and intentions: in 1929, for example, Ezras Noschim interrogated over six hundred women. Assenting to communal requests, after 1922 immigration authorities permitted female passengers to disembark only after checking with their relatives, who had to claim them at the port. The Sociedad de Protección a los Inmigrantes Israelitas, or Soprotimis, created in 1922, aided incoming women. In 1929 it found jobs for 245 women and encouraged 16 girls to get married, thus endeavoring to keep them out of promiscuity and prostitution.[15]

Inmates in the Jewish girls' orphanage were closely watched. Some were related to traffickers; all seemed to be at risk simply because they were single and not under family supervision. The Sociedad de Damas Israelitas de Beneficencia continued to monitor the girls even after they left the institution, to ensure that they were leading a moral life. Promoted and financed by these philanthropists, the girls' marriages were highly publicized celebrations representing the philanthropists' victories over potential dangers to the orphans and Argentine Jewry.[16]

Even Jewish women's vaunted attractiveness could harm their image. Beginning in the 1930s, Ana Rovner and other Jewish women entered beauty contests sponsored by Jewish groups and the broader society. Chosen Miss Collectivity of Rosario in 1931, Dr. Anita Berlatsky embodied the "grace, loveliness, intelligence" of the prototypical Jewess, according to a Jewish periodical.[17] Berlatsky exemplified the sedate beauty that Jewish leaders wanted women to project, far removed from prostitution or unbridled sensuality.

Prominent Jews rejected coreligionists who threatened to besmirch the community's reputation. The young German emigrés of the Riegner group decided they could best support each other and observe Jewish rites by living under one roof. They considered their living arrangement practical, yet it struck members of the main German-speaking Jewish institutions, who included wealthy immigrants of long standing in Argentina, as potentially immoral. Their view was ironic because one of the Riegner group's reasons for cohabitation was to protect women from white slavers. German Jewish philanthropists were reluctant to give the group the assistance they offered other refugees.[18]

Neither Jewish nor Catholic Argentines taught daughters about their bodies or sexuality. When the married women in a Syrian family joked about sex, they banished single girls from the room. Few young Jewish women learned about sex from their mothers; some sought information from their equally ignorant classmates.[19] Ignorance was thought to ensure purity, parental control, and honor, but it also instilled anxiety. Traumatized by her family's silence, the middle-class Polish immigrant Miriam Turjanski, who reached adolescence in the 1930s, could not speak about intimate matters with anyone. The shame she felt when she needed her first brassiere erased her memory of how she acquired it. A girl of Aleppine descent who married when she was eighteen, in 1946, delayed having relations with her husband for a year out of fear. Intimidated by sex as well as maternity, the actress Cipe Lincovsky's (see chapter 3) first menstrual period terrified her.[20]

Jews protected their spaces in Argentine society by trying to keep young women innocent and moral, restricting them to a code similar to or more rigid than that followed by other Argentines. Such rules often conflicted with Eastern European customs but coincided with those of the Mediterranean region. The allure of the forbidden, however, prompted some adventurous girls to defy the code.

From Arranged Marriage to Freedom of Choice

Arranged marriages seemed to reinforce parental authority, family stability, and honor. Mediterranean men frequently returned to their homelands to marry in this manner and brought their brides to Argentina. This was the case for Luna de Mayo, who wed at her guardian's command in 1919, when she was seventeen, and sailed with her husband from Izmir to Posadas (see chapter 1).[21] The custom lingered in Argentina, where some parents apparently chose spouses for their children without consulting them. In the 1910s in Buenos Aires, Rachel Mesulam refused several candidates for the hand of her daughter Vida without asking her. Instead the parents looked favorably on Eliaú, the father's employee; whether they took Vida's wishes into account is unclear. In another instance, a twenty-year-old from Izmir went with his Catholic friends to meet girls at church in the early 1920s. When his father found out, he asked his brother to find a Jewish match. The young man's uncle selected an impoverished twelve-year-old employee, and the father ordered his speechless son to marry her.[22]

Many Ashkenazi couples arriving in Argentina in the late 1800s and early 1900s had already made arranged marriages in Eastern Europe. Numerous other arranged marriages followed in the early years of settlement, when matchmaking became a favorite leisure pursuit. Parents searched for possible spouses for their children, friends told eligible bachelors about young women they knew, and elderly women in the colonies prided themselves on bringing couples together. One farmer decided to marry off his daughter during the harvest, although his wife discouraged him since it was the busiest time of the year. Nevertheless, he joked, "I know my merchandise," and he found her a husband.[23]

When such efforts failed, parents could hire a marriage broker; ads for them appeared in *Mundo Israelita* as late as 1940. One male broker, who arrived in Colonia Mauricio soon after its founding in 1891, ran between the settlers' tents and shacks, matching up single women and men of all ages. Other matchmakers were female. According to an observer, once the colonies were established, there was little need for matchmakers, for in these small communities everyone knew each other.[24]

In early-twentieth-century Buenos Aires, privileged Ashkenazim still called on brokers to find professional men for their daughters and women with large dowries for their sons. Once the two sets of parents and the matchmaker reached an initial accord, they set up a meeting between the young man and woman, and if the couple consented, a well-chaperoned courtship ensued. Love was supposed to come after the marriage ceremony, if at all. Yet many youths confounded these norms by asking their parents to arrange matches with persons they found attractive, while others fell in love with their promised spouses during the *noviazgo*.[25]

Renewed immigration after the First World War—and fear of prostitution—breathed new life into arranged marriages, despite the decline of this custom in Eastern Europe. Not all such marriages worked out, however. A family in Poland exchanged letters with a contact in Argentina, arranging for the betrothal of their daughter and the contact's son. When the woman arrived in 1934, she formed a dislike for her fiancé, married him only to avoid repatriation, and quickly left him. This was one of many cases in which men sent for women whom they hardly knew, and the relationships never blossomed. To end this practice, Ezras Noschim negotiated an agreement among sponsoring agencies and Polish officials requiring men who applied to bring fiancées from Poland to provide information on the courtship, as well as the previously required certificate of morality.[26] Jewish organizations wanted not only to keep pimps from importing prostitutes, but also to prevent marital instability.

As Marion Kaplan explained for Germany, arranged marriages gave way to "arranged situations," which perpetuated a degree of parental control. A German Jew overheard two young men speaking German on the bus in Buenos Aires. Judging that they were of good Jewish families, she invited them for dinner; one eventually married her daughter. The scarcity of young women in the German-speaking Avigdor colony in Entre Ríos prompted residents to send for Ashkenazi girls from the Jewish orphanage in Buenos Aires, three of whom wed local men.[27]

The social season offered ample arranged situations for wealthy young Mediterranean and Ashkenazi Jews. During the fall and winter, Buenos Aires was the scene of social activities capped by the Sociedad de Damas's grand ball in benefit of the girls' orphanage, held annually in the exclusive Plaza Hotel. The season also featured coming-out parties, in which parents presented their elegantly dressed daughters.[28] These events duplicated ones among Catholic Argentines.

As time passed, women increasingly fought their elders for the right to make their own marital choices. One can see traces of debates on this issue as early as 1912, when *Juventud*, a magazine read by young Ashkenazi intellectuals, printed the poignant tale of a woman who loved one man but was forced by her parents to marry another. According to the female author, while her parents may have wanted the best for their daughter, they killed her soul. By 1921, "Ruth," the presumed author of a women's column in the Moroccan Jewish newspaper *Israel*, claimed that Argentine girls "will never permit their parents to select their *novio*. Even further: they don't even want to ask for advice."[29] Confirming this statement, when Judith Cohen (better known by her married name of Isaharoff) was in her teens in the late 1920s, members of the Bukharan community began to make offers to her father. Her mother wanted Judith to marry her first cousin, but she insisted on a distant relative whom her parents did not see as a good prospect. He had declared his love on a secret date, when Judith was fifteen and he was twenty-six.[30]

Miriam Turjanski's brother David tried to marry her off. He was keen on one of his employees, for if Miriam married that man, David would be assured of two reliable workers. With such a match, there was no need for the girl to study. Miriam fought off David's ploy, graduating with a degree in pharmacy and marrying the man she chose. Nor did she have a dowry when she married in 1945; that she found its absence worthy of mention suggests that dowries were still common.[31]

Dowries were popular among the Ashkenazim, but it is uncertain how typical they were among other Argentines. Since the 1869 civil code did not require dowries, Catholic Argentines may not have given them after that date; perhaps brides' parents helped newlyweds without giving their assistance that name. The same may have been true for Mediterranean Jews in Argentina, who instead emphasized the brides' trousseaus, consisting of embroidered linens, towels, lingerie, and clothing. Dowries declined in importance in Ashkenazi agricultural settlements, according to some accounts, yet they persisted among urban Ashkenazim of all classes through the 1940s. They varied from the 8,000 pesos offered to a surgeon in the 1940s to a more common 270 pesos, which a weaver saved from her wages and gave her fiancé in 1938. Sometimes the bride or her family paid cash, helped a groom establish a business, or bought him a sewing or weaving machine.[32]

Accompanied by dowries or not, marriages tended to follow certain patterns. Ashkenazi daughters commonly married in order of age; a woman would delay her nuptials or even conceal a courtship until her older sister wed. The ideal husband had already launched his career; the ideal wife was younger and unsullied. Before the 1940s, many Mediterranean women married as teenagers; their husbands were typically relatives and at least ten to twenty years older.[33]

Working-class Ashkenazim usually found their own spouses, although relatives and friends often facilitated matches. It would have been difficult for them to afford matchmakers—and even more difficult to prevent contact between men and women in factories, tenements, neighborhood clubs, and leftist libraries.

As customs loosened, women found ways of exercising freedom and meeting men. The brave or foolhardy scanned *El Correo Sentimental*, a set of personal ads published in the Yiddish press starting in 1938, or daringly

11. A dance in Colonia Avigdor, 1938.
Centro Marc Turkow, Buenos Aires.

placed their own ads. In Germany and Eastern Europe, Jews had used this method to find a spouse. Through this service one working-class woman met and married a carpenter in 1941, but the relationship soured when she discovered his "bad reputation."[34] Like Catholic Argentines, Jewish women strolled down small-town boulevards or circled urban plazas, pretending to ignore the stares and compliments they received from men standing around.[35] Jewish men and women also crossed paths in boardinghouses, apartment buildings, synagogues, and businesses.[36]

Women found compatible partners as they pursued social, cultural, and political activities. Fanny and Bernardo Edelman began to converse at a proletarian art exhibition and wound up married and in the Communist Party. Bruria Elnecavé met her husband in the Socialist Zionist Hashomer Hatzair in her native Bulgaria in 1930. A resort in the Córdoba hills attracted young German Jews, some of whom married each other. One young man and young woman noticed each other at a party at the Aleppine Círculo Social Pueyrredón in the 1940s and eventually wed. Jewish social spaces provided occasions for youths to pair off—and for reinforcing community borders.[37]

Migration, industrialization, incorporation into the world market, and secularization transformed families and relaxed sexual customs on both sides of the Atlantic at the beginning of the twentieth century. Challenging community vigilance and conservative norms, many Argentine Jewish women took advantage of these transnational currents. Yet by choosing their own boyfriends and husbands, Turjanski, Cohen, and other Jewish women also drew upon the sense of liberty they associated with Argentina. In schools, patriotic celebrations, and everyday encounters, Jewish women absorbed the nation's liberal freedoms, including the belief in individual happiness, sometimes even before they mastered Spanish.[38]

Courtship

Courtship was often the best part of the relationship between a man and a woman, the time when the woman felt noticed and pampered. One woman confessed to Ruth, the *Israel* columnist, that if she could do it all over again, she would spend her whole life as a novia and never marry. As Carolyn Heilbrun observed, "it is the part of their [women's] lives most constantly and vividly enacted in a myriad of representations—to encourage the acceptance of a lifetime of marginality."[39]

In the early 1900s, at least for old-fashioned men, courtship began with a respectful visit to the woman's home. When young Isaac Nissensohn met an attractive liceo student, Sofía Rabinovich (see chapter 1), on the street in Buenos Aires in 1911, his father sent a relative to tell her family that he would return with Isaac. It was understood that the latter wanted to become acquainted with the young lady. The two men arrived for tea on a Sunday afternoon, and Nissensohn and Rabinovich discussed Zionism and found that both favored it. Since few girls were interested in the topic at this time, she made a good impression on her suitor. He left praising the food, which according to custom meant he would return.[40]

A young physician used both his charm and his profession to woo a female dentist in the 1930s. First he sent her patients, then flowers. Later he invited her to go out with him and to accompany him when he visited his patients. The persistent doctor vaccinated her family against smallpox, and when her father fell ill, he performed X-rays. As her father neared death, the two families agreed on an engagement.[41]

Matilde Yadid's boss, Marcos Chami, reached her heart through that of Farida, her mother. He pined for Matilde, but she showed little interest. Still, she let him take her and her siblings to carnival. Expected home at midnight, they arrived much later, provoking Farida's anger. Chami told her not to worry about Matilde's reputation, for in two months he would marry her. Taken aback, Farida, accustomed to privation, blurted out that her daughter had no suitable underwear. He assured his future mother-in-law that he would supply a trousseau.[42]

Fearing parental disapproval, other women courted secretly. The unconventional Judith Isaharoff delayed announcing her noviazgo because her suitor was not wealthy. When her parents predictably decried his prospects, she asked them if his conduct was unsuitable. They said no. And if one married a rich man, she asked, how could one know he would stay rich? They could not answer. Isaharoff won the battle, insisting she would not be sold into marriage.[43]

Other Jewish women refused to be bought. A barometer of public debate on gender, Ruth's *Israel* column featured a letter in September 1920 from a woman who criticized prosperous men for purchasing "a beautiful 'social doll'" to marry. Once their passion cooled, they often turned elsewhere for new conquests.[44] The transaction resembled legalized prostitution. The letter writer justified women's rights in the marriage market by raising the specters of disorderly sexuality and, as did Isaharoff, commercial sex.

Broken noviazgos wounded women, as in the case of Ilse Katz (see chapter 1). Her love for her boyfriend was so natural that "we accepted it as one accepts the rain, the sun and the soft breeze that blew across the fields of Entre Ríos." But Katz decided to work in Buenos Aires to help support her beleaguered family, whose farm was in shambles. Her boyfriend's parents pressured him to marry a cousin in Germany to rescue her from Nazism and obtain her large dowry. He seemed to welcome Katz's decision to move to Buenos Aires; as she was leaving in any case, he could marry his cousin, please his family, and relieve his guilt over the cousin's fate. Realizing he had hurt Ilse's feelings, he apologized and asked her to stay, but the devastated young woman left.[45]

Spurning one's novia could ruin her life. Matilde Yadid loved her first novio, but his family rejected her because she worked in a factory. She longed for him even after her employer began to court her. Still, she was lucky to have a new suitor, as many Syrian men in this era wanted nothing to do with women who had been engaged, whom they regarded as defiled.[46]

Courtship placed women in the center, perhaps for the only time in their lives. In this transition between parental and spousal control, their fiancés lavished attention on them. Yet the financial underpinnings of their engagements humiliated women,[47] as did broken noviazgos.

Marriage

Women married for reasons not always related to love, parental pressure, or a sense of duty. Many believed it was their destiny, as they could aspire to nothing else. Ruth reflected public opinion when she wrote in her *Israel* column that there was nothing sadder than an old maid, who lived a "dry and solitary life." At least marriage meant not being alone. Some women sought to escape parental domination, conflicts at home, or poverty. Several brothers brought a woman named Schiffre, then twenty-one, from Poland in 1931, and one of them, who was forty, wed her. Discovering that he was already married and did not support his existing family, Ezras Noschim asked Schiffre why she stayed with him. The woman, an impoverished orphan, replied that she felt gratitude and feared she could not survive on her own.[48]

The Sociedad de Damas sought to marry off the orphans under its care to keep them out of prostitution, help perpetuate Argentine Jewry, and strengthen the communal image. In fact, the girls' so-called sexual health depended not only on marriage but on leaving the institution for a good home relatively early in life. *Mundo Israelita* claimed that it was not appropriate for young women to live together for prolonged periods, hinting at lesbianism.[49]

Brides and their parents wanted to ensure that grooms had a good reputation. To find out if fiancés were traffickers, already married, had treated other women unscrupulously, or were really Jewish, Ezras Noschim checked their backgrounds through contacts in the interior and other countries. Between 1930 and 1935, for example, it investigated 435 cases.[50]

Arranged marriages could turn out surprisingly well. One man fell in love with a woman he spotted at the port of Rhodes. Marrying an unknown man sixteen years her senior frightened this orphan, but her grandmother thought his generosity in paying wedding expenses augured well. He told his bride that once she got to know him, she would love him—even more than he loved her, he slyly added. They lived together for fifty years in Buenos Aires, working together in their store and raising two children.[51]

Good sexual bonds strengthened marriages. On Fridays, Farida Yadid and the other Syrian wives in her building visited the mikvah. Returning from the ritual bath refreshed and perfumed, they dressed in their finest clothes and jewelry. After the Sabbath dinner came the awaited intimacy.[52]

Some husbands went to great lengths to please their wives. Chami lifted Matilde Yadid out of poverty, paying for her trousseau and preparing an apartment for them in an elegant neighborhood. He encouraged her to study journalism by sending a car to pick her up at school daily. In addition, he accepted her family's presence and included them in outings.[53]

Other marriages were more patriarchal. A woman from Izmir married her uncle when she was sixteen and he was twenty-seven. He insisted on ruling the household; as he did so in a loving manner, she complied. At his request, she learned from his mother how to cook Turkish style. Submission, fulfillment of emotional needs, and appeals to the stomach were typical women's tactics. Like other wives, and according to Jewish custom, this woman valued and absorbed her husband's knowledge and piety. In their interviews, however, men rarely acknowledge learning anything from their wives.[54]

Women's and men's common interests and work signaled an evolution toward more egalitarian marriages. Fanny Edelman shared a political commitment with her husband, one that led them to participate in the Spanish Civil War. A lawyer, he defended her and other female members of the Communist Party in court. Bruria and Nissim Elnecavé dedicated their partnership to Zionism and communal social life, while an Ashkenazi teacher and her husband, a school principal, were devoted to education. "I was always very much his companion," observed Catherine Hassid (see chapter 1), who worked alongside her spouse in their store.[55]

Transgressing Sexual Frontiers

Women who engaged in what their elders and Ezras Noschim considered promiscuity could expect repercussions. An eighteen-year-old who left Poland in the mid-1930s to join her father in Buenos Aires proved too rebellious for him to handle. Discovering that she had several lovers, Ezras Noschim blamed her behavior on her "uncontrollable" need for sexual satisfaction. Evidently believing that normal women did not have such desires, the group claimed she was retarded and might become a prostitute.

To prevent this danger, the organization placed her with a family that watched her carefully.[56] In this and other cases, it linked sex outside marriage with commercial sex.

Some men used the lack of virginity—or suspicion thereof—as a pretext for extortion. When Marta married her fiancé in 1938, her parents gave the young man a dowry of 300 pesos and furnished the couple's home. After the first night together, he accused his wife of having had relations with other men. Although two doctors verified that Marta had only recently been deflowered, her husband demanded an additional 2,000 pesos. Insisting on her honor, Marta blamed her spouse's accusations for ruining her life.[57]

Some women faced the consequences of bearing children out of wedlock. Elisa, a seamstress who arrived from Romania in 1931, when she was twenty-two, fell in love with a man who abandoned her when she became pregnant with his child. The relatives who had brought her to Buenos Aires and lodged her then kicked her out. A kind family sheltered Elisa and her baby and employed her as a servant. After she left this home, she had a succession of affairs. Elisa told Ezras Noschim that she would continue her behavior unless she met a man willing to marry her. According to the organization, she offered herself to men because she had lost her self-esteem. One might also conjecture that this lonely young woman, repudiated by her lover and relatives, sought affection, or simply enjoyed sex and expressed her desires in terms that Ezras Noschim would accept.[58]

Another man who impregnated a woman also marginalized her. Engaged to a man for three years, this woman had sexual relations with him when he promised marriage. After their baby was born, he stopped visiting her. Instead of seeking a wedding, which was unlikely because he seemed to come from a higher class than she did, she asked Ezras Noschim in 1942 to convince her former fiancé to recognize their son, possibly as a first step toward demanding support. The manner in which she related her story indicated her desire to prove her honor. The man refused to admit he was the father or take a blood test, although he confessed to having had sex with her.[59]

Leftist and working-class couples, including Ashkenazi ones, often cohabited outside the bounds of religious or civil marriage because they found it convenient to do so, or because they rejected religious and governmental rules. Some Jews were separated from spouses who refused to grant them a religious divorce, or guet. When these individuals found new partners, they lived together outside marriage. Unlike Catholics, if Jews received a guet, they could remarry in a religious ceremony.[60] Ezras Noschim helped many Jews acquire these divorces to formalize their new relationships, thus promoting marital stability and the appearance of propriety.

As long as marital partners fulfilled their duties, even if they cared little for each other, they generally remained together. Women were supposed to maintain a clean home, cook adequate meals, and raise the children, whether or not they worked for wages; men would provide most of the income and abstain from beating their wives. They would have sexual relations and accord each other a minimum of respect. Infringing these boundaries was grounds for ending a marriage. Ezras Noschim files mention husbands who requested separation because their wives did not cook, attend to their needs, or remain at home. For their part, women left spouses who were impotent or could not support their families.[61]

The stress of persecution, migration, and resettlement also weakened marriages among Central European Jews. According to one observer, a disproportionate number sought divorces.[62] How their community institutions responded is unclear.

Some Jewish immigrants left families behind in their homelands and began new ones outside matrimony in Argentina. A penniless carpenter abandoned his wife in Poland and impregnated a minor in Buenos Aires. Equally poor, the girl's parents pushed him to straighten out his affairs and marry their daughter, but his first wife would not grant a divorce without a cash payment, which he could not afford. After several years, in 1939, the Polish wife finally agreed to a divorce; whether the couple married is unclear.[63] What is clear is that by retaining the relationship, the girl asserted her own desire for happiness and violated propriety.

Some women affirmed their freedom by leaving their families for other men. In 1935 Berta, who had been married for seventeen years, took one son and went to live with a non-Jew, leaving three other children with her husband. She transgressed in three ways: by going off with her lover, taking up with a Catholic, and giving up her children, thus challenging the notion of obligatory maternity. She then transgressed a fourth way. Refusing to give her husband a guet, she said "let him find a woman, like I found another man."[64]

Crowded tenement conditions gave rise to tales about women who committed adultery with boarders. Ana, who arrived with her husband and baby from Poland in 1928, took boarders as her lovers. Claiming Ana was a prostitute, Ezras Noschim may have conflated this practice with her rooming-house business and paramours.[65] In the organization's eyes, sex outside marriage was equivalent to prostitution, and both hurt Argentine Jews.

Whatever Ana's motives, love and desire impelled Berta Singerman, the reciter (see chapter 3), into affairs. She and her husband shared a family, career, and affection, but there was little spark in their marriage. Instead she sought passion in the arms of others, including one man who was her great love. Violating boundaries had its costs: "generations of women of my Orthodox family, who had repressed their feelings out of respect for the law, morality and duty weighed on me."[66]

Intimacy with Catholic men was the ultimate transgression. The closely knit nature of Jewish colonies, and the construction of criollo men as racialized other, meant that the only imaginable relationship between a Jewish woman and a non-Jewish man was a *rapto*. Also common among non-Jews, these ritualized "kidnappings" implied that women were victims, which maintained the borders between Jews and gauchos.[67] Yet Ashkenazi women were often willing accomplices.

In his fictionalized account of the Entre Ríos colonies, Alberto Gerchunoff wrote of Miryam, the lovely daughter of a pious Jewish farmer, and his employee, the handsome, honorable criollo Rogelio. Lacking a common tongue, they shared their feelings through song. When neighbors spotted them alone together, Miryam's father reluctantly fired Rogelio, driving the courtship underground rather than ending it. Mounted behind Rogelio, Miryam "defiantly" glared at the villagers as the two galloped out of town.[68] Her agency was obvious. After her "abduction" and no longer with her gaucho lover, the real-life Miryam returned for a visit before moving to Buenos Aires. Whether she felt repentance or shame is unknown. Her brothers welcomed her, but her parents shunned her, treating her as dead.[69]

Other parents reacted differently. Raquel was the oldest daughter of a pious family in Colonia Mauricio. Her knowledge of French helped her get a job with the JCA administration and communicate with Pedro, a criollo ranch foreman of French descent, who regularly conducted transactions at the JCA office. One day Raquel disappeared, seemingly taken forcibly by Pedro; the police discovered, however, that they eloped and married by joint consent. The couple then rescued her parents. As the family had only one son and large debts, the JCA had threatened to throw it off its plot. Raquel's desperate father accepted Pedro's offer to work with him on his land, and Pedro fought to secure the JCA's consent. The unforgiving community, however, cast Raquel out and dismissed her father as cantor.[70]

Some Jewish urban girls like Raizla, a fifteen-year-old Polish immigrant, feigned kidnapping. A week after her disappearance in 1934, which her parents reported to the police, the girl reappeared. Raizla claimed that two men had grabbed her and forced her to drink a narcotic beverage. In truth, she had run away with an Italian youth, who sent her home when he realized that Ezras Noschim was tailing him. The couple concocted the story Raizla told the police, and her parents confirmed it to save her reputation.[71] Raizla wanted it both ways: to cross sexual and communal borders, yet pretend she had not done so.

Some such pairings were temporary, but others were permanent. Although her parents forbade thirteen-year-old María from seeing her non-Jewish boyfriend, the two ran off together and had sexual relations. The police arrested him for statutory rape, and a judge placed her in a state institution. The young man's family tried to arrange a marriage, but María's parents, backed by Ezras Noschim, opposed it, declaring he might force her into prostitution. Asserting her own wishes, María defied them and married her lover.[72]

The notion that sex with a gentile might lead to prostitution influenced a distraught father's perception of his sixteen-year-old daughter Tauba, who ran off with Albian, a Catholic eleven years her senior. When they had disappeared previously, the police had forced him to return her, but the second time, in 1927, the father attributed the authorities' inactivity to Albian's political connections. He feared Tauba's seducer, who spent his days in a cafe and lived off her wages. As cafes were associated with prostitution, the suggestion was that Albian was pushing Tauba into sex work. María's and Tauba's cases show how Jews fanned fears of white slavery to highlight the danger of illicit sexual relations and enforce the community's borders.[73]

Not all Jewish women who desired Catholic men married them. In one fictionalized saga, a working-class Ashkenazi girl fell in love with an attractive young Christian around the 1930s. Each Sunday afternoon, in the standing-room section of the Teatro Colón, they held hands as they listened to classical music. He wrote her a love poem on a concert program, which she kept long after the hidden courtship ended. Unable to escape her milieu, she married "not the boy of the poem, but the one of the tradition."[74] This account seemed emblematic of Jewish women who remained within their community's confines.

One Ashkenazi woman inculcated the "iron laws" of endogamy in her children. Fearing her disapproval, her daughter, born in 1931, dated Catholics secretly. She married a Jewish man, but as soon as her mother died, she separated from him. No longer pressured to be with a Jew, she formed a lasting relationship with a Catholic.[75]

Fiction writers attempted to dissuade young Jews from forming relationships outside the faith. A young Jewish woman published a story in an Ashkenazi periodical describing a doomed affair. A Catholic youth wanted to take his Jewish girlfriend to live somewhere where no one would know her religion. The spiritual young woman refused, insisting that God would know. They died together, and their ghostly figures, dressed in white, were visible on calm nights. This ultraromantic tale suggested that a love affair between a Jew and non-Jew could never end happily.[76] A similar message pervaded some *novelas semanales*, short stories published weekly for a mass audience. In one such story, Sonia, an impoverished Jew, eloped with Sergio, a fellow medical student and wealthy Catholic. Their marriage sent her mother to an early grave and reduced her father to destitution and insanity; moreover, Sergio died of complications resulting from drug addiction. The non-Jewish author sympathized with his heroine yet implied that her rebellion could only have destructive consequences.[77] This conclusion echoed the standard view of the Jewish community.

In actuality, not all such relationships were doomed, nor did all Jewish parents reject children who married gentiles. An Ashkenazi couple outwardly accepted their daughters' marriages to Catholics in the 1940s, although inside may have harbored regrets. Decades later Sara Salón (ch. 1) found it more difficult to accept the fact that a son and a daughter married Catholics. Intermarriage conflicted with her Turkish Jewish upbringing and memories of anti-Semitism in Corrientes. Yet the love and respect she felt from her daughter- and son-in-law and their enthusiasm for Jewish holidays changed her mind.[78]

Some parents welcomed non-Jewish suitors. Steaming toward Argentina in 1942, a Swiss businessman fell in love with an Austro-Hungarian Jewish refugee. She longed for children and a home far from war and dislocation; fleeing Nazism, unconsciously she also may have sought to hide her Jewish identity. Moreover, she wanted to please her assimilated parents, who became close to the man during the voyage. Thus, she married this Christian.[79]

Among the first two generations of Ashkenazim in the interior, endogamy was the rule. However, the Mediterranean men who worked in provincial towns often could not find local Jews to marry. Over time the small rural communities witnessed an exodus of young people. Some of the remainder probably found non-Jewish spouses.[80]

Initially there was a high degree of endogamy among Moroccans, German-speakers, and other urban Jews, reflecting their linguistic and social bonds. By the late 1920s, however, the situation had changed for some groups. *Tribuna Hebrea* warned in 1929 that Turkish Jewish women in Villa Crespo were marrying Christians. It urged Ottoman organizations to increase Jewish awareness among young people, especially women.[81]

In the 1920s, Mediterranean and Ashkenazi rabbis and leaders debated whether to allow Christian marital partners to convert to Judaism and permit mixed couples and their offspring to join community institutions and be buried in Jewish cemeteries. These discussions suggest the frequency of intermarriage. While they focused on Jewish men who married non-Jews,[82] some Jewish women did the same.

The earliest scholarly study of intermarriage in a major Argentine city is based on the 1960 census. Its authors, U. O. Schmeltz and Sergio Dellapergola, conclude that 20 to 25 percent of Jews in greater Buenos Aires were marrying Christians. Rates may have been nearly as high in the 1950s. While this and other works suggest that larger numbers of men than women seek marital partners outside their community, Rosa Geldstein warns that demographers may undercount women in mixed couples.[83]

Unions also took place between Jews of different backgrounds. Soon after their arrival in the Moisesville area, offspring of the Lithuanian and Ukrainian colonists began to intermingle and marry. The Turkish Mesulam sisters married Syrian men during and after the First World War.[84] The most novel "mixed marriages" among Jews united Ashkenazim and Sephardim. An early case occurred in rural Entre Ríos in the early 1900s. Since the Aleppine groom did not speak Yiddish and his pronunciation of Hebrew differed from the Ashkenazi style, the bride's family sought proof that he was Jewish before permitting the marriage.[85]

While many Mediterranean parents wanted their daughters to marry within the community, a few preferred Ashkenazi spouses. A couple from Rhodes and Egypt disagreed over the ideal husband for their daughter. The father thought an Ashkenazi would treat the intellectual girl more equitably than a Sephardi. The mother, however, thought Ashkenazi men allowed women too much freedom to pursue activities outside the house.[86]

Some Ashkenazi and Sephardi voices alike encouraged Jewish intermarriage to tear down barriers between Yiddish, Ladino, and Arabic speakers.[87] Indeed, the marriages between communities that took place may have represented the culmination of this process. They demonstrated that Jews of varied backgrounds shared neighborhoods, workplaces, cultural spaces, and some synagogues.

By engaging in sex outside marriage, bearing children out of wedlock, forming and breaking consensual unions, and seeking partners of other backgrounds, Jewish women contested walls built by Jews and other Argentines. They also tested the freedoms of a modern liberal society. At the same time, their parents and Ezras Noschim tried to restrain them and clean up disreputable behavior.

Abuse and Exclusion

Rather than exercise liberty, some women were coerced into sex. Drawn to girls who were "white, clean, full of grace," claimed Marcos Alpersohn, a few criollos raped female colonists. He insisted that gauchos simply took what they wanted, be it cattle or women, both of which he and other male colonists seemed to regard as theirs. Furthermore, they saw locals as racial intruders, ones who did not even confine themselves to the unmarried. A man attacked a midwife carrying her baby and accompanying another woman to the ritual bath in Mauricio. Tossing the infant to the side, he raped and trampled her, while her friend ran for help. The rapist escaped, but from then on armed men escorted their wives to the mikvah. Similar incidents persisted into the 1930s. Sympathetic to the gauchos with whom he was raised, an educator born in Entre Ríos in the early 1900s asserted their attacks were infrequent and usually limited to women they thought had shown interest in them.[88]

In Buenos Aires, the assailants included Jews. Shortly after arriving in 1938, a young woman met a seemingly respectable man who she claimed proposed to her. One evening he invited her to a restaurant and served her a suspicious drink. Feeling ill, she asked him to take her home, but instead he took her to a house with many rooms, implying a brothel, and raped her. Alarmed about the attack and hint of prostitution, Ezras Noschim accompanied her to the police. The youth admitted that he had sexual relations with her, but he claimed she threatened to accuse him of rape if he did not pay her. The police and Jewish organization sided with the woman.[89]

Sometimes young women did falsely accuse men of rape, as may have been true of Cecilia Wajovsky. Cecilia and Catalina Wajovsky, twenty-five and twenty-two, respectively, had emigrated with their penniless Eastern European family in the early 1920s. When their mother became ill, Rosa, the manager of the tenement where they lived, invited Cecilia to sleep in her room. The young immigrant believed that Rosa had enticed her into her room and drugged her, enabling two other residents to rape her in her sleep and transmit a venereal disease. The family fled to another location, and Cecilia sought medical aid. To receive free medicine, she had to obtain a certificate testifying to her poverty from the police, who added that she was a prostitute. Humiliated, convinced that the authorities would not prosecute her assailants, and anxious to assert her honor, Cecilia decided to kill herself. Catalina, distressed by her sister's shame, joined her. The double suicide in 1925 shocked Jewish porteños.

Concerned about the case even before the suicides, Ezras Noschim consulted two doctors, who asserted that Cecilia's disease existed only in her mind; whether she was a rape victim also was questionable. Malnutrition and stress might have sent her over the edge into insanity. Yet the physicians and Ezras Noschim had biases that could have skewed their perceptions of Cecilia. They may have linked her actions to hysteria, promiscuity, and work outside the home, which Argentine health experts often conflated. Whatever her problems, the marginalized young woman needed help, and many Jews wondered why community charities had not provided it.[90] The latter had not ignored her, but their conception of communal honor did not coincide with her notions of personal honor.

Abuse within families also threatened to harm Jewish girls and besmirch Jewish communities. To thwart this danger and prevent children from witnessing sexual relations, the JCA's homes had at least two bedrooms, one for parents and one for their offspring. Perhaps this measure curbed sexual predation in the colonies, but in Buenos Aires entire families shared tenement rooms, and here there were cases of abuse. In 1941, María accused her alcoholic husband Jacobo of raping one of their nine children. One night as she slept, her husband attacked their fifteen-year-old daughter Flora, who afterwards tried to kill herself. When Jacobo returned home from jail, awaiting trial, María sent Flora to live with her grandparents and tried to place five other children in the orphanage. Insisting she had had relations with her Catholic boyfriend, Jacobo depicted Flora as deviant, but she did not alter her story.[91]

Other parents' abuse had sexual overtones. In 1937, a man asked Ezras

Noschim to find his fifteen-year-old daughter. The agency discovered that years before, her parents had pulled her out of school, put her to work, and insisted she bring money home; they also dressed her inadequately and often punished her. These conditions led her to run away repeatedly. When police returned the girl after her third flight, her parents stripped her so she could not leave. They seemed to assume she was a prostitute and degraded her as such, or tried to push her into this trade; nevertheless, her uncle believed she was "decent." Ezras Noschim found the girl and informed the father that her "moral health" required her to live elsewhere.[92]

Raped and abused women sometimes wound up as prostitutes. One girl left school when she was nine, possibly because she was retarded. When she was fourteen, she was raped; a year later she was living among prostitutes. Her parents placed her in the Jewish girls' orphanage under the tutelage of the public defender of minors.[93]

Believing that marital stability strengthened the community's reputation, Jewish agencies persisted in trying to reconcile wives and battering husbands. Throughout their eleven-year marriage, Salomon had abused Berta. After a particularly vicious beating in 1933, Berta turned to Ezras Noschim, which prodded them to stay together. Salomon did not alter his behavior, however, and after a year Berta complained anew to the agency.[94]

German émigrés Regina and Leonhard settled in a colony in Entre Ríos in 1940. Close to giving birth, Regina fled to Buenos Aires, charging that her husband beat her. This was not the first time she had left him for this reason. Ezras Noschim and other Jewish groups interceded and hospitalized her. Doubting he was the father of the child, Leonhard refused to answer his wife's letters or requests that he pay her medical bills.[95]

Addiction also led to abuse. In 1940, long-suffering Berta had been married to Gregorio for thirty-one years. Periodically abandoning his home for drinking and gambling sprees, he provided only a meager sustenance even when he lived there. Another woman left her husband several times because of his alcohol-influenced maltreatment.[96]

Abandoning one's family was not uncommon. Poverty, shame, and marital strains led the Damascene Isaac Liniado to desert his spouse Elena in Buenos Aires in 1923 (see chapter 2). He sent no money to his desperately needy wife and seven children, nor did he appear when one child died of scarlet fever. Jewish neighbors urged Elena to seek aid from community organizations, but she proudly refused.[97]

Desertion not only deprived many Jewish women of financial means, but it left them in limbo. Under Jewish law, they could not remarry without acquiring a guet from their husband or proof of his death. These provisions, however, did not apply to men.[98] Jewish agencies feared some abandoned wives would turn to prostitution to provide for their families.

Argentine law required a husband to feed and clothe his wife and children if he was legally married, but the law often went unenforced. Ezras Noschim received numerous pleas from women seeking their husbands' support. In one case, a Turkish man, León, left his wife Rosa in 1932, after ten years of marriage and four children. By 1937 he had sent her only 20 pesos, forcing Rosa to place her two daughters in the Jewish girls' orphanage. Afflicted with rheumatism, Rosa worked sporadically in a textile shop, where she earned 2 pesos a day. A tailor, León refused Ezras Noschim's entreaties for alimony, insisting that Rosa was a prostitute who had ruined his name, and his girls' residence in the orphanage was preferable to Rosa's raising them as "libertine" women. The tone of his letter, as well as his imprisonment for disorderly conduct, suggested that León was unbalanced. Nor did his use of the prostitution argument win the agency's sympathy. Its investigation revealed that he could afford to support his wife and progeny but was irrationally jealous and had left them four times. After two years of pleading with León, Aslán asked a Jewish charity to help the beleaguered family.[99]

Women also abandoned their husbands, sometimes for good reason. An Ashkenazi woman in Bahía Blanca in 1938 claimed her cousin's depravity "sowed hatred and revulsion" within his family. Suspected of arson, he had caught a venereal disease from one of his many lovers. At various times he had left his family; even when he lived at home, he spent on himself the money needed for their sustenance. His wife finally left him, taking their three children, and eked out a meager living washing and mending clothes. Using language designed to appeal to Ezras Noschim, the spiteful husband insisted his wife had run away with a non-Jew, and his cousin, who was caring for one of his daughters, was having an extramarital affair.[100]

Men cheated on their wives, as one new bride discovered to her dismay. In Rosario in 1942, Juana, an Ashkenazi dentist, married a surgeon and gave him a hefty dowry. After a few months, Juana realized that her husband had a pregnant mistress. When she confronted him, he left her to live with his lover. Some scholars have attributed complaints of male infidelity to women's increasing power and independence. Yet these traits did not help Juana recover her marriage settlement.[101]

Ezras Noschim tried to convince another woman to accept her husband's affair. Having settled just outside Buenos Aires in 1930, a man sent for his wife and child from Poland three years later. The revelation that he had a criolla mistress embittered her, and she spurned her husband's attempts to revive their relationship. Ganopol urged her to "resign herself," as had countless other women, and he comforted her by noting that she would feel better over time, although he admitted in his notes that did not always happen.[102] Preserving the marriage and the community's image mattered more to his agency than the woman's pain over her husband's rejection.

Conclusion

The theme of state formation permeates Jewish efforts to guard women, as well as women's choices. Ashkenazi leaders attempted to include Jews in the nation by enforcing moral behavior. They believed that order within the family—with spouses remaining together, husbands supporting wives and progeny, and women observing decorum—would facilitate Jews' acceptance in Argentina. To combat possible stigmatization, they policed individuals deemed vulnerable or unrespectable. Reinforcing gender and community borders, they conflated prostitution with premarital sex and relations with Catholic men. Even though it was female-led, Ezras Noschim did not denounce the double standard, women's inferior status in Jewish communities, or the lack of well-paid jobs for women as contributors to family conflicts and sex work.[103] Ironically, calling attention to Jewish prostitution and promiscuity may have heightened public awareness of these problems, thus reinforcing the Jews' bad reputation.[104]

Sometimes Ezras Noschim and other agencies straightened out marriages and families. Insufficient resources and resistance from the presumed beneficiaries, however, impeded efforts to reform violators of sexual and social norms. Some noncompliant women, as well as those who tried to control them, deployed the prostitution argument to justify their behavior. Sometimes women also justified their desire for sexual freedom by utilizing the language of liberalism.

By choosing their own paths, rebellious Jewish women linked their destinies to a liberal democratic nation, as did women who chose their own spouses. At the same time, women who accepted customary gender practices could pride themselves on upholding family and community honor. In this manner they, too, claimed spaces in the nation. As described in succeeding chapters, Jewish women also claimed such spaces through leftist and communal activities.

Many women lived on the sidelines. Before and after marriage, they were confined to their homes and strict oversight. A brief period of courtship sweetened and punctuated a lifetime of marginality. A number of Jewish and non-Jewish men, including rural criollos apparently attracted by their whiteness, raped Jewish women, who also suffered from abuse, abandonment, and other forms of degredation. Other Jewish women, however, enjoyed happy relationships and life in the mainstream.

Fighting communal and familial pressures, some women crossed borders in their intimate lives. Absorbing transnational currents of liberalization, they challenged bourgeois respectability by bearing children out of wedlock, engaging in extramarital affairs, and abandoning their husbands and offspring. Workers lived in consensual unions, separated from their spouses, and found new partners, all the while ignoring religious and government strictures. Many other women took smaller yet significant steps that challenged sexual and community confines. Girls sought information on sexuality, refused to give dowries, and insisted on selecting their husbands, including Jews of other backgrounds and non-Jews. Some wives rejected spouses they found incompatible, even if the husbands fulfilled their obligations; others neglected their domestic duties in favor of diversion. All contested limits imposed by parents, husbands, and Jewish leaders.

Many other women, however, did not challenge the boundaries. Some were content with their fiancés and husbands; others simply acquiesced to arranged marriages within their communities of origin and to the practices of dowries and trousseaus. Before marriage they submitted to their parents, and after marriage to their husbands. They stayed with and remained faithful to their spouses, even if they did not love them. Abandoned wives demanded money from derelict husbands and sought community aid to obtain religious divorces and halt abuse. Such actions did not constitute rebellion against gender norms since the Jewish communities and the wider society expected husbands to support families and treat wives with some respect. Still, these battered and neglected women resisted marginalization.

The themes of this book cannot fully encapsulate women's rich intimate stories, replete with laughter and tears. One hungers to know how the narratives ended. Like so many documents, however, the incomplete case files and other sources offer only snapshots of the past.

CHAPTER SIX

"What Surrounds Us Dissatisfies Us"

Leftists and Union Members through the 1930s

What surrounds us dissatisfies us.
—Guitl Kanutsky, interview

In the struggle of the producer class, there should be no distinction between men and women.
—Flora Absatz, *El Obrero Textil*

Arriving in Argentina in 1924, Guitl Kanutsky brought from Poland tailoring skills, organizing experience, and a desire to end the exploitation and poverty she saw around her. Kanutsky was among the Ashkenazi women who devoted themselves to leftist and workers' causes in Argentina. They helped construct the values that nourished leftist politics and created social capital—if one may apply this term to anticapitalist movements.[1] Seeking a socially just, pluralistic, and democratic Argentina and world, these women engaged with the liberal project and transnationalism.

Politics was a masculine public space in Argentina, as Jocelyn Olcott notes for Mexico in the 1930s.[2] Women who dared to trespass often were repressed by the larger society and disparaged by male comrades, as Flora Absatz hinted in the quotation above, when she argued for equality between male and female workers. Professing women's liberation, a notion intertwined with popular liberation, Absatz and other militants contested their marginalization.

Female activists of Ashkenazi origin navigated multiple borders. Militants of diverse backgrounds interacted in leftist and union movements. Some Jewish women, however, maintained community boundaries by participating in Yiddish-speaking groups. Often entering the left through cultural activities considered appropriate for them,[3] women nevertheless confronted gender strictures. To cross these barriers required commitment, rebelliousness, and fortitude.

Local conditions and prior experience helped determine Jewish women's affiliations. At the beginning of the twentieth century, a classically liberal elite ruled Argentina, permitting substantial freedoms except on election days. Demanding free elections and universal male suffrage, the Unión Cívica Radical (known as Radical, or the UCR) challenged the oligarchical "conservative" parties, so called because they perpetuated themselves in power. Securing these rights helped the UCR win the presidency between 1916 and 1930. Doubtful of regaining power through legal means, the conservatives, along with the radical rightist Nacionalistas, supported a coup in 1930 that ousted UCR President Hipólito Yrigoyen. A Nacionalista-leaning dictatorship ruled until 1932, followed by the conservative Concordancia alliance that governed through fraudulent elections until 1943. Centrist and conservative parties offered little room for Argentine women until they acquired the vote in 1947, apart from small feminist circles in the UCR. Jewish centrist and rightist women tended to remain outside politics or become Zionists (see chapter 8). Poverty, activism in Eastern Europe, and family militancy impelled most Jewish female political activists toward the left.[4]

Most activists were of Eastern European descent. The problematic identities (see chapter 2) and refugee status of Central Europeans and Italians tended to keep them from joining political groups, although some would openly oppose fascism (see chapter 7). Mediterranean women had not participated in unions or political parties in their homelands and rarely did so in Argentina; the Yiddish-speaking character of some of these groups further excluded them. Despite their Ashkenazi origins, however, some female activists may not have considered themselves Jews because they had divorced themselves from the religion and community institutions. Others identified themselves as secular Jews.

Divided into sections on anarchists, Socialists, Communists, and union members, this chapter traces women of Jewish origin in these groups roughly until the 1930s, concentrating on particular individuals and moments. The literature on politically active Argentine women has barely begun to treat female Communists or rank-and-file leftists and union members, especially after 1930.[5] I examine women whose lives illustrate the themes of this book, reflect broader leftist tendencies, and provide insights into the mass base.

Anarchists

Anarchism predominated among urban laborers in Argentina before the First World War. While this movement contained different tendencies, it aimed to destroy capitalism, government, organized religion, and marriage, substituting a new society based on freedom, equality, cooperation, and rationalism. Its emphasis on secularism and liberty overlapped liberalism slightly, but anarchism fought this hegemonic project. Argentine anarchists created unions and labor federations, of which the most important was the Federación Obrera Regional Argentina (the FORA), newspapers such as *La Protesta*, libraries, and other centers. In their periodicals, anarchist women rejected capitalist, religious, and male exploitation, urging women to form free relationships with men.[6]

Jews were overrepresented in anarchist groups in Russia, and the same was true in Argentina. Precisely how many of the women who attended anarchist meetings, read and contributed to anarchist periodicals, and joined FORA affiliates were of Ashkenazi backgrounds, however, is difficult to ascertain.[7] To evade official monitoring and persecution, anarchists often wrote anonymously and worked clandestinely.

Some Jewish anarchists joined Yiddish-speaking groups or sectors of unions. For a time, *La Protesta* published a page in this language. The use of Yiddish smoothed the entry into the anarchist movement of female immigrants, who were more likely to work at home and learn Spanish slowly. Some made use of Yiddish connections only initially, while others retained them longer.[8] Others stressed their internationalist convictions and immediately affiliated themselves with larger, Spanish-speaking groups. In these border spaces, some families of Ashkenazi origin created networks of friendship and intimacy with others of varied ethnic backgrounds, which reinforced their militancy and anarchist identities.[9]

Rosa Chanovsky was an internationalist and one of the few female anarchists of Jewish origin who emerges from anonymity. Already revolutionaries, she and her husband Adolfo Dubovsky fled Odessa, she for France and he for Argentina. They reunited in Argentina in 1905, when she was about twenty-two, establishing themselves in Santa Fe's anarchist circles. Dubovsky's politics resulted in his dismissal from one job after another, so he left carpentry to work with Chanovsky, an upholsterer, in their home.[10]

Chanovsky tried to stem the exploitation of women around her. To prevent sexual abuse, she admonished male anarchists that "free love" did not mean indiscriminate sex. A reader of anarchist classics, Chanovsky loaned books to penniless anarchist women and founded a library for them, probably the Biblioteca Femenina Popular.[11] She advised female workers in a match factory on organizing and strike tactics. Chanovsky continued to spread her views among women when the family relocated to the Buenos Aires area in 1930, conversing with female residents of her tenement building while they waited in line to wash clothes.

Chanovsky also was involved in general anarchist activities. She attended meetings, distributed propaganda, and served as secretary of the Emilio Zolá Library, where FORA affiliates congregated in Santa Fe. She opened her house to visiting anarchists, and the police frequently searched it for fugitives and anarchist documents, which Chanovsky hid under a table. Chanovsky inculcated her children with anarchist ideas and debated texts with them; the entire family carried food to jailed comrades. Two daughters and a son braved the growing persecution after 1930 and became militants. While Chanovsky gradually curtailed her activism, she attended cultural events and meetings of the Federación Anarco Comunista Argentina (the FACA), later called the Federación Libertaria Argentina (the FLA), until she was in her eighties.[12] Through her words and deeds, Chanovsky helped propagate the anarchist values of resistance, solidarity, women's equality, and the free exchange of ideas, as well as creating a home that embodied them.

Sara Dubovsky entered anarchism by helping her mother distribute fliers and accompanying her to meetings. An article she wrote for *Nuestra Tribuna*—an anarchist women's journal of the early 1920s edited by, among others, Juana Rouco Buela, Chanovsky's friend—provides insight into her beliefs. Egotistical people, Dubovsky claimed, used intellectual advances to exploit and hurt others. Moral progress could temper knowledge and reduce the divides of class, nationalism, and religious sectarianism, which sowed hatred. Nourished on healthy ideals, young people would institute this moral change, concluded Dubovsky, a member of the generation she had in mind. Tall and energetic, Dubovsky devoted much time to the FACA and the FLA. Defying fears that limited women's political engagement, she visited jails, keeping track of inmates and bringing them food and supplies. Dubovsky herself was imprisoned for her activism.[13]

More visible than most, Chanovsky and Dubovsky were emblematic of anarchist women of Ashkenazi origin. Some joined groups that discussed anarchist philosophy, disseminated literature, and painted slogans on buildings. A few challenged convention by making speeches and writing for anarchist publications. Yet as a woman from Bernasconi noted in *Nuestra Tribuna*, women's most important contribution to anarchy was to raise healthy children free of religion, nationalism, hypocrisy, and flirtatious behavior. Some women of Jewish origin participated in anarchist theatrical and choral performances and literary evenings (*veladas*), designed to awaken consciousness of social problems and spread anarchist ideals. They helped organize festivities that strengthened camaraderie, bring children into the fold, and shape anarchist culture.[14]

The Liga de Educación Racionalista arose in 1912 to spread knowledge among workers and their children in a free, secular manner. Although some Socialists participated in this endeavor, it was primarily an anarchist one. Rosalía Granowsky taught dressmaking, anatomy, and physiology for the Liga, served on its board, and recited poems and delivered speeches at its functions. In a talk in 1913, she explained that education had subjugated people by emphasizing notions that were theological in origin, such as the afterlife and obedience to authority. Schools also encouraged inequality by classifying and grading students. Only a rationalist education could create a true individualism, without fostering divisions, religion, or nationalism.[15]

Contrasting with Granowsky's desire to overcome religious and ethnic barriers, other anarchists reconciled their politics with their Jewish roots. While these groups were small, their hybridity merits attention. A circle of relatives and close friends formed around the brothers Berish and Meier Bursuk, renowned as intellectuals and contributors to a Yiddish anarchist periodical, *Dos Freie Wort*. They established the local anarchist library and theater in the colony of Narcise Leven, La Pampa, then moved to an area near Charata, Chaco, in 1922–23, when the government opened lands for settlement. Each of the six interrelated families at the core of this group occupied 100 hectares and planted cotton and other crops. Farming proved unprofitable, but constructing a cooperative society and Jewish anarchist identities, rather than earning money, was their foremost interest.

The Bursuk clan represented anarchism with a Yiddish flavor, in transition toward a local blend. At night after dinner, Yosl Bursuk, the brother of Meier and Berish, read aloud *Dos Freie Wort* and other Yiddish publications to his wife Bruje and their children. Their daughter Nelia, born in 1921, read aloud *La Protesta* and *La* FORA. She, her cousins, and their friends founded the Biblioteca Brazo y Cerebro, and their parents created the Biblioteca León Jazanovich, named for a progressive journalist whose denunciations of JCA abuses had led to his deportation from Argentina.

The languages of their texts and the names of the libraries illustrated the generational change and the young people's claim on Argentina.[16]

Their area included Spanish, Czech, and Polish farmers, some of them anarchists, and criollo migrant laborers. The Bursuks reached out to neighbors and workers to cultivate anarchist values and networks. Nelia, her mother, and her aunt Taibe participated in the Bursuk theatrical troupe, directed by Meier and Berish. By the 1930s, non-Jews had joined the productions, which were then in Spanish. The troupe produced a play every three months, drawn from a repertoire of Yiddish, anarchist, and European works that dignified workers and their struggles. Nelia acted in such social dramas as *Hambre*, which presented a mother who lacked food for her family. One showing roused such emotion that a member of the audience cried out, "Steal a chicken!" The troupe performed in fields and neighboring communities, raising money for unions and anarchist causes.[17]

The girls of Brazo y Cerebro organized biweekly literary evenings, attended by Jews and non-Jews alike, in which they recited and discussed humanist and anarchist works written in Yiddish and Spanish. *La* FORA reported on an anarchist velada held in the fields near Charata in 1934 that attracted about 400 people.[18] Who organized this event is unclear, but it demonstrated the vitality of the anarchist project that the Bursuk women helped foster.

The Charata experiment faded by the 1940s, when the clan left the land. Nelia and her relatives resettled in Buenos Aires, where she frequented the Juventud Libertaria, a FACA affiliate. A seamstress, Nelia recited poetry and acted in anarchist productions, sold literature, and distributed propaganda in night schools, while battling fear of the police and male discrimination against female comrades. By this time, anarchists as a whole and anarchist women in particular were endangered species. Nelia's appearances in anarchist events were cultural performances that demonstrated her talents and presence in a society and movement that marginalized her.[19]

She and the older generation from Charata also participated in the Asociación Racionalista Judía. Active from 1916 to 1978, the Racionalista represented the confluence of several earlier Ashkenazi anarchist tendencies. A few hundred people congregated regularly in this porteño cultural center at its height. They spurned religion and Zionism but regarded anarchism as the culmination of the Yiddish humanistic tradition they cherished. Racionalista members organized as Jews, yet maintained ties with non-Jewish anarchists.[20]

Twenty to twenty-five women were among the sixty-odd core activists, but they were on the sidelines. Two of the ten young people who translated classic Yiddish works into Spanish for publication were women, and some may have volunteered in the library. At Racionalista events, Nelia Bursuk declaimed in Yiddish, and Bruje and other women served Ashkenazi foods. Female members had little voice, even as they reinforced ethnic borders—ones that soon collapsed. The politically minded among their children, who mainly spoke Spanish, joined broader leftist groups instead of Jewish ones.[21]

Socialists

Women of Jewish origin who were inclined toward socialism found little space in the Argentine branches of the Socialist Zionist Poale Sion and the Bund, which favored Jewish cultural autonomy yet opposed a Jewish homeland.[22] Instead they joined the Argentine Socialists, who believed in a melting pot; thus Jews in this party rarely identified themselves as such and forswore ties with community institutions. Socialists may have offered women, including those of Jewish backgrounds, greater scope than other political movements before 1930.[23] Since the party usually operated legally, it is easier to trace them than anarchists.

Historians usually have emphasized the moderate, proliberal character of the Socialist Party, founded in 1894. The more recent literature, however, highlights tensions between radicals and reformers, and between the minimum program and the long-term goal of socializing the means of production. The reformers and minimum program prevailed, yet debates continued. Socialists supported free trade (before the 1930s), secular education, women's rights, and the liberal freedoms and heroes, yet they completed and transcended the liberal project by favoring genuine democracy, cooperatives, and aid for workers and tenant farmers.[24]

The early history of Socialist women is intertwined with that of a family of Jewish origin, the sisters Fenia, Mariana, and Adela Chertkoff, and Fenia's daughter Victoria Gucovsky. Of the three sisters, Fenia stood out. Born in 1869 in Odessa, she became a primary-school teacher. As a young woman, she was already known for her intellect, educational outreach to farmers and workers, and socialist activism. Married to a socialist poet, Gabriel Gucovsky, she gave birth to Victoria in 1890. In 1894, after Gabriel Gucovsky's death, Fenia emigrated with her family to Colonia Clara, Entre Ríos, where she established a library, gave classes in Russian

12. Fenia Chertkoff. Archivo General de la Nación, Dpto. Doc. Fotográficos.

and Spanish, and translated for the Socialist press. Feeling isolated, she headed for Buenos Aires and Europe. In 1897–98, she studied pedagogy and child psychology at the Sorbonne and the University of Lausanne, where she earned a degree in Froebelian kindergarten education.[25]

Back in Buenos Aires, Fenia, with her sisters and brother, Naúm, frequented Socialist circles and met the party's leaders. A network of families arose: Mariana married Juan B. Justo, the party's founder and head; Adela married the future congressman Adolfo Dickmann; Fenia married Nicolás Repetto, another future congressman and future vice presidential candidate; and Naúm married Justo's sister, Sixta.[26] Eventually Victoria Gucovsky wed the future congressman Antonio De Tomaso. By marrying people of Catholic origin and spurning religious and government sanction for their unions (as was true of many Socialists), the Chertkoffs and Gucovsky defied convention.

Fenia wanted to implement socialism in both the home and society. She implored male workers to encourage their wives to participate in Socialism and accept their intellectual growth. Ushering women into the party, Fenia and her sisters were among the founders of the Centro Socialista Femenino (the CSF) in 1902, which held May Day parties for children, a practice Fenia inaugurated. Its tasks expanded to welcoming "all the women who work and suffer," as Fenia put it, through lectures, cultural events, and creation of female networks. Challenging women's absence from politics, the CSF lobbied male politicians to make divorce legal, regulate women's and children's labor, ban alcohol, lower consumption taxes, and make the schools genuinely secular. Fenia contested her own party's marginalization of women by representing the CSF at the party congresses of 1903, 1908, 1910, and 1914; she was the sole woman in the 1903 sessions. The CSF's aim was the social, political, and economic liberation of women within a socialist framework.[27]

Fenia devoted herself to women laborers. She worked with the Unión Obrera Textil in Avellaneda, and in 1903 she founded the Unión Gremial Femenina, which created women's unions, supported strike actions, visited workplaces, and lobbied employers and government officials. Competition with anarchists apparently led to its demise, and the CSF took over some of these activities. Fenia wrote petitions, gave talks, and organized meetings for groups of female workers, often voicing support of a bill regulating women's and children's labor. Once the bill became law in 1906, Fenia set up a CSF committee to ensure its enforcement. She checked workplaces and reported infractions, becoming the Labor Department's best inspector, according to the Socialist newspaper *La Vanguardia*. Fenia also monitored the enforcement of the law regulating piecework, as well as other presumed legal protections for women laborers. Her initiative to prod employers into giving their female workers chairs was signed into law in 1919.[28]

Chertkoff analyzed and participated in women's causes. She helped organize the International Feminine Congress in Buenos Aires in 1910, which she described as part of the initial stage of South American women's liberation. Contesting reactionaries who opposed women's participation in public life, she wrote, delegates had assumed "their duties of citizenship and motherhood, had defended with heat and passion the rights that unreservedly belong to them as to any human being who knows how to think and feel."[29] Like other supporters of women's rights, Fenia did not separate women's activism from maternalism, but she considered women to be workers as well as mothers. During the First World War, she commended women in combatant countries for assuming men's jobs, predicting too optimistically that they would retain these occupations in peacetime.[30]

Yet her advocacy of women's suffrage was tepid. Chertkoff wrote that women needed to prepare themselves for this responsibility by becoming active in unions and party centers, and she proposed a literacy requirement for voting, which was mitigated somewhat by her support for building schools. Her views seemed to contrast with those of the CSF, which by 1910 supported unrestricted universal suffrage. However, Fenia favored permitting women to testify in court, dispose of their own income, receive salaries equal to those of men for the same work, and control their children. These issues and organizing female workers probably engaged her more than the vote.[31]

One admirer claimed that "Fenia Chertcoff was above all else a teacher." Chertkoff saw her role as one of educating "the family in Socialism," a notion that reinforced Juan B. Justo's view of the party as "a school of culture and civics" that would raise workers' cultural level and train them to conscientiously exercise their political rights. Fenia helped found the Escuela Libre para Trabajadores in La Boca in 1897, where she and her sister Mariana gave classes. She also taught in the Sociedad Luz, a Socialist popular university.[32] When a leftist anticlerical teacher was fired in 1903 from a suburban public school, Fenia helped organize a progressive secular school under the ousted instructor as principal. Fenia taught in this and another secular school, in La Boca.[33]

Chertkoff sought to educate impoverished children. She followed young beggars home, urged their parents to send them to school, and asked the police to follow up. In 1904, she and the CSF created a center where newsboys could eat, bathe, and study, but the establishment press refused to fund this Socialist project.[34] Beginning in 1913, Fenia led an effort to provide after-school care for poor children. Children gathered for several hours daily in these *recreos infantiles*, located in Socialist centers in worker neighborhoods, to play, work on arts and crafts, read, and eat nutritious snacks. Female teachers helped them with their homework and encouraged them to read and cooperate with each other. The recreos took children on excursions and sent them outside the capital for vacations. Headed by Fenia, the Asociación Bibliotecas y Recreos Infantiles (the ABRI) was founded in 1914 to collect funds and oversee the recreos. While Fenia created the first recreo without any official support, eventually the ABRI received funding from the municipal assembly and the national congress. By 1928, perhaps 45,000 children had passed through the nine recreos.[35]

In the late 1910s, Fenia established another set of educational enterprises, in Tío Pujio, Córdoba, on an estate owned by the Repettos and

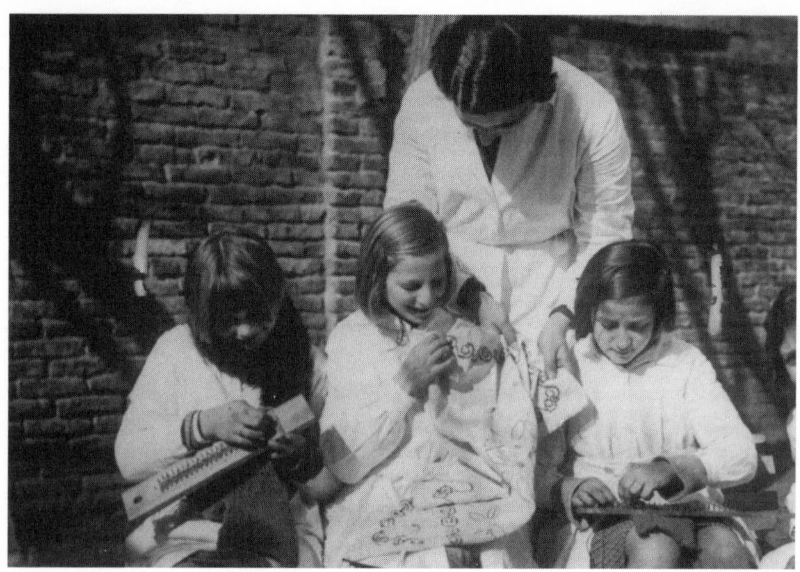

13. A *recreo infantil* (after-school center). Archivo General de la Nación, Dpto. Doc. Fotográficos.

Justos. Her tutoring sessions for local children expanded into a school affiliated with the public system. One room in the house became a lending library; as its secretary, Fenia invited guest speakers to address local people on hygiene, agrarian reform, agronomy, education, and alcoholism. She and her husband organized a consumers' cooperative and medical clinic.[36] Educating disadvantaged children led to educating their parents as well.

An admirer claimed that Fenia, who died in 1928, was the first Socialist woman in Argentina. Perhaps her main achievement was to put a human face on Socialism by giving of herself to the young and the needy.[37] Fenia epitomized the Socialist values of secular education, democracy, cooperation, and inclusion of laborers, women, and children. Thus she strengthened party efforts to complete and transcend liberalism and install a Socialist project.

Victoria Gucovsky enjoyed an activist career as prominent as her mother's. Known as an intellectual, she graduated from the prestigious Liceo Nacional de Señoritas, obtained a college degree in biology from the Instituto del Profesorado, and taught in the Liceo and other secondary schools for thirty-two years. She also wrote for many periodicals, including *La Nación* and *La Vanguardia*, whose literary supplement she edited between 1918 and 1923, and she authored several collections of short stories on rural themes. Sharing Fenia's interests in education and women, Gucovsky worked in the children's May Day festivities, the CSF, Sociedad Luz, and the ABRI, which she eventually headed. She founded the Liga Pro Alfabetización de Adultos, which supported literacy training in tenements and workplaces, and participated in the Socialist El Hogar Obrero cooperative. Gucovsky urged women to form unions, study the Socialist platform, spread party doctrine, and educate themselves. As a leader of the Comité Socialista Nacional Pro Sufragio Femenino, she favored a Socialist bill to grant women the vote without restrictions. A party insider, she served in the leadership of its porteño branch.[38]

While Fenia had pioneered women's political and union activism, Gucovsky excelled at writing and especially lecturing: her voice, elegant expression, and deep understanding of topics set her apart. "In the feminine oratory of our country, Victoria Gucovsky occupies first place," noted one observer. Indeed, as one of the few female public speakers at this time, she faced little competition. Beginning at age seventeen in 1907, Gucovsky addressed audiences of Socialists and workers, as well as many institutions in Argentina and other countries, on a wide range of subjects. Using her insights as a writer and pianist, Gucovsky analyzed music, composers, and authors as diverse as Tolstoy, Shelley, Shaw, Bergson, Maerlinck, and Dostoevsky.[39]

Gucovsky was particularly eloquent on social and political issues such as education and cooperatives, which she and other Socialists saw as foundations of a more equitable society. Outlining the history of Argentine primary schools for the CSF, Gucovsky, citing Sarmiento, defined politics as the art and science of forming citizens through policies promoting education and welfare. In another speech to this group, Gucovsky explained how cooperatives embodied strength through unity and could empower women. Acting as ministers of finance in their homes, housewives appreciated the money and hours they could save by purchasing through a cooperative. Women could devote this extra time to their cultural growth by creating a library under the cooperative's auspices. Furthermore, administering cooperatives would sharpen their abilities.[40]

Touring major cities in 1929 with a group of Argentine educators, Gucovsky acquainted U.S. audiences with Argentine Socialist programs on education, cooperatives, and women. Back in Argentina, she related her impressions of U.S. society. The Socialist traveler did not care for its death penalty, wealth differences, or racism, whose existence she blamed on capitalism. In her view, "pigment absorption" was a more effective solution

14. Victoria Gucovsky. Archivo General de la Nación, Dpto. Doc. Fotográficos.

to racial problems than segregation, which suggests that she favored assimilation of darker-skinned people in Argentina as well. Such U.S. government initiatives as the income tax and the Labor Department with its women's office, however, appealed to her. She also admired the settlement houses, numerous educational establishments and libraries, and the wide distribution of land ownership. Argentina should imitate the last policy, she believed, for the typical criollo was "Juan without land." The existence of such a large federated country and its unguarded border with Canada led her to wonder why South American countries had not unified, and how one could build a peaceful globe. Substituting cooperatives for capitalism could eliminate the need for national borders and armies, she concluded.[41] The trip inaugurated her transnational peace campaign, which will be discussed in chapter 7.

Gucovsky's life intersects with the themes of this book. Starting at an early age, she crossed multiple boundaries, challenging norms that silenced women and rising into the ruling circle of a political party. Gucovsky helped include female and male workers in Socialism and the

Argentine nation. Her intellectual and organizing efforts reinforced the Socialist values of equality, peace, cultural enrichment, and cooperation. By promoting networks, learning, and discussions among women, she and her mother stimulated the creation of social capital, which would eclipse the liberal state.

Berta Wainstein de Gerchunoff, who came to Argentina from Russia in 1890, when she was five, focused her activism on education and women. The sister-in-law of writer Alberto Gerchunoff, this schoolteacher joined the Centro Socialista Femenino in 1909 and involved herself in its May Day children's parties. She lectured for the Sociedad Luz and helped found the Socialist Ateneo Popular, a workers' educational institute, in 1910. Gerchunoff served on its board, taught courses, and covered global labor news for its periodical. She also was an officer of the Unión Feminista Nacional (UFN), created by Dr. Alicia Moreau de Justo and other Socialists in 1918, which promoted the social, economic, and political emancipation of women, including giving women the vote. Editor of the UFN's journal *Nuestra Causa*, Gerchunoff wrote children' stories and articles on the international women's movement. She served as poll watcher in the women's mock election of 1920, in which feminists campaigned for office and voted for their candidates.[42] Through her participation in this election, she helped foster democratic procedures among women, a form of social capital.

Women's status preoccupied Gerchunoff. One hundred million women around the world were voting, she noted; when would Argentine women join them? The French Revolution had assured the rights of men; who would proclaim them for women? Yet the indifference of many women about their own marginality disillusioned her to the point of giving up on her generation. Gerchunoff left Socialism for reasons that are unclear, but she continued to press for women's advancement through Zionism (see chapter 8).[43]

Rosa Scheiner's views of women's liberation were more far-reaching than Gerchunoff's. This dental surgeon had joined the Centro Socialista Femenino by 1909, and in the 1930s she wrote for *La Vanguardia* and spoke at Socialist women's gatherings and on radio.[44] While she followed in Gucovsky's footsteps as a Socialist female intellectual, Scheiner's radical voice contrasted with that of her predecessor. Gucovsky's humanistic speeches transcended party walls, whereas Scheiner addressed other Socialists on ideology, tactics, and the conditions for change.

In many articles and talks, Scheiner dissected women's exclusion throughout history. Women's biological roles had given men the excuse to confine them in the home, and men used their economic control over women to force them into submission. The French Revolution had liberated men but not women from organized religion, another source of oppression. Capitalism had seemingly freed women by helping them flee their "domestic prison" for outside labors and collective life, but the double or triple day and economic hardship limited this "emancipation." The Socialist Party was the first to address the need to take "the Argentine woman out of her subaltern position" and support women's political rights. Even as voters, however, women ran the risk of becoming tools of capital. Women's lower status was part of the larger social problem rooted in capitalism. The workers' movement had inaugurated the struggle for women's liberation, and only Socialism could fulfill it.[45]

Transgressing the views of her party and society, Scheiner contested maternalism. She blamed the upper class and the clergy for using motherhood to deny women the vote. Many women were not mothers, she daringly admitted, and even those who were sometimes delegated the care of their offspring to others, or at any rate did not spend a lifetime raising them. Large numbers of women, then, did not play maternal roles, nor should these roles eliminate them from political participation.[46] Unlike the Chertkoffs, Gucovsky, and Gerchunoff, Scheiner did not involve herself in child-related Socialist activities.

Yet Scheiner believed that suffrage was a means rather than an end. Capitalist democracy was one of form, not content. Voting alone would not accomplish the Socialist mission of creating "the social justice . . . of a society without classes, without exploiters and without exploited." Until workers developed sufficient class consciousness to build Socialism, however, activists should use the democratic arena to organize support and highlight abuses.[47] The project that Scheiner endorsed went far beyond that of liberals or Socialist moderates.

Scheiner found much to admire in Communism. Despite the enmity between Communists and Socialists, the two groups agreed on socializing the means of production. Socialists have never forgotten this goal, she quipped, as if to remind party leaders. Communists opposed Socialist gradualism, yet Marx and Engels often had favored it, noting that one could not force a revolution. Still, proletarian control of Russia, despite its lack of industries, pleased her. There was no rigid Marxist blueprint to follow; Lenin himself implemented a reformist economic policy, demonstrating that one had to work within a given context.[48]

Scheiner broke the mold in many ways. Like the Chertkoffs, Gucovsky, and Gerchunoff, she sought to include women; unlike them, she rejected maternalism. Her tough rhetoric, lucid revolutionary analysis, and Marxist project contested the bourgeois reformism of party leaders. It is not surprising that she, with fellow radicals, left the Socialists in 1937 to form the Socialist Worker Party[49] and later probably joined the Communist Party.

How many women of Jewish origin were Socialists is unknown, but the number of prominent Jewish women in the party suggests that many entered the ranks. Readings, speeches, and family discussions acquainted women with Socialism. In some rural and urban Jewish families, *La Vanguardia* was read aloud. This daily newspaper was sold in Villa Domínguez as early as 1903, and Socialist orators, including Jews, visited that and other towns. One Jewish girl's compassion for her laborer father in his work-stained clothes led her to join the party. Women frequented Socialist centers in colonies and porteño neighborhoods with large Jewish populations. Some helped workers in nearby factories establish or revive unions. Jewish women were on the podium and in the audience during lectures and literary evenings sponsored by UFN affiliates, the Sociedad Luz, and female sectors of Socialist centers, which they joined and sometimes led.[50]

A few Mediterranean women departed from custom through limited participation in Socialism. A socialist sympathizer, Judith Isaharoff, originally from Samarkand (see chapter 5), heard Dr. Alicia Moreau de Justo speak on the Palestinian Jewish labor federation, the Histadrut—which led Isaharoff to form an Argentine Jewish auxiliary, Amigas Sefaradíes de la Histadrut, in 1945. One Socialist merchant of Turkish origin took his daughter to party demonstrations despite his wife's opposition.[51]

In the 1930s, Scheiner and other Socialist women also crossed gender borders by publicly campaigning. One woman of Jewish origin recalled that "for the first female pioneers who went into the street it was not easy." In her initial foray, this woman shouted from a perch on a fruit crate outside a subway station. Men gathered to listen, but women approached female orators only when they spoke in enclosed locations. Few women openly rebelled against silence and political exclusion.[52]

The Communist Party

The International Socialists, who had broken off from the Socialists in 1918, formed the Communist Party in 1920. Tensions arose in the party between those who subordinated themselves to Moscow and those who were more interested in grounding themselves locally. The former predominated in the leadership, and the party's shifting strategies reflected the Comintern's influence. Nevertheless, Communists were active on many fronts and formed the strongest leftist movement in Argentina after 1930.[53] Chapter 7 discusses Communism's nuanced relationship with liberalism. Membership data on the frequently outlawed Communist Party is scarce. Nevertheless, the disproportionate representation in the party of Jews in general, at least in the late 1920s,[54] along with Jewish women's militancy in Eastern Europe and visibility in Communist-linked unions, auxiliaries, and cultural activities in Argentina, strongly suggest that this party became the predominant leftist current among Jewish women in the 1930s and 1940s.

One Communist pioneer was Ida Bondareff de Kantor, a Russian dentist and founding member of the party, who addressed crowds in Russian, Yiddish, and Spanish in the early 1920s. By 1924 she was the head of the Comité Central Femenino, which delegated her and other *compañeras*, including the dental student Mika Felman, to guide female strikers in the textile and match industries and recruit factory women. Bondareff also taught a weekly course on Marxism for the Comité in 1925.[55]

In her speeches and articles in the Communist *La Internacional*, Bondareff insisted that women were emancipating themselves in the Soviet Union, where day care and collective kitchens liberated them from domestic tasks, the sexes were legally equal, and women participated in unions and other organizations. In Argentina, however, few women took part in the struggle, and men seemed more interested in retaining male privileges than in recruiting women. By extolling motherhood and women's place in the home, Socialists ignored women's need for paid labor to help their families and thus hindered women's progress. Only a Communist revolution would free women, but they had to work for it.[56]

Bondareff ran afoul of internal politics when, paradoxically, she led a group advocating an alliance with the Socialists. Expelled from the Communist Party in 1922, her name reappeared in the party newspaper in 1924–25, when she assumed several posts. In 1926, however, she was ousted again and departed for the Soviet Union. There, Bondareff and her husband reentered the party despite the Argentine leaders' continuing campaign against them.[57]

Strengthened by Polish Communist immigrants, Communism spread through Ashkenazi communities in the 1920s and 1930s. Jewish women joined Communist-oriented clubs in neighborhoods like Villa Crespo, where they participated in discussions, read Communist periodicals in Yiddish, socialized with like-minded people, and sometimes met their future husbands. The women helped organize events that bound Communists together. Party members went on lecturing and recruiting tours in Jewish communities in the interior. As of 1927, the Agrupación Comunista Israelita was the party's second largest ethnic or foreign-language section in the capital, after the Italian. Its official purpose was to gather Yiddish speakers together, but members also saw it as a means of strengthening a secular and leftist Jewish identity. To stem this particularism and independence, Communist leaders reined in the foreign sections in the late 1920s. When the party became illegal in Argentina after the coup of 1930, however, it shifted its operations to semiautonomous allied groups that could function openly. Some of these organizations again fenced off a "progressive" Jewish identity.[58]

One such organization was Procor, which promoted Jewish colonies in the Soviet Union. Founded in 1924 in Buenos Aires, this group attracted about 2,500 adherents in cities and colonies. It raised funds, prepared candidates to move to Russian farms, and created an alternative to Zionism. When the Soviet Union made Birobidjan an autonomous Jewish region, Procor became the Sociedad Pro-Colonización Israelita en Birobidjan. Although Jewish agriculture there did not prosper, Birobidjan was a means of mobilizing Jews for Communism. Pointing to anti-Semitism in Argentina and the world, a manifesto of 1935 insisted that only the Soviet Union truly included Jews, as evinced by Birobidjan. Jewish women numbered among the small Argentine contingent that settled there.[59]

It was Soviet policy, on and off, to promote Yiddish, but Yiddish also harmonized with the experiences of Ashkenazi working-class women and men in Argentina. To them, Yiddish was more than a language: it stood for their past and for class-conscious humanitarian values expressed in an extensive literature. Moreover, Yiddish formed part of the women's sphere. Many Jews distinguished between Hebrew as the language of the synagogue and study hall, which Communists of Jewish origin rejected, and Yiddish as the language of the home and hearth. Since the latter was the female domain, women had a key role to play in Jewish Communism. Yet this linguistic emphasis excluded non-Yiddish speakers.

Women were active in the progressive Yiddish school movement, founded in 1922; they taught classes, recruited students, and raised money. Plagued by persecution, the schools reached a low point in 1937, when the federal police's infamous Special Section, which smashed labor and leftist organizations and tortured its prisoners, closed seven schools in the capital, and the provincial police did the same to four suburban schools. Educational authorities defended these actions by claiming the schools were filthy and unhealthy; there was no physical proof for this assertion, but perhaps the authorities equated Communism with dirt. The police imprisoned teachers, activists, and pupils, and confiscated materials from the premises and teachers' homes. A Procor and school activist, Teresa Gílenberg (see chapter 2) tried to forestall prosecution of a school leader by removing such evidence from his room. The schools remained closed, but new ones opened a few years later.[60]

Founded in the 1930s, the Teatro Popular Israelita Argentino, or Idische Folks Theater (IFT), was another progressive Yiddish institution that engaged women. Cipe Lincovsky, Golde Flami, María Fux, and other female performers appeared on its stage. Women sang in its choir and helped raise money for IFT activities. They were among the dues-paying members, totaling 1,000 in 1938, who attended IFT-sponsored plays, concerts, movies, and lectures. Girls entered its acting program and participated in children's theater. The plays provoked men and women in the audience to think critically about class, gender, and political issues. In the mid-1950s, Spanish began to replace Yiddish, yet the productions remained socially conscious.[61] The IFT tied women into the Jewish Communist web of sociability, learning, and activism.

Labor

Socialists and anarchists like Chertkoff and Chanovsky, respectively, had organized workers in the early 1900s, and Socialist women in particular continued to participate in unions in the 1930s. Yet Communist women gained sway in this arena at this time. They were part of the Communist drive that created the most dynamic unions in the interwar period.[62]

One Communist activist was Rosa Ziperovich (see chapter 3), who led her first strike in 1929 to prevent the firing of her mentor, the director of the normal school she was attending. When she began teaching in Moisesville in 1931, Ziperovich joined the Círculo de Maestros, founded by several Jewish women and other instructors, which affiliated with the Santa Fe provincial teachers' federation. One goal was to institute a policy of hiring based on merit, rather than political influence, which lowered the caliber of teaching and encouraged sexual abuse. Ziperovich and her colleagues joined a national struggle that finally implemented this change in 1958. She and the Círculo also fought for the right to be paid promptly. Teachers often waited months, if not years, for their meager salaries. In 1933, the Círculo held a rally—at which Ziperovich made the opening remarks—protesting a nine-month delay in salaries. When local teachers' unions met in Moisesville the following year, they elected Ziperovich vice president of the county-level junta. These experiences inaugurated her long union career.[63]

Guitl Kanutsky, who managed a triple day (see chapter 2), was one of many Ashkenazi women in needle-trade unions. She had little if any schooling but a strong desire to make things better, "because what surrounds us dissatisfies us." Born in poverty in Poland in 1897, Kanutsky started sewing at an early age and propagandizing for her union and the Bund. Shortly after she arrived in Buenos Aires in 1924, she found a job and looked for a union to join. Kanutsky's appearance at the overwhelmingly Jewish and male garment union startled its militants. To paraphrase Alice Kessler-Harris's observation for U.S. Jewish women workers, Kanutsky had to court the labor association that should have courted her to become its first female member. Union leaders recovered from their shock and used her experience, placing her on their governing committee and assigning her to address workers in Yiddish at events where she usually was the lone woman speaker. The mostly female garment workers thrilled to hear "Compañera Guitl." Further contesting notions of female passivity, Kanutsky helped lead a two-block long column of female garment workers in the May Day demonstrations of 1929.[64]

Kanutsky and her husband, a militant in the carpenters' union, helped found the Bund in Argentina in 1925, but she left this group in 1930 to focus on labor organizing. She and other garment workers belonged to the Obreros Cortadores, Sastres, Costureras y Anexos (the UOCSCA), which arose in the mid-1920s. They labored in talleres, producing clothing for large enterprises. When workers complained about poor working conditions and low salaries, the sweatshop owners, who were also Jewish and only slightly better off than their employees, replied they themselves were squeezed by retailers. Fighting two bosses, garment workers also faced a labor surplus and seasonal unemployment. Their struggle mounted by June 1929, when telleristas locked out female workers demanding a raise. Kanutsky, the secretary of the Villa Crespo section, asked the UOCSCA for its support. While the results of this strike were unclear, another strike the following year won a salary increase.[65]

Pursuing recognition of their union, better wages, job security, and "a humane workplace," as Kanutsky put it, garment workers again went on strike in 1934, this time united with the talleristas against the retailers. Kanutsky and other organizers also managed to attract thousands of lowly paid, mostly non-Jewish pieceworkers. After seven weeks off the job, the union was victorious, although it took much time to implement the agreement. A union and Communist militant, Julio Liberman, praised Kanutsky, among others, for leadership. But there was more to be done. In *El Obrero de la Confección*, Kanutsky noted that while female garment work ers had never been as involved as in 1934, the union needed to organize a female section to ensure their participation. It took this step in 1935.[66]

Kanutsky and other militants often faced arrest. Official repression worsened with the 1930 coup and the creation of the Special Section. The Federación Obrera del Vestido (the FOV), formed when the UOCSCA merged with another union, was in Communist hands, and by now Kanutsky had gravitated toward this party. The police repeatedly raided and closed union headquarters, broke up meetings, and imprisoned and brutalized men and women. The repression worsened under the dictatorship of 1943–45 (see chapter 7), forcing FOV members into clandestine activity. In spite of these circumstances, Kanutsky continually entreated female workers to transcend submissiveness and fear.[67]

Kanutsky was one of many Ashkenazi women who were activists in garment unions. Rank-and-file Jewish women attended assemblies, monitored shop floors, engaged in strikes, and performed at celebrations of union victories. They helped organize fundraisers for strikers, as well as the communal kitchens that fed them. Jewish women in the garment union's female section recruited pieceworkers, offered courses, organized a library, and marched in May Day parades.[68]

Ashkenazi women were equally active in textile unions. Many Jews joined the Federación Obrera Textil, which arose in 1921 and created a short-lived section for the mostly female Jewish knitters. Later in the 1920s, a Communist and largely Jewish group split off from the Socialist-dominated Federación. Influenced by the Popular Front strategy, Communists rejoined the larger union, now called the Unión Obrera Textil (UOT), in 1936. By the end of the decade, Communists and Socialist Workers dominated it.[69]

Like their garment-worker counterparts, Jewish women textile workers participated in recruitment drives, strikes, demonstrations, and cultural activities. They and other members of the Feminine Commission pushed for a minimum salary, wages equal to those of men doing the same work, the implementation of labor laws, and the improvement of air quality. One important voice was Flora Absatz, whose education had fallen prey to poverty and a hostile boss (see chapter 2). Her low earnings in the silk mill led her into the union in the mid-1930s, where she remained until she retired in 1952. A Communist, Absatz rose quickly in the union, by 1935 becoming her factory's delegate, responsible for collecting dues, enlisting members, and scrutinizing management. That year, a thousand silk workers struck for three weeks. The only member of the strike committee not to be arrested, Absatz visited the other leaders in the Villa Devoto prison and carried their instructions to the membership. The strike ended with workers winning salary and other concessions.[70]

Absatz's most radical contributions may have been her articles in *El Obrero Textil* criticizing the exclusion of women. Absatz noted that despite women's preponderance in the industry, they did not occupy corresponding roles in the union. We are the lowest-paid workers and the bosses use our submissiveness to exploit us even more, she complained, echoing Kanutsky. Rather than serving as tools against us, these weaknesses should inspire action: "through our union organization we should continue in the struggle for the woman's emancipation."[71]

Many women did not understand how exploited they were, Absatz observed. In order to pay women less and set them against men, employers helped spread the myth that women were inferior to men, hurting both sexes as a result. Pointing to women's double and triple days, Absatz implied that exploitation reached into the home. Yet "in the struggle of the producer class, there should be no distinction between men and women." She wanted women to play equal roles in the labor movement and hinted that men should assume household duties.[72]

Dora Genkin also challenged male as well as capitalist domination. Her parents had been militants in Poland, where she was born in 1916, and they kept these memories alive for her as she grew up in Argentina. Genkin entered the mills at age seventeen and the union at twenty, marrying fellow Communist Jorge Michellon, who led the UOT from 1939 to 1946. Bright and bold, she spoke at public gatherings, wrote for the union magazine, and served as secretary of its Feminine Commission. In 1942, as one of four female delegates at the congress of the Argentine labor federation, the Confederación General de Trabajo, Genkin criticized male unionists for making sexist comments and ignoring problems that women brought to their attention. That year she also appeared at a women's assembly seeking to revise the maternity law. As secretary of the organizing committee and a UOT delegate, Genkin addressed an audience of over 1,500 female workers from diverse industries.[73]

Genkin peppered her speeches and writings with trenchant denunciations of bosses' abuses. In 1939, she denounced an employer-organized meeting on workers' health for not inviting laborers. The congress president owned stock in rat-infested mills whose workers had high rates of tuberculosis. Everyone knew about the poor conditions in the textile factories except for conference participants, she sarcastically observed.[74] Their forthright rhetoric and defiance of exclusion distinguished Genkin, Kanutsky, and Absatz.

Conclusion

Nourished by foreign experience and dissatisfied by the conditions around them, female anarchists, Socialists, Communists, and union members of Ashkenazi origin fought to include women and other downtrodden people. Anyone—especially a woman—who participated in such causes was on the fringe. Through their activism and calls for rights and social justice, militants of Jewish backgrounds pushed to enter the mainstream of their movements and society.

Some of these women favored what they called female liberation, a term with multiple meanings. It signified ending capitalist exploitation and escaping the home through education and participation in broader struggles. Winning rights such as the vote formed part of women's emancipation, at least for Socialists, whereas freedom from oppressive institutions meant liberation for women anarchists. Most of the women discussed above tried to emancipate their sex by contesting male control, although Scheiner was the only one who tied female oppression to maternalism.

Female militants negotiated borders. Many joined groups containing persons of other origins; Yiddish-speaking anarchists and Communists, however, erected ethnic walls. Yet these were porous. Through public speaking, writing, demonstrating, lobbying, striking, and going to prison, many women defied passivity, domesticity, and fear. Leftists broadened spaces considered acceptable for women, although it proved difficult to cross from these educational and reproductive activities to the domain of male intellectuals and strategists. Anarchists, Socialists, and Communists sought to create a socially just world without national borders or capitalism. Involvement in transnational causes grew with the Spanish Civil War, as chapter 7 will show.

Claiming spaces in the nation, Ashkenazi women activists engaged in state formation. By participating in the building of social capital, they sought to make Argentina more democratic. They helped construct leftist values that challenged hegemonic projects, such as fraternal solidarity, class struggle, rationalism, and the inclusion of women and the poor. Leftist and union women accepted some aspects of the liberal project, such as secular education, while rejecting its economic program. The next chapter continues to explore how leftists addressed liberalism.

CHAPTER SEVEN

"A Dike Against Reaction"

Contesting Anti-Semitism, Fascism, and Peronism

By defending the Jewish people . . . we also
defend the integrity of our beautiful fatherland.
—Berta B. de Drucaroff, *Nuestros talleres*

We will build "a dike against reaction."
—Agrupación de Intelectuales, Artistas,
Periodistas, y Escritores, *Unidad*

Argentina seemed relatively tolerant before the 1930s, with a few important exceptions, but growing right-wing extremism made some Jewish women question whether the country truly included them. By this time, the radical rightist Nacionalistas were competing for hegemony with liberals. Unlike the essentialist nationalists of the early 1900s (see chapter 1), who accepted Jews and other immigrants who adopted local ways, the Nacionalistas, drawing sustenance from European fascism, argued that Jews could never fit in the nation. In response, many Jewish women considered it vital to contest whatever resembled fascism. They defended their spaces in Argentina and tried to strengthen its capacity for pluralism, democracy, and social justice.[1] I trace their efforts to construct dikes against reaction chronologically through the years 1930 to 1945.

These Jewish women—mostly leftist Ashkenazim—formed part of a broader Argentine antifascist campaign. Recent work has shown that it was massive and complex, yet we do not yet fully comprehend women's involvement in this cause.[2] This chapter contributes to such an understanding.

The struggle against anti-Semitism and fascism was transnational.

Women like Berta B. de Drucaroff believed that events on one side of the Atlantic influenced those on the other side. Just as European fascism nourished the local brand, Argentines who aided the Allies and Jewish refugees tried to spread humanitarianism and freedom overseas. At the same time, they hoped to protect Argentina from the dangers of external and internal fascism.

Intolerance and persecution threatened to shunt Jewish women to the sidelines. By resisting fascism, anti-Semitism, and dictatorship, Jewish women battled outsider status. They fought not only for their rights but for those of other oppressed persons, such as political prisoners.

In this context of Nacionalismo and repression, Jewish female militants continued to negotiate borders. They contested fear and notions of proper female behavior as well as the newer anti-Jewish barriers. These activists bridged ethnic and religious divisions between antifascists. They also helped break down national boundaries by aiding opponents of fascism overseas, even as they erected dikes against fascism at home.

Anti-Semitism, Nacionalismo, and Early Responses

Even before the 1930s, sporadic attacks on Jews had awakened doubts about their acceptance by other Argentines. Ashkenazi participation in labor and leftist movements, and the Russian origins of most Jews in the early 1900s, promoted the equation of Jews with revolutionaries. During the centennial of Argentine independence in 1910, which witnessed conflicts between anarchists and the authorities, vigilantes struck Once, targeting a Jewish socialist organization and raping several women there. Convinced the Russian Revolution had reached Argentina, government forces and mobs assaulted strikers and worker sites during the Tragic Week of January 1919. Once again, civilians and police entered Once, demolishing several Jewish institutions. In one foray the military attacked an apartment where it claimed snipers were hidden, shooting a fifteen-year-old girl armed with a revolver. Crying "Death to the Jews! Death to the Maximalists [revolutionaries]!," marauders burst into households, tossed the occupants' belongings into the streets and burned them, and thrashed men, women, and children. Others fired at, beat, and dragged Jews to police stations. The detainees included women such as Rosa Wainstein, a dressmaker and the fiancée of Pinie Wald, a Bund member accused of heading a supposed Soviet. Wald was tortured, but Wainstein complained only of rough treatment. At least one person died and over 150 were wounded in this pogrom, or government-sponsored attack on Jews; one was nine-year-old Aída Stimbaj, who tried to accompany her father to jail.[3]

Most Jews hid indoors, although this did not guarantee safety. Defying fear, one Jewish woman left her front door open. When her husband accused her of jeopardizing their security, she replied that she did not want to feel guilty if an innocent person died for lack of refuge.[4] Her solidarity with others contrasted with the government's and vigilantes' restrictive view of the nation.

The persecution did not affect only Russian Jews in Once. The forces of order attacked *La Vanguardia*'s printing press, located in the Bajo. A resident of this Turkish neighborhood, Estela Mesulam (see chapters 2 and 5) saw the flames and heard the shooting. Braving the turbulent barricaded streets, her mother had gone to La Boca to help Estela's sister Vida give birth. It was the first time she had heard the word "Jew" spoken with hatred, Estela recalled. Although the Mediterranean contingent often escaped notice as Jews, the violence and anger hurt them, too.[5]

The Tragic Week sparked the first organized female responses to anti-Semitism. *Israel*'s female correspondent in Río Cuarto, Córdoba, created a fund administered by the magazine to benefit Jewish victims. Prominent women's charities joined other Jewish institutions in Buenos Aires and Rosario to protect Jews from slander, help the wounded and imprisoned, and lobby the government. These efforts were elitist, however, in that their authors disassociated themselves from leftists, asserting that most Jews were conservative and law-abiding.[6] Thus privileged Jews marginalized other Jews.

Anti-Semitism plagued Villaguay, Entre Ríos, in the Jewish agricultural zone. After the Tragic Week, marchers protesting Jewish "maximalism" headed from Gualeguaychú to Villaguay, where they joined a demonstration led by Alberto Montiel, a conservative caudillo who presided over the local Liga Patriótica Argentina brigade. The Liga recruited bourgeois citizens from around the country to protect private property from workers and leftists. The first important radical rightist group in Argentina, it stood for essentialist nationalism, favoring immigrant submission to Argentine "customs" such as obedience to employers. The Liga brigades of Villaguay and surrounding areas clashed with union members and Socialists in February 1921, resulting in many casualties and arrests among laborers. Although there were Jews on both sides, most Jewish residents disliked and feared the Liga.[7]

After Jews began to arrive en masse, some influential Argentines had criticized their presence. A few called Jews an inferior race.[8] In forums on immigration around the time of the Tragic Week and after, opinion makers favored the arrival of Northern and Latin Europeans. Russians, urban proletarians, and leftists—synonyms for Jews at that time—met with disapproval. Several speakers lumped Jews, Middle Easterners, East Asians, and blacks together as undesirable. This juxtaposition suggested that its framers considered Jews to be nonwhite, although most of the criteria used were cultural, political, and ethnic, rather than biological.[9]

The legacies of the Tragic Week and Villaguay resurfaced in the 1930s, combining with new influences. If only briefly and partially, the coup of 1930 brought to power radical rightist Nacionalistas. They participated in General José F. Uriburu's dictatorship (1930–31), which tortured its opponents and outlawed the Communist Party. The succeeding Concordancia ruled through electoral fraud until 1943, reversing the democratic trend of the previous two decades. Nacionalistas and their powerful allies regarded Spanish Catholic authoritarianism as the foundation of argentinidad. The democracy and liberalism with which numerous Jews had identified lost sway as extreme right-wing views gained influence. This shift took place during the Great Depression, when many Argentines perceived their country to be in decline and criticized its long-standing subservient relationship with Great Britain. Under these circumstances, fascist-inspired ideas and prejudices won converts, not only among Nacionalistas. These factors set off a more pervasive anti-Semitism than Argentina had previously experienced.[10]

Nacionalistas denounced Jews and assertive women. They believed that the foundation of a powerful nation was the hierarchically constituted heterosexual family, with its rigid distinctions between male and female roles. Ideally maternal and pure, women should remain within the home; if they left it, they ran a much greater risk than men of falling into moral decay and leftism. Nacionalistas blamed Communism for fostering promiscuity, the decline of the family, and social disorder, all of which they identified with Jews, whom they also blamed for prostitution and pornography. They aimed most of their anti-Semitic slurs at men, whom they depicted as grotesque racialized bodies, white slavers, and greedy financiers who doubled as revolutionaries. Jewish men, they feared, would corrupt Catholic females and assume control of Argentina by marrying elite women. Occasionally Nacionalistas referred to Jewish women, describing them as sensual, cold-blooded, and leftist, terms that contradicted the feminine ideal. Nacionalistas also tended to stigmatize

Jewish women as prostitutes, reinforcing Jewish anxiety over being seen through the lens of the sex trade. In sum, Nacionalistas thought Jews did not belong in Argentina.[11]

The prominent politician Matías Sánchez Sorondo agreed. In a Senate debate in 1936 over his bill to outlaw Communism, this Nacionalista-influenced conservative wondered why Communist schools taught Yiddish. Why did only Jews attend these schools, and why did Communists send their children only to Jewish institutions?[12] His exaggerated claims further marginalized Jews.

Anti-Semitism became more common and open. Nacionalistas proclaimed their views in publications, in the streets, and on the radio, sometimes urging the murder of Jews in the name of patriotism. They shouted anti-Semitic slogans in demonstrations, bombed synagogues, attacked movie theaters, assaulted Jewish men, and lobbied to keep them out of government and university positions. Their periodicals contained advertisements from state agencies, demonstrating their inroads into ruling sectors—which, as the writer Alberto Gerchunoff discerned, used fascism as a shield for their privileges. There were numerous cases of schools that discriminated against Jewish students and hospitals that banned or mistreated Jewish doctors.[13]

Jewish women were among these targets. A music instructor in the Liceo No. 2 de Señoritas in 1936 told her pupils there were too many Jews in the school; Jews should convert to Catholicism or be suppressed. Teachers in a school in a lower-middle-class barrio in the early 1930s singled out a Jewish girl to check her hair and nails, seemingly expecting the rusita to be dirtier than other girls. In 1942, a group of medical students tried to expel the pharmacist Beatriz Gogosch from the Hospital Piñero in Buenos Aires because she was Jewish. Gogosch stubbornly resisted, despite threatening phone calls and being barred from the dining hall and sleeping quarters. The Dirección de Asistencia Pública finally agreed to investigate the matter, but the result is unknown. As already noted (see chapter 3), anti-Semitism pushed Dr. Sara Schnitman out of the Hospital Rivadavia in the 1930s.[14]

Anti-Semitism touched women to varying degrees. Only a few were violently attacked, as happened in 1910 and 1919. Yet even homemakers could experience anti-Semitism directly through right-wing radio broadcasts and indirectly through the experiences of loved ones. They discerned Nacionalista impunity and links to the government, military, police, and Catholic Church. Some women felt prejudice in educational institutions, hospitals, and public spaces; others witnessed but did not suffer from it. Events in Europe led many to fear that Nazism was taking root in Argentine soil. Some still felt accepted; indeed, Jewish women's organizations held events in swank porteño hotels when such locales in the United States excluded Jews. Anti-Jewish attitudes were spreading but did not harm all Jewish women.[15]

The equivocal nature of anti-Semitism was evident in Villaguay, where memories of 1921 lived on. Sometimes allied with Nacionalistas, the anti-Jewish Montiels continued to lead conservative forces. In the early 1930s, Nacionalistas hung anti-Semitic posters in Villaguay and left ugly fliers at Jewish homes in the area. When they threatened to hold an anti-Semitic march in 1933, law-enforcement officials permitted Jews to carry arms and helped guard them, a rare favor from the Argentine police. An Ashkenazi women's charity loaned Jewish men money to purchase guns. These women resisted anti-Semitism and asserted their right to belong to the nation—with support from the provincial Radical government.[16]

Antifascism

By the late 1920s, women of Jewish origin were contesting bellicose nationalism at home and abroad. Opposing the views of radical rightists, the Socialist Victoria Gucovsky affirmed a "sane nationalism that without separatist sentiment will stand in solidarity with other nations." She predicted that narrowly defined nationalisms would die out, as the "law of evolution"—in which she and other Socialists believed—meant the development of less homogeneous and discrete forms over time.[17] Gucovsky was the secretary of the Socialist Comité Pro Paz, formed in 1931, which sought peace through disarmament, education, arbitration, and the free movement of goods, peoples, and ideas. In her view, the Chaco War (1932–35) between Bolivia and Paraguay, two countries united by soil and history, was fratricide and should never have happened. "Boiled, sterilized, the bacillus dead, water becomes drinkable," she noted; similarly, "germs of hatred" did not infect people "sanitized" by rational and humane thoughts and actions. Spending on development rather than war, and lowering tariffs to promote economic cooperation were among her "sanitizing" proposals.[18] Thus Gucovsky advocated breaking down national borders and creating a Southern Cone common market.

A pacifist and spiritualist, Gucovsky considered it vital to reason with others and spread understanding. Acceptance of ideological differences and dialogue was part of her oppositional project, which contrasted markedly with Nacionalista authoritarianism. These views led her to trespass on enemy territory by attending a Nacionalista rally on August 20, 1932, in the Plaza del Congreso in Buenos Aires. When she asked to speak, the radical rightists, taken by surprise, allowed her access to the podium. Gucovsky appropriated the Nacionalistas' Catholic-inspired discourse for her own ends to urge moderation and concord. Repelled by her interaction with right-wing extremists and appeals to their religious sentiments, Socialist leaders demanded and received her resignation from the party. In her statement of resignation, Gucovsky defiantly asserted her right to spread "truth, good, and peace."[19] Despite her expulsion, Gucovsky continued to push for these values and women's rights.[20]

Other leftist women of Ashkenazi origin warned about the fascist threat. Speaking in her town of Villa Domínguez on May Day 1936, Dr. Clara Schliapnik (see chapters 1 and 3), a former member of the leftist student group Insurrexis, claimed that German, Italian, and Austrian elites had created fascism to foment religious and racial divisions in order to aid capitalism and dispel leftism. Schliapnik urged Argentines of all classes to form an antifascist popular front under the banner of liberty and social justice. In subsequent speeches and writings, she called specifically on women to fight fascism.[21]

This and other pleas prompted the creation of antifascist groups throughout Argentina, many in Jewish communities. For example, the Jewish Acción Antiracista Entrerriana had forty branches throughout the province. In this context, the Delegación de Asociaciones Israelitas Argentinas (the DAIA), which arose as an intermediary between Jews and the government, proclaimed a week of mourning to protest Kristallnacht, the Nazi pogrom of November 1938, starting with closing businesses for a day. Many non-Jewish shops also closed.[22]

Some of the antifascist groups were leftist. Communist-aligned intellectuals founded the Comité contra el Racismo y el Antisemitismo (the CCRA) en Argentina in 1937 as part of the Communist Party's transnational popular-front strategy. This large organization attracted prominent politicians and professionals, including Jews. In 1933, Ashkenazi Communist men and women created what became known as the Organización Popular contra el Antisemitismo to compete with the more conservative DAIA. Its periodicals *Alerta* and *¡En Guardia!* informed readers about Nacionalistas and their opponents, anti-Semitism, and government repression.[23]

Divided by class and ideology, many Ashkenazi women joined the struggle against fascism. Through the Comité de Damas Israelitas pro Ayuda a los Expulsados de Alemania in Buenos Aires, privileged women raised money for 8,000 Jews of Polish descent expelled by Germany in 1938. In contrast, the leftist Comité Juvenil contra el Fascismo y el Antisemitismo in Moisesville, led by the militant teacher Rosa Ziperovich, among others, raised political consciousness rather than funds. In 1935, the Comité Juvenil, the Partida Demócrata Progresta (PDP), and Communists demonstrated against the flagrant murder of PDP Senator-elect Enzo Bordabehere on the Senate floor, a crime widely perceived as a Nacionalista and conservative warning against PDP denunciations of British control of the meatpacking industry and its kickbacks to government officials. At this demonstration, the teacher and activist Sara Segal placed the killing in the context of rising fascism at home and abroad. She urged women to join the antifascist struggle, "since any mother would give her life for her children, and to fight against fascist barbarism is the same as saving one's children."[24]

Whether leftist or centrist, these antifascist activities caught the authorities' attention. They scrutinized the Communist-backed groups, Acción Antiracista Entrerriana, and DAIA-supported business closures alike. The government seemed more interested in limiting peaceful opposition to anti-Semitic authoritarianism than controlling violent Nacionalistas. This bias further convinced many Jewish men and women of their diminishing stature in an increasingly rightist Argentina.[25]

Some Jewish women participated in the broad cultural resistance to fascism. One example is the Agrupación de Intelectuales, Artistas, Periodistas, y Escritores (the AIAPE), founded in 1935. Overlapping with the CCRA, its prominent members included intellectuals associated with the Communist Party. The AIAPE rallied cultural producers to build a "dike against reaction" and construct a leftist nationalism to compete with the right-wing variant. By identifying with Sarmiento, Alberdi, and other liberals, who had vanquished Spanish colonialism and Juan Manuel de Rosas's conservative dictatorship (1829–32 and 1835–52), the AIAPE positioned itself within an ongoing Argentine revolutionary tradition. The organization defended basic freedoms, secular education, and other aspects of the liberal program endangered by the shift to the right; it and other leftist antifascists considered it progressive to do so. But the AIAPE also broke with liberalism by tying itself to the struggles of laborers and subaltern nationalists. By 1937, the AIAPE had 2,000 members and twelve branches in the interior. Its adherents of Jewish origin included Isa Kremer, the folksinger discussed below; the Socialist writer Ethel Kurlat; the Communist educator Berta de Braslavsky (see chapter 3); and the Communist sculptor Cecilia Marcovich.[26]

Writing in an AIAPE publication in 1941, Kurlat, a Russian-born playwright and journalist, passionately asserted that no honorable intellectual could disengage from politics at this critical juncture. To fail to advocate freedom and justice, "to close one's heart and eyes to this calamity [fascism] . . . to refuse out of fear, coldness, or calculation to serve Man, is to hand over one's brothers and oneself—though some might think the reverse—to a sinister form of death."[27] Given the global surge of fascism, neutrality was impossible.

Following the AIAPE's lead, the author Serafina Warshaver, a Socialist turned Communist, criticized the Nacionalistas' reverence for Spain, noting that it had fostered the Inquisition and coerced gold from the Indians. "The lived reality of the people and not a medievalist philosopher's dusty cabinet" was the true source of the Argentine character, she wrote, discrediting the rightist movement's claim to nationalism and affirming her own. This article appeared in *Contra-fascismo*, the voice of the Communist-linked Comité Antifascista Argentina, which Warshaver served as treasurer.[28]

On a smaller scale than Kurlat and Warshaver, Ashkenazi grass-roots antifascists carved out niches in Argentina by appropriating gaucho customs and liberalism. The Comité Juvenil and sympathizers danced the pericón at their festival in Moisesville in September 1935. In that town, activist Jewish women teachers lectured on Sarmiento and other nineteenth-century liberals, stressing their support for universal secular education and immigration, measures important to Jews and opposed by Nacionalistas. The DAIA in 1938 asked Jews to commemorate Sarmiento, a Nacionalista target. In one program, the inmates of the girls' orphanage in Buenos Aires sang a song celebrating his achievements and gave recitations and speeches in his honor. These performances featured versions of expansive liberalism and of nationalism that opposed the right-wing variety. Furthermore, they demonstrated Jewish women's contestation of Nacionalista and government marginalization.[29]

Nourished by European experience, exiles created antifascist networks. A few Italian Jewish families sought refuge in the interior, where they formed friendships in schools and universities with other Jewish and non-

Jewish fugitives from Germany, Italy, and Spain.[30] Central European Jewish girls who attended the anti-Nazi German-language schools and Jewish actresses in the Freie Deutsche Bühne formed similar relationships with their non-Jewish colleagues, reinforced by their common tongue and culture.

The stage offered another space for resisting fascism at home and abroad. Jewish women and fellow participants in anarchist, IFT, and other radical productions celebrated progressive humanistic values at odds with Nacionalista ones. Jewish and non-Jewish troupe members of the Freie Deutsche Bühne aimed to save German culture from Nazism. The Teatro del Pueblo, including Jewish women performers such as María Fux, epitomized freedom of expression and modern theater for the masses, and in this way struggled against fascism.[31]

The Spanish Civil War

Support for the antifascist Republicans in the Spanish Civil War (1936–39) attracted more mass involvement in Argentina than any political movement from the 1930s to the mid-1940s. The Spanish origin of many Argentines does not completely explain this popularity. While Argentine liberals and leftists had often scorned the nation's Spanish roots, now that Spain had transformed itself from an authoritarian country into a beleaguered republic, they saw it as akin to Argentina. In their view, both nations were struggling to overcome rightist opposition to democracy and social justice. The Socialist Rosa Scheiner believed that Argentina was moving toward a Spanish-style conflagration. Although it may be inaccurate to reduce the Spanish conflict to one of democracy versus fascism, numerous Argentines saw it this way.[32] In the political maelstrom of the 1930s, they, like Kurlat, thought they had to choose one side or another, neither of which they defined precisely. Furthermore, they understood that a rebel victory would strengthen the Nacionalistas in Argentina, whereas a Republican victory would weaken them. This was a transnational struggle, waged on both sides of the Atlantic and intensified by the movement of peoples and ideas back and forth.

Leftist allegiances aside, many Ashkenazim felt a particular affinity with the Spanish Republic.[33] Solidarity, democracy, and idealism dictated Jewish support for this cause, as did the rebels' anti-Semitism and their ties to Hitler and Mussolini, declared the Comisión Israelita de Ayuda al Pueblo Español (the CIAPE).[34] Through the Republican network, Jews could assert their Argentine identity by working with local democrats and strike a blow against the pro-Franco Nacionalistas. It was a transnational campaign with national goals.

Jews found many ways of aiding the Spanish Republicans. Whipping up support for them, the Yiddish Communist press devoted more attention to the Spanish Civil War than any other issue, even the struggle against local anti-Semitism. Men and women joined the CIAPE, whose fifteen affiliates collected money for the Spanish embassy, and the Communist-leaning Federación de Organismos de Ayuda a la República Española. Jewish girls in the Jóvenes Amigos de España Leal in Quilmes solicited donations and organized benefit picnics and veladas. Such efforts were common in Villa Domínguez, Moisesville, and other towns and barrios heavily populated by Jews. Even after the fighting ended, many Jews, like other Argentines, sent aid to Spanish refugees and protested Franco's policies.[35]

The Spanish Civil War made militants out of many young Ashkenazi women. Neighborhood aid committees and the collection of aluminum foil, clothing, and contributions introduced them to leftist politics. A participant in fundraising events, the young Polish immigrant Perla Wasserman accompanied her mother to pro-Republican demonstrations, including that of May 1, 1938, in which about 200,000 people filled the Avenida de Mayo in Buenos Aires. Everyone sang "The International" in his or her own language, her mother in Yiddish. Their performance of an Argentine nation proud of its diversity contested Nacionalista xenophobia. The rebel victory hit Wasserman hard, but her experience set her on a path that led through anarchist activities, the IFT, the Socialist Party, and the Madres de la Plaza de Mayo.[36]

Perhaps several hundred Argentines, mostly Communists, went to Spain, including several Ashkenazi women. Sara Segal was one of two Jewish women who left from Moisesville. Raquel Levenson, wife of the prominent Communist Juan José Real, traveled through Spain in the last stages of pregnancy as a party organizer. An officer of the Comité Argentino de Mujeres Pro Huérfanos Españoles (CAMHE), which helped Spanish children, Fanny Edelman worked for the Communist-sponsored Socorro Rojo in Spain, soliciting food and clothing for combatants and their families. Joining her husband in Spain in 1934, Berta Baumkoler guarded Communist headquarters, organized dining halls and literacy courses, and worked for schools of revolutionary soldiers, among other activities. Back in Argentina in 1941, after detention, Baumkoler, like other returning activists, applied her experience to local political chores.[37]

Mika Felman followed the most interesting path to the Spanish front. A dentist born in Moisesville, she moved from anarchism to the radical student group Insurrexis, the Communist Party (see chapter 6), Communist Worker Party, and Trotskyism. She and her partner Hipólito Etchebehere enrolled in the Trotskyite Partido Obrero de Unificación Marxista militia in Spain when the war broke out. Continuing to fight after Etchebehere's death, Felman became a captain. After Franco's victory, she wrote for antifascist publications in Argentina and returned to Europe after 1945.[38]

Berta Singerman's leftism, love of Spanish poetry, and trips to Spain put her on the Loyalist side: "We all dreamed of the revolution, of the Republic. We thought the world could be different." The Spanish Republic symbolized a project of social justice and freedom that she and many other Ashkenazi women favored. Berta and her sister Paulina performed at pro-Republican benefits. After the defeat, Berta signed numerous anti-Franco manifestos and refused to set foot in Spain for seventeen years.[39]

The government regarded Jewish and other Republican sympathizers as subversive. Policemen harassed pro-Republican demonstrations, including the large one of 1938, and canceled a benefit festival in Moisesville in 1939. The Jewish *chaqueño* anarchists paid a price for their Republican allegiance. During the Civil War, Spanish farmers hosted and attended the Bursuks' plays, the proceeds of which went to Spanish refugee funds, and sponsored the troupe. The mobilization around the Republican cause, which coincided with strikes by cotton farmers, caught the eye of authorities, who raided and destroyed the Brazo y Cerebro library.[40]

Help for the Allies

Many Argentines braved repression and continued to participate in transnational antifascist campaigns, which shifted toward helping the Allies. Thousands of men and women joined a myriad of groups. Perhaps the largest was Acción Argentina (AA), supported by Socialists and some Radicals and conservatives. Like other antifascist organizations, it aimed to strengthen Argentine democracy, which it believed was dependent on the future of European democracy. Female adherents knitted goods for Allied soldiers, studied nursing, gave speeches, and conducted democratic practices.[41]

Duplicating roles that women played in AA, Jewish women joined pro-Allied Jewish groups throughout the country. Unlike AA, these organizations also sought to help beleaguered coreligionists. The Comité Israelita

Pro Ayuda a Gran Bretaña had its Comité de Damas; so did the Comité Pro Socorro a las Víctimas de Guerra y Refugiados, created by the DAIA. Some joined the Junta de Ayuda Judía a las Víctimas de Guerra; affiliated with it was the Taller de Costura para Refugiados (Tacor), founded in April 1944, which acquired and made children's clothing. Women residing in the German Jewish old-age home outside Buenos Aires worked with Tacor, as did Hungarian Jewish women.[42] Some Jewish women's aid groups maintained community borders, even as Tacor crossed them.

Other organizations attracted Communist-linked Ashkenazi women. Initially such efforts as the Organismo de Ayuda Directa a las Víctimas Judías de la Guerra en Polonia, which included women, solely helped Polish Jews. After the German invasion of the Soviet Union, however, Communists formed pro-Allied groups. One was the Comisión Central Femenina Israelita de Ayuda, with over 10,000 members and 50 workshops in cities, industrial suburbs, and colonies. According to a Comisión leader, by knitting and sewing for the Allies, women expressed their solidarity with those who fought for freedom and the existence of the Jewish people.[43]

All the Jewish female pro-Allied organizations made and collected clothing and raised money, but in other respects they differed. The bourgeois groups were philanthropic; the Communist-aligned ones tried to raise women's consciousness. Members of the latter criticized Nazis for confining German women to the kitchen, nursery, and church. According to an Ashkenazi Communist garment worker, through the aid movement, women learned that "the people's struggle for democracy is also the woman's struggle for her liberation."[44]

In 1942, Delila Saslavsky, a Communist sympathizer, recalled that she had learned in school that Argentina was her country and she should love and defend it. Now, however, the Nacionalistas denied her the right to be Argentine. The best way to claim this identity, according to Berta Blejman de Drucaroff, a former leader of progressive Yiddish schools, was to participate in the aid effort: "By defending the Jewish people . . . we also defend the integrity of this, our beautiful fatherland."[45]

Much Communist rhetoric exalted the Soviet Union and its heroic stand against Hitler. Many listeners did not see the Soviet Union as democratic, which was how Communists portrayed it, but now it faced Germany in a battle that would determine the future of the world and its Jewish population.[46] This was sufficient reason to join the campaign to aid the Allies.

The Communist Party was instrumental in creating the largest pro-Allied group of non-Jewish and Jewish women, and perhaps the largest women's political group before Peronism. When Germany invaded the Soviet Union, the Communist Cora Ratto and the Communist sympathizer María Rosa Oliver decided to draw upon the Republican relief campaign and the bourgeois suffragist Unión Argentina de Mujeres (the UAM), founded in 1936, to build this movement. Their principal motive was to protect socialism, as they defined it, but they wanted to appeal to a broad antifascist spectrum. The Junta de la Victoria began its operations in September 1941 under President Ana Rosa Schlieper de Martínez Guerrero, head of the Inter-American Commission of Women, secretary general of Acción Argentina, and a member of the Radical Party and the UAM. Schlieper had worked with Jewish organizations in an unsuccessful attempt to bring thousands of Jewish refugee children to Argentina.[47] She, Ratto, and Oliver were not Jewish.

The Junta saw its campaign as transnational. According to Rosa Scheiner, the Junta understood "up to what point and how intimately linked the struggles unfolding on distant Russian steppes, and the no less distant British front, are with our own struggles for liberty and democracy." Working for democracy abroad entailed reinforcing it at home. The Junta aimed to strengthen allegiance to the constitution and laws, respect for others, and social justice.[48]

The Junta's connections with the highest circles helped it thrive. Members of the Catholic elite, like Schlieper and Oliver, were among its officers. The organization established cordial relations with political leaders, Allied ambassadors, and wealthy businessmen, who donated goods and money. The Junta held benefit teas for diplomats' wives, cocktail parties, cultural events, and star-studded shows.[49] Seemingly an aristocratic group, the Junta may have highlighted its upper-class elements to obtain backing and operate in safety. Its Jewish contingent demonstrates that it was more than an elitist social gathering.

Women of Jewish origin had a large presence in the Junta, although we lack statistics. Its governing board included the Communists and sympathizers Rosa Scheiner, Clara Helman, Cecilia Marcovich, and Dalila Saslavsky; in addition, Berta de Braslavsky worked on the press committee and the Junta's magazine. Jewish women filled affiliates in the porteño neighborhoods of Almagro, Villa Crespo, Caballito, and La Paternal; Bahía Blanca, Concordia, and other provincial cities; and Jewish colonies.

Dr. Clara Schliapnik, president of the Villa Domínguez chapter, and Rosa Ziperovich, secretary of the Palacios unit, near Moisesville, were among numerous Jewish officers. The Junta branches in the tiny Jewish agricultural centers of Moisesville and Basavilbaso attracted 400 and 426 members, respectively, only a few less than the 500 in the large city of Córdoba.[50] This comparison is a revealing measure of Jewish commitment.

Adherents of Jewish origin were diverse. Sister of a famed movie director, scion of a rich assimilated family tied to the grain trade, and the wife of a non-Jewish aristocrat, Saslavsky belonged to the Argentine elite. Junta members also included the German Jewish photographer Annemarie Heinrich and the Viennese psychoanalyst Marie Langer. Eta Engel, with her husband, owned a tiny news and refreshment stand in working-class Almagro. Fanny Edelman and Raquel A. de Monín, the Polish wife of a railroad laborer, were of humble origins.[51]

Such backgrounds were typical of Junta members. Employees, factory workers, farmers, professionals, and especially housewives—women of varying classes and ethnic origins, both immigrants and native born—filled the ranks. By June 1943, the Junta de la Victoria had mobilized about 45,000 women in 125 chapters around the country.[52]

Jews crossed lines of class and ethnicity to mingle with other Junta members. One Russian Jewish woman translated for French and Eastern European women at Junta headquarters. The Jewish farmers who formed the bulk of the chapter of Delfín Huergo, Buenos Aires, elected a Catholic aristocratic rancher president and used her car for Junta business. At the office in San Fernando, north of Buenos Aires, Monín, an elected representative, and well-off Christian Englishwomen and Argentine wives of Englishmen knit clothing and held teas and raffles. Engel and her Jewish friends went to the homes of fellow Junta members in high society to make bandages together. Jews and members of the elite mixed but did not become friends. Still, at a time when only charity, commerce, or domestic service brought together women of different classes, the Junta allowed them to become acquainted. Creating another form of social capital, Jewish women helped construct these rare spaces of interaction and a model of pluralism.[53]

This pluralism encompassed religious differences. The Junta did little to recruit Jews, who had strong motives to join, yet the Church's rightist tendencies made it necessary to launch special appeals to devout Catholics. Reminding Argentine women that the German regime persecuted the Church, Junta representatives asked them to help assure freedom of religion for all. One of these representatives was Eugenia Silveyra de Oyuela, a contributor to *Orden Cristiano*, the lone Argentine Catholic publication that sympathized with Jewish victims of Nazism.[54] In an age before religious ecumenicalism, Jewish and Catholic Junta members came together and challenged Catholic Nacionalista intolerance.

The Junta labored to aid the Allies. Members collected apparel, hospital items, food, and goods for recycling to make weapons and for other wartime uses, as well as materials for its workshops. In hundreds of these locations, women made clothing, bedding, bandages, and first-aid kits, while others picked up goods and sewed or knitted at home. As of May 1943, Rebeca de Malajovich of Moisesville, who at 95 was the oldest Junta member, had knit 150 pairs of socks for Soviet soldiers. Her poor eyesight, she said, forced her to use dark wool during the day and light wool at night. Dues, contributions, magazines, and benefits brought in revenue. Women in Jewish colonies rode horses and sulkies on muddy roads to collect funds from their distant neighbors. Thanks to such efforts, the Junta had raised almost 288,000 pesos in cash alone by late 1942.[55]

Berta and Paulina Singerman, Golde Flami, and Paloma Efron were among the stars of Junta benefits in large theaters. Explaining her participation, Berta Singerman wrote that fascist countries did not permit the freedom vital for artistic production. Thus she stood with those who defended "liberty and equality, without racial or religious distinctions."[56] She and other antifascists sought to protect the liberal freedoms and extend the Argentine liberal project.

A frequent participant in benefits hosted by the Junta and other pro-Allied groups was Isa Kremer. Trained in opera, the Russian-born Kremer had crossed the line from, in her words, "the silks and satins of opera singing . . . [to] the woolens and the homespun of the music made by the people." Kremer gathered folk songs from many countries and sang in sixteen languages, including Yiddish, Ladino, and Hebrew. Yiddish was the heart of her repertoire, and Jews the core of her audience. She sang in Argentina for the first time in 1934, incorporating folk songs of the provinces into the repertoire she took back to the United States.[57]

This intermediary between countries returned in 1938 to settle in Córdoba with Dr. Gregorio Bermann, who had created the Argentine medical brigade that served in Spain and would head the AIAPE. Through Bermann, Kremer became close to Communists and Spanish Republicans. Her performances had always been political in the sense that she diffused the music of the dispossessed and exalted her Jewishness, but now they

15. Isa Kremer. Instituto Científico Judío (IWO).

were explicitly leftist and antifascist. Often appearing with María Teresa León, an exiled Spanish Republican writer, Kremer sang at events supporting the Allies, Jews who were being persecuted, and strikers. Her transnational experiences and witnessing of Nazism in Europe heightened the urgency of her music. Kremer imported the Red Army anthem, music of the Spanish Republican militias, and a song celebrating the Soviet Union's supposed lack of anti-Semitism for her repertoire.

Owing to its feminist roots, the Junta's greatest preoccupation apart from aiding the Allies was to strengthen women's participation in democratic procedures. As the Junta prepared its second national convention in May 1943, Helman, Edelman, Saslavsky, and other leaders from Buenos Aires visited chapters in the interior to solicit their involvement. Junta chapters set their agendas democratically, compiled reports on their work, and elected representatives for the meeting. Through these activities, Jewish women helped contribute to civic democracy. Yet the Junta's democratic activities lacked social content. According to Rosa Ziperovich, better conditions for the poor hinged on the triumph of democracy. The Junta claimed it would promote industrialization, health, and education when the war ended. In the meantime, like the rest of the pro-Allied campaign, the Junta emphasized political rather than economic democracy.[58]

The Junta's pluralistic democratic project and ties to the Allies challenged the Axis-leaning Nacionalistas. The roles that Junta members assumed outside the home also defied the Nacionalistas' rigid gender notions. Nacionalistas jeered at the group's Jewish, Communist, and oligarchical members; support for the Soviet Union; and aid for a cause they considered irrelevant and antinational. They assaulted at least two Junta branches.[59]

Originally the Junta won official recognition, but the increasingly repressive government of Ramón Castillo (1940–43) turned against it. The police prohibited a number of Junta events and broke up its *Victory Review* at the Gran Rex Theater, organized by Braslavsky and featuring the Singerman sisters and other stars, in December 1942. When women in an impoverished porteño neighborhood resisted orders to close their chapter in February 1943, the police hauled them off to the dreaded Special Section. In a separate incident, the authorities imprisoned Braslavsky and other members of the downtown chapter, stole their keys, and robbed their homes. Resisting U.S. pressure, the military regime that assumed power in June 1943 closed down the Junta and all pro-Allied aid organizations.[60] Antifascists, in its view, were anti-Argentine.

Exclusion and Struggle, 1943–46

The Nacionalista-influenced military dictatorship of 1943–45 constructed Argentine identity as largely Spanish and Catholic. José Ignacio Olmedo, interventor of the Consejo Nacional de Educación, that is, a military government-imposed head, declared that schools must conform to "the soul of the race" by identifying "with the Christian home." Voiced in these terms, the imposition of Catholic education seemed to bar Jews from the nation. The military jailed Communists, anarchists, union militants, and students and appointed Nacionalistas to positions in the universities and cultural institutions. It silenced dissidents, including Jews, who also lost government jobs. Claiming that instructors from other countries "who do not feel or love our traditions" could not adequately teach children about Argentina, federal education officials expelled numerous teachers, perhaps 250 of whom were Jews and many of them women. New laws forbade the use of Yiddish in public gatherings and the ritual slaughter of animals.[61]

Jews in Entre Ríos felt particularly threatened. Interventor Lieutenant Colonel Carlos María Zavalla closed Hebrew schools, withdrew government recognition of Jewish organizations, changed street names honoring Baron Hirsch (see chapter 1), and harassed Jewish residents. Police raided Jewish institutions, removing the picture of liberal President Bartolomé Mitre (1862–68) from the Villa Domínguez library because they thought he was a bearded Jew.[62]

Zavalla also persecuted women. In 1944, Luisa Furman (see chapter 3) and five other Jewish women teachers in Villa Domínguez laughed at a speech given by President Edelmiro Farrell (1944–45). Their principal denounced them, and Zavalla fired them, claiming they were immoral and unpatriotic Communist sympathizers. In reality, they were known for their devotion to Sarmiento and ties to the Socialist Party, both of which were out of favor. Insisting that one of them had said that the Day of the Race, the celebration of Columbus's arrival in the Americas, meant nothing to Jews, the government in effect asserted that Jews could not be Argentine. Zavalla followed this action by dismissing all Jewish teachers in the province, who numbered between 100 and 200. The government mistakenly threw out a few Christian instructors of German descent, but it reinstated them when they complained. Backed by teachers' unions and community supporters, Jewish educators protested until the next interventor, General José Humberto Sosa Molina, took office. He slowly reincorporated the teachers, also overturning other measures his predecessor had taken against Jews. The new head of the Consejo Nacional de Educación in 1945 reversed many of the dismissals carried out around the country, admitting they were arbitrary and sometimes anti-Semitic.[63]

This episode was significant for several reasons. The Jewish teachers' victory signified that rightists could not deny the Jews' Argentine identities or their place in the schools. It demonstrated that, under certain circumstances, Jewish women could negotiate the content of nationalism with even a Nacionalista-tinged dictatorship. As Sosa Molina was close to Perón, his conciliatory measures also suggested that the future Peronist government would distance itself from Nacionalismo and include Jews.[64]

As news of the liberation of Paris spread through Buenos Aires in August 1944, the Junta de la Victoria, operating clandestinely, invited women to gather in the Plaza Francia. Many others joined them in what became a massive display of opposition to fascism abroad and dictatorship at home. Among the women were Perla Wasserman and her friends, carrying Spanish Republican banners, and Jewish and non-Jewish girls who were skipping classes. A throng of roughly 200,000 listened to Berta Singerman recite the "Marseillaise." Mounted police scattered the crowd with tear gas; the parents of one Jewish girl rescued her and took her home. Still, the authorities could not dispel the exuberance. Singerman repeated her recital several times over the next few days.[65] The question was whether victory overseas would translate into victory at home.

Sensing that the regime was in retreat, students, professionals, leftists, and the Junta mobilized. The end of the war raised their hope that Argentina would embrace democracy, which happened in a manner that antifascists did not anticipate.[66] They threw their support behind the Unión Democrática, which opposed Juan Perón's presidential candidacy. An army officer who had admired fascism, Perón had garnered support from the Church and the Nacionalistas. As labor secretary for the military regime, he had implemented social-welfare policies that won him popularity among laborers, union leaders, and reformers. Conservative antifascists denounced these measures for class reasons; progressive antifascists criticized their opportunism and cooptation of leftist programs. Tying Peronism to fascism, a Jewish Socialist woman circulated around Buenos Aires in her party's truck, declaring through a loudspeaker: "Argentine women! Nazi-Peronism threatens the tranquility of your homes, the lives of your children!" A majority ignored such pleas. Unconvinced by antifascist arguments that social justice was tied to the consolidation of democracy, they preferred Perón's concrete record to the Unión's antifascist rhetoric, opposition to Perón's redistributive efforts, and ties to the United States.[67] His election stunned his opponents, including most Jews. Antifascists had helped defeat their enemy overseas, but the person they regarded as its local incarnation had bested them.

Solidarity with Political Prisoners

Long before Perón's election, the Argentine government had imprisoned and abused political activists. Human-rights violations swelled after the coup of 1930, diminishing somewhat after Agustín P. Justo assumed the presidency in 1932. Among those persecuted were Jewish women. In November 1933, police dragged a twenty-two-year-old Polish Jewish seamstress from her apartment to the Special Section, which kept her incommunicado and hungry for six days. An interrogator forced her to sign a blank confession sheet and threatened her with gang rape if she did not discuss her union activities and name her compañeras. Another official warned he would jail her with prostitutes in the Asilo de San Miguel unless she agreed to leave the country. Falsely charged with carrying arms, she was incarcerated at San Miguel for three weeks. Other Jewish female militants complained of beatings and torture; lack of food, blankets, and bathroom facilities; and filth and illness. One spent two weeks of solitary detention naked. Jailers tried to force young Jewish women to have sex with them, or copulated with prostitutes before their eyes.[68]

Conditions worsened after the coup of 1943, when the regime imprisoned perhaps 10,000 activists, many of them Communists. Jewish women once more suffered abuse; at least three in 1945 complained of severe torture.[69] Nor had the situation improved much by April 1955, under Peronism, when police detained a nineteen-year-old student of Jewish Polish origin for giving a package to striking metallurgical workers. After passing through the Special Section, she spent a month in San Miguel, where she and other political prisoners shared a crowded room with over two hundred prostitutes, beggars, and drunks. The rats, disease, and stench recalled the Buchenwald concentration camp, observed *Tribuna*. The Special Section mistreated all its detainees, but this Jewish Communist organ claimed it was especially abusive toward Jews.[70]

Human-rights organizations arose throughout the country, including Jewish areas such as Moisesville, after 1930. The most important was Socorro Rojo Internacional, a Communist group in solidarity with political prisoners, deportees, and their families. As the need for its services grew and the popular-front strategy emerged, Socorro Rojo became the Liga Argentina por los Derechos del Hombre in December 1937 and expanded its mission to protecting the basic freedoms. Prominent left-of-center intellectuals and politicians joined the Liga, but Communists provided the main impetus.[71] This demonstrates once more how leftists appropriated and expanded the liberal project, extending it to safeguard the rights of so-called subversives, whom most liberals stigmatized.

Ten years ago, observed *Mundo Israelita* in 1937, no one would have imagined the need for a group like the Liga. Times had changed, however; men sporting swastikas did not bother the authorities, who instead singled out patriots loyal to the national anthem's refrain of "liberty, liberty, liberty."[72] Even this organ of the Ashkenazi elite praised the left-leaning Liga.

Rosa Scheiner, Fanny Edelman, and Dalila Saslavsky belonged to the Liga's visible level, which raised money and awareness of racism, fascism, and human-rights abuses. It provided lawyers for political prisoners, including during the military regime of 1943–45, which did not recognize the Liga as lawful. Even members of this level of the organization were not immune from police persecution.[73] Edelman and others organized a benefit meeting of Socorro Rojo for July 1936 at the weekend home of one of its leaders, Dr. Augusto Bunge, outside Buenos Aires. As participants deliberated converting Socorro Rojo into what would become the Liga, police and Special Section agents raided the premises, carting away Bunge's papers and 109 well-dressed persons, including Edelman and thirty-three other women. According to *La Nación*, many detainees apparently were "of Hebrew ascendance, but native-born, and of good social position." Bunge agreed, claiming policemen attacked his home because they identified Jews with Communism.[74]

The Liga provided legal aid for beleaguered Ashkenazi women such as fourteen-year-old Catalina Kuper, detained in 1941 for selling a Communist-linked youth paper. When Catalina's mother, Rosa Wladimersky, also a militant, tried to claim her, a judge placed the girl in a reformatory, citing a law on abandoned delinquent children. Although Catalina was neither abandoned nor delinquent, the authorities regarded Communism as criminal and her politicized Jewish family as unsuitable. The judge sent inspectors to evaluate the Kuper home and refused to permit the Liga's lawyer to speak to them. Prominent Communists, Socialists, union leaders, and even the influential cleric Monseñor Miguel de Andrea questioned whether Wladimersky should lose her rights to her daughter. Another Liga lawyer, the distinguished Socialist deputy Carlos Sánchez Viamonte, finally was able to review court documents, which he found inaccurate and anti-Semitic, and free Catalina. Nevertheless, the police continued to harass the girl and her mother.[75]

The Liga's subterranean level consisted of grass-roots women, many of them organized in foreign-language or ethnic sections. Among these, the Comisión Israelita Femenina stood out, according to the Liga. Even in times of relative freedom, Comisión members like Teresa Gílenberg—veteran Procor, school, and CIAPE activist—and other women of solidarity operated mostly in the shadows to evade persecution.[76]

These women aimed not only to help prisoners, but also to incorporate the masses in class struggle through acts of "proletarian solidarity," which they distinguished from charity. Carrying her infant daughter, Gílenberg went from door to door, asking for contributions and spreading awareness of repression in the early 1940s. When an arrest occurred, she and other committee members headed to the police station or jail, met with

16. Relatives of political prisoners in Villa Devoto prison, 1941.
Archivo General de la Nación, Dpto. Doc. Fotográficos.

the family, and spread the news in the prisoner's neighborhood, workplace, and union; if the incarceration was lengthy, they notified Liga leaders. Tying the campaign to broader anticapitalist efforts, they extended it beyond the barrio or factory, soliciting funds, urging friends to visit the prisoner, and recruiting new Liga activists.[77]

A vital part of the women's mission was taking provisions to the penitentiary. Gathering and fixing food linked women to a chain of solidarity and the construction of a revolutionary society. Rather than buying prepared foods, some women made the meals to further invest themselves in the prisoners' fate. Gílenberg and her comrades, however, asked their butchers and vendors to donate meat and produce, which they assembled in packages with cigarettes and chocolate. The Comisión did not restrict its solidarity to Jews; Gílenberg asked her Italian vendor for food to take to the imprisoned tango musician Osvaldo Pugliese. What she called "an army of women" carried these heavy parcels to male political prisoners in the Villa Devoto prison, and to women confined in San Miguel. Another Comisión member washed the jailed militants' clothing. These solidarity workers also sent goods to prisoners in the even harsher Rawson prison in Patagonia, and other jails.[78]

Brave working-class women specialized in these semiclandestine and dangerous activities. Berta Baumkoler, a participant in the Spanish Civil War, was among them. Having entered the Liga out of Communist conviction and to help her oft-incarcerated husband, she herself became a political prisoner. So, too, did the legendary figure known as "old Zlate," later described by the magazine *Antinazi* as one of the two best known women of solidarity. Tiny, elderly, and fierce, Zlate Dlugates was the proletarian mother of several prisoners. Fighting uncooperative correctional officers with her fists landed her in jail several times.[79]

Prison visits were harrowing. Indeed, merely to present oneself at the jail was frightening. Prison officials opened all packages, cut through bread and cold cuts, and often sent food back, claiming it was excessive. Zlate would insist that one portion was for a fictitious grandson and a second portion was for another supposed grandson; true or not, such tactics helped supply more prisoners. Sometimes forbidden from seeing or touching detainees, the Liga women nevertheless reduced the prisoners' isolation and demoralization and helped keep their militancy alive. Prisoners wrote letters of appreciation to the women who brought them packages, who in turn formed friendships with their families. In this manner, Jewish and other solidarity activists helped create networks that strengthened the Communist party and fought for a society that recognized human rights.[80]

Peronism

Repressive in some respects, the Peronist administration was complex. Perón accepted ethnic differences and recognized immigrants and their descendants as part of the nation. He included previously marginalized groups, such as workers, Jews, and women. While identified with domesticity, women achieved suffrage and greater legal rights and mobilized in large numbers under Eva Perón and the Partido Peronista Femenino. Perón appropriated and popularized some of the Nacionalista agenda, namely social Catholicism, economic nationalism, anti-Marxism, and authoritarianism, yet he incorporated new elements. His project emphasized planning, social welfare, and engagement with the people, as well as top-down control and unity.[81]

Perón's relationship with Argentine Jews was multifaceted. His government improved their—and other Argentines'—economic position; opposed discrimination; courted Israel; and legitimized the status of the many Jews who had entered the country illegally in the 1930s and 1940s. It first softened Catholic education in the schools, then eliminated it entirely in 1955. Through such measures, the creation of the Organización Israelita Argentina (the OIA), and support for Zionism (see chapter 8), it sought Jewish votes—and U.S. favor. While many Jews appreciated these policies, few genuinely backed the administration. Some Jewish women, such as Clara Krislavin, the wife of Interior Minister Angel Borlenghi, were active Peronists, but their numbers appear to have been small.[82] The repression of leftists and other opponents; anti-Jewish violence by Nacionalista Peronists during the campaign of 1946; the emphasis on conformity; and policies restricting Jewish, while promoting non-Jewish, immigration reinforced the perception that Perón was a fascist, although as president he distanced himself from Nacionalismo. Jewish periodicals and organizations praised Peronism, but their words seemed prudent rather than heartfelt.[83]

Peronism had a complicated impact on Jewish workers. During the Second World War, work increased and conditions improved for garment and textile laborers. In 1945, garment workers joined together in the Federación Obrera Nacional del Vestido (FONIVA), which shared the benefits Perón extended to labor. Outspoken Communists such as Kanutsky, however, were no longer welcome. Jews who remained in FONIVA had to conduct meetings in Spanish rather than Yiddish, although sometimes policemen left the room to permit non-Spanish speakers to talk. Eventually the Spanish, Italian, and Arab immigrants who arrived after 1945 replaced Jews in the needle trades and unions.[84]

The Communist-dominated textile union, the UOT, declined under the military regime of 1943–45. It operated secretly, and many of its leaders, including women, were imprisoned. The Peronist government favored the Asociación Obrera Textil (the AOT), created in 1945. The UOT and Socialist splinter textile unions dissolved, their members joined the AOT, and Dora Genkin and Flora Absatz faded into obscurity.[85] Ironically, as unions entered the mainstream of Argentine society, their Ashkenazi women leaders were relegated to the fringe.

The Communist Party decided in 1946 to disband its unions and infiltrate Peronist ones. Still, militants like the teacher and activist Rosa Ziperovich were fired or imprisoned. Ziperovich lost her post as principal of a school in Rosario, and the government closed the Santa Fe provincial teachers' federation in 1950. Clandestinely, Ziperovich remained active in the union, serving as secretary. She resisted marginalization by continuing "to speak loudly, to write, to rebel, to overcome fear, to fight within the union alongside one's comrades."[86]

Under Peronism the status of Argentine Jewry was changing from predominantly lower- to middle-class. By the 1950s, the number of Jewish workers had declined, as some moved into retirement or entrepreneurship, and their children entered commerce and the professions. Kanutsky set up a cosmetics business with her son, and some Jewish couples wove textiles in their new plants. The Peronist government's stimulus for small industry, wage increases, and social-welfare policies enabled many Jews to prosper.

Upward mobility and social measures convinced some Jewish workers to join the Peronist ranks, but most progressive Jews remained loyal to the Communist Party. Nevertheless, some Communist Jews accorded Perón a grudging respect. While she despised what she saw as his fascism, Mina Ruetter, a former activist in the Organización Popular contra el Antisemitismo, recognized that his social policies helped the common people. She vacationed in hotels in the Córdoba highlands, where the government allotted rooms to workers. Ruetter enjoyed the unease displayed by members of the elite when forced to share the facilities with the laborers they disdained. Another Communist woman of Jewish origin criticized Perón for not taking advantage of his popular support and carrying out a genuine revolution. Yet she saw that he compelled vineyard owners in Mendoza to build homes for their workers, who had previously slept in barns and fields.[87]

The Peronist government excluded leftist performers. It blacklisted the Singerman sisters for refusing to praise Perón on the radio. Berta's opposition to Franco and fascism had made it hard for her to acquire a passport, and these difficulties continued after 1946. Nor could Isa Kremer appear on stage after 1952.[88]

Under Peronism, leftist movements faced enormous challenges. As labor secretary and then president, Perón stole the Socialists' thunder by implementing women's suffrage, wage hikes, and other measures they had long favored. Socialists who viewed Perón favorably left the declining party or were expelled. Anarchists were few and divided, and the government largely controlled the unions. It was difficult to compete with a government that benefited workers or to survive under persecution.[89]

Military and Peronist repression hurt at least one Jewish woman associated with Socialism. Dr. Clara Schliapnik had written for the Socialist *Vida Femenina* and engaged in leftist activity in Villa Domínguez. She fought the arrest and expulsion of her son from school for protesting against the dictatorship of 1943–45. When Schliapnik and her family moved to the capital in 1945, her political past kept her from finding work. Influential Peronist friends managed to clear her police file, enabling her to obtain a position in a municipal hospital. However, copies of her original file still circulated, the police raided her home, and she could not leave the country without an official certificate of good conduct.[90]

Communist Party

Marginalized under Peronism, Jewish Communists gravitated to Idischer Cultur Farband (ICUF). A transnational Jewish cultural movement sponsored by the Soviet Union, ICUF was founded in 1937. It promoted a secular, progressive version of popular Ashkenazi culture, drawing on Yiddish roots. ICUF opposed Zionism as a diversion from class struggle, in which it wanted Jews to participate while retaining their cultural identity. Thus it also employed Yiddish, as opposed to the Zionist use of Hebrew. Beginning its activities in 1941, the Argentine branch of ICUF faltered under the repressive Castillo and military governments but recovered in 1945, with the opening to democracy. At the same time, ICUF offered spaces for some Communists banished from meaningful union activity, such as Kanutsky. In 1946, it included twenty-five cultural institutions, such as schools, children's summer camps, and the IFT theater, with 9,000 members.[91]

Recognized as inculcators of Yiddish culture—although that culture was increasingly expressed in Spanish—women were included in ICUF ventures. The veteran antifascist Mina Ruetter translated works from Yiddish to Spanish for the ICUF's publication series and periodicals and wrote for the periodicals, as did Kanutsky.[92] The largely female teaching corps taught girls and boys not only letters, culture, and history, but engagement with the state: how to live "an active, useful, and dignified life, that understands and feels . . . the ideals for which one should fight" in Argentina, as one female teacher put it. Not all instructors were Communists, however. The teachers knocked on doors, registering students and soliciting money. Women's committees maintained facilities, raised funds, and organized transportation and scholarships for students in ICUF schools and summer camps. Alumni clubs joined the Federación de Instituciones Juveniles Israelitas Argentinas (the FIJIA), an ICUF affiliate. In 1948, it created women's committees in all its branches, which sponsored cultural, sports, and aid activities and encouraged women to become ICUF teachers.[93]

ICUF also encouraged women to depart from customary roles. The 120-strong committee of the I. L. Peretz School in Santa Fe invited intellectuals to lecture in 1954. It participated in a local pedagogical conference as well as campaigns for peace, tolerance, and the formation of democratic fronts. Women's school committees organized reading circles, mostly among working- and lower middle-class housewives with little education. By 1956, over 1,000 women belonged to forty reading circles in greater Buenos Aires, Rosario, Córdoba, Mendoza, and Santa Fe. Some circles read in Spanish, some in Yiddish, and some in both languages; all pondered topics that crossed gender and domestic borders. Kanutsky's group in Buenos Aires read and commented on current politics, whereas the Mendocinas perused materials on education and peace and organized literary evenings. Circle members attended cultural events and demonstrations together. Their participation in these organizations spurred women to express themselves, which promoted more egalitarian relations with their husbands. In addition, the circles stimulated members' leadership abilities and desire for knowledge.[94]

They also included women in broader struggles. The circles formed the base of ICUF's Organización Femenina (the OF), which was created in 1947. Leike Kogan, a French-educated Polish teacher in ICUF schools, the first director of the Zumerland summer camp, and a critic of women's marginalization, was its principal leader; *Di Idische Froi* (the Yiddish woman) was its voice. Beginning in 1951, this bilingual periodical reported on women's activities in ICUF and encouraged women to contribute articles. Its circulation in 1956 was 1,500, but this may not be an accurate estimate of its readers, as women probably shared copies and read them aloud at circle meetings.[95]

The OF faced the thorny problem of how to deal with Israel. Many Jewish Communists were proud of the new Jewish nation, but they saw it as one among many Jewish communities. This stance pitted them against the mainstream Jewish organizations, which were Zionist. Mirroring broader Jewish Communist backing for Israeli workers, the OF sent aid to children of progressive Israelis.[96]

While many Communist-aligned groups campaigned against U.S. cold-war policies, memories of the Holocaust and fascism made the OF particularly interested in peace and tolerance. Its members demonstrated in favor of disarmament, German demilitarization, and Ethel and Julius Rosenberg, whom the United States executed as spies. It also collected signatures for a DAIA petition asking Congress to outlaw discrimination and anti-Semitism, a measure Perón appropriated.[97]

Nevertheless, as Kogan observed, the OF "collided with the cold walls of Peronist oppression." At times, the government and Communists reached out to each other; at other times, they clashed. Turning against the Communist Party, the administration repressed ICUF and its women's branch after 1952. It closed the IFT, prohibited ICUF events and publications in Yiddish, and detained some ICUF leaders. The police raided Gílenberg's reading circle and confined the women in San Miguel for two weeks. This time, Gílenberg benefited from other women's solidarity and food packages. Kanutsky's reading circle and cultural center retreated underground.[98]

Some activists evaded persecution. In 1952, Kanutsky and other members of her cultural center founded a credit union so they could operate in the open. While Jews formed the core of the credit unions, non-Jews also joined. By 1956, Jewish Communists and sympathizers had created ten credit unions in the capital, five in the suburbs, and six in the interior. All had women's committees and progressive cultural events.[99]

The Jewish establishment and the Communist Party also repressed ICUF. A long-simmering conflict between progressive and Zionist Jews boiled over when the former refused to accept the DAIA's condemnation of the Stalinist trials of Jews in Prague in 1952. Disenchanted, some Jews left ICUF and the Communist Party. This quarrel prompted the DAIA to oust progressive Jewish organizations; the Jewish educational network to expel ICUF schools; and the Asociación Mutual Israelita Argentina, the Ashkenazi communal organization, to cut its ties with ICUF. Progressives were now on the fringe of the Ashkenazi community. ICUF institutions lost substantial subsidies, and Jewish leaders assented to the heightened official persecution of Communists. Meanwhile, leftist Jewish groups faced renewed pressure to dissolve and integrate into the Communist Party.[100]

Jewish, government, and Communist Party opposition weakened ICUF and its cultural mission, as did the rise of the Spanish-speaking generation. Recognizing these limitations, ICUF increasingly adopted Spanish.[101] Nevertheless, it continued to exist.

ICUF women resisted amalgamation into Perón's anti-Communist "New Argentina" and helped sponsor a critical view of Argentine society that rejected the Peronist benefactor state as the ideal.[102] While both Peronism and the OF emphasized women's maternal roles, the Jewish progressives—unlike Peronist leaders—encouraged women to question authority. The official ideology stressed assimilation, although it recognized ethnic minorities through their mainline corporate institutions that accommodated to Peronism. Instead, ICUF women helped maintain progressive Ashkenazi identities that opposed Zionism and Peronist authoritarianism.

Meanwhile, some women of Jewish origin resisted the Peronist project through Communist cultural activities. In 1952, a member of the Sociedad Argentina de Escritores, Serafina Warshaver, along with other Communist writers, denounced its submission to Peronism and demanded freedom of expression and measures to improve authors' standard of living. Berta de Braslavsky wrote for the Communist-sponsored intellectual periodicals *Orientación* and *Cuadernos de Cultura*, and in the mid-1950s, she also served as secretary of the Instituto Cultural Argentino-Ruso. Veterans of the AIAPE and the Junta de la Victoria, Braslavsky and Cecilia Marcovich participated in the Agrupación Intelectual Femenina. Created in 1947, it brought together female professionals, artists, and writers and linked them to women's groups in working-class neighborhoods, including those with large Jewish populations, to offer health services and educational activities for women and children. Seeking to include the masses in high culture and critical thinking, the Agrupación contested a Peronist cultural project that emphasized practical knowledge, technical education, and ideological conformity.[103]

In contrast to these cultural initiatives, which may have only touched small numbers of people, Fanny Edelman headed an effort to mobilize many women. At the Eleventh Party Congress in August 1946, she insisted that a genuine mass movement for social and national liberation required women's involvement on a large scale. The Junta de la Victoria, which had reappeared in 1945, was unsuitable for this task, as Communists worldwide spurned antifascist, multiclass alliances after 1945.[104] The Junta melted away, and the Unión de Mujeres Argentinas (the UMA, founded in 1947) became the new vehicle for attracting women. The OF and the Agrupación supported it, as did grass-roots women's groups. Edelman became the UMA's secretary-general, a post she exercised for almost twenty years, with some time off when she directed the Party's Comisión Nacional Femenina. The UMA fought for women's economic and political rights and against U.S. foreign policy and the high cost of living under Perón. The size and composition of its membership is difficult to gauge, since much of its activity was secret. Edelman and her colleagues frequently landed in jail.[105]

Communist militancy cost women dearly. Jobs and political duties left the oncologist Rosa Woscoboinik de Levin (see chapter 3) little time for her family or herself. Events and social occasions all had a political

17. Fanny Edelman. Archivo General de la Nación, Dpto. Doc. Fotográficos.

purpose, and no one lingered when they ended. Nor did women discuss the dilemmas of being females, Communists, professionals, and mothers. Levin's medical career suffered, as hospitals either denied her positions or fired her because of her Communist affiliation. Devoted to the Communist Party and her crippled husband, Edelman regretted not having been closer to her children.[106] Communist activism often foreclosed personal and professional ties.

Motherhood and the need to arrange child care tended to exclude women from other activities; they often had to reduce their militancy or abandon it altogether. Ruetter hired servants to care for her children while she worked afternoons and evenings for the Communist Party. Gílenberg and other working-class women, who could not afford such help, took their children to functions. Some simply could not combine maternity with Communist activities.[107]

Conclusion

The Peronist triumph seemed to erase the labor and leftist struggles that preceded it. Jewish women militants and the causes in which they had participated disappeared from view. Only recently have historians rediscovered the antifascist movements. The participation in them of Jewish women, many of modest backgrounds, demonstrates that such groups were diverse. It also shows that women in the ranks inserted their own meaning into issues and strategies devised by male leaders above them.[108] For obvious reasons, antifascism resonated among Jewish women activists.

They took part in a transnational struggle. The fascist threat had infected the world; through Nacionalismo, anti-Semitism, and creeping authoritarianism, it had entered Argentina. Combating these dangers abroad meant strengthening freedoms at home, including women's right to be active outside the home. As Drucaroff noted, the defense of the Jewish people in Europe meant the defense of Argentina and its democratic institutions.

Jewish leftist women negotiated borders. They helped lower ethnic, class, and religious walls in the Junta de la Victoria. Although sewing for the Spanish Republicans and Allies and gathering food for jailed militants represented customary female roles, many women pushed through gender barriers, becoming unfeminine street agitators, outspoken wives, and political prisoners. The dikes they built against reaction did not protect them from persecution.

Jewish women who opposed fascism, Nacionalismo, and Peronism engaged with the state. Creating social capital, many worked to strengthen democracy inside and outside their organizations, as well as to disseminate culture and humanism. This democratic position characterized some Communist-aligned groups as well, despite their support for the Soviet dictatorship. Jewish women's oppositional projects stressed the acceptance of diversity, popular participation, solidarity, peace, women's rights, and critical thinking, with the Communists also emphasizing class struggle and alternatives to Zionism. Antifascists' use of liberalism tied those women in general to regressive economic policies and eventual electoral doom. Yet Jewish female activists continued to focus on aspects of liberalism that they found attractive, such as universal secular schooling, immigration, women's rights, and the basic freedoms.

Excluded by Nacionalistas, leftist Jewish women sought to be part of the nation. Fighting fascism alongside Argentines of other backgrounds was a means of ensuring their acceptance, as was supporting a pluralistic democracy that would truly encompass Jews and other minorities, the poor, and women. The Communist Party also included Jewish women in another sense, by offering them a rare opportunity to assert their ethnic identities outside their homes and communities. ICUF women did not have to submerge their backgrounds to be political, as did Socialists of Jewish origin. Yet the Peronist surge, repression, and the difficulties of combining militancy with family and profession left many Jewish leftist women on the edges of society and their political movements. In contrast, the next chapter shows how Jewish female philanthropists and Zionists remained on the margins of their communities but entered the Argentine mainstream.

CHAPTER EIGHT

"We the Women Have to Do Something"

Philanthropies and Zionism

We the women have to do something!
—Adela de Maldavsky, interview

[The Jewish woman] quickly understood that
through her struggle for the liberation of her people
she was attaining her own emancipation.
—*OSFA*, May–June 1945

Jewish women on both sides of the Atlantic had long cared for the needy.[1] By the early 1900s, Jewish women were working for Zionism, efforts that also were philanthropic in that they helped Jewish pioneers in Palestine. All these caregivers devised incremental ways of meeting basic needs.[2] In the face of social problems, "we the women have to do something," as the Zionist Adela de Maldavsky put it. Yet women's communal activism also had other meanings.

This chapter treats women's philanthropies and Zionist groups thematically, analyzing how they functioned and intersected with the broader arguments of the book. It examines Eastern European, Central European, and Mediterranean organizations side by side, rather than separately, as most scholars have done,[3] and highlights commonalities, differences, and relations between them. I also compare Jewish women's charities with their non-Jewish counterparts.[4]

The philanthropists and Zionists in Argentina drew upon influences from abroad and sent aid there. By participating in global networks, several Argentine Jewish women shaped organizational practices in other countries. Yet Argentine as well as foreign models influenced these activists. Interplay between the local and transnational characterized some Jewish associations.

Most charities reinforced the linguistic and regional boundaries around Jewish communities. Over time, some philanthropies and Zionism helped reduce these barriers and create wider Jewish identities. Charities also laid bare the divisions among Jews. Members of these organizations crossed, but did not eliminate, lines of class to help the poor.

Female community activists engaged with the state in many ways. Philanthropists addressed the shortcomings of liberal rule, which provided inadequately for the poor, by filling in cracks, rather than advocating broader socioeconomic change.[5] Thus they challenged liberalism to be more inclusive, but not as directly or thoroughly as leftist Jews did. Charity work offered a means of demonstrating respectability, countering the image of Jewish women as prostitutes, and claiming spaces in the nation. Even as they helped create Israel, Zionist women asserted their argentinidad and forged a constructive relationship with Peronism.

Through their voluntary associations, some women contested marginalization in the Jewish and larger societies. They asserted power and performed tasks that fellow Jews appreciated. Yet Jewish communities tended to sideline women by assigning practical matters to them and leadership and ideological issues to men. By challenging this and other gender norms, a number of women struggled for emancipation. They also negotiated with the government to secure resources and fulfill their missions.

The Rise of Women's Groups

Women's charity work began with mass Eastern European immigration. Poverty among the early Russian Jewish colonists aroused the pity of women associated with the Congregación Israelita de la República Argentina (the CIRA), made up largely of prosperous Western Europeans. In 1892, they founded the Sociedad Israelita de Beneficencia, dedicated to assisting the Jewish Colonization Association and the impoverished immigrants. Soon thereafter the Sociedad faded away. But it reconstituted itself in 1908, having added well-off Eastern Europeans; eventually it changed its name to the Sociedad de Damas Israelitas de Beneficencia. It helped needy Jews and opened a girls' orphanage, the Asilo Argentino de Huérfanas Israelitas, in 1919.[6]

Moroccan Jews in Buenos Aires initiated the next organized effort. By 1899, members of the Sociedad de Beneficencia Damas de Sión were visiting bedridden compatriots and supplying expectant mothers with provisions and money. In general, Mediterranean groups were associated with temples, as was the Comisión de Damas El Socorro, created by women of the Balkan Etz Hajaim synagogue in 1908.[7]

Female charities were also being formed in Ashkenazi colonies. The first were informal circles of pious elderly women in Moisesville and possibly other locations that provided husbands and trousseaus for poor women, and mourners for funeral processions. Not necessarily wealthy, the members of these circles quietly gathered money from the rich to distribute to the needy. More permanent associations, such as the Sociedades de Damas of Colonia Clara and Moisesville, arose in the early 1900s.[8]

From the 1890s to the mid-1930s, Ashkenazi women founded at least thirty-five beneficent societies throughout Argentina, and Mediterranean women at least thirteen. The societies were located in rural areas, industrial suburbs, and cities alike. In addition, in Buenos Aires in 1936, German speakers formed the Sociedad de Socorro Femenina or the Frauenhilfsverein, the women's section of the Asociación Filantrópica Israelita, which helped refugees fleeing Nazism. The Hermandad Femenina of the German Jewish cultural association Jüdische Kulturgemeinschaft was created in 1940 to aid the sick, elderly, and poor, and help defray funeral expenses.[9]

While charitable experiences abroad influenced the Sociedades, so did local non-Jewish beneficent societies. The most important was the upper-class Catholic Sociedad de Beneficencia, created in 1823. The Argentine government gave it subsidies to administer orphanages, hospitals, and other institutions.[10]

Transnational linkages were crucial in constructing the most ambitious Argentine Jewish women's group. Some Ashkenazi participants in efforts to resettle Jews displaced by the First World War became interested in Zionism. Aided by Dr. Uriel Benzión, a Sephardi representative of the London-based World Zionist Organization, they founded the Comité de Damas del Fondo Nacional in July 1925 in Buenos Aires. In the meantime, the Women's International Zionist Organization (WIZO), founded in London in 1920, began to set up branches in other countries. Engaged in this endeavor in Chile, Ida de Benzión, Uriel's wife, went to Mendoza, where she helped found the first Argentine WIZO chapter in 1926. Word of her mission inspired the porteño Comité de Damas to become the core of the Organización Sionista Femenina Argentina (OSFA) and affiliate with WIZO. Benzión helped the new group, and, as time passed, she and other WIZO delegates toured Argentina to offer their skills, lecture on Palestine, and strengthen ties between the local and global movements. In turn, OSFA leaders attended WIZO congresses, visited Palestine and WIZO centers in other countries, and corresponded with the central office. These transnational contacts helped convert OSFA into the largest Jewish women's group (indeed, the largest Jewish group) in Argentina and the only truly national one.[11]

An umbrella organization also arose to bring women's philanthropies together. Delegates from these groups—including Ezras Noschim, OSFA, the Frauenhilfsverein, the Sociedad de Damas Israelitas de Beneficencia, and the Balkan Sociedad de Damas Israelitas de Beneficencia La Unión—met in October 1937 to form what was eventually known as the Consejo de Mujeres Israelitas de la Argentina (CMI). CMI sought to coordinate women's aid to growing numbers of Jewish refugees. Its founders envisioned CMI as a female DAIA, a central organization of women's groups. The focus would be charity, however, rather than the DAIA's tasks of defending Jews against anti-Semitism and speaking on their behalf with the government. The new association established a list of aid recipients, so that affiliates would know who was already receiving help, and a used-clothing depository to which constituent groups were supposed to contribute, instead of sponsoring their own. These and other CMI initiatives, however, made little headway, as discussed below.[12]

CMI received sustenance from councils of Jewish women in other countries. The National Council of Jewish Women (the NCJW) contacted CMI shortly after its founding, and in 1939, a CMI member visited the NCJW and took information on its activities back to her organization. Another CMI leader established ties with the French, Swiss, and Palestinian councils. A distinguished philanthropist and long-serving officer of the German council moved to Argentina in 1933 and shared her expertise with CMI. Although the Argentine group claimed the NCJW as its model, there were differences between the two. The NCJW's original base consisted of the German Jewish elite, and it created its own network of affiliates throughout the United States. In contrast, CMI drew upon existing institutions in the various Jewish communities. While social work and settlement houses influenced NCJW programs, CMI's activities fit in the local mold of upper-class women's charities.[13]

Functions

Beneficent societies shouldered the "difficult but noble human task of mitigating the pain and carrying a bit of consolation and inspiration to disinherited and suffering people," as the Ashkenazi Sociedad de Damas of Basavilbaso put it.[14] They visited the poor and the sick to assess their needs and gave them small loans or grants, food, clothes, and medicine. Societies contributed to medical facilities in their towns and financed trips to Buenos Aires to obtain treatment unavailable locally. An Ashkenazi beneficent society in Villa Domínguez maintained a hospital bed for indigents, while one in Carlos Casares created its own childbirth facility. Often societies donated money to other Jewish institutions.[15]

The Sociedad de Damas Israelitas de Beneficencia in Buenos Aires prepared individuals to support themselves. They gave women sewing machines and arranged for tubercular patients to sell cigarettes. To aid impoverished Eastern European women who arrived after 1918, the Damas helped establish a sewing workshop, placed its apprentices in businesses, and provided other menial jobs, housing, and small subsidies. By assisting the immigrants economically, the Damas tried to keep them out of prostitution, thus protecting the Jews' reputation and place in the nation.[16] The employment the Damas offered, however, was not very remunerative.

Respectability also concerned other beneficent societies. The Ashkenazi Damas Israelitas Pro-Maternidad y Niños Ezrah of Carlos Casares specified that its members had to be of "honorable occupation and irreproachable moral antecedents." Following a common practice for female charities, two *socias* had to present and vouch for potential members. Indeed, as charity suggested affluence and confirmed women's caregiving nature, it was inherently respectable.[17] It made Jewish practitioners similar to elite Catholic female philanthropists, thus inserting the Jewish women into the center of society. Through philanthropy and self-policing, societies like that of Carlos Casares strengthened the reputation of Argentine Jewish womanhood, albeit at the expense of women deemed unsuitable for membership.

Echoing the sentiments of female Zionists elsewhere, OSFA regarded itself as the first Jewish women's group in Argentina to break from "the old norms of philanthropy, exchanging them for a systematic plan of social work to help the woman and child" in Palestine, later Israel. What truly distinguished this endeavor from charity was the role it played in constructing a Jewish homeland.[18] To meet this broader goal, OSFA trained its members to conquer their households for Israel. It told women to put its collection box in a place of honor in their homes and instruct their families that "it represented the determination of a people to acquire their own liberation." Although OSFA was not religious per se, it recommended that members teach their children Hebrew and Jewish history, light Sabbath

18. Leaders of the Moisesville OSFA (Organización Sionista Femenina Argentina) center, 1939. Museo Histórico Comunal y de la Colonización Judía Rabino Aaron Halevi Goldman (MHC).

candles, and celebrate religious holidays to strengthen Jewish and hence Zionist identity. It encouraged mothers to send their children to OSFA after-school programs, parties with Zionist and Jewish historical themes, and Hebrew courses. "Young WIZO" members engaged in cultural and fundraising activities, practiced giving speeches, and corresponded with pen pals in Palestine, later Israel. This was the training ground for OSFA.[19]

Rural Jewish communities were starved for entertainment, and women's groups supplied it. A fundraiser ball hosted by the Damas of Moisesville in 1924 attracted 250 youths from the town, surrounding countryside, and as far away as Santa Fe. In May 1937, they organized a benefit velada, featuring local amateurs. As the town's Jewish newspaper put it, "our public flocks to . . . [such events] like believers to the synagogue."[20]

Insiders and Outsiders

The wealthiest Ashkenazi philanthropies were located in Buenos Aires, and the dances, concerts, and lectures they sponsored made up the annual winter season. Its climax was the gala ball of the Sociedad de Damas Israelitas.[21] While its ostensible purpose was to benefit the girls' orphanage, this ball permitted the Damas and their circle to tighten friendships and youths to find marriage partners. The season helped consolidate an Ashkenazi bourgeoisie. The charity balls affirmed the income gap between the elegantly dressed guests and those who needed the Damas' aid, between Jewish insiders and outsiders.

The balls demonstrated to society at large that some Jews had made it and could imitate the Catholic Sociedad de Beneficencia. According to one Jewish critic, conventional manners, a superficial veneer of culture, and the desire to flaunt their fancy clothes—rather than genuine charity—motivated the Damas Israelitas. He censured them for absorbing local customs by assuming the materialism, noblesse oblige, and submissive domestic roles of aristocratic Catholic ladies.[22]

While the Catholic Sociedad de Beneficencia of Buenos Aires was upper-class, middle- and even working-class women joined non-Jewish beneficent societies in smaller localities. A similar hierarchy may have characterized Jewish women's philanthropies, headed by the Sociedad de Damas Israelitas in the capital—whose prestige, however, did not match that of the Catholic group. The Ashkenazi and Mediterranean beneficent societies in large cities recruited the most affluent women. All held balls that celebrated their prosperity; all cemented their ties to wealth through contacts with rich male benefactors. Small-town groups may have recruited more widely. Dues were as low as the fifty cents a month charged by the Ashkenazi Sociedad de Socorros de Damas Israelitas of Carlos Casares. Still, few lower-class women may have been able to spend even this amount or spare the time. Nor could middle-class women farmers easily afford dues during economic downturns.[23]

Some Damas had risen out of poverty, as the case of Luna de Mayo of Posadas demonstrates. Originally a poor peddler, her husband eventually established a general store (see chapter 1). In the early 1930s, she headed the women's committee of the Asociación Mutua Israelita Hijos de Sión, which raised money, paid the rabbi's salary, and distributed food to the poor of the Izmiri community. Mayo's participation in the Damas highlighted the distinction between her "impoverished past and present status" as a benefactor, demonstrating to the underprivileged that they, too, could become insiders. Thus some female philanthropies of the interior united their communities around the possibility of upward mobility.[24]

Broader-based than the beneficent societies, OSFA welcomed women of all classes, whose efforts it deemed necessary to spread Zionism, and had them address each other as "comrades." Before the 1940s, almost all the members were Ashkenazi. In 1931, Moisesville boasted 222 members, Villa Domínguez 205, and Basavilbaso 193, compared to 100 in the city of Córdoba. In some agricultural settlements, most women, both rich and poor, joined, despite the dues. So numerous were OSFA chapters in such areas in Entre Ríos that this province became the site of OSFA's first regional grouping. Anti-Zionist leftists, however, joined neither OSFA nor the charities.[25] Frequent critiques of OSFA members' "low cultural level"—a code phrase for class—indicated its plebian character.

As already noted, rural Jewish women were more active in voluntary associations than were their urban counterparts, and arguably more influential.[26] While some neighborhoods in Buenos Aires and other metropolitan centers had sizable Jewish populations, none were majority Jewish, unlike the colonies. There was no anonymity in the Ashkenazi agricultural settlements and small Mediterranean communities of the interior. Most women knew and could persuade each other to join groups.

Fundraising

Women's organizations united their communities around fundraising. They received dues from members, money and goods from benefactors, and some subsidies from male-run community organizations. Groups solicited contributions at weddings, bar mitzvahs, and other festivities and charged admission for teas. In search of money, they knocked on doors and stood on street corners. One OSFA member traveled thirty kilometers by sulky to collect dues from twenty-five farmers "in the heat of summer, the cold of winter, the rain on mud-covered roads." Associations held benefit dances, cultural evenings, raffles, and other events that reinforced community borders. Governments also helped fund some beneficent societies and their projects, most notably the girls' orphanage. Hosting few benefits, CMI relied on dues from member institutions and the annual sale of an annotated date book.[27]

Although it also sponsored benefits, OSFA broke new ground. It increasingly depended on yearly campaigns organized around themes, and on its members, whom it encouraged to contribute on family birthdays, bar mitzvahs, and other occasions. Each member had a little blue box with a Star of David in her home, in which relatives deposited spare change. This money went to the Jewish National Fund for the purchase of land and trees in Palestine, later Israel. Using visual symbols, tangible goals, and calendar dates tied to the reproduction of family and community, OSFA's

19. Women selling flowers and candies for the Asilo Argentino de Huérfanas Israelitas, 1925. Archivo General de la Nación, Dpto. Doc. Fotográficos.

innovative fundraising was almost too successful. WIZO officers frequently criticized the Argentine affiliate for concentrating on collecting money and neglecting cultural uplift.[28]

Funding, however, could be precarious, as diverse organizations, both male and female, competed for scarce resources. The local OSFA center complained in 1929 that Moisesville was saturated with events and collections. Benefits were not always profitable; the Moroccan Damas de Caridad of Rosario earned only 51 pesos for a dance in the late 1920s. Low income during the Great Depression forced the Sociedad de Socorros of Carlos Casares to curtail its subsidies to impoverished women in 1932. Furthermore, as Jews moved out of the rural communities, local women's associations and their revenues shrank.[29]

Difficulties plagued the Damas of Basavilbaso, whose records in 1923 were so disorganized that they did not know how much money they had. They needed to finance the building of their headquarters on land acquired from the Jewish Colonization Association (JCA) in 1916. The economic crisis that accompanied the First World War hampered fundraising, and their efforts to aid war refugees and fulfill local needs diverted funds from their goal. By 1925, the JCA was threatening to take back the land if the Damas did not begin construction. When the JCA presented its final ultimatum in 1929, the Damas scurried to raise money as never before. Subventions from Jewish organizations, a grant from the provincial governor, and special donations produced enough funds. Finally recognized and included, the Damas opened their building in 1935.[30]

Borders

Their financial woes notwithstanding, philanthropists tried to fortify their communities. In 1925, the Sociedad de Damas Sefaradiot of Buenos Aires raised money for a school to teach Hebrew and Jewish culture. "This way our children will not grow up ignorant" or "be ashamed when they hear themselves called Jews," said the Damas.[31]

Also strengthening community borders, the Frauenhilfsverein set up a day-care center in 1938 in the Belgrano neighborhood, where most German Jews lived. The organization hired several German Jewish women to care for the children, with the help of volunteers. Children of working parents spent the day at the Kinderheim, and a few children lived there. Those old enough attended a nearby public primary school, where they learned Spanish. The Kinderheim inculcated German-style discipline, taught German literature, put on German plays, and on one occasion took older charges to a performance of Mozart's *The Magic Flute* at the Teatro Colón. These shared experiences in German culture inspired lifelong friendships among many Kinderheim alumni.[32]

The Sociedad de Damas Israelitas de Beneficencia La Unión of Buenos Aires, a group founded in 1922 with 200 members, directed its efforts toward the Balkan community. Its visibility and prestige grew after the dynamic and well-connected Esther Gedalievitch de Chami became president in 1933. Even as her organization reinforced ethnic boundaries, Chami had crossed them. Born to a Russian Jewish family in the cosmopolitan city of Galata, Turkey, in 1888 and married to Mois Chami, a prominent textile producer from Rhodes, she embraced Mediterranean Jewish culture. By the 1930s, La Unión's work focused on Ottoman Jews in impoverished Villa Crespo who attended the synagogue and Hebrew school run by the Comunidad Israelita Sefaradí (the CIS). Securing money from wealthy Balkan Jews and elegant benefit teas and dances, and clothing from manufacturers like Chami's husband, La Unión distributed goods and grants to needy families, handing out 8,000 pesos in 1936. It gave winter garments to poor children at the CIS school in May 1933. Demonstrating her acquaintance with the students, Chami also sent clothing to underprivileged pupils whose names had not appeared on the recipient list.[33] The organization's strong contacts with all sectors of Balkan Jewry enabled La Unión to reinforce community identity.

The Sociedad de Damas Israelitas de Beneficencia did much the same for Ashkenazim, particularly through its orphanage. Like the orphans in institutions overseen by the Catholic Sociedad de Beneficencia, the girls attended public school for six years and sewed to earn money for the orphanage and themselves. In contrast to the Catholic children, however, who spent most of their time working, the Jewish *asiladas* took dressmaking, secretarial, bookkeeping, and nursing courses, and some attended normal schools, acquiring credentials for "a dignified and remunerative occupation," in the Damas' words. The girls received a Jewish education and French lessons and were treated to lectures, sports, excursions, movies, and plays, activities that went far beyond those provided by the Catholic Damas. Unlike the latter, some Jewish Damas knew their charges personally; one woman, for example, paid for an orphan's singing lessons. The Damas placed orphans in agricultural settlements for vacations and invited Ashkenazi performers to give concerts in the facility. They asked Jews to tour the Asilo and attend its celebrations of religious and national holidays, as well as the annual ceremony that recognized girls' achievements, which attracted sizable audiences.[34] The Damas connected orphans to the Ashkenazi community.

The Damas also helped reproduce and tighten that community. Professors regularly tested the girls on their knowledge of Hebrew and Jewish history, and the Jewish press reported the results. As Donna Guy points out, these newspapers showed little interest in the male orphans' religious education. This preoccupation evinced concern over preparing the girls to be good Jewish mothers, a goal the Damas constantly reiterated. The orphans studied homemaking and practiced cooking, ironing, and cleaning. As already noted, the Damas sponsored their weddings and monitored their behavior after they left the Asilo.[35]

OSFA bound Ashkenazi women together. To belong to the movement meant being a "sister" of all the other comrades in the "great and beloved Republic," one member noted,[36] and until the 1940s, this mostly meant Ashkenazim. National officers' visits to centers in the interior further linked women of Eastern European descent throughout Argentina.

Even as some women's organizations shored up walls around their communities, other groups sought to lower them. A few beneficent societies in the interior included both Ashkenazi and Mediterranean members. Also blurring the lines, eventually 35 percent of the orphans in the Damas' Asilo were of Mediterranean descent. Sephardi communities contributed to the institution, and the Sephardi press frequently praised the Asilo for including Mediterranean girls.[37] Despite the orphanage's Ashkenazi links, it became one of the most visible spaces encompassing Jews of diverse backgrounds.

CMI also intended to be such a space. It planned to represent all Argentine Jewish women's organizations and stimulate cooperation between Jewish women "without distinction of the nationality of origin." Delegates from Eastern European, German, and Mediterranean groups attended the initial meetings, and Esther Chami and a German representative became vice-presidents of the provisional directorate. A conflict broke out immediately, however, when an Ashkenazi philanthropist disagreed with Chami's claim that Sephardim went only to Sephardi relief agencies. Soon after this debate, La Unión dropped out, followed a few years later by the Frauenhilfsverein. Personality clashes, protection of ethnic and jurisdictional boundaries, and the desire of all constituents to retain autonomy weakened CMI.[38]

A more successful attempt to unite Jewish women evolved within Zionism. Although for nearly two decades, most spokeswomen were Ashkenazi, Mediterranean women demonstrated interest in Zionism. When Ida Benzión toured Argentina in 1926, a Mediterranean beneficent society cosponsored a tea for her in Buenos Aires. Benzión then visited Rosario, where she inspired the formation of the Círculo de Damas Sionistas, which affiliated with OSFA and included Ashkenazi and Mediterranean women. One was Hortensia de Ambram, a Tangier-born writer and president of the Moroccan Damas de Caridad in Rosario, whose writings and lectures lauded women's roles in reviving Jewish life in Palestine.[39]

OSFA in Buenos Aires reached out to Mediterranean women as early as 1929, when it invited La Unión to help plan an event. OSFA's first national congress in 1933 decided to compile a list of potential Sephardi, German, and English recruits. This effort only slowly bore fruit, but contacts between Ashkenazi and Mediterranean women continued, as Esther Chami hosted a tea in her home in 1937 and divided the proceeds between OSFA and La Unión.[40] The Círculo in Rosario was not the only OSFA center with a diverse membership. In 1937, María Adler, who had participated in WIZO in Belgium and Holland, and her daughter, Anny Weil, helped create a new chapter in Belgrano. It attracted well-off Syrian, Turkish, and Central European women—"a better class of local Jewry" previously absent from Zionism, claimed one observer. Adler also joined the OSFA executive board.[41]

Members of the Belgrano chapter shared another trait: they did not speak Yiddish. Although almost all OSFA documentation was in Spanish, some members conversed and gave speeches in Yiddish until the 1950s, a practice that excluded women of other backgrounds. When Ashkenazi Zionists asked Judith Isaharoff (see chapters 5 and 6) how they could appeal to a wider spectrum of Jews, she told them to speak French to Mediterranean peoples, not Yiddish.[42] Although OSFA increasingly reached out to non-Yiddish speakers in the 1940s and 1950s, the language problem lingered.

Julieta Camji played a critical role in stimulating Zionism among Mediterranean Jews. She imbibed this ideology from her father, José Camji, president of the Macabi sports club, whose longing to return to his birthplace, Jerusalem, led him to cofound the Centro Sionista Sefaradí. Julieta, her relatives, and Ashkenazi friends they had made in OSFA children's circles formed the Zionist youth group Avukah. In 1940, when she was fifteen, Camji delivered her first speech, on the poet Chaim Nachman Bialik and the Zionist Theodor Herzl, to an audience at Chalom, where prosperous Balkan Jews congregated. One of a handful of women interviewed by *Mundo Israelita* in a special series on Jewish female activism, she analyzed Ashkenazi Zionist meetings and pondered applying these lessons to Ladino- and Arabic-speaking communities.[43]

Camji and other members of the Departamento de Juventud del Centro Sionista Sefaradí, created in 1940, believed that working effectively for a Jewish nation required Mediterranean unity. Under Camji's presidency, the Juventud invited representatives of youth clubs in these communities to join its board and attend its gatherings. In 1944, it inaugurated the custom of convoking the communities to raise money for the Jewish National Fund through an annual Purim ball. Over 1,200 youths whose families came from Damascus, Aleppo, Jerusalem, Salonika, Bulgaria, Rhodes, Izmir, Istambul, Bukhara, and Birobidjan attended the dance; in 1948, Moroccans joined them. According to *Israel*, never had so many young Argentine Jews of these diverse origins appeared at an event. Their participation demonstrated that "the youth no longer understand the old distinctions"; most were now criollos, united by tastes, language, and an amorphous sense of Zionism. Candidates nominated by youth groups competed for the titles of Queen Esther and Miss Congeniality, the latter won by Camji. In 1945, the single title "Miss Sefaradí" replaced the two earlier ones.[44]

The word "Sephardi" had appeared in the press, organizational titles, and conversation, but regional loyalties diluted its substance. The Gran Baile de la Colectividad Sefaradí and the crowning of Miss Sefaradí symbolized the merging of the communities into a larger Sephardi identity. Only with the advent of Zionism did "Sephardi" become a reality in Argentina.

The Comisión de Señoritas del KKL (Keren Kayemeth Leisroel), a young Jewish women's group in support of the Jewish National Fund of the Centro Sionista Sefaradí, founded in 1945, reinforced the new pan-Sephardi identity. Camji and other Señoritas placed National Fund collection boxes in homes in various communities. They compiled lists of young people to recruit for Zionist chores and temple members to whom to send publicity.[45]

The rise of a Jewish nation after 1945 and the enormity of its needs convinced many Mediterranean women to join Zionist organizations. The question was whether to mobilize within OSFA or separately. Some women did both by organizing a Sephardi sector within OSFA, to avoid the marginalization fostered by the use of Yiddish and to promote cultural autonomy. Working with OSFA leaders Berta de Gerchunoff (see chapter 6) and Raquel Shuster de Tov, the wife of a Jewish Agency official, the Señoritas identified and recruited potential members. Drawing on transnational contacts, OSFA invited the president of the Sephardi WIZO center in Uruguay to speak to her paisanas in Buenos Aires. The center opened in 1946 with 300 members drawn from wealthy Ladino and Arabic speakers.[46] A year later it collected more money for Palestinian construction projects than any other center. Chapters in Buenos Aires and eight other cities had 1,340 members by 1955 and were organized in a separate division.[47]

OSFA tapped potential Sephardi leaders. Bruria Elnecavé, the Bulgarian Zionist (see chapters 2 and 5) and a member of the OSFA Sephardi center in Buenos Aires, caught Gerchunoff's eye. Impressed with her border skills, intellectual bent, and command of Hebrew, Gerchunoff asked her to join OSFA's executive board as cultural director in 1950.[48]

Like the Sephardim, recent European immigrants organized separately within OSFA. By 1947, a Hungarian center had formed in the capital, followed by an Italian chapter in 1954. The most important segment of OSFA, apart from the women of Eastern European and Sephardi descent, was that of German speakers. Two hundred German, Austrian, and German-speaking Czech and Hungarian women formed a Central European center in 1946, which collaborated with the Belgrano chapter. Lisbeth Wind, a founder of the Central European center, helped organize affiliates in Rosario and six agricultural colonies; all of these formed part of the Central European division that Wind headed for many years. In the 1960s, WIZO sent her to Germany to create new chapters and strengthen existing ones.[49] There Wind applied the expertise she had acquired in Argentina, demonstrating that WIZO influences crisscrossed the Atlantic.

Judith Isaharoff overcame gender and regional barriers to create a Zionist project outside OSFA. When she began her crusade, male leaders told her: "You are crazy, the Sephardi woman is useless." Rejecting their view that these women would rather dress up and play cards than work for a cause, Isaharoff urged the latter to leave their homes and narrow communities for Zionism. She founded the Amigas Sefaradíes de la Histadrut (Israeli labor federation), later called Naamat, in early 1946. Its adherents were of Greek, Moroccan, Bukharan, Aegean, Turkish, Syrian, and perhaps other origins. The 600 members of its central group and affiliates in Flores, Villa Crespo, and Rosario sent money and clothing to Palestine, later Israel.[50]

Meeting in 1948, the Segunda Convención Regional Sefaradí Argentina created the Consejo Central de Damas Sefaradíes to engage women in Zionism, raise money for Israeli Sephardim, and forge Sephardi unity. It invited women from Zionist, beneficent, and social organizations to participate, drawing some away from OSFA. OSFA officials protested to male Sephardi leaders, but they refused "to heed our plea that we are a People with a common ideal."[51] Divisions persisted even within the Consejo, as porteñas of Aleppine, Damascene, Italian, Palestinian, and Moroccan descent grouped separately. By 1952, the Consejo had added affiliates in four provinces. It held cultural events and sent medicine, bedding, clothing, and hospital equipment to Israel, along with large sums to the United Campaign for Israel. Sephardi groups in Israel, as well as the Alliance Israélite Universelle, were among the recipients of the Consejo's aid. We did not do big things, but necessary ones, said one longtime member, Chola Tawil de Ini (see chapter 2); "we filled holes."[52] Like other Jewish women's groups, the Consejo devised practical solutions for tangible needs.

Regional and jurisdictional divisions notwithstanding, Zionist women worked together. Representatives of Naamat, the Consejo, OSFA-Sefaradí, and other groups attended the meetings of the women's committee of the Delegación de Entidades Sefardíes de la Argentina, the Sephardi umbrella organization.[53] Nor did the initial rivalry prevent the Consejo from adding a wing for small children to the OSFA-sponsored Afulah women's agricultural school in Israel. WIZO officials there praised the Consejo for paying twice as much as requested and being willing to raise even more money.[54] Nevertheless, the Consejo, Naamat, and OSFA-Sephardi sector created Sephardi versions of Zionism.

Zionist women helped convert the abstract term "Sephardi" into a reality, but that was still tenuous. So, too, was the category of Jews, which OSFA helped construct by bringing together a mix of women. After all, its affiliates of Central European, Italian, Hungarian, Mediterranean, and Eastern European descent organized separately, albeit under a single organization.

Some Jewish women helped lower walls not only between their communities but also between Jews and non-Jews. OSFA attracted a massive audience, including diplomats and politicians, to its benefit in 1943 to raise funds to send Jewish children from Europe to Palestine. The Socialist leader Alicia Moreau de Justo gave a speech, as did President Ana Rosa Schlieper of the Junta de la Victoria.[55] The Damas Pro-Maternidad in Carlos Casares established a Jewish maternity clinic, yet they also contributed money to the municipal hospital's maternity ward. That reinforced respect and cooperation among the various immigrant groups in Carlos Casares, known for its tolerant climate.[56]

As Argentine Jews became more prosperous, such contributions became common. The Sociedad de Damas in Carlos Casares and other groups sent donations to the victims of the San Juan earthquake in 1944. By the late 1950s, CMI, now called CAMI (for Consejo Argentino de Mujeres Israelitas), had opened its programs to all and established ties with government agencies and non-Jewish social service institutions.[57] Jewish philanthropists claimed spaces in Argentina through their assistance to people of various faiths.

Engaging with the State

Jewish women's groups explicitly identified with Argentina. In their orphanage, the Damas oversaw "the formation of future mothers . . . saturated with healthy principles of Argentinism, who will help strengthen the solid concept of the fatherland." Indeed, the Damas' promotion of domesticity represented absorption of Argentine mores. By "intensifying their respect and love for their Argentine fatherland," CMI sought to make Jewish youth "good Argentine citizens." Yet while female philanthropists helped "nationalize" Jews, they integrated them into a nation they saw as more pluralistic than Nacionalistas or most liberals did.[58]

Regarding Argentina as democratic, female activists tried to govern themselves accordingly. OSFA, CMI, and the beneficent societies deliberated issues and elected officers. Yet these practices were occasionally faulty. The Damas of Moisesville failed to attract a quorum to their annual general assemblies four times between 1925 and 1932, which meant they had to postpone elections and the dispersal of funds. Apathy, distance, and arduous working days kept rural activists from attending meetings in various towns. Several members of the Basavilbaso beneficent society resigned in protest when it refused to grant a petitioner a loan. Although they rejoined when they realized that the man did not need the money, the incident revealed an inability to accept group decisions. Leaders often remained in office year after year; Isaharoff, for example, presided over Naamat for four decades. Thus the social capital created by Jewish women activists was sometimes fragile.[59] Nor did non-Jewish groups and the local polity always meet democratic ideals.

The very importance of women's charities suggested identification with local culture. Mediterranean Jews brought the custom of male leadership in charities, but over time they shifted toward the Argentine pattern emphasizing women's primacy. Founded in 1916, La Unión split into male and female branches in 1922. Claiming charity was women's natural vocation, the men's section disbanded and handed its treasury, archive, and duties to the female one. For this reason, as well as La Unión's proven competence, in 1942 the Comunidad Israelita Sefaradí delegated funds and all charitable tasks to this women's group. The history of this organization illustrates how Jewish women—and men—Argentinized themselves through philanthropy.[60]

Through their charities, Jewish women performed argentinidad. The female orphans practiced criollo dances and celebrated national festivals in the Asilo. To raise money for the German Jewish old-age home outside Buenos Aires, women helped organize an annual Argentine-style barbeque. La Unión and other beneficent societies claimed national space by distributing goods to the poor on Argentine holidays.[61]

Zionists also tied themselves to a cosmopolitan Argentina. In 1945, Hortensia de Ambram lamented that Holocaust victims had not lived in "this very noble Nation, crucible of humanities that extends its blue and white pavilion to shelter men of good will who come from all the latitudes . . . A Hebrew legion . . . loves, elevates, venerates, defends, and respects it."[62] Another Zionist woman juxtaposed her attachments in a poem titled "Argentine and Jewess":

Argentine by birth
Jewess by tradition . . .
In this beloved fatherland
All is greatness and love
In that dreamed-of fatherland
Its soil covers blood and pain . . .
The two arose in May . . .
with bravery they fought
to conquer liberty.
Their beloved flags
have the same colors.[63]

Liberty, valor, and common symbols bound Argentina and Israel together, and reverence for one meant reverence for the other.

Zionist women saw no contradiction between the two nationalisms. By the late 1940s, few questioned the patriotism of Argentines of Italian and Spanish descent, although many held double nationality—a status that Jews could not enjoy. Jews struggled for a homeland to become more like these compatriots and, hence, more Argentine.[64]

Cordial relations with business and government made women community activists feel they belonged in Argentina. The municipality of Buenos Aires loaned the Teatro Nacional Cervantes to OSFA for events and sent leafy branches to the group to help it celebrate the Jewish holiday of Sukkot. Women's organizations leased space in prestigious hotels and ordered kosher food for their balls and banquets, even during the years of Nacionalista ascendancy.[65]

Some beneficent societies, most notably the Damas who ran the orphanage, received government subsidies. In the 1920s, they invited high-ranking officials to visit the facility, including President Marcelo T. de Alvear, who praised it. When Regina Pacini de Alvear, the president's wife and a former opera singer, asked the Asilo to admit a talented Jewish orphan and provide her with voice training, the Damas complied. This cultivation of government figures facilitated the Damas' lobbying efforts. In 1923–24, they acquired their first subsidy of 1,800 pesos from the national congress and a one-time payment of 5,000 pesos from the municipal council. The national subventions resumed in 1927, and in 1928, the semiofficial Sociedad de Beneficencia added its own contribution, which it provided for four years. Before the mid-1940s, the national government's annual subsidy ranged from a high of 24,250 pesos, awarded in 1928, 1929, and 1930, to a low of 8,000 in 1938–39.[66]

Peronism

Soon the Damas had to deal with the military dictatorship of 1943–45 and the presidency of Juan Perón (1946–55). These governments rationalized and centralized control over welfare, which they regarded as social justice rather than charity. The venerable Catholic Sociedad de Beneficencia could not coexist with these policies. In 1946, the Peronist administration intervened in it, and two years later the new National Directorate of Social Assistance absorbed most of its institutions. The Eva Perón Foundation arose in 1948 to address needs not covered by other welfare agencies. The question was how the Jewish Damas—and other Jewish women's groups—would engage with the Peronist benefactor state.[67]

Official funding for the orphanage became uncertain. The first subsidy from the military regime, in 1943–44, was 8,100 pesos, half of what the Asilo received the previous year. For 1945–46, the government supplied only 4,500 pesos, paid in the first half of 1945, supplemented by 2,500 from the official petroleum monopoly. In 1946–47, the Peronist administration contributed 13,500 pesos, covering the second half of 1945 as well as 1946, but it was still behind. Whether the Damas received the 9,000 pesos promised by the Ministry of Labor and Social Welfare for 1947 is unclear. If they did, this was the final payment.[68]

This funding situation made sense in the larger context. To streamline and coordinate welfare institutions and save money, ministries cut off subventions to a host of charities, including the Jewish Damas. The 3,052 philanthropic institutions that had been partially financed by the government stopped receiving official funds in 1948, about the same time as the orphanage.[69]

Already operating under a deficit, the Damas faced even larger problems when the subsidies ended. Yet the government did not close the Jewish Sociedad or take over its Asilo, as happened to the Catholic Sociedad and its facilities. Jews had expected European refugee children to enter the orphanage, but Peronist policies encouraged Italian and Spanish immigration and prevented Jews from arriving. The reduced flow of Jewish immigrants and rising community prosperity, in part resulting from Peronist economic measures, meant there were fewer orphans to shelter. To use the empty space in the orphanage, the Damas lodged young women from the interior studying to be Hebrew teachers. The facility moved to a smaller building and limped on until 1980.[70] Official policies that both aided and hurt Argentine Jews contributed to its demise.

Declining poverty and immigration removed the conditions that prompted the creation of CMI. Furthermore, philanthropy seemed to clash with the new hegemonic view of social assistance. As a consequence, official inspectors lurked around the premises of CMI and other private aid groups and asked questions. Alarmed CMI officials hid internal records in members' homes; some of the documents were never recovered. Partly to dispel any possible impression that its efforts—however limited and faltering—overlapped those of the government or the Eva Perón Foundation, CMI announced a new mission of spreading Jewish-Argentine culture and acquainting Jewish women with broad issues. It offered courses, music recitals, social functions, and lectures on diverse topics. CMI's shifting purpose, combined with financial and leadership problems, led to a loss of members and persistent calls for reorganization.[71]

Transnational collaboration reinvigorated CMI. The organization's president, Hélène de Aslán (see chapters 4 and 5) renewed ties with the NCJW when she visited its headquarters in 1946. The NCJW and the American Jewish Joint Distribution Committee, a Jewish refugee agency, helped two young women from Argentina study social work in the United States in the late 1940s to early 1950s. The idea was that when the women returned home, they would train social workers for Jewish institutions, a project CMI had long been interested in. By 1955, these and other members of a new generation interested in social work had become active in what was called the Consejo Argentino de Mujeres Israelita (CADMI), and later that year some of them took office in the organization. Felisa Favelukes de Kohan, a member of the Sociedad de Damas Israelitas, became president. At the same time, the International Council of Jewish Women (the ICJW) was revived after the war and sought Latin American branches. Its president visited Argentina in February 1956 and helped convince CADMI to focus on social service and the training of social-work volunteers. The Argentine organization affiliated with the ICJW later that year. In 1957, the

NCJW arranged for Favelukes de Kohan to study volunteer work in the United States, where she learned about programs for the elderly. This discovery inspired CADMI's new Club Edad de Plata.[72]

Contacts with the NCJW and the ICJW and the contributions of Argentine women trained abroad injected new life into CADMI. But the influences did not only flow in one direction. Favelukes de Kohan and other CADMI members would serve as high-ranking ICJW officers, shaping this global network, helping it attract new affiliates, spreading awareness of Latin American conditions, and strengthening transnational cooperation among Jewish women.[73]

CMI's and CADMI's main problem had been a lack of purpose, which had antedated Peronism. Nevertheless, fear of the government's perceptions of charity work and possible opposition to international ties may have delayed the organization's revitalization. That CADMI adopted welfare-related duties and joined an international federation only after Perón's overthrow in September 1955 does not appear accidental. Yet Peronist social measures facilitated one of CADMI's most important initiatives: the old-age pensions inaugurated by Perón insured that senior citizens would have the leisure time to join the Club Edad de Plata.[74]

OSFA did not conduct local beneficent activities that could have impinged on government roles, as was true of the Damas and possibly CMI. Instead it helped construct another country, and these connections had begun to create problems in the late 1930s. A 1939 government decree requiring that voluntary organizations have Spanish names forced this WIZO branch to call itself OSFA and eventually change the title of its periodical from *Revista WIZO* to *OSFA*. In 1948, under Peronism, OSFA informed WIZO that it could not reissue the WIZO periodical in Argentina, as WIZO had requested, since a law forbade the publication of foreign materials.[75]

Sending aid to the new state of Israel posed the most crucial dilemma. The desperate needs of children arriving there preoccupied one OSFA member, Adela Maldavsky, who exclaimed, "We the women have to do something!" The question was how to do it. A decree of 1949 forbade collections for overseas purposes. The peso was weakening against the dollar and the Israeli pound, limiting OSFA's ability to transfer funds even under the best of circumstances. OSFA also found it difficult to send used clothing. In 1949, the government allowed individuals to ship only two parcels at a time to Israel, and travelers to include just a few boxes in their luggage.[76]

OSFA negotiated with the government to create a method that satisfied both sides. Juan Perón was courting Zionists, believing that a pro-Israeli stance could win over Argentine Jews and in particular U.S. Jews, who he thought heavily influenced their government. To improve Argentina's image, the Eva Perón Foundation aided the needy in Europe and Latin America, and Eva Perón wanted to spread such efforts to Israel. According to a high-ranking OSFA member, Berta de Gerchunoff made a deal with Evita that allowed OSFA to ship cases of goods under the Foundation's seal and government auspices, as well as continue to send aid the usual way. In its initial shipment under this agreement in 1950, OSFA inserted ten cases of used clothing into a larger Foundation donation of garments and food. In another instance, Evita permitted the organization for the first time to transmit a large quantity of new clothing. When each shipment arrived, WIZO leaders in Israel expressed gratitude to Evita and the Argentine ambassador, Pablo Manguel. During a visit to Argentina, Golda Meir, then the Israeli labor minister, personally thanked Evita for the Foundation's gifts. These performances did not hide the fact that OSFA was the source of much of the goods. The shipments continued after Evita's death.[77]

Evita made similar arrangements for other Zionist groups. Supplies for the Weizmann Institute, a medical research facility, arrived in Israel through her Foundation. So did clothing, provisions, and bed linen sent by the Comité Central de Damas Sefaradíes and the Amigas Sefaradíes de la Histadrut.[78]

Like many Argentine organizations, OSFA eulogized Evita after she died. OSFA centers and other Jewish women's groups held moments of silence or otherwise shared in public grieving for the former first lady. The OSFA executive board sent flowers to the Ministry of Labor and Social Welfare, where Evita had worked, and a telegram to the president's press office. Dedicating a page in its periodical to her memory, OSFA linked itself to Evita: both helped needy women and children, and the Zionist group had sent goods to Israel through her. It praised her for understanding and addressing Israel's problems.[79]

Rituals of appreciation of Eva Perón were political necessities, and they seemed small prices to pay for helping Israel. The administration's willingness to overlook local economic problems and nationalistic principles was noteworthy. Peronism included male Jewish leaders—whom anti-Peronists ironically perceived as almost too close to the government—and female Zionists in its populist project.[80] CMI and the Damas did not fare as well, but the Damas were treated better, and CMI no worse, than comparable non-Jewish groups, allowing them to feel they belonged in Perón's New Argentina, for better or for worse.

Did voluntarism liberate women? They often felt torn between household and outside duties. Group leaders recognized their members were "neglecting their homes" to complete their work. Only the need to alleviate communal poverty or construct a Jewish homeland could justify women's temporary crossings from the domestic to the organizational spheres. Rather than transform women's roles, activism added a new task, as OSFA's periodical realized.[81]

Nevertheless, OSFA insisted it "taught the woman her true mission, and she quickly understood that through her struggle for the liberation of her people she was attaining her own emancipation." Emancipation entailed the realization that one could accomplish what one had "never dreamed of being capable of fulfilling." Initially women doubted their ability to serve as officers and produce publications, but mutual encouragement and teamwork helped them overcome their fears. Many were equally apprehensive about public speaking and had to train themselves to give speeches in meetings and congresses.[82] Through writing, oratory, and organizing, OSFA women developed skills and self-esteem.

OSFA claimed its members no longer were "timid, humble, diminished" creatures disconnected from life outside the home. An extension of maternal caregiving, the member's work in OSFA nevertheless "demonstrated that the Jewish woman knows how to be energetic and enterprising at the same time as tender and sweet." Through OSFA, she was transforming herself into an "active element," thus "breaking the false concept that the woman is a passive factor that 'accompanies,' by inertia, her husband or brother."[83]

To spur women's liberation, female Zionists encouraged identification with Palestinian and, later, Israeli women. OSFA often pointed to these women's advances in professional and public life, as well as their entry into novel fields such as construction, agriculture, and the military. Indeed, OSFA and CMI contributed to the women's agricultural school at Afulah, which promoted nontraditional roles, although it also taught home economics. While OSFA exaggerated the extent of women's progress in Palestine and Israel, this discourse favored women's equality.[84]

Of the Jewish women's groups in Argentina, only OSFA and CMI deployed the rhetoric of liberation. CMI's use of the words "women" instead of "ladies" (*damas*), and "council" (*consejo*) instead of "society" imitated NCJW practice and suggested a desire to escape the old-fashioned gender and class connotations of philanthropy. By the late 1940s, CMI had set itself the goals of raising women's level of accomplishment and carving out for women "a preponderant place in the collectivity and its institutions,"[85] although it was unable to fulfill them.

Women opened spaces through philanthropy and Zionism, albeit not as expansively as CMI intended. The struggle of the Damas of Basavilbaso to acquire their own building, described above, symbolized their quest for autonomy. CADMI's training of women to be qualified volunteers was a pioneering activity, as was its Club Edad de Plata. Women crossed into new territory by conducting meetings, managing budgets and programs, and publicizing their efforts. The Damas, through their orphanage, and OSFA offered women the chance to administer massive fundraising campaigns and organizations. Indeed, OSFA leaders headed 32,000 women in 311 centers in 1954—the second largest WIZO federation in the world, after Israel.[86]

Leadership opportunities were few for women of any background in the communal and national arenas before 1950. Women were absent from the boards of the most important Jewish organizations. Nor could Argentine women as a whole vote until 1947, and even then they found it difficult to advance within political parties, except the Peronist women's branch and the marginalized Communist Party. Zionism and philanthropy offered Jewish women roles they were unlikely to find outside the left.

Women used their unique attributes to excel in these positions. Esther de Chami's deep familiarity with her community and ties to businessmen enabled her to mobilize and distribute resources. Judith Isaharoff's and Julieta Camji's cultural savvy and connections stretched across the Sephardi spectrum. Familiarity with the Ashkenazi milieu added to Camji's and Bruria Elnecavé's talents. Rather than simply dispense charity, Felisa Favelukes de Kohan wanted to learn more about the people she helped. This search led her to take case histories at clinics and study volunteer work in the United States before becoming president of CADMI.[87] All broke new ground for Argentine Jewish women.

Two capable women headed OSFA for many years, alternating in the presidency and imposing their very different personalities on the organization. One was Sofía Rabinovich de Nissensohn (see chapters 1 and 5), an early graduate of the prestigious Liceo de Señoritas in Buenos Aires. Married to a distinguished Zionist, she entered OSFA at its beginning and was its first vice-president. She guided the organization in its infancy, serving as president from 1927 to 1936 and again in the group's adulthood, from 1948 to 1955, holding other posts in the interval. Her education, rare among early members, helped propel her into the leadership. What kept her there, aside from ability and dedication, was her tact and delicacy. A "lady in every sense of the word," Doña Sofía governed with "her measured word, discreet gesture, and tranquil opinion."[88]

Forceful and direct, Berta de Gerchunoff was Doña Sofía's opposite. A secondary-school teacher, union member, and small business owner, Doña Berta, along with her husband, left the Socialist party and became active in the Jewish Ezrah Hospital. Her involvement in its Comisión de Damas failed to satisfy Gerchunoff, however, and after her husband died, she accepted Nissensohn's invitation to join OSFA in 1933. At times their personality differences set them apart, but these did not hurt the movement. Soon Gerchunoff became OSFA's vice-president and, between 1936 and 1948, its president, overseeing a vast expansion of members and centers. Her feminist background led her to promote women's emancipation. Doña Berta won accolades for her warmth, intelligence, versatility, and energy.[89]

Throughout her long career in OSFA, Gerchunoff moved back and forth between Jewish and non-Jewish circles. She taught until the 1940s, enjoyed friendships with fellow educators, politicians, and cultural figures, and utilized these contacts to OSFA's benefit. Traveling to other Latin American countries to create WIZO chapters, Doña Berta called upon those nations' first ladies to explain the organization's purpose. By promoting Zionism, Gerchunoff tore down barriers between Jews and non-Jews.[90]

Gerchunoff played a transnational role in Zionism. She visited all Latin American countries as WIZO's ambassador, founding WIZO centers in many of them; as director of WIZO's Latin American publicity and propaganda department, she edited and distributed publications throughout the region. WIZO President Rebecca Sieff called her the "mother, guide and leader" of the organization in Argentina and Latin America. Doña Berta regularly journeyed to Palestine and Israel, and to annual WIZO conferences and other world Zionist meetings.[91] Through these activities, and the seat she took on the WIZO executive board beginning in 1939, she helped shape women's Zionism throughout the World. Gerchunoff, Lisbeth Wind, and other colleagues created a two-way exchange between WIZO and OSFA.

Defying a gender limit that persisted into the 1950s, Gerchunoff and other OSFA members often traveled alone. They attended distant conferences and toured Argentina's interior and other countries to organize centers, deliver speeches, and inaugurate fundraising campaigns. Shortly

20. Berta de Gerchunoff (seated, center) at the Villa Crespo OSFA center, 1939. Instituto Científico Judío (IWO).

after joining the movement, in the winter of 1938, Rosa Pascaner, a future OSFA executive officer, attended the first regional congress for Entre Ríos in Basavilbaso. She needed to return to Paraná on a Sunday, when there was no direct train or bus service. The plucky young woman took a cargo train, heated only by a small brazier, to Villaguay, where she ran to catch the bus to Paraná. Pascaner arrived exhausted, but she left two days later for an OSFA congress in Buenos Aires. Elnecavé also had adventures touring South America, where some of her hosts patronized her for being Sephardi and spoke about her in Yiddish, not realizing that she understood them.[92]

Zionism and philanthropy fostered women's emancipation through self-expression as well as mobility. Women produced *Revista WIZO*, *OSFA*, and CMI's *Boletín Mensual* for a female audience. CMI's *Almanaque-Agenda*, an annotated date book that appeared for over a decade, published selections from Argentine Jewish women authors and described Jewish women's organizations and contemporary and historical figures. It communicated the message that these women were worth remembering. Another periodical that showcased women's words and skills was *Hanoar Hasefaradí*, which first appeared in 1948. The organ of the Departamento de Juventud del Centro Sionista Sefaradí, it was not published by or directed solely toward women, but it was largely Julieta Camji's creation. Having studied journalism and written for Jewish publications, Camji had the experience to manage a magazine. *Hanoar Hasefaradí* printed extracts from

Jewish writers and news clips from Israel, as well as editorials and stories of interest to Sephardi Zionists.[93]

Occasionally the beneficent societies featured intellectual discussions.[94] More consistent were CMI and Zionist efforts to educate women and expand their horizons. During the military dictatorship and Perón administration, CMI hosted many talks, usually delivered by women. OSFA centers, the Consejo Central de Damas Sefaradíes, and Naamat held numerous poetry recitations, musical performances, and presentations on Jewish history and Palestine or Israel. OSFA also offered Hebrew courses.[95]

Women's groups created spaces for speakers like Dr. Clara Schliapnik (see chapters 1, 3, and 7). Only the rise of Nazism had convinced this socialist to support a Jewish nation. Schliapnik's intellect and experience in cultural institutions led her to serve as OSFA's director of culture for Entre Ríos. Her belief that knowledge of one's heritage made one more comfortable with a Jewish identity and better equipped to confront anti-Semitism, as well as her desire to acquaint Jews with their leftist heritage, helped determine her publicist role in Zionism.[96] She continued to deliver speeches after she entered the Organización Femenina del Sionismo Obrero, or Pioneer Women, and became its president. Unlike the nonpartisan OSFA, the Pioneer Women were tied to the socialist Poale Sion party and the Histadrut. Schliapnik stressed that they worked for collectivism and gender equality in the new Jewish nation.[97]

Schliapnik and other female orators challenged the gender divide between women's practical work and male intellectual endeavors. Philanthropists and especially Zionists labored to free themselves further from subservience and domesticity, developing organizational skills, traveling, and expressing themselves in print. Their interaction with men, however, was the true indication of women's emancipation.

Contesting Male Exclusion

Negotiating with their husbands was the first step some women took toward the center. Some spouses, like Bruria Elnecavé's husband Nissim, an ardent Zionist, were supportive. He encouraged her to join OSFA, put her name on the OSFA pamphlets she produced, and travel, although when one of her trips abroad stretched beyond the scheduled time, he implored her to return. Nissim accompanied Bruria to a Latin American WIZO meeting in Brazil, where he introduced himself as her secretary. After realizing this was a joke, Bruria's fellow delegates adopted this title for their spouses. Other husbands described themselves as OSFA's chauffeurs. The organization's magazine called them the husbands of OSFA and lauded them as "these admirable men who not only sympathize with their wives' work that subtracts attention from their homes and children, but also help WIZO in every way." This statement underlined women's transgression, even as it thanked men for overlooking it. Similarly, the "husbands of CAMI" received certificates from the grateful organization. Some men, however, may never have accepted their wives' activity. Others, like Judith Isaharoff's husband, struggled to overcome their jealousy and fear of what their wives were doing.[98] Perhaps it was no accident that single women, such as Pascaner and Gerchunoff, figured prominently among OSFA leaders.

Men's groups did not always comply with requests for funds from women's groups, and when they did, they sometimes tried to wield control through financial leverage. When the male sector of La Unión disbanded in 1923 and gave its treasury to women, it also assigned them two male advisors. In the 1940s, the CIS handed money and responsibility to La Unión, at the same time instructing it on fundraising and other operations. After the Chevra Keduscha, the Ashkenazi burial society and center, awarded 25,000 pesos to the girls' orphanage in 1928, some members complained that the Asilo was insufficiently Jewish. While a visit to the facility persuaded them otherwise, it did not rid them of the notion that their grant gave them power over the Damas who ran it.[99]

Male organizations formed female branches to enlist women's aid, but sometimes curbed their influence. The president of the Servicio Sanitario Israelita of Colonia Clara, Entre Ríos, formed a female auxiliary in 1928 to raise money for a new addition to the hospital that the Servicio administered. The Servicio permitted the women to speak at meetings but not to vote.[100]

Nor did men want to share power with women. In 1930, the Damas of Buenos Aires proposed to two male organizations that they pool resources and coordinate aid to maximize efficiency. Although the male groups agreed, one of them, the Chevra Keduscha, did not fulfill its commitment.[101] The Chevra, with the largest budget of the three, did not want to relinquish funds or authority.

Men did not always welcome female criticism. The Damas of Basavilbaso provided bed linen for the local Jewish hospital and inspected it regularly. When they discovered the sheets and hospital kitchen were filthy, they considered cutting off aid. Instead they confronted the male committee that ran the hospital, which treated them rudely and refused to address the problem.[102]

The uncooperative hospital board assigned a low priority to the Damas' needs. In 1926, the Basavilbaso women requested to meet with the men to plan a fundraiser for their long-delayed building. The male committee postponed this encounter until after the Damas had organized their event, then demanded they reschedule it so the men could hold their own benefit for an X-ray machine on the same day. Then the men proposed a joint event to be held later that would give women only a third of the proceeds. The Damas stood firm and held their planned event on the original date, but partly as a peacemaking gesture they contributed money for the X-ray machine.[103]

Some men criticized OSFA for "assaulting" them for money in the streets, instead of confining their soliciting to women. In turn, OSFA officials decried the subordination of their collections to the male-run United Campaign for Israel. Nor did OSFA receive the percentage of the proceeds promised by United Campaign officials when they participated in this fundraising effort.[104]

One reason OSFA claimed it was not a traditional charity was to win male approval. Yet although it was the largest Zionist group in Argentina, OSFA received little male respect. Even when men praised OSFA, they tended to patronize it. Recognizing OSFA's advances in its first decade, *Mundo Israelita* declared in 1936 it was no longer a "timid group that once in a while held meetings to celebrate the Zionist calendar." A WIZO official observed in 1948 that OSFA had not attained the position it deserved in the Zionist arena.[105] OSFA's successful negotiations with the government suggested it enjoyed a higher status in national than in Jewish circles.

Women fought for admission into community bodies. By 1948, OSFA had placed two delegates in the Consejo Central Sionista, but it is unclear whether they had any voice or vote. It achieved a larger victory in 1952, when the Consejo seated three delegates, including Gerchunoff, who became vice-president. Five years later, Schliapnik won a seat in the DAIA as CADMI's representative. Often the lone female speaker at Sephardi Zionist affairs, Judith Isaharoff joined the board of the Organización Sionista Sefardí Argentina in 1950, but only as an honorary member.[106] Men only grudgingly and tardily accepted women's participation in these organizations.

Men gave women's groups some support but tended to oppose women's autonomy and power and subordinate female to male goals. Gender prejudice relegated many capable women to the sidelines of Jewish institutional life and deprived it of valuable talent, as Schliapnik observed.[107] As of the mid-1950s, Jewish women had not overcome this discrimination.

Conclusion

Marginalization by men was only one of the challenges that women's groups faced in 1955. Growing prosperity, new welfare policies, and declining Jewish immigration had reduced the need for charities. The decreasing Jewish population had prompted the closure of beneficent societies in the interior, where women had exercised the most influence. Schliapnik's departure from Villa Domínguez in the 1940s symbolized the migration to Buenos Aires and the resulting blow to women's organizations.[108]

It was difficult for organizations to attract younger women, even in the cities. Some professionals joined OSFA, CADMI, and other women's groups, but few had time for voluntarism. The lack of turnover in leadership positions also may have alienated potential members.[109]

Transnational ties, however, infused new life into CADMI and OSFA. These contacts helped CADMI find a purpose and OSFA expand and diversify its membership. In turn, OSFA and CADMI leaders influenced practices in global networks. The perhaps inaccurate perception that Israeli women were becoming equal to men inspired their Argentine coreligionists. Thus, Jewish women seemed poised to assume larger roles in their communities after 1955.

Community activists both reinforced and weakened borders. Some retained customary women's duties, whereas others took on new roles. Philanthropic work often fortified the class and regional markers that separated Jews. These charities were declining, however, and newer groups traversed cultural divisions. Despite their ties to the older pattern, the Damas mobilized a spectrum of Jews to support their orphanage. From the start, CMI tried to bring women of varied backgrounds under its umbrella, although it had limited success. It was primarily the Zionist organizations that helped unify Argentine Jewry, around the goal of a Jewish nation. In the process, Mediterranean women helped forge a broad new sense of Sephardi identity that superseded narrow particularisms. Female activists also began to cultivate ties with non-Jewish Argentines.

In addition, they engaged with the state. Jewish women's charities addressed needs neglected by the liberal state and contributed to civil society by creating social capital. Not always as democratic as intended, their practices sometimes mimicked the Argentine milieu instead of contesting its flaws. One exception was the Jewish Damas, who treated orphans more equally than their Catholic counterparts did. Even as Jewish women aided their communities and the nascent state of Israel, they highlighted their Argentine identities and expanded the sense of who belonged in the nation. The favorable treatment they often received from the government helped them feel a part of Argentina and demonstrated Peronist inclusiveness. While CMI's and the Damas' experiences were not as positive as those of the Zionists, the Peronist administration did not discriminate against them.

Believing that "we the women have to do something" to alleviate poverty and create a Jewish nation, Jewish women's charitable and Zionist organizations carved out niches in their communities. These spaces fostered a sense of emancipation that sometimes brought Jewish women into conflict with Jewish men. Women's struggles for respect, resources, and power had only limited success. To the extent that the wider society included women, Jewish philanthropists and Zionists won insider status while remaining outsiders in their own communities. In turn, female community activists both included and excluded poor Jewish women.

CONCLUSION

"The miracle takes place: they have become Argentines," observed Violeta Nardo de Aguirre of Ashkenazi colonists, as noted in chapter 1.[1] The conclusion of my book explores what this signified for early generations of Jewish women. It links their perceptions and experiences to the themes of borders, inclusion and exclusion, transnationalism, state formation, and race, and it analyzes their impact on the historical literature. Putting Jewish women at the center reshapes Argentine history by highlighting previously unexplored events and processes and offering new perspectives on familiar topics. It shows the power of women's history to change existing narratives.

Borders

First we turn to borders and their multiple meanings. The Argentine countryside and cities alike offered a plentitude of sites where Jewish women interacted with Jews of different origins and non-Jews. To what extent did they cross cultural boundaries, and to what extent did they remain inside them? Each woman answered these questions in her own fashion, yet all inhabited an ever-shifting cultural borderland of movement between the old and new.

There were many ways of retaining borders. Some Jewish women used their native tongue both inside and outside the household, socializing in Italian or Arabic, putting on plays in German or Yiddish. They used decorations brought from their homelands to convert their homes into ethnic enclaves. Jewish women handed down their linguistic, culinary, musical, and storytelling heritage to their children. They welcomed paisanos as boarders, fostered Jewish education, promoted sociability, and helped the poor of their communities. Some German women became more German and Jewish in their new surroundings than they had been in the old. Women were at the center of events that reproduced the communities, such as weddings, holiday meals, and matchmaking; they also reproduced leftist beliefs through cultural and educational activities. Some reinforced community borders by monitoring other women's sexual behavior.

Yet Jewish women also crossed cultural and gender borders. They learned Spanish in the streets and schools, and prostitutes became fluent in lunfardo. Adopting local customs, they held barbeques, celebrated carnival, and attended Spanish-language movies and plays. Many housewives prepared "Argentine" foods for everyday consumption and foods from their homelands for special occasions; the substitution of local for foreign ingredients, however, transformed even imported dishes. Jews absorbed Argentine gender notions of female spirituality, domesticity, and primacy in charity. Countering both local and Jewish customs, many women sought learning and some entered the professions, including unusual fields for women such as orthopedic surgery. As a doctor, Victoria Simsolo challenged the gender divide in her Sephardi community. Domestic help, support networks, and expertise acquired abroad enabled women to climb over hurdles, as did the border skills of innovation, flexibility, and adaptation. Eugenia Sacerdote, Berta de Braslavsky, and others used these skills to reinvent themselves and forge new careers.

Some women sought to tear down walls dividing Jews from Catholics and Jews from Jews. Slowly, OSFA and Jewish philanthropies reached out to non-Jewish causes. Rosa Chanovsky, Fenia Chertkoff, and Berta de Braslavsky entered the mainstream of their respective political movements, rather than remain in Ashkenazi political orbits. Even the Bursuks, however, were not completely isolated from the rest of anarchism, nor were ICUF women from the Communist Party. Jewish women of Eastern, Central, and Western European origins joined non-Jews in the Junta de la Victoria. The Sociedad de Damas Israelitas de Beneficencia included Mediterranean as well as Ashkenazi girls in its orphanage. Zionists recruited women of varied class and regional backgrounds and helped create broader Sephardi and Jewish identities.

Many women contested borders in their private lives. They questioned the confining norms of female seclusion, dowries, arranged marriages, and endogamy. Prostitutes moved back and forth between their private and professional lives, and between reputable and disreputable behavior. Adulterous and "promiscuous" women, sex workers, unwed and uncaring mothers, and women with Catholic lovers all transgressed acceptable female deportment.

So did women activists. Rebelling against notions of female passivity, Ashkenazi militants carved out new spaces for women in party and union halls, prisons, and the streets. Less overtly, Zionists also contested gender norms by organizing, traveling, and making speeches. Zionists and leftists alike challenged the division between women's practical or reproductive tasks and men's ideological leadership. Although they often resorted to maternalist rhetoric, OSFA, union members, and leftists weakened gender barriers.

Through coercion or choice, however, many women behaved conventionally. They accepted the prevailing moral code, roles within the home, and spouses from their community—sometimes picked by their parents. Even many leftist and community activists deferred to male authority and performed the usual female tasks of organizing social events, nurturing, and fundraising.

Inclusion and Exclusion

Jewish women inhabited both the margins and the center; first we will examine the former. Poverty doomed many Jewish women to shacks and tenements, little schooling, and a double or triple day, and some women to dependence on Jewish welfare institutions. Gender norms limited their access to technology and channeled them into hard manual labor, while impoverishment and family pressures thrust some women into prostitution. Poor women in outlying neighborhoods rarely tasted the delights of Buenos Aires. Many refugees from European fascism lost, at least temporarily, the bourgeois lifestyles and careers they had once enjoyed. The financial woes of some women's charities showed even their marginality; ironically, their membership and aid practices further marginalized needy Jewish women in some respects.

Jewish communities further excluded women. Customarily barred from learning, girls often had less access to education or the professions than boys. Community leaders founded a college preparatory institute to attract men to the Jewish teaching corps, but created only a normal school to train female instructors. The Jewish Colonization Association did not permit women other than widows to own land, nor did the rural cooperatives encourage female participation. The most important Jewish organizations kept women out of leadership roles throughout most of the period studied in this book. Male community activists accepted and subsidized female philanthropists and Zionists, yet also slighted and subjugated them. Expelling Communists in the early 1950s, Jewish groups shunted progressive men and women to the fringe.

Restrictive gender norms and the perception that inclusion in the nation rested on women's reputations tended to marginalize women. Many women were isolated in their homes; when they left them, some could not navigate the outside world. Keeping girls in ignorance about sexuality helped ensure their purity and submission, as well as pregnancy and exclusion if they strayed. Chaperones and arranged marriages also limited women's freedom. The image of Jewish women as sensual other objectified them; communal pageants that defined beauty in a genteel fashion communicated suspicion of sexuality, which also shackled women. Rape, abandonment, and abuse further degraded women, as did pimps' and madams' exploitation of prostitutes, although the degree of this control varied. Ezras Noschim listened to beleaguered Jewish women, secured divorces for them, and pressured derelict husbands. But the organization's insistence on propriety meant sidelining unconventional women and propping up dubious and abusive marriages.

Exclusion varied by origin. The earlier German arrivals helped yet disdained the later ones, who also felt rejected by Eastern Europeans. In the period under study, Mediterranean women often had less autonomy and education than their Ashkenazi counterparts. Perceiving them as different and backward, Ashkenazi women tended to marginalize the Sephardim and compounded this exclusion by speaking Yiddish in some organizations. Yet Ladino and Arabic speakers also were insiders in that they were less distinguishable as Jews than rusas and polacas, and hence less likely to suffer from anti-Semitism.

Before 1930, Jewish women felt prejudice, most notably during the Tragic Week of 1919. Even if not meant as insults, the common use of words like rusas underlined the women's difference. Anti-Semitism and discrimination spread after 1930, with the growth of Nacionalismo and its appeal to clerics, military officers, and ruling conservatives. Some women experienced prejudice directly, others indirectly. Anti-Semitism reached a height under the dictatorship of 1943–46, whose vision of a Catholic corporatist Argentina excluded Jews. While Jewish women responded in varied ways to the military's Catholic education project, some considered it anti-Semitic.

More insidious was the feeling that inclusion rested upon muting one's Jewishness. As long as she did not call attention to her background, a Jewish woman could become a beauty queen in Argentina, a decade before

Bess Myerson was crowned Miss America. Unlike Ana Rovner, however, Myerson did not attempt to pass as non-Jewish. Critics cast suspicion on Cipe Lincovsky's assertions of the Jewish component of her identity.

Sometimes it is difficult to say which factors—ethnic, gender, political, or others—motivated discrimination, for they were intertwined. Both her sex and her ethnicity hurt Sara Satanowsky; age and language did the same to Hedy Crilla, and poverty and politics to María Fux. In other cases, a single factor was primary. Gender norms shunted women doctors into gynecology and pediatrics, and activists to the fringes of unions and political organizations. Leftist and union credentials made some Ashkenazi women vulnerable to repression, blacklisting, and, in at least one case, the loss of children. Their respective parties restricted Braslavsky's voice and silenced Victoria Gucovsky.

While a lucky few were born or married into wealth, most Jewish women in the center had moved there from the margins. Some used political connections and Catholic mentors to enter the professions. Unique skills enabled others to circumvent discrimination or the lack of contacts. Circuitous journeys through institutions outside academe took Braslavsky and Sacerdote to the center of their disciplines. Paloma Efron's and Sara Satanowsky's combativeness helped them succeed in male-dominated fields.

Many women pushed their way out of poverty, the home, and the brothel. They overcame unwilling parents and the lack of resources to acquire some education. Some girls and mothers established school cooperatives to feed and equip impoverished pupils. Others evaded limits on their sexuality and created marriages that were partnerships. Prostitutes tried to assert control over their bodies and earnings, sometimes managing to finance a reentry into respectable life. Escaping household routines, women entered labor, political, and community groups. Thus the masses of Jewish women attained a degree of inclusion.

Ashkenazi activists fought for a more pluralistic society. Leftist and union militants agitated for women, workers, and other marginalized people. Through human-rights groups, they worked for a polity that accepted a full range of opinion. Contesting anti-Semitism, Ashkenazi women participated in a variety of antifascist groups and helped men in Villaguay prepare against anticipated attack.

Jewish philanthropists and Zionists struggled for acceptance in the Jewish and Argentine arenas. Philanthropy made Jewish women respectable; charitable organizations, as well as Zionist ones, attained recognition from the government and the society at large. Faring as well as, or better than, other female groups, Jewish women's associations were on the inside track in the larger society. Although they had won limited representation in Jewish umbrella organizations by the mid-1950s, female activists were still on the margins of their communities.

In many respects, the larger society had included Jewish women by the mid-1950s. They had achieved stature in education, the liberal professions, entertainment, and voluntarism. In Argentina, unlike in the United States, universities did not have quotas for Jews, and hotels and neighborhoods were not segregated. Neither Peronists nor the old elite, however, accepted Jewish or other leftists. Moreover, many Jews perceived an undercurrent of anti-Semitism that the Peronist administration had not completely repressed. In this sense, Jewish women still were outsiders.

Leftists, unionists, Zionists, and—to a limited extent—CMI members worked for what they called women's emancipation. Militants linked it to the creation of socialism, and Zionists to the creation of a Jewish nation. For both, women's liberation mainly signified expanding one's horizons, cultivating skills and confidence, and participating in broader struggles outside the home. Rosa Scheiner, Flora Absatz, and Clara Schliapnik were among the few who publicly—and largely unsuccessfully—criticized male privilege and the gendered assignment of roles.

State Formation

Through a myriad of quotidian practices, Jewish women tied themselves to their adopted land. The very creation of hybrid identities signified a connection to the nation. So did reading Spanish-language texts, attending public schools, and migrating alongside other Argentines to large cities in search of higher education. Marriage, childbearing, and celebrations of rites of passage demonstrated Argentine roots and faith in an Argentine future, as did participating in independence-day festivities, dancing the pericón, and becoming citizens. In these performances, Jewish women claimed the gaucho, Argentine flag, and other local symbols as their own, thereby expanding constructions of the nation to include their communities. The beauty queen Ana Rovner even became a symbol of Argentine identity. The struggle for a Jewish homeland made its proponents similar to locals of Italian and Spanish descent who helped their countries of origin, and hence made the Jews more Argentine.

Many Jews believed that the existence of secure spaces for them in

Argentina hinged on the respectability of Jewish women and families. Therefore the Ashkenazi elite tried to ensure propriety, particularly among working-class Jews. Yet the attention given to such issues may have had the unintended consequence of further conflating Jews with prostitution.

Some Jewish women obtained government recognition. They received subsidies for midwifery studies, philanthropy, and rural libraries, and OSFA, Naamat, and the Consejo Central de Damas Sefaradíes won concessions from the Peróns. Politicians helped some Jewish women enter normal schools and obtain teaching positions. These experiences reaffirmed Jewish women's sense of belonging in Argentina.

Many Jewish women had an abiding relationship with liberalism. They appreciated its support for mass secular education, the basic freedoms, immigration, voluntarism, individual upward mobility, and mild feminism. Heeding Sarmiento's call for women to mold young minds and improve the nation, aspiring teachers absorbed liberalism in normal school. By choosing their spouses and seeking learning, many Jewish women identified with a liberal Argentina. Some also accepted racist precepts of the liberal project. Liberalism was changing: by the early 1900s, leading liberals were becoming less cosmopolitan and egalitarian, as evident in education. Rosa de Ziperovich and other female Jewish teachers contested this shift, stretching liberalism much further than its Argentine founders had intended. By meeting the needs of the Jewish poor that the liberal state did not address, Jewish philanthropists also expanded liberal pluralism. Political and community activists sought to deepen liberal democracy by creating social capital.

Like Ziperovich, other leftists appropriated and reworked liberalism. Fenia Chertkoff enhanced the secularism and inclusiveness of the liberal education program. In the 1930s, Braslavsky and other leftist intellectuals linked themselves to liberalism to demonstrate their homegrown revolutionary roots. Yet all contested liberal socioeconomic ideas by demanding social justice.

Leftist women of Ashkenazi origin helped construct national projects that rested on proletarian solidarity. Female militants supported labor control of production, a healthy and respectful workplace, equality between men and women, popular access to culture and education, and, in general, human dignity and freedom. By the 1930s, this list included ending war, imperialism, and human-rights violations.

From the 1930s on, new projects emerged and battled for hegemony. The first was Nacionalismo, whose Catholic authoritarian vision of Argentina excluded Jews and marginalized women. Jewish women's assertions of Argentine identity in the 1930s and 1940s contested Nacionalista nativism, as did philanthropists' aid to immigrants. Their activism in antifascist groups and support for women's rights challenged Nacionalista notions of women as passive homemakers. Through this involvement, Jewish women insisted they were part of the nation.

While Perón inherited some of the Nacionalistas' ideas, such as anti-Communism and a reluctance to admit Jews into the country, he proved to be malleable and pluralistic. Juan and Evita Perón envisioned an Argentina that encompassed immigrants and non-Catholics. They included Zionists but excluded leftists—both Jewish and non-Jewish—who contested the Peronist benefactor state.

Some Jewish women never engaged with the state. The refugee women who returned to their native Italy after 1945 did not cast roots in their temporary shelter. At home neither in their old or new settings, some German Jewish women considered themselves citizens of the world rather than of Argentina. The regimented patriotism and Catholic education classes in schools may have numbed some Jewish women students into indifference. Other Jewish women were too restricted to their home or fearful to participate in any form of politics.

Transnationalism

Many Jewish women engaged in transnational exchanges. Global economic forces conditioned their journeys and choices, as did the rise of Communism, fascism, Zionism, and other "isms" and the liberalization of sexual mores on both sides of the Atlantic. In the sex trade, women, capital, and management techniques circulated among countries.

Influenced by experiences in their homelands and events in Europe and Argentina, many Jewish women of varied ideologies and origins attempted to construct a more equitable and peaceful world. They linked fascist advances overseas with those at home and helped launch transnational struggles against them. These women used the campaigns for Spanish Republicans and the Allies to strike out against anti-Semitic rightists in Europe and Argentina, situate themselves among local democratic forces, and further women's liberation at home and abroad. Particularly influential in antifascist groups, the Communist Party was itself transnational. ICUF members continued working for world peace in the cold war era.

Zionist and charitable groups engaged in transnational reciprocity with global organizations. WIZO was vital in creating and stimulating OSFA, which in turn supplied WIZO with funds and talented leaders like Lisbeth Wind and Berta de Gerchunoff, who served as intermediary between Latin American and world Zionism. The National Council of Jewish Women nourished what was eventually known as CAMI, which from the mid-1950s on furnished officers for the International Council of Jewish Women and furthered its understanding of Latin America.

Several Ashkenazi women conducted cultural exchanges across borders. Isa Kremer, Berta Singerman, and Cipe Lincovsky performed in many countries, acquiring in each one additions to their repertoires. Singerman carried poetry and messages of social justice across boundaries, serving as a bridge between Spanish-speaking countries and between them and Brazil.

Race

The study of Jewish women contributes to the incipient debate on whiteness in Argentina. The tolerance that characterized most daily encounters, especially before 1930, suggests that Jews largely fit within the white category. So did notions of Jewish women's light-skinned beauty, as epitomized by Golde Flami and Ana Rovner. A spectrum of Jewish women, ranging from colonists to prostitutes, claimed whiteness by setting themselves apart from criollos. Distinguishing herself from a black Miss South America, Rovner insisted she would whiten the continent's image. Ziperovich rejected such tactics, however, when she fought discrimination against dark-skinned pupils.

Rovner's remarks seemed defensive, hinting that Jews feared they were not white. Hers was not the only image of Jewish beauty that asserted claims to whiteness and refinement. Journalistic comments on Cipe Lincovsky's African or gypsy appearance indicated that Jewish fears were not unreasonable. So, too, did the fact that some public figures associated Jews with blacks and Asians, all deemed unacceptable immigrants on apparently racial grounds. Characterizing Jews as undesirable, Nacionalistas racialized Jewish men in anti-Semitic cartoons. Unperturbed about possible perceptions, however, Efron popularized jazz, socialized and studied with African Americans, and invited them to Buenos Aires.

The Argentine racial hierarchy and Jews' places in it remain opaque. In some instances, Jewish women were seen as white, in others possibly not. Their experiences complicate the notion that Argentines consistently have regarded all European and Mediterranean immigrants as white. Oscar Chamosa points out how, over time, some indigenous Argentines were whitened into criollos.[2] Evolving racial constructions of European immigrants are also worthy of study.

Argentine History

The theme of race suggests how Jewish women's experiences recast Argentine history. Another area for revision is the coverage of Argentine Jews. Focusing on men, previous studies have concentrated on community organizations and politics, the Ashkenazi-Sephardi divide, relations with the broader polity, anti-Semitism, and entry into the middle class. The insertion of women shifts the focus from institutions and discourses to the daily lives of multifaceted individuals. It shows that the processes of inclusion and exclusion were more complex than the simple dichotomy of anti-Semitism and acceptance. Spousal abandonment of women, their exploitation as workers, and their need for charity prove that upward mobility was not easy or inevitable. That many Mediterranean women worked for wages, established early charities, and participated in Zionism indicates that Sephardim differed less from Ashkenazim than some have thought. The study of Jewish women further undermines the Ashkenazi-Sephardi binary by highlighting those who fit in neither category in Argentina, such as German speakers. Works on Jewish "gauchos" have tended to idealize their relationships with criollos; focusing on Jewish women shows that one should not romanticize these contacts. Finally, the absence of women from most historical works on Argentine Jewry has suggested that they were bystanders, an impression dispelled by this book.

How typical were Jewish women? The greater residential segregation of Jewish porteñas is one way they differed from other Argentine women. In the early years, foreign-born female Jews were less literate than other female immigrants, yet their daughters closed the gap. By the 1960s, a smaller percentage of Argentine Jewish women than of Argentine women as a whole participated in the labor force, yet those Jews who did so were more likely to occupy professional and white-collar positions. Indeed, Russian Jews were overrepresented among pioneering female physicians in Argentina. Ashkenazi women also may have been disproportionately involved in Communism and the Junta de la Victoria. The stigma of prostitution affected Jews more than women of other backgrounds.

In other respects, Jewish women seem to have resembled their non-Jewish peers. Jewish and other women of immigrant descent were excluded from landownership and full participation in community institutions. Leftist movements, antifascist campaigns, charities, and other voluntary associations attracted diverse non-Jewish women, yet we know little about their experiences. Christian women entering the professions also must have confronted barriers; whether these were comparable to those faced by Jews is unknown. Nor is it clear if other groups of women felt the same tension as both insiders and outsiders. One hopes this book will stimulate research on women of varied origins and facilitate comparisons between them.

Inserting Jewish women helps revise long-held notions of Argentine politics.[3] This work adds to the recent literature showing that the local political culture consisted of more than electoral practices, deal making between male politicians, and violence. It highlights how women helped construct the political culture long before they won the vote. In classrooms and teacher organizations, female educators interpreted, reshaped, and spread political ideas. Through their voluntary associations, both partisan and nonpartisan, Jewish and other women forged social networks, established trust, debated issues, worked on civic projects, and set up norms of governance that enhanced the country's democratic potential. Neither beneficent societies nor leftist-tinged groups like the Junta de la Victoria, however, fully democratized the polity, as was also the case with nineteenth-century Latin American civic organizations.[4] Female militants strengthened leftist movements by encouraging sociability, disseminating culture, integrating the youth, organizing solidarity, and coping with fear. Such activities indicate how people at the grass-roots level lived as Communists, Socialists, and anarchists, and how they formed leftist identities.

Ashkenazi women's involvement provides insight into leftist movements. Their presence in leftist circles in the interior demonstrates that these groups were found throughout the nation, not just in Buenos Aires. Women's lively activism shows that Socialism and anarchism lasted past 1930, although few studies of these political forces go beyond that year. Participation by women of Jewish origin calls attention to the dynamic radical wing of the Socialist party. The Communist presence in schools, unions, and antifascism underlines this party's pivotal role in the 1930s and 1940s, and not only in Argentina.[5] Ashkenazi Socialist and Communist women's involvement also points to global peace campaigns and, therefore, "conversations that different groups of women maintained across national boundaries."[6]

One should note that women of Jewish descent continued to participate in leftist and human-rights movements after 1955, in such groups as the Ejército Revolucionario del Pueblo and Madres de la Plaza de Mayo. Two of the women I interviewed for this study, Perla Wasserman and Clara Gertel, were Madres. While there is a large literature on such movements, scholars have not focused specifically on the participation of women of Jewish origin.

Centering on Jewish women illustrates the ongoing construction and transformation of the liberal project. The liberal elite may have imposed its worldview from above, but many Jewish women—and probably a wide range of other Argentines—adapted this hegemonic project to fit their lives. This process continued into the 1930s and 1940s, when the ruling conservatives lent support to the Roman Catholic Church, and Nacionalistas attacked the foundations of liberalism. Aspects of the besieged liberal program now seemed almost radical, and as such leftists absorbed them. Jewish women's appropriation and contestation of liberalism demonstrate that it was not static, and different versions existed simultaneously.[7] How other ordinary Argentines engaged with liberalism deserves scholarly attention.

Female Zionists' encounters with Peronism demonstrate its inclusiveness. This government's concessions to OSFA fit within a larger pattern of accommodating Zionism, suggesting the government's desire not only for good relations with Jews, Israel, and the United States, but also for the incorporation of all Argentines into the polity. Further research is needed to understand the relations between other immigrant communities and Peronism, as well as its pluralistic model of nationhood.

Historians, including this author, have tended to identify Argentine nationalism with its most strident proponents, the Nacionalistas. The cosmopolitan and democratic forms constructed by many Jewish women, however, indicate that nationalism was not confined to radical rightists. Scholars should examine how other Argentines at the grass-roots level manifested nationalist sentiments in the twentieth century.[8]

Conclusion

The lives and choices of Jewish female immigrants, their daughters, and their granddaughters demonstrate the many ways they became Argentine. They crossed, contested, and retained borders and chose whether or not to engage with the state. While carving out spaces in the nation, some of the women participated in transnational causes and exchanges. We have learned not only about women but also about their often unequal relations with men. The women were both insiders and outsiders. Some of their experiences fit within and alter our understanding of old frameworks, while others suggest the need for new frameworks.

But this summary does not do them justice. The themes of this study do not completely encompass the pathos and joy, bitterness and resignation, and defeat and triumph expressed in the stories of Argentine Jewish women. The power of their thoughts, dreams, experiences, and memories transcends the boundaries of this book.

APPENDIX

Available statistics on Argentine Jews are limited and incomplete, although they suggest some patterns.[1] Official censuses have included only professed Jews, omitting unbelievers and those reluctant to divulge their identity. Focusing on Jews registered with community institutions, other studies overlook the many people who were unaffiliated. Demographers have disagreed over Jewish population figures and found fault with census results.[2]

It is difficult to compare Jews with other immigrant groups, as Jews include the native- and foreign-born, whereas the census categories of Spaniards and other groups include only the foreign-born. Nor can one conflate Russians with Jews, even in the early years of Jewish settlement, as some Russians were Christians, and of course some Jews were not Russian. Nevertheless, to compensate for holes in the data, I offer here some tables on women by nationality.

The censuses provide only limited information on Jews. Of those within the approximate years under study in this book, the national censuses of 1895, 1947, and 1960 and the Buenos Aires municipal censuses of 1909 and 1936 specified Jews as a category. These national censuses indicated Jewish population solely by location; that of 1895 broke this population down by sex and foreign- versus native-born, while those of 1947 and 1960 did not. The municipal census of 1909 provided the population of Jewish men and women by neighborhood and divided Jews into native- and foreign-born. Along with the indicators studied in the 1909 census, the 1936 Buenos Aires census correlated religion with birthplace, and literacy with sex, age, religion and nationality.

Notes

1. Elkin (*The Jews*, 192, and 194–95) also discusses statistical limitations.

2. Rosenwaike, "The Jewish Population of Argentina"; Schmeltz and Dellapergola, "The Demography of Latin American Jewry"; and S. Weill, *Estudios*.

TABLE 1. Jewish Agricultural Population

Year	Population in Colonies	Percent of Total Jewish Population
1895	5,000	82
1904	9,126	NA
1920	27,096	21
1925	33,135	20
1934/35[a]	25,796	12

Sources: Rosenwaike, "The Jewish Population of Argentina," 197 and 204; Argentina, Comisión Directiva del Censo, *Segundo censo*, 2:36; and Schmeltz and Dellapergola, "The Demography of Latin American Jewry," 65.

[a] The Jewish population in the colonies in 1934 equaled about 12 percent of the total Jewish population in 1935.

TABLE 2. Literacy Rates for Women over Six Years Old, by Origin, 1914

Origin	Percent Literate
Argentine	59.8
Austro-Hungarian	59.7
German	85.9
Italian	52.4
Ottoman	19.0
Russian	48.2
Spanish	55.3
All foreign-born	55.6
Total female population	58.5

Source: Argentina, Comisión Nacional del Censo, *Tercer censo*, 3:329.

TABLE 3. Origins of Families Registered in Mediterranean Jewish Communities in Buenos Aires, 1960

Origin	Percent of Registered Families
Moroccan descent	4.2
Ladino speakers	35.5
Aleppine descent	28.7
Damascene descent	31.6

Source: Margalit Bejarano, "Los sefaradíes en la Argentina: Particularismo étnico frente a tendencias de unificación," *Revista Rumbos*, nos. 17–18 (1986): 146, cited in Epstein, "Aspectos generales de la inmigración," 159.

TABLE 4. Foreign-Born Jewish Population in Buenos Aires by Birthplace, 1936 (selected countries)

Birthplace	Total Jews	Jewish Women
Eastern Europe		
Latvia	202	89
Lithuania	1,056	532
Poland	31,172	14,168
Romania	5,175	2,602
Russia	23,171	11,309
Southeastern Europe		
Bulgaria	164	79
Greece	175	83
Italy	330	142
Turkey	2,978	1,459
Yugoslavia	42	12
Central Europe		
Austria	1,092	522
Czechoslovakia	203	71
Germany	1,376	534
Hungary	499	226
Switzerland	44	18

(continued on next page)

TABLE 4. *(continued)*

Birthplace	Total Jews	Jewish Women
Western Europe		
France	261	144
Great Britain	289	147
Spain	179	91
Middle East and North Africa		
Arabia	23	14
Egypt	181	88
Iran	31	16
Morocco	195	86
Palestine	388	176
Syria-Lebanon	3,408	1,564
Tanger	24	15

Source: Argentina, Municipalidad de Buenos Aires, *Cuarto censo*, 3:310–23.

TABLE 5. Jewish Population in Argentina, by Province and Territory

Province/Territory	1895	1909	1936	1947[a]
Federal Capital	753	16,589	120,195	166,190
Buenos Aires	670			32,725
Catamarca	0			157
Chaco	0			2,744
Chubut	0			94
Comodoro Rivadavia[b]	NA			122
Córdoba	47			5,925
Corrientes	0			1,377
Entre Ríos	3,880			11,876
Formosa	0			334
Jujuy	1			122
La Pampa	5			1,408
La Rioja	0			170
Mendoza	2			2,439
Misiones	0			579

TABLE 5. *(continued)*

Province / Territory	1895	1909	1936	1947[a]
Neuquén	0			237
Río Negro	2			718
Salta	0			629
San Juan	0			909
San Luis	1			218
Santa Cruz	1			51
Santa Fe	721			16,724
Santiago del Estero	1			781
Tierra del Fuego	0			14
Tucumán	1			2,787
Total	6,085			249,330

Sources: Argentina, Comisión Directiva del Censo, *Segundo censo*, 2: clxxix; Argentina, Buenos Aires, Dirección General de Estadística Municipal, *Censo general*. . . 1909, 1: 88-93; Argentina, Municipalidad de Buenos Aires, *Cuarto censo*, 3: 294-95; Argentina, Presidencia de la Nación, Ministerio de Asuntos Técnicos, *Cuarto censo*, 1: 20.

Note: The 1909 and 1936 censuses are for the Federal Capital and do not supply numbers for the rest of the country. The censuses of 1895 and 1947 are national ones.

[a] I. Horowitz ("The Jewish Community of Buenos Aires," 200) finds the 1947 figures low. Schmeltz and Dellapergola ("The Demography of Latin American Jewry," 65) agree, estimating the total Jewish population at 286,000. Argentina, Dirección Nacional de Estadística y Censos (*Censo nacional de población 1960*, 112–13) provides figures only for Jews five years of age and older.
[b] Not listed in the 1895 census.

TABLE 6. Percent of Women in the Labor Force by Age, in Greater Buenos Aires, 1960

Age	Percent All Women	Percent Jewish Women
14–19	34.6	24.7
20–29	43.4	38.8
30–44	27.2	20.3
45–64	16.7	12.7
65 +	5.1	4.8
All ages	26.4	19.9

Source: Adapted from Syrquin, "The Economic Structure of Jews," 125.

TABLE 7. Percent of Jewish Women Age Fourteen and Older in the Labor Force by Birthplace, in Greater Buenos Aires, 1960

Birthplace	Percent
Argentina	26.4
Americas and Western Europe	16.7
Eastern Europe	10.9
Asia and Africa	7.0

Source: Syrquin, "The Economic Structure of Jews," 126.

TABLE 8. Literacy Rate for Women by Age and Origin, in Buenos Aires, 1936

	Jewish[a] (%)			French	Italian	Spanish	Argentine
Age	*Foreign*	*Native*	*Total*	(%)	(%)	(%)	(%)
15–19	99	99	99	100	98	98	99
20–24	97	100	98	100	95	95	98
25–29	94	100	96	99	92	92	98
30–34	91	99	92	99	89	88	97
35–39	83	96	84	99	82	85	96
40–44	75	98	76	98	77	80	95
45–49	66	90	66	97	72	76	94
50–54	59	86	59	97	70	71	93
55–59	53	25	53	97	66	67	93
60–64	47	100	47	97	61	63	92
65 +	38	50	38	91	53	58	89

Source: Argentina, Municipalidad de Buenos Aires, *Cuarto censo*, 2:294–95 and 306–27, and 3:242–47.

[a] The category Jewish includes all origins; the other categories include Jews.

TABLE 9. Literacy Rates for Women Age Fifteen and Older, in Buenos Aires, 1936

	Percent of All Women	Percent of Jewish Women
Native born	97	99
Foreign born	80	79
Total	90	84

Source: Argentina, Municipalidad de Buenos Aires, *Cuarto censo*, 2:298 and 3:244–47.

TABLE 10. Occupational Distribution of Women in the Labor Force Age Fourteen and Older, 1960

Occupation	Percent of All Working Women	Percent of Jewish Working Women
Clerical	14.60	24.20
Commerce	7.30	21.80
Executives and Administrators	.80	2.30
Factory and Craft Workers	22.40	14.10
Farmers, Fishermen, Hunters, Loggers, and Miners	4.30	.02
Professionals and Technicians	16.30	20.00
Service, Sport, and Recreation	26.40	8.50
Transportation and Communication	.02	.02
Unclassified	7.70	8.70

Sources: Elkin, *Jews*, 151; Argentina, Dirección Nacional de Estadística y Censos, *Censo . . . 1960*, 1: 103.

Note: Totals do not equal 100 percent because of rounding.

NOTES

Introduction

1. Jeffrey Lesser, personal communications; and Anderson, *Imagined Communities*.

2. Barrancos ("Historia") does not mention works on immigrant women in Argentina per se. Stolen (*The Decency of Inequality*), Gandolfo ("Del Alto Molise"), and Frid de Silberstein ("Immigrants and Female Work") discuss female immigrants. Most of the women studied by Lobato ("Women Workers") were immigrants.

3. Morris, *Odyssey of Exile*; and Jurkowicz de Eichbaum, *Cuando las mujeres*. Short works and articles on Jewish women's history include Blank (*La mujer judía*), Guy ("Women's Organizations"), Y. Levin ("Posturas genéricas"), and Deutsch ("Changing the Landscape" and "Women"). Portions of the last two articles, in different form and to make different points, are scattered throughout this book.

4. Elkin inserted women in *The Jews*, but the few secondary sources prevented her from elaborating on the topic.

5. Rein, "Together yet Apart," 3. Guy's *Sex and Danger* is the key work on prostitution. Chapter 4 below discusses the historiography.

6. On nonprostitutes' sexuality, see Caulfield (*In Defense of Honor*), Rebhun (*The Heart Is Unknown Country*), Barrancos ("Moral sexual"), Tinsman ("Good Wives" and *Partners in Conflict*), and Cosse ("Cultura y sexualidad").

7. As Argentines did not use the word "Mizrahim" during the years studied, I do not use it either.

8. "A Jew is a descendant of Jews," quoted by Guber ("Identidad cultural," 78).

9. Gilman, *Love*, 184–92.

10. Lesser and Rein ("New Approaches") note that Jews unaffiliated with the community are still Jews and should be studied as such.

11. Hall, "Ethnicity."

12. Ibid.; Clifford, *The Predicament of Culture*, especially 277–346; Antler, *The Journey Home*; and Schneider, *Futures Lost*. Schneider includes persons who did not declare themselves to be Italo-Argentine (ibid., 35).

13. See, for example, "Gender and Sexuality in Latin America." Yet Scott (*Gender and the Politics of History*, especially 22–27) sees gender history as part of women's history.

14. Deutsch, "Visible," *Counterrevolution*, "Gender," "What Difference," *Las derechas*, and "Los nacionalistas."

15. Levins Morales, *Medicine Stories*, 26–27; Sklar, "Considering," 148. Also see Boxer (*When Women Ask the Questions*, especially 144–46).

16. Staudt and Spener, "The View from the Frontier"; Sánchez, *Becoming Mexican American*, 9; Vila, *Crossing Borders*; Martínez, *Border People*; Anzaldúa, *Borderlands*; and Stephen, *Transborder Lives*.

17. Staudt and Spener, "The View from the Frontier," 6. Gilman (*Jewish*, 1–31) applies border and center-periphery notions to Jewish studies without discussing women.

18. Guy, "Parents Before the Tribunals."

19. Biale, Galchinsky, and Heschel (Introduction, 5) note that Jews often have occupied the margins and center. I extend this analysis to women. Wenger ("Jewish Women of the Club," 333) concludes that Atlanta's Jewish clubwomen were both integrated into and marginal to the larger society.

20. Quote in Schiller, Basch, and Blanc-Szanton, "Towards a Definition of Transnationalism," ix; Topp, *Those Without Country*; and Tyrell, "American Exceptionalism"; and personal communications from Cheryl Martin, Margaret Power, Kathleen Staudt, and Barbara Weinstein.

21. Joseph and Nugent, *Everyday Forms of State Formation*; Applebaum, Macpherson, and Rosemblatt, *Race and Nation*; Johnson, "Engendering Nation"; Vaughan, *Cultural Politics in Revolution*; and Beezley, French, and Martin, *Rituals of Rule*.

22. Molyneux, "Twentieth-Century State Formation," 43. Pioneering works include Guy ("'White Slavery'"), Dore and Molyneux (*Hidden Histories*), and Vaughan (*Cultural Politics in Revolution*).

23. Prell (*Fighting to Become Americans*) prompted some of these thoughts.

24. Biale, Galchinsky, and Heschel, Introduction, 5; and Jaher, *The Jews and the Nation*.

25. On liberalism, see Nállim, "Conflictive Legitimacies," "The Crisis of Liberalism," and "Del antifascismo al antiperonismo"; Halperín Donghi, "¿Para qué la inmigración?"; Escudé, *El fracaso del proyecto argentino*; Shumway, *The Invention of Argentina*; Botana, *El orden conservador*; Plotkin, *Mañana es San Perón*, especially chapter 1; Bushnell, *Reform and Reaction*; Guy, *Performing Charity*; Criscenti, *Sarmiento and His Argentina*; Halperín Donghi et al., *Sarmiento*; Senkman, "Nacionalismo e inmigración"; and Sábato, *The Many and the Few*.

26. Putnam, "Bowling Alone." On Latin American voluntarism, see Gutiérrez and Romero (*Sectores populares*) and Forment (*Civic Selfhood*). Moya ("A Continent of Immigrants," 27–28) attributes Argentine voluntarism largely to immigrants.

Ogilvie ("How Does Social Capital Affect Women?") claims that social capital hurt women, yet she studied male-controlled organizations, unlike many of the ones I examine.

27. Exceptions to these historians are Nállim ("The Crisis of Liberalism") and Plotkin (*Mañana es San Perón*). Guerin-Gonzales (*Mexican Workers and American Dreams*) influenced my view of the liberal promise. Kirkendall (*Classmates*) examines how generations of male law students redefined liberalism.

28. On rightism and Peronism, see note 14 and Rock (*Authoritarian Argentina*), Buchrucker (*Nacionalismo y peronismo*), Lvovich (*Nacionalismo*), Zanatta (*Del estado* and *Perón*), Finchelstein (*Fascismo*), Spektorowski (*The Origins*), Torre (*Los años peronistas*), and Plotkin (*Mañana es San Perón*).

29. Rein, *Argentina, Israel, and the Jews*; and Bell, "In the Name of the Community" and "Bitter Conquest."

30. One exception is Delaney ("Imagining *El Ser Argentino*"). For the 1800s, see Bertoni (*Patriotas, cosmopolitas y nacionalistas*).

31. Roediger, *Working toward Whiteness*; and Jacobson, *Whiteness of a Different Color*.

32. Lesser, *Negotiating National Identity*.

33. Chamosa, "Indigenous or Criollo"; Andrews, *The Afro-Argentines*; Grimson, "Ethnic (In)Visibility"; Quijada, Bernard, and Schneider, *Homogeneidad y nación*; and Rotker, *Captive Women*, especially 20–22.

34. Moya, "A Continent of Immigrants," 20.

35. See the appendix.

36. Quote in Parush, *Reading Jewish Women*, xiv. Also see Heilbrun (*Writing a Woman's Life*, 24 and 64) and M. Kaplan ("Tradition and Transition," 204).

37. T. Kaplan, *Taking Back the Streets*, 181; and James, "Tales Told."

38. See especially Gluck and Patai (*Women's Words*); also see Farnsworth-Alvear (*Dulcinea in the Factory*, 204). However, Rose ("Gender History/Women's History," 91) and other historians advocate accepting and trusting the stories of minority women.

39. Farnsworth-Alvear, *Dulcinea in the Factory*, 236–37.

40. James, "Tales Told," 35; French and James, "Oral History," 298; and Tinsman, *Partners in Conflict*, 16–17.

41. Hunt, "The Objects of History," 542–46; Parush, *Reading Jewish Women*, 10); and Leo Spitzer, personal communication.

42. See Stanchina (*Tanka Charowa*) and Schalom (*La polaca*).

43. Conversations with Rachel Hollander, Mischa Klein, Nancy Nemeth-Jesurun, Thomas Orum, Beth Pollack, and especially Yael Halevi-Wise enriched my understanding of the use of fiction, as did Owensby (*Intimate Ironies*).

44. Anderson (*Imagined Communities*) highlights the importance of reading in constructing a nation.

ONE *Jewish Women in the Countryside*

Epigraph sources: Bela Trumper de Kaller, quoted by Kaller de Gutman, interview, 1989, AP; Nardo de Aguirre, "Canto a la Colonización Judía," 75 *aniversario*, n.p.

1. Kaller de Gutman, interview, 1989, AP.

2. Alpersohn, *Colonia Mauricio*, 23 and 208 (quote).

3. See especially Gerchunoff (*The Jewish Gauchos*). Also see Senkman (*La identidad judía*, 62–68) and Kreimberg, interview, 1991, AP. Former colonists attend anniversaries of their colony's founding, and those living in Israel gather there.

4. Maldavsky, "Raíces" (quote) and her 1998 interview with author.

5. Elkin, *The Jews*, 54–55.

6. Argentine Jews generally distinguish between "Ashkenazim," or Eastern European Yiddish speakers, and "Central European" Germans, Austrians, Czechs, and Hungarians.

7. Rosenwaike, "The Jewish Population of Argentina," 204; *Mundo Israelita*, 31 March 1928, 4; Schmeltz and Dellapergola, "The Demography of Latin American Jewry," 65; E. Levin, *Historias de una emigración*, 63; and Schwarcz, *Y a pesar de todo*, 179–89.

8. Brodsky, "The Contours of Identity," 30–36, and personal communication; Mayo, interview with author, 2000; Mirelman, "Sephardic Immigration," 22–23 and 28; Epstein, "Aspectos generales de la inmigración," 162–65 (statistic on 162); *Presencia sefaradí* (44 and 55).

9. Epstein, "Maestros marroquíes"; and Mirelman, "Sephardic Immigration," 20–21. On the AIU, see Rodrigue (*Images of Sephardic and Eastern Jewries*, especially 34, 49–50, and 80–93), G. Weill ("The Alliance Israélite Universelle"), and Laskier ("Aspects of the Activities").

10. Guy, "Women, Peonage, and Industrialization"; statistics in Hollander, "Women in the Political Economy of Argentina," 52 and 56.

11. On Italo-Argentine farm women, see Stolen (*The Decency of Inequality*, 55, 66, and 190–91). On rural U.S. Jewish women, see Calof (*Rachel Calof's Story*) and Schloff ("'We Dug More Rocks,'" 92–93). Little is known about Jewish female agriculturalists in Bolivia, Brazil, the Dominican Republic, and Uruguay. Spitzer (*Hotel Bolivia*, 131) mentions a Jewish woman poultry farmer in Bolivia.

12. *Tierra de promesas*, 48–49; Serie Colonias Administración, Archivo Samuel Kogan, Carpeta 9, Subserie "Administración JCA," "Informe especial sobre los colonos instalados entre 1935–1940," Montefiore, 28 January 1941, MHRC; Alpersohn, *Colonia Mauricio*, 209; Zimerman de Faingold, *Memorias*, 7–8, and 11; Gutkowski, *Rescate de la herencia cultural*, 64, 67, 176, and 184; Frank (2000) and Schvartz de Pitasni (1997), interviews with author; Caplan (1989), Koval Magrán (1989), Voloshin de Lisnofsky (1989), Kaller de Gutman (1989), Grimberg and Trumper (1989), Ojberg de Aisicovich (1989), Sichel (1996), and Fuks (n.d.), interviews, AP;

Escliar, *Mujeres en la literatura*, 26 and 36–37; and I. Katz, *De raíces y sitios*, 236, 238. Guy ("The Economics of Womanhood") finds that many Arizona widows worked and homesteaded. Other contributors to Scadron (*On Their Own*) and to Kertzer and Laslett (*Aging in the Past*), however, note widows' dependence on children and charities.

13. Movimiento, "*Pioneros*," 136–138 (quote on 137); and sources in note 14.

14. Bortnik de Duchovny, *Recuerdos*, 15–18; Caplan, interview, 1989, AP; *Jewish Chronicle*, 23 January 1903, 23; *El Campo*, 20 May 1928, 3 and 6; and Y. Levin, "Posturas genéricas," 52–55.

15. Epstein, "Maestros marroquíes," 357.

16. Wolf, interview with author, 1998; "Los pesares"; Fuks, interview, n.d., AP; Frank, interview with author, 2000; Sichel, interview (1996), AP; and I. Katz, *De raíces y sitios*, 231–32, and 235.

17. Fuks, interview, n.d., AP; I. Katz, *De raíces y sitios*, 266–71; and Sauer, interview, 1997, AP.

18. Italo-Argentine women did not enjoy landownership rights, according to Stolen (*The Decency of Inequality*, 67). Few Latin American women did, even after agrarian reform: see Tinsman (*Partners in Conflict*), Deere and León de Leal (*Empowering Women*), and Olcott (*Revolutionary Women*). U.S. Jewish women filed for deeds under the Homestead Act: see Schloff ("'We Dug More Rocks,'" 93) and Calof (*Rachel Calof's Story*, 25).

19. Y. Levin, "Posturas genéricas," 60–62; and Elkin, *The Jews*, 112.

20. Cooperativa Fondo Comunal, Libro de Actas, 1927–1931, Archivo del Fondo Comunal; *El Campo*, 10 March 1928, 1, and 30 October 1928, 6; and Y. Levin, "Posturas genéricas," 62.

21. Schvartz de Pitasni, interview with author, 1997; and *Tierra de promesas*, 246–48.

22. Mayo (2000) and Hassid de Treves (1998), interviews with author.

23. Mayo and Salón de Esperanza, interviews with author, both 2000; Zimerman de Faingold, *Memorias*, 42; Knopoff (n.d.) and Maladietzky (1989), interviews, AP. On Jewish women's work in U.S. rural family businesses, see Weiner ("Jewish Women") and Schloff ("'We Dug More Rocks'").

24. Serie Las Colonias, Carpeta 9, Friedman, 28 January 1941, MHRC; Eidman de Tkach (n.d.) and Yagupsky (1984), interviews, AP; and Bercovich de Zlotnitsky, interview with author, 1997. Chapter 4 discusses prostitution.

25. Yagupsky, interview, 1984, AP; Garfunkel, *Narro mi vida*, 260; Schvartz de Pitasni, interview with author, 1997; and Movimiento, *Pioneros*, 139. Calof (*Rachel Calof's Story*, 46 and passim) relates similar problems in North Dakota.

26. Kipen, interviews, AP (1989) and with author (1997); and *El Colono Cooperador*, March 1972, 8–9.

27. Ropp, *Un colono judío*, 52; *Rescate de la herencia cultural*, 67–68; and *El Alba*,

16 March 1937, 2. *Juventud*, Carlos Casares, 1 June 1925, 8, and *Sarmiento*, 14 March 1936, 8, displayed midwives' ads.

28. López de Borche, *Cooperativismo y cultura*, 24; *Tierra de promesas*, 164; and Sichel (1996), interview, AP. Chapter 3 discusses professionals.

29. *El Alba*, 16 July 1922: 3, 17 January 1928: 3, and 28 July 1936: 3; and A. Kaplan, *Memoria de un médico*, 22.

30. Itzigsohn, *Una experiencia judía contemporánea*, 11–12 and 101, and "La atención médica," 22.

31. Filer, interview with author, 1999; and Itzigsohn, "La atención médica," 25.

32. Ropp, *Un colono judío*, 73.

33. Sigwald Carioli, *Colonia Mauricio*, 116; Glombovsky, *Los gringos*, 121; *Di Idische Froi*, nos. 22–23 (August–September 1956): 6; and Lieberman, *Los judíos en la Argentina*, 151–52.

34. Jewish Colonization Association, *Rapport . . . 1898*, 11; and Makoff de Sevi, interview, 1989, AP.

35. Camín de Efron (1989) and Benchik (n.d.), interviews, AP; and Tolcachier, "Movilidad socio-ocupacional."

36. Spalding, "Education in Argentina," 45.

37. Efron, "La obra," 72–78; and Norman, *An Outstretched Arm*, 126. Children who lived outside JCA colonies attended state schools from the beginning. The non-Jewish Federación Agraria Argentina was also concerned about education; see T. Gutiérrez ("La educación del colono pampeano").

38. Argentina, Comisión Nacional del Censo, *Tercer censo*, 3:329. Itzigsohn ("La atención médica," 19) notes that many female colonists were semiliterate. Other groups besides Russians in table 2 must have included Jewish women, but their numbers are unknown because the 1914 census did not separate Jews as a category. On Russian Jewish women, see Parush (*Reading Jewish Women*), Adler ("Jewish Girls"), and S. Brumberg (*Going to America*, 26, 29).

39. Sauer (1997), Fuks (n.d.), and Neumark (n.d.), interviews, AP; Wolf, interview with author, 1998.

40. Jewish Colonization Association, *Rapport . . . 1898*, 8.

41. Bercovich de Zlotnitsky, interview with author, 1997; and Spalding, "Education in Argentina," 54.

42. Alpersohn, *Colonia Mauricio*, 210.

43. Garfunkel, *Narro mi vida*, 277; Camín de Efron, interview, 1989, AP; *Jewish Chronicle*, 23 January 1903, 23; Sigwald Carioli, "Fueron," 126, 55.

44. Kipen, interview, 1989, AP; and Hecker de Uchitel, *Vivencias*, 22.

45. *Tierra de promesas*, 120; Garfunkel, *Narro mi vida*, 278; Gutkowski, *Rescate de la herencia cultural*, 200; and Literat-Golombek, *Moisés Ville*, 125.

46. Ropp, *Un colono judío*, 45; *Juventud*, no. 49 (July 1916): 35; López de Borche, *Cooperativismo y cultura*, 117–18; and Furman de Bendersky, interview with author, 1997. On non-Jewish cooperatives and mothers' groups, see Spalding ("Education

in Argentina," 38), Stolen (*The Decency of Inequality*, 207), and Vaughan (*Cultural Politics in Revolution*, 176).

47. Inspector's entry, Escuela Elemental La Capilla, Libro de Actas, 9 September 1933, MHRC; Bortnik de Duchovny, *Recuerdos*, 73; and Salomón de Susman, interview, 1989, AP.

48. Escuela Elemental La Capilla, Libro de Actas, 5–7 August 1919, MHRC. On liberalism in schools, see Plotkin (*Mañana es San Perón*).

49. Escudé, *El fracaso del proyecto argentino*, 25–50.

50. Spalding, "Education in Argentina," 47.

51. Waisman (n.d.), Caplan (1989), and Salomón de Susman (1989) interviews, AP; Bercovich de Zlotnitsky, interview with author, 1997; Gutkowski, *Rescate de la herencia cultural*, 200; *El Alba*, 30 March 1926: 1, 6 March 1928: 1, 14 August 1928: 1, and 21 July 1936: 1; and López de Borche, *Cooperativismo y cultura*, 103. On the United States, see Klapper (*Jewish Girls*, 105–42).

52. Mayo and Salón de Esperanza, interviews with author, both 2000.

53. Kipen, interview, 1989, AP; and Ropp, *Un colono judío*, 52. For similar attitudes in the United States, see Klapper (*Jewish Girls*).

54. Furman de Bendersky and Schvartz de Pitasni, interviews with author, both 1997; Efrón de Boianovsky (1989), Grimberg and Trumper (1989) and Knopoff (n.d.) interviews, AP; Kipen, interviews with author, 1997, and AP, 1989; Ropp, *Un colono judío*, 51; Bortnik de Duchovny, *Recuerdos*, 24–26; Olga de Sajaroff, 18 July 1920, no. 5037, Archivo Miguel Sajaroff, SI, MHRC.

55. Besedovsky de Farber, Furman de Bendersky and Kipen interviews with author, all 1997; Nissensohn de Stilerman, interview, 1991, AP; and Bortnik de Duchovny, *Recuerdos*, 22–23.

56. Anderson, *Imagined Communities*, 121–22.

57. Bortnik de Duchovny, *Recuerdos*, 38–40. On teaching careers, see chapter 3. On the importance of teaching for Latin American women, see Palmer and Rojas Chaves ("Educating Señorita," especially 63–68) and Vaughan (*Cultural Politics in Revolution*, especially 93 and 169).

58. Rippberger and Staudt, *Pledging Allegiance*.

59. Yagupsky, interview, 1984, AP; and Bargman, "Un ámbito," 55–56. Plotkin (*Mañana es San Perón*, 5) notes that even anarchist and Communist teachers imparted "patriotic indoctrination."

60. *Israel*, 30 May 1924: 13, 27 March 1925: 12, 28 September–5 October 1928: unnumbered page; and *La Luz*, 24 April 1931, 77–78.

61. Ades de Galagorsky, "Pantallazos," 39, 52, MHC; Wolf (1998) and Frank (2000), interviews with author; Neumark (n.d.) and Sauer (1997), interviews, AP; and Bargman, "Un ámbito," 54.

62. Meyer Malamud, in Sociedad Kadima, *Boletín del 25 aniversario*, unnumbered page.

63. Anderson, *Imagined Communities*, 44.

64. Hecker de Uchitel, *Vivencias*, 24–25; Maldavsky (1998) and Frank (2000), interviews with author; Camín de Efron and Ojberg de Aisicovich, interviews, both 1989, AP. How reading affected Mediterranean households remains to be studied. On Jewish women readers elsewhere, see Parush (*Reading Jewish Women*) and Klapper (*Jewish Girls*, 206–13).

65. I. Katz, *De raíces y sitios*, 265; and Frank, interview with author, 2000.

66. Zimerman de Faingold, *Memorias*, 14; and Salomón de Susman and Camín de Efron, interviews, both 1989, AP. *Israel*, 14 December 1945, 12, complained that Sephardim read few Spanish-language Jewish periodicals.

67. *Israel*, 3–10 April 1925: 32 and 19 June 1925: 22; *Mundo Israelita*, 9 January 1943: 10; *El Campo*, 1 February 1927: 1 and 1 November 1927: 1; *El Alba*, 1 January 1928: 3, 8 November 1938: 1, and 15 October 1939: unnumbered page; Alpersohn, *Colonia Mauricio*, 212; López de Borche, *Cooperativismo y cultura*, 41; Bortnik de Duchovny, *Recuerdos*, 33–34; Ades de Galagorsky, "Pantallazos," 69–70, MHC; and Magrán, interview, 1988, AP. Public libraries collected dues and sometimes received state subsidies. Argentina (Comisión Nacional del Censo, *Tercer censo*, 9:232 and 234) lists the Moisesville and Villa Domínguez facilities in its compilation of public libraries.

68. Gutiérrez and Romero, *Sectores populares*, 12–13 and passim.

69. Riegner (1997), Sauer (1997), and Sichel (1996), interviews, AP; and Avni and Senkman, *Del campo al campo*, 275–76.

70. Sociedad Kadima, *Boletín del 25 aniversario*, unnumbered page.

71. Gutman de Landman, interview with author, 2000; Kaller de Gutman, interview, 1989, AP; Gutman, interview, 1990–91, HUJ; Libro de Actas, 3–4, 13, and 19, Seminario de Maestros Hebreos de Moisesville "Iosef Draznin"; Ades de Galagorsky, "Seminario," MHC; "Primera inmigración judía organizada," MHC; and *El Alba*, 15 October 1939, unnumbered page.

72. *El Alba*, 15 October 1939, unnumbered page; *La Luz*, 10 February 1933, 57; and Mayo, interview with author, 2000.

73. *Tierra de promesas*, 136 and 142–3; Koval Magrán (1989), Knopoff (n.d.), and Sichel (1996), interviews, AP; and Gutkowski, *Rescate de la herencia cultural*, 201–2. Klapper (*Jewish Girls*, 215–19, 221) discusses similar activities among U.S. Jews.

74. For this and the following paragraph, see *Juventud*, Carlos Casares, 20 August 1925, 23; *Sarmiento*, 4 March 1936, 16; *Israel*, 30 April 1918: 325, 15 July 1918: 424, and 30 July 1918: 444; *Tierra de promesas*, 136–37; Maladietzky (1989), Rosenthal de Garber (1989), and Riegner (1997), interviews, AP; and Schvartz de Pitasni (1997), Gutman de Landman (2000), and Filer (1999), interviews with author. Mexican voluntary associations sponsored entertainment; see Forment (*Civic Selfhood*, 264–65).

75. Ballhorn (1989), Riegner (1997), Ehrenfeld (1996), and Sichel (1996), interviews, AP; Frank, interview with author, 2000. German Jews sponsored an Avigdor group performance in Buenos Aires in 1942.

76. Wolf (1998) and Salón de Esperanza (2000), interviews with author; Neumark (n.d.), Maladietzky (1989, quote), and Sichel (1996), interviews, AP; "Los pesares"; *El Alba*, 16 April 1929: 1 and 25 April 1933: 4; Gutkowski, *Rescate de la herencia cultural*, 202; and *Colonia Mauricio*, 66. On socializing among Italian immigrant women, see Stolen (*The Decency of Inequality*, 202–4). Spitzer (*Hotel Bolivia*, 126) mentions rural Jewish women's social life.

77. *El Alba*, 24 October 1919, unnumbered page; Hassid de Treves (1998) and Levi (2000), interviews with author. Chapter 2 describes Mediterranean marriage customs.

78. *La Luz*, 10 February 1933, 69; *El Alba*, 24 June 1932: 20 and 30 November 1934: 14; *Mundo Israelita*, 23 March 1935: 4 and 5 October 1935: 6; Speckman de Klein, interview, n.d., AP; and Hassid de Treves, interview with author, 1998.

79. *Israel*, 9 February 1945, 13.

80. Ehrenfeld (1996), Neumark (n.d.), and Sichel (1996), interviews, AP.

81. Alpersohn, *Colonia Mauricio*, 111–14; Bortnik de Duchovny, *Recuerdos*, 67–68; N. Rapoport, *Desde lejos hasta ayer*, 53–56; and Pascaner, interview with author, 1997.

82. Diner, *Hungering for America*, 60; and Ferris, "'From the Recipe File,'" 265–66. I see Ashkenazi, Mediterranean, and German cooks creating hybrid identities, rather than what Kirshenblatt-Gimblett described as "Kitchen Judaism." On this hybridity, see Lockhart ("Is There a Text in This Gefilte Fish?," 112–13).

83. Frank (2000) and Wolf (1998), interviews with author; and Riegner (1997) and Ehrenfeld (1996), interviews, AP.

84. Mayo (2000), Salón de Esperanza (2000), and Hassid de Treves (1998), interviews with author.

85. *Colonia Mauricio*, 66 and 78; *Tierra de promesas*, 286–97; and Filer, interview with author, 1999. Women used the word "fanatic" in interviews.

86. Literat-Golombek, *Moisés Ville*, 29; Ambasch, interview with author, 1998; and Caplan and Efrón de Boianovsky, interviews, both 1989, AP.

87. Ades de Galagorsky, "Seminario," MHC; Libro de Actas, 19, Seminario de Maestros Hebreos; Literat-Golombek, *Moisés Ville*, 25–27; Ballhorn, interview, 1989, AP; and Y. Levin, "Posturas genéricas," 64–66. Also see Hyman (*Gender and Assimilation*, 48), Sartori ("'The Most Beautiful Jewish Innovation'"), M. Kaplan (*The Making of the Jewish Middle Class*, 69–84), and Sarna ("A Great Awakening," 52).

88. Rotker, *Captive Women*, 38.

89. Mayo, interview with author, 2000; Sichel (1996), Ehrenfeld (1996), Yagupsky (1984), Voloshin de Lisnofsky (1989), and Grimberg and Trumper (1989), interviews, AP.

90. Hecker de Uchitel, *Vivencias*, 12–13, 18, and 20; *Tierra de promesas*, 31 and 40–41; Alpersohn, *Colonia Mauricio*, 304–12; *Colonia Mauricio*, 70 and 72; I. Katz; *De raíces y sitios*; Riegner (1997), Yagupsky (1984), Grimberg and Trumper (1989), and

Notvovich (1989), interviews, AP; Salomón, "Las escuelas judías," 35; *Israel*, 1 April 1950, 21; and Freidenberg, *Memorias de Villa Clara*.

91. Schvartz de Pitasni and Lifchitz de Hamburgo, interviews with author, both 1997; Efrón de Boianovsky and Maladietzky, interview, both 1989, AP; and *Raíces que dieron alas*, 203. Chapter 5 discusses Jewish women's relations with non-Jewish men.

92. Freidenberg, *Memorias de Villa Clara*; Bargman, "Un ámbito"; Schallman (1991) and Neumark (n.d.), interviews, AP; Ruggiero, "Gringo and Creole"; and Lynch, *Massacre in the Pampas*. After Jews left the land, criollos administered their properties and moved into their houses.

93. Hassid de Treves (1998) and Salón de Esperanza (2000), interviews with author; Speckman de Klein, interview, n.d., AP; Zimerman de Faingold, *Memorias*, 3; *Presencia sefaradí*, 57.

94. Yagupsky, interview, 1984, AP; Salón de Esperanza, interview with author, 2000; and Avni and Senkman, *Del campo al campo*, 112.

95. Salón de Esperanza, interview with author, 2000; Yagupsky (1984), Eidman de Tkach (n.d.), and Speckman de Klein (n.d.), interviews, AP; *Jewish Chronicle*, 20 May 1898: 20 and 27 May 1898: 14; Garfunkel, *Narro mi vida*, 287–96; Alpersohn, *Colonia Mauricio*, 67, 127, 236–43, and 344–45; Itzigsohn, "La atención médica," 22; and Y. Levin, "Posturas genéricas," 57. On rape, see chapter 5. Gerchunoff (*The Jewish Gauchos*, 71–74) offers a fictional account of a murder.

96. Caplan (1989), Knopoff (n.d.), Efrón de Boianovsky (1989), and Eidman de Tkach (n.d.), interviews, AP.

97. As Bolivian Jews may have done; see Spitzer (*Hotel Bolivia*, 130).

98. Gerchunoff, *The Jewish Gauchos*; Senkman, "Identidades colectivas," 436, and *La identidad judía*, 200–1; Bargman, "Un ámbito," 54–55; *Tierra de promesas*, 205; Mónica Szurmuk, personal communication; and Slatta, *The Gauchos*.

99. *Israel*, 15 January 1919, 744–45; Efrón de Boianovsky (1989), interview, AP; Itzigsohn (1997) and Gutman (1990–91), interviews, HUJ; and Senkman, "Identidades colectivas," 421–22 and 433–35.

100. See, for example, Bortnik de Duchovny (*Recuerdos*, 30–31). See also chapter 3.

101. La Escuela Elemental La Capilla, Libro de Actas, 28 May 1917, MHRC. *El Campo*, 20 May 1927, 6; and Gerchunoff (*The Jewish Gauchos*, 11–15) also describe celebrations.

102. Anderson, *Imagined Communities*, 145.

103. *El Alba*, 9 July 1922: 1, 16 July 1922: 1–3 (quote), and 23 May 1933: 5; *Israel*, 17 June 1921, 18; and Olga de Sajaroff to Vera Sajaroff, no. 5054, 17 May 1924, Archivo Miguel Sajaroff, SI, MHRC. On philanthropy, see chapter 8.

104. Olga de Sajaroff to Vera Sajaroff, no. 5057, 26 May 1924, MHRC; and Bortnik de Duchovny, *Recuerdos*, 47.

105. *El Alba*, 27 May 1924: 1 and 25 August 1936: 2; and Gutkowski, *Rescate de la herencia cultural*, 129.

106. Sichel (1996) and Sauer (1997), interviews, AP; Mayo, interview with author, 2000; and Bortnik de Duchovny, *Recuerdos*, 47.

107. Schechner, *Performance Studies*.

108. Bertoni, *Patriotas, cosmopolitas y nacionalistas*. Also see Solberg (*Immigration and Nationalism*), Payá and Cárdenas (*El primer nacionalismo argentino*), Rock ("Intellectual Precursors"), and Escudé (*El fracaso del proyecto argentine*). Delaney ("Imagining *El Ser Argentino*") does not see cultural nationalism as necessarily essentialist, intolerant, or static.

109. Criscenti, *Sarmiento and His Argentina*; Halperín-Donghi, "¿Para qué la inmigración?," 444–51 and 463–68; and Lewin, *Cómo fue la inmigración judía*, 102–3.

110. According to Dwight Conquergood, quoted in Schechner (*Performance Studies*, 19), "performances simultaneously reproduce and resist hegemony" and "accommodate and contest domination."

111. Mactas, *Los judíos de Las Acacias*.

112. Ufford and Merkx, "Ich Hab' Noch einen Koffer in Berlin," 101–2; and Ehrenfeld, interview, 1996, AP.

113. Sichel, interview, 1996, AP.

114. Gerchunoff confirmed these identities, according to Szurmuk ("At Home in the Pampas").

115. Vila, *Crossing Borders*.

TWO *Jewish Women in Buenos Aires*

Epigraph sources: Furman, 1997, interview with author; Elnecavé, *Crisol de vivencias judías*, 59.

1. E. H. (2000, quote) and Furman (1997), interviews with author.

2. On Jewish immigration, see Avni (*Argentina and the Jews*), Mirelman (*Jewish Buenos Aires*), and *Presencia sefaradí*.

3. The higher percentage is in S. Weill (*Estudios*, 82); the lower is in Brodsky ("The Contours of Identity," 28).

4. Newton, *The Nazi Menace*, 141–42; and Schwarcz, *Y a pesar de todo*, 51.

5. Smolensky and Vigevani Jarach, *Tantas voces*, 21.

6. Argentina, Municipalidad de la Ciudad de Buenos Aires, *Cuarto censo*, 3:300, and Argentina, Presidencia de la Nación, *Cuarto censo*, 1:20. There are many works on immigration; see, for example, Moya (*Cousins and Strangers*), Baily (*Immigrants in the Lands of Promise*), and Schwarzstein (*Entre Franco y Perón*).

7. Jewish women in Savannah, Georgia, did the same: see Greenberg ("Savannah's Jewish Women," 758). Also see *La Luz*, 4 March 1932: 101; Epstein

("Aspectos generales de la inmigración," 161 and 166–67); Levi, interview with author, 2000; *Presencia sefaradí* (47); and Mirelman ("Sephardic Immigration," 23).

8. Sofer, *From Pale to Pampa*, 66–69.

9. Simsolo, interview with author, 2002; Levy, *Crónica de una familia sefaradí*, 44, 70; Bertoni, "De Turquía a Buenos Aires," 73, 75, 77, and 79; Mirelman, "Sephardic Immigration," 26–27; and *Presencia sefaradí*, 55–56.

10. *Raíces que dieron alas*, 34–36, 121, and 130–31; Levy, *Crónica de una familia sefaradí*, 48, 50, 52, 54–55, and 56; *Presencia sefaradí*, 80; and Mirelman, "Sephardic Immigration," 27. In Syria, many Jewish families shared buildings; see Levy (*Crónica de una familia sefaradí*, 93).

11. *Presencia sefaradí*, 80–81; Sofer, *From Pale to Pampa*, 69–79; Maldavsky, interview with author, 1998; *Israel*, 31 March and 7 April 1939; Boulgourdjian and Epstein, "Armenios y judíos"; Korn et al., *Los huéspedes del 20*; Kamenszain, "Los barrios judíos . . . Once"; and Green, *Jewish Workers*, 94–95.

12. Yadid de Chami, interview with author, 1998. This was probably the same kind of drum, the *dumbelek*, played by Regina Mendes (see chapter 1). Gutkowski (*Erase una vez*) describes music and other customs brought by Mediterranean Jews to Argentina.

13. Tawil de Ini, interview with author, 1998; Kamenszain, "Los barrios judíos: Flores"; *Presencia sefaradí*, 65 and 80; and Mirelman, "Sephardic Immigration," 29. On peripheral lots, see Walter (*Politics and Urban Growth*, 84); González Leandri ("La nueva identidad," 214); and Mónica Szurmuk and José Moya, personal communications.

14. For statistics in this and the next paragraph, see Sofer (*From Pale to Pampa*, 79, 83). And for the two paragraphs, see also Chromoy (*Un barco*, 138–39); Emanuel, interview, 1988, AP; Kamenszain ("Los barrios judíos: Villa Crespo," 24–29); Kowalska ("La emigración judía," 261).

15. Sampedro, *Madres e hijas*, 33–37; and Lightman, 1 August 1944, #1073, AJJDCA. González Leandri ("La nueva identidad," 207) finds that it was difficult for laborers to enter the middle class. Sofer (*From Pale to Pampa*, 95) argues the same for Jewish workers.

16. Sampedro, *Madres e hijas*, 185; and Blutrajt (1986) and Reiser (n.d.), interviews, AP.

17. *Presencia sefaradí*, 67–68 and 81; Brauner Rodgers, "La comunidad judía alepina," 50; Schwarcz, *Y a pesar de todo*, 157; and Ufford and Merkx, "Ich Hab' Noch einen Koffer in Berlin," 108.

18. Smolensky and Vigevani Jarach, *Tantas voces*, 58–59 and 70 (quote); Mendes, 3 Nov. 1936, #1067, File 2, AJJDCA; Sommer, interview with author, 2000; Brummer, interview, 1972, AP; and Rojer, *Exile in Argentina*, 43.

19. Kaufman and Pardo, especially 101.

20. Moya, *Cousins and Strangers*, 180–87 and 481, note 163; and Sofer, *From Pale to Pampa*, 80 and 83–85.

21. Sampedro, *Madres e hijas*, 35; also see Singerman, *Mis dos vidas*, 18. Liniado (*Recuerdos imborrables*, 114–21) describes Peronist inspectors.

22. Soriano, interview with author, 2000.

23. Brummer, interview, 1972, AP.

24. Liniado, *Recuerdos imborrables*, 44; see also 42 and 44–48. On tenement life, see Fridman ("La familia Fridman"), Evans ("Setting the Stage for Struggle," 55–56), and Hollander ("Women in the Political Economy of Argentina," 104).

25. Teper, interview, 1986, AP; Yadid de Chami, interview with author, 1998; Green, *Jewish Workers in the Modern Diaspora*, 43; and Jurkowicz de Eichbaum, *Cuando las mujeres hacen memoria*, 46. Middle-class Brazilian homemakers sewed fashionable clothes to maintain prestige; see Owensby (*Intimate Ironies*, 100). On laborers' budgets and consumption, see *La Vanguardia*, 2 June 1930, 1–2, and Ferreras ("La cuestión de la alimentación" and "Evolución").

26. *Juventud*, no. 31 (1 January 1914): 54 (quote); *Mundo Israelita*, 28 December 1940, 2; and Donna Guy, personal communication. These conditions prompted philanthropic activity, as discussed in chapter 8. Desertion (see chapter 5) was common among U.S. Jews; see Friedman ("Founders," 28–30) and Glenn (*Daughters of the Shtetl*, 67).

27. Farja, interview with author, 2000.

28. Yadid de Chami, interview with author, 1998.

29. Baum, Hyman, and Michel, *The Jewish Woman in America*, 68–70 and 74; and Hyman, *Gender and Assimilation*, 94.

30. Shilo, *Princess or Prisoner?*, 113, 117–18, and 121–23; S. Itzigsohn, et al., *Integración y marginalidid*, 115; Levy, *Crónica de una familia sefaradí*, 28 and 31; Yadid de Chami, interview with author, 1998; and Gutkowski, *Erase una vez*, 114–15, 319, 329, 348, and 355.

31. Maldavsky (1998), Hassid (1998), Soriano (2000), Levi (2000), Farja (2000), Eissler (2000), Galante de Franco (1997), Guelman de Belmes (1997), Monín (1997), and Salzman (2000), interviews with author; Brummer (1972), Schallman (1991), Zak (1985), and Tarica (n.d.), interviews, AP; Zimerman de Faingold, *Memorias*, 65–66 and 68; Wolff and Shalom, *Judíos y argentinos*, 18; Knaphais and Bresler, *Album de oro judeo-argentino*, 171–72; *Raíces que dieron alas*, 21, 96, and 238; Jurkowicz de Eichbaum, 55, 73; Arcuschin, *De Ucrania a Basavilbaso*, 25; Poch and Turjanski de Gold, *Orígenes y trascendencia*, 125–26; Graziani-Levy, *Wanderings*, 66; Fridman, "La familia Fridman"; and *Israel*, 2–9 October 1925: 32–33, 6 May 1927: cover, and 10 June 1927: cover. For other examples of Mediterranean seamstresses, see Dios de Martina (*Mujeres inmigrantes*, 88–89); Jurkowicz de Eichbaum, 48–49; and Adida de Bentata et al., interview with author, 2000. Sewing was important for Argentine women of other backgrounds; see Frid de Silberstein ("Immigrants and Female Work," 212), Baily (*Immigrants in the Lands of Promise*, 158), and Hollander ("Women in the Political Economy of Argentina," 56, 85, and passim).

32. Wenger, "Budgets, Boycotts, and Babies," 186; and Glenn, *Daughters of the Shtetl*, 75–76. On the construction of women workers as homemakers, see Veccia ("'My Duty as a Woman'"); on tropes obscuring women's labor, see French and James ("Squaring the Circle," 10). Chapter 5 discusses respectability.

33. Quote in Kanutsky, interview, 1985–86, AP; Judkowski, *El tango*, 43; *Mundo Israelita*, 20 July 1923: 5 and 6 September 1930: 2 (statistics); and Lewintal, interview, 1985–86, AP. How many Jews were among the Eastern European female meatpackers is unknown; see Lobato (*La vida en las fábricas*, 109 and 113–14). According to Hollander ("Women in the Political Economy of Argentina," 61), the Great Depression disproportionately affected women.

34. *El Obrero de la Confección*, 1 December 1934, 2; and *El Obrero Textil*, no. 11 (May 1936): 11.

35. Furman interview with author, 1997; Lewintal (1985–86) and Teper (1986), interviews, AP; *El Obrero Sastre*, nos. 49–50 (June–July 1935): 7; and Schloff, "'We Dug More Rocks,'" 91. On garment and textile production, see Tuccio ("La mujer obrera argentina," 42–46 and 49), J. Horowitz (*Argentine Unions*, 50–54), and Sofer (*From Pale to Pampa*, 99–106). On needle workers in earlier years, see Guy ("Women, Peonage, and Industrialization") and Lavrin (*Women*, 72–74).

36. Absatz (1986), Reiser (n.d.) interviews, AP; and Gesel, interview with Ruetter, n.d.

37. Tuccio, "La mujer obrera argentina," 47, 55, and 57; Absatz, interview, 1986, AP; Wasserman, interview with author, 1998; Arnaiz and Chomnalez, *Mujeres que trabajan*, 38–39 and 83–85; and Hollander, "Women in the Political Economy of Argentina," 108, 111–12, and 116. Compare with conditions in meatpacking; see Lobato (*La vida en las fábricas*, especially chapter 4). U.S. Jewish women workers also faced sexual abuse; see Glenn (*Daughters of the Shtetl*, 147–48).

38. Schapira, *Argentina, mi arbol*, 32, 35–37, and 43–44; and *La Vanguardia*, 2 June 1930, 1. Even union activity did not usually achieve such happy endings; see chapter 6.

39. Gílenberg, interview with author, 1997.

40. Kanutsky, interview 1985–86, AP. On her activism, see chapters 6 and 7.

41. Furman, interview with author, 1997.

42. E. Levin, *Historias de una emigración*, 65, 70, and 73; Smolensky and Vigevani Jarach, *Tantas voces*, 170; Cohn, Halperin, Eissler, and Sacerdote de Lustig, interviews with author, all 2000; *Filantropía*, no. 591 (April–May 1989): 24; Brummer, interview, 1972, AP; Mendes, 16 Oct. 1936, #1067, File 2, AJJDCA. German Jews in Brazil faced similar limitations; see Lesser ("In Search of Home Abroad," 172). On how some women changed careers, see chapter 3.

43. M. Kaplan, *Between Dignity and Despair*, 7–8, 17, 28–30, 55, 59–60, and 63–65.

44. Abstract, 28 Dec. 1937, #1059, File 1, Mendes, 3 Nov. 1936, AJJDCA (quote). See also Annemarie Schlesinger archive, 1034/15–16, IWO; #1067, File 2, Borchardt and Glick, 10 June 1939; #1069, File 1, Hirsch, 18 Sept. 1942; and #1070, File 1,

AJJDCA; E. Levin, *Historias de una emigración*, 73; Sommer, Eissler, E. H., and Smilg, interviews with author, all 2000; Schwarcz, *Y a pesar de todo*, 36–37; Smolensky and Vigevani Jarach, *Tantas voces*, 64, 108, 123, 170, and 279; and Riegner, "Un proyecto," 161–62 and 166–72.

45. Schallman, *Pela Szechter*, 38, 45, 47, and 49; and Gartenstein-Faigenblat, interview with author, 2000.

46. Hollander, "Women in the Political Economy of Argentina," 84; and Friedman-Kasaba, *Memories of Migration*, 123–29. According to Frid de Silberstein ("Immigrants and Female Work," 210 and 213), Italian women participated much less in the labor force than other women in Rosario did, and work in family businesses also obscured their involvement.

47. Elkin, "Latin American Jewry Today," 29; Syrquin, "The Economic Structure of Jews," 125–26; and Argentina, Dirección Nacional de Estadística y Censos, *Censo . . . 1960*, 1:80.

48. Levy, *Crónica de una familia sefaradí*, 39, 47, 68–69, and 76–77. Other examples were discussed in Levi (2000), Wasserman (1998), and Yadid de Chami (1998), interviews with author.

49. Yagupsky, interview, 1984, AP; and Poch and Turjanski de Gold, *Orígenes y trascendencia*, 109 and 118. While many of the Italian women Gandolfo ("Del Alto Molise") studied were illiterate, they and their husbands approved of education for their daughters, some of whom became teachers. Also see S. Weinberg ("Longing to Learn," especially 114–18) and Glenn (*Daughters of the Shtetl*, 86–87).

50. *Mundo Israelita*, 8 June 1923: 4, 1 September 1923: 3, 6 October 1923: 2, 8 March 1924: 4, 14 June 1924: 2, 19 September 1925: 5, and 26 December 1925: 1; Guy, "Women's Organizations"; and G. Lerner, "La historia del Asilo Argentino."

51. Smilg and Cohn, interviews with author, both 2000; Schwarzstein, "Entre la tierra perdida," 134–35; Schwarcz, *Y a pesar de todo*, 120–23; and Smolensky and Vigevani Jarach, *Tantas voces*, 58 and 82.

52. Levinsky, *Herencias de la inmigración judía*, 139; and Smolensky and Vigevani Jarach, *Tantas voces*, 60–61 and 70.

53. Sarlo, *La máquina cultural*, 52–56 and 276–77; Grimson, "Ethnic (In)Visibility," 26; and quote in S. Weinberg, "Longing to Learn," 119. Hogar Infantil Israelita Argentina, Libro de Actas, 3 Oct. 1933, f. 50, 31 Oct. 1934, f. 153, IWO describes impoverished Jewish children in unsanitary conditions; I thank Donna Guy for sending me this information. On lice, see Chromoy (*Un barco*, 31 and 40).

54. Wasserman, interview with author, 1998; and Schapira, *Argentina, mi arbol*, 26–28.

55. Poch and Turjanski de Gold, *Orígenes y trascendencia*, 97.

56. Schapira, *Argentina, mi arbol*, 28; and Monín, interview with author, 1997.

57. Zadoff, *Historia de la educación judía*; Green, *Jewish Workers in the Modern Diaspora* 98–101; Barrancos, *Anarquismo*, 225–27; P. Katz, *Páginas selectas*, 79–80 and 106–8; and Mirelman, *Jewish Buenos Aires*, 147–60.

58. Levy, *Crónica de una familia sefaradí*, 57; *Israel*, 28 October 1921: 13 and 9 May 1924: 7; Tawil de Ini, interview with author, 1998; Brauner Rodgers, "La comunidad judía alepina," 52; and *Presencia sefaradí*, 91.

59. Edelman, *Banderas*, 19; *Juventud* 5, no. 43 (May 1915): 43; and Mayo, interview with author, 2000. Also see Juanita Kleinbort Archive, 1154/19; Sociedad Israelita Pro Cultura Musical, 225/43; Asociación Musical Israelita Ioel Engel, 225/35 and 225/19; Sociedad Israelita Cultural Musical, 1009/1, all in IWO. Jewish women also joined musical associations with no ethnic affiliation.

60. Chromoy, *Un barco*, 103; Yadid de Chami (1998) and Wasserman (1998), interview with author; Mónica Szurmuk, personal communication. On New York Jewish women workers who studied, see S. Weinberg ("Longing to Learn," 108–22).

61. *Mundo Israelita*, 25 June 1932, 4; *Juventud*, no. 10 (1 April 1912): 15–16, no. 13 (1 July 1912): 15, and no. 16 (1 October 1912): 15; Farja, interview with author, 2000; and Dreier, *Five Months in the Argentine*, 119 and 122. Owensby (*Intimate Ironies*) shows that middle-class and upwardly mobile Brazilian men took courses.

62. *Juventud* 3, no. 33 (March 1914): 60; Edelman, *Banderas*, 60; and Barrancos, *La escena iluminada*.

63. Gutiérrez and Romero (*Sectores populares*) conclude that such institutions accepted the status quo, but this was not true of the Socialist ones, or many Jewish ones. See González Leandri ("La nueva identidad," 222–23 and 230–31).

64. *Juventud* 3, no. 38 (August 1914): 61; Centros Culturales Peretz Hirschbein, letter, 6 July 1923, IWO; *Mundo Israelita*, 30 March 1929: 2 and 30 November 1935: 14; and *Israel*, 29 August 1930, 13.

65. *Juventud* 5, no. 46 (August–September 1915): 132–36 and 138, no. 47 (October–December 1915): 191 (quote), 193, and 195, and no. 48 (April 1916): 43. P. Katz (*Páginas selectas*, 43–44) and Mirelman (*Jewish Buenos Aires*, 175–76) describe this organization.

66. *Mundo Israelita*, 22 February 1941, 2. The Ateneo, AJIA, and Asociación Hebraica later merged to form the Sociedad Hebraica Argentina.

67. *Israel*, 8 December 1922, 15.

68. On these and other women's appearances, see: *Mundo Israelita*, 13 June 1925: 2, 8 June 1929: 2, and 30 November 1935: 14; *Israel*, 7 October 1921, 16; *La Luz*, 2 October 1931, 476; *El Israelita Argentino*, no. 12 (15 December 1913): 23–24; and Radio Glaserman, 1116/18–5–1939, IWO.

69. *SHA*, September 1949: 5 and November 1949: 10–11; lists of candidates in Box 116; all in IWO.

70. Donna Guy, personal communication; also see chapter 8.

71. *Presencia sefaradí*, 50; Sommer and Levi, interviews with author, both 2000; Sociedad Cultural Israelita Jüdische Kulturgemeinschaft, *Estatutos* (Buenos Aires: n.p., n.d.), 232/43, and *1937 JKG 1942* (Buenos Aires: n.p., n.d.) 232/2, IWO; Emanuel,

interview, 1988, AP; and Poch and Turjanski de Gold, *Orígenes y trascendencia*, 114–15 and 120.

72. Yadid de Chami, interview with author, 1998; Schwarcz, *Y a pesar de todo*, 70; Spitzer, *Hotel Bolivia*, 75, 78, and passim; and Schwarzstein, "Entre la tierra perdida," 120.

73. Radio Glaserman, 1116/9, IWO.

74. Guelman de Belmes, interview with author, 1997; Sociedad Hebraica Argentina, "Por una casa digna y de puertas abiertas," n.d., Box 116, IWO; Sociedad Hebraica Argentina (*Memoria y balance*, 115–20); and *Mundo Israelita*, 8 June 1923: 2, 22 June 1923: 5, 25 August 1923: 2, and 25 April 1925: 1.

75. Smolensky and Vigevani Jarach, *Tantas voces*, 62, 80, 85, and 274; and Schneider, "La política," 308–9.

76. Smolensky and Vigevani Jarach, *Tantas voces*, 319; Sociedad Hebraica Argentina, *Vidas*, 183; and Yadid de Chami (1998), Tawil de Ini (1998), and Simsolo (2002), interviews with author.

77. Zanders de Silber, interview, 1986, AP; Riegner, "Un proyecto," especially 138; and Schwarzschild, 25 Nov. 1937, and Lew, 11 May 1938, #1069, File 1, AJJDCA.

78. Farja, interview with author, 2000.

79. *Mundo Israelita*, 8 June 1940, 2; *Israel*, 30 April 1918, 325; *La Luz*, 13 March 1931, 17; Hassid and Tawil de Ini, interviews with author, both 1998; and Jurkowicz de Eichbaum, *Cuando las mujeres hacen memoria*, 162. *Israel*, 25 November 1921: 12 and 15, and 24 March 1922: 17–18, describes other prestigious Mediterranean weddings.

80. Haboba (1998), Hassid (1998), Tawil de Ini (1998), Guelman de Belmes (1997), and Cohen de Isaharoff (1997), interviews with author; Cohen de Isaharoff, interview, 1992, AP; and Levy, *Crónica de una familia sefaradí*, 63–64.

81. *Filantropía*, no. 607 (April–May 1992): 16; and Sociedad Cultural Israelita Jüdische Kulturgemeinschaft (*1937 JKG 1942*, 15), 2/232. IWO.

82. Kaufman and Pardo, 105–107. Whether the Nazis permitted circumcision among Jews is unclear, according to David Hackett, Robin Judd, and Marion Kaplan, personal communications.

83. Farja (2000, Tawil de Ini (1998), Guelman de Belmes (1997),Yadid de Chami (1998), and Sommer (2000), interviews with author; *Israel*, 10 June 1932, 12; *Mundo Israelita*, 14 December 1940, 2; Schapira, *Argentina, mi arbol*, 38–39 and 41; Sociedad Hebraica, *Vidas*, 186; Kohen, *El color de la nostalgia*, 65, 67–68, 70, and 72; Edelman, *Banderas*, 28; Jurkowicz de Eichbaum, 149; and Smolensky and Vigevani Jarach, *Tantas voces*, 62 and 80. González Leandri ("La nueva identidad") discusses leisure in Buenos Aires.

84. Smilg (2000), Halperin (2000), Tawil de Ini (1998), and Cusien (2000), interviews with author; Radio Glaserman, Box 1116, IWO; *Israel*, 4 January 1935: 15 and 13 December 1935: 15; and Ballent and Gorelik, "País urbano o país rural," 164–71.

85. Mernissi, *Dreams of Trespass*; Kohen, *El color de la nostalgia*, 51 (quote) and 55; Levy, *Crónica de una familia sefaradí*, 67, 77, 84–85, and 87; and Farja, interview with author, 2000.

86. *Mundo Israelita*, 2 December 1940, 2; and Jurkowicz de Eichbaum, *Cuando las mujeres hacen memoria*, 162.

87. *La Luz*, 4 December 1931: 647, 22 July 1932: 429, and 10 March 1933: 117.

88. Simsolo (2002), Soriano (2000), and Elnecavé (1997), interviews with author.

89. Zanders de Silber, interview, 1986, AP; and Schwarcz, *Y a pesar de todo*, 129–34.

90. *Noticias Gráficas*, 17 June 1932: 11, 19 June 1932: 15, and 21 June 1932: 11; also see other issues from 20 April through 4 July 1932. I thank Adela Harispuru for this material. Argentine beauty contests assumed importance in the 1930s; see Lobato (*Cuando las mujeres reinaban*). The Brazilian press also sponsored beauty contests; see Besse ("Defining a 'National Type,'" 96).

91. *Mundo Israelita*, 25 June 1932, 1; Elia Pérez, personal communication; and Avni, *Argentina and the Jews*, 85. R. López ("The India Bonita Contest") and Besse ("Defining a 'National Type'") discuss race and national identity in beauty contests; Lobato (*Cuando las mujeres reinaban*) focuses on work, politics, and women's roles. Banner (*American Beauty*, 249–70) treats these pageants' multiple meanings.

92. Dworkin, *Miss America 1945*, especially 92, 109, 124, 131, 145, 147–48, 179–80, 182, 196, 199–200, and 203; and Pamela Nadell, personal communication. Whether U.S. Jewish women won local titles comparable to Miss Capital before 1945 is unclear.

93. Schneider, "La política," 307–9; Newton, "The Evanescent Community"; Terracini, "Una inmigración muy particular," 362–63; and Smolensky and Vigevani Jarach, *Tantas voces*, 170–71, 179, 299, and 301.

94. Schwarzstein, "Entre la tierra perdida," 123, 131–32, and 136; Schwarcz, *Y a pesar de todo*, 66–69 and 119; Riegner, "Un proyecto," 172; Lesser, "In Search of Home Abroad"; Smilg and Sommer, interviews with author, both 2000; Zanders de Silber, interview, 1986, AP; E. Levin, *Historias de una emigración*, 83, 87, and 101; and Ufford and Merkx, "Ich Hab' Noch einen Koffer in Berlin." German Jews in Bolivia felt differently; see Spitzer (*Hotel Bolivia*).

95. Kohen, *El color de la nostalgia*, 63.

THREE *Pathway into the Professions*

Epigraph sources: Alianak, *Israel*, 2 and 9 October 1925, 33; Fux, *Danza*, 1.

1. Abeijón and Lafauci (*La mujer*), Lieberman (*Los judíos en la Argentina*), and other works briefly describe some women's careers, and there are biographies of

prominent individuals. The few works that critically examine women's professionalism include Morgade (*Mujeres en la educación*), Kohn Loncarica, Sánchez, and Agüero ("La contribución"), and Kohn Loncarica and Sánchez ("La mujer . . . primera década" and "La mujer . . . segunda década"). I do not treat musicians, artists, photographers, or scientists (except in medicine). Few Argentine women, Jewish or non-Jewish, entered the law until they attained the vote in 1947. See *Guía anual israelita* (138–39) and Oficina Nacional de la Mujer (*Evolución de la mujer*, 83). A few writers appear in succeeding chapters, and some social workers in chapter 8. I follow some women's continuing careers after 1955.

2. On overrepresentation as employers and self-employed, see Elkin (*The Jews*, 150–51) and Argentina, Dirección Nacional de Estadística y Censos (*Censo . . . 1960*, 1:103).

3. The sources did not indicate where these Jewish women were born.

4. Kinzer, "Women Professionals in Buenos Aires," 179.

5. That was also true for Jewish women in New York, according to Antler (*The Journey Home*, 181) and Ford (*The Girls*, 4). It was not the case for Germany; see M. Kaplan ("As Germans," 211).

6. Markowitz, *My Daughter, the Teacher*, 2. On the appearance of Jewish teachers, see *Tierra de promesas* (237); Shijman (*Colonización judía*, 102–3); Escuela No. 8, Carlos Casares, Caja Escuela No. 8, I-3, 150/209, and Dirección General de Escuelas, Registro General de Aspirantes, 1916, 11–12, Caja Educación: Maestros: Asociación de Maestros, AHAM; and *El educador Pablo A. Pizzurno* (309–10).

7. Braslavsky, interview with author, 2000; Diament, *Testimonios*, 30; and Levinsky, *Herencias de la inmigración judía*, 198. Also see Kohen (*El color de la nostalgia*, 201 and 203). On immigrant teachers, see Sarlo (*La máquina cultural*, 20–23 and 25–27).

8. *Israel*, 2 and 9 October 1925, 32–33.

9. Salzman de Glombovsky, interview with author, 2000.

10. Morgade, "La docencia"; and Yannoulas, "Maestras de antaño." Barrancos ("Moral sexual," 207), however, claims that female teachers enjoyed prestige. Bellucci ("Sarmiento") notes that the president elevated women's roles.

11. Sanjurjo, "Rosa Ziperovich," 12 and 14; and Rajschmir, "Rosa Ziperovich." On another mentor of Jewish women teachers, see "Para Ti Maestra Cecilia Borja," Album, 1950, and *El Oeste*, 1981, clipping, Caja Educación: Maestros: Asociación de Maestros, AHAM; Carlson (*¡Feminismo!*, 76–77); and Luiggi (65 *Valiants*, 176–80).

12. Braslavsky, interview with author, 2000; and Diament, *Testimonios*, 32. On classist student cliques, see Spalding ("Education in Argentina," 49).

13. Ziperovich, "Memoria de una educadora," 244.

14. Soriano, interview with author, 2000.

15. Salzman de Glombovsky (2000), Besedovsky de Farber (1997), Furman de Bendersky (1997), Kipen (1997), Kohen (2000), Morgade (2000), and Trumper

(1998), interviews with author; *Clarín*, 19 April 1993, 48; Bortnik de Duchovny, *Recuerdos*, 31; Glombovsky, *Los gringos*, 116–17; and Spalding, "Education in Argentina," 50.

16. Braslavsky, interview with author, 2000; Diament, *Testimonios*, 36; and Levinsky, *Herencias de la inmigración judía*, 199. New Yorkers also needed political influence to obtain teaching jobs in the 1930s; see Markowitz (*My Daughter, the Teacher*, 87, 90, and 92).

17. Walter (*Student Politics in Argentina*), Mazo (*La reforma universitaria*), and Deutsch (*Las derechas*, 195–217) describe the context.

18. Argentina, Congreso Nacional, *Diario de Sesiones de la Cámara de Diputados*, 4 (Dec. 3, 1936), esp. 839–40, and (Dec. 9, 1936), esp. 905–6; *La Vanguardia*, 4 December 1936, 5–7; Braslavsky, interview with author, 2000; Diament, *Testimonios*, 25, 29, and 39; and Levinsky, *Herencias de la inmigración judía*, 199. I thank Adela Harispuru for giving me the material in *La Vanguardia*. Markowitz (*My Daughter, the Teacher*, 44–48, 53, 56–74, 151, and 159) describes persecution of leftist Jewish women educators in New York, in the 1930s through 1950s.

19. José Lieberman, "Profesora ciencias biológicas," *Israel*, 6 March 1925, 13–14. Lieberman soon became a well-known author.

20. *Juventud*, no. 44 (June 1915): 48; *Israel*, 1 February 1935, 14; and Spalding, "Education in Argentina," 58.

21. Kohen, interview with author, 2000.

22. Furman de Bendersky, interview with author, 1997; *Crónica*, 28 August 1981, unnumbered page (quote); and *El Heraldo*, 29 April 1994, unnumbered page. Morgade ("La docencia," 98) notes that many retired teachers dedicated themselves to philanthropy.

23. *El Litoral*, 16 January 1995, unnumbered page; Sanjurjo, "Rosa Ziperovich"; and Rajschmir, "Rosa Ziperovich."

24. Ziperovich, "Memoria de una educadora"; and Sanjurjo, "Rosa Ziperovich." On educational reformism, also see Puiggrós ("La educación argentina," 58–65 and 69–71).

25. Braslavsky, interview with author, 2000; Diament, *Testimonios*, 40–41 and 158; and Deutsch, *Las derechas*, 223–24. Argentines commonly identified Jews as leftists; see chapter 7.

26. Perelstein, *Positivismo y antipositivismo*; Braslavsky, interview with author, 2000; and Diament, *Testimonios*, 158. On her activism, see chapter 7.

27. This and next paragraph rely on Braslavsky, interview with author, 2000; and Diament, *Testimonios*, 42–46, 51–58, 135, 153–155, and 222.

28. On such domination, see Morgade ("La docencia," 96–97).

29. Mónica Szurmuk, personal communication; Glombovsky de Edelman, interview with author, 2000; Rein, *Argentina, Israel, and the Jews*, 44–52, and "Nationalism"; Escudé, *El fracaso del proyecto argentino*, 83 and 90; Plotkin, *Mañana es San*

Perón, 87–88; Ivereigh, *Catholicism and Politics in Argentina*. On the military regime and Jews, see Lvovich (*Nacionalismo*, 521–50).

30. Glombovsky de Edelman and Soriano, interviews with author, both 2000. Avni (*Argentina and the Jews*), however, claims that Jews exempted from Catholic instruction did not experience discrimination; see also Rein ("Nationalism," 170).

31. Salzman de Glombovsky (2000) and Besedovsky de Farber (1997), interviews with author.

32. Anonymous, 1997, interview with author.

33. *La Congregación*, no. 6 (27 August 1943): 6; no. 48 (26 May 1950): 5, no. 50 (4 September 1950): 13, and no. 63 (10 July 1953): 5.

34. Sulkin (2001) and Rollansky (2000), interviews with author. Weisbrot (*The Jews of Argentina*, 152) finds that in the 1970s, nine-tenths of the teachers in Jewish schools were women. Sephardi women had less access to Jewish education (see chapter 2) and, therefore, to teaching.

35. Zadoff, *Historia de la educación judía*, 203, 348–50, and 354–56; Rollansky, interview with author, 2000; Weisbrot, *The Jews of Argentina*, 152; *La Congregación*, no. 6 (27 August 1943): 8 and no. 50 (4 September 1950): 13; and Literat-Golombek, *Moisés Ville*, 232.

36. *La Congregación*, no. 68 (26 August 1954): 2.

37. S. Novodvorsky, interview, 1985, AP; Capizzano de Capalbo and Larisgoitia de González Canda, *La mujer en la educación*, 215–16; 7.9/10, Sara Fischer archive, AYAJE; and *In Memoriam*, 4–5.

38. 7.7/16, Fischer archive, AYAJE; Capizzano de Capalbo and Larisgoitia de González Canda, *La mujer en la educación*, 216–17; and *In Memoriam*, 4–7, 9, and 11–12.

39. *In Memoriam*, 6–7; and 7.7/16, Fischer archive, AYAJE.

40. 7.7/14 (quote), 7.7/16, 7.9/11, Fischer archive, AYAJE. Another preschool educator of Jewish origin was Fenia Chertkoff; see chapter 6.

41. Details on her life and career come from Sacerdote de Lustig, interview with author, 2000; Sacerdote de Lustig (*De los alpes*); Smolensky ("Una mujer italo argentina," 128–41); Smolensky and Vigevani Jarach (*Tantas voces*, 157–63) and Levinsky (*Herencias de la inmigración judía*, 66–71). Centuries earlier in Italy, the family name of Cohen was translated into Sacerdote.

42. Almaráz, Corchon, and Zemborain, *¡Aquí FUBA!*, 32.

43. Levinsky (*Herencias de la inmigración judía*, 66).

44. Langer, *From Vienna to Managua*, 33–34, 37–39, 47–48, 63, 68–69, 76–90, and 93–94; and Plotkin, *Freud in the Pampas*, 93.

45. Langer, *From Vienna to Managua*, 94–95, 98, 103; and Plotkin, *Freud in the Pampas*, 94–97 (quote on 94).

46. This and the next paragraph rely on Langer (*From Vienna to Managua*, 39, 95–102, and passim) and Plotkin (*Freud in the Pampas*, 57, 88, 94, and 97).

47. Kohn Loncarica and Sánchez, "La mujer . . . segunda década," 91 and 102,

and "La mujer . . . primera década," 113–38; Pavlovsky in www.planetariogalilei.com.ar/ameghino/biografias/pavlov.htm (accessed 20 July 2009); and Benarós, "Rosa Pavlovsky."

48. Abeijón and Lafauci, *La mujer*, 43; and Blank, *La mujer judía*, 15–20 and 28–29.

49. Spalding, "Education in Argentina," 56.

50. Parush, *Reading Jewish Women*, 295, note 54.

51. Oficina Nacional de la Mujer, *Evolución de la mujer*, 82–83.

52. Kohn Loncarica and Sánchez, "La mujer . . . segunda década," 97–98. German Jewish women also disproportionately entered medicine; see M. Kaplan ("As Germans," 211).

53. Kohn Loncarica and Sánchez, "La mujer . . . segunda década," 101–2.

54. Kohn Loncarica, Sánchez, and Agüero, "La contribución," 52 and 56; Kohn Loncarica and Sánchez, "La mujer . . . segunda década," 102 and 104; and Winocur, *Desarrollo*. Brumberg and Tomes ("Women in the Professions," 284) find similar patterns in the United States.

55. Kohn Loncarica, Sánchez, and Agüero, "La contribución," 51–53; Kohn Loncarica and Sánchez, "La mujer . . . segunda década," 102–3; Sosa de Newton *Diccionario biógrafico*, 430–31; Sel, "La cirujana Sara Satanowsky," 184, quote; and Perruelo, "Sara Satanowsky." Despite her pediatric specialty, surgery and orthopedics were male fields. Women entered Argentine professional organizations late; see Allegrone (*La mujer y el poder*).

56. Perruelo, "Sara Satanowsky," 169 and 176–77; Sel, "La cirujana Sara Satanowsky," 189; and Senkman, *La identidad judía*, 448.

57. Oficina Nacional de la Mujer, *Evolución de la mujer*, 82–83; Lázaro Schallman, "Las primeras agrupaciones de mujeres judías en la Argentina," OSFA, no. 306 (December 1972): 37; Abeijón and Lafauci, *La mujer*, 43; and *Guía anual israelita*, 182–84 and 223–28.

58. Simsolo, interview with author, 2002; and *Israel*, 12 January 1934: 13 and 8 November 1946: 10. Another early Sephardi woman physician was Dr. Victoria Balaciano, who graduated in Rosario in 1933 or 1934; see *Israel*, 12 January 1934, 14.

59. *Democracia*, 28 November 1993, 28; Weinstein and Gover de Nasatsky, *Escritores judeo-argentinos*, 2:170–71; A. Kaplan, *Memoria de un médico*, 77–79; and Lvovich, *Nacionalismo*, 453–54.

60. Woscoboinik de Levin, interview with author, 1998.

61. Woscoboinik de Levin (1998), Hirsch (2002), and Guelman de Belmes (1997), interviews with author; and *El Israelita Argentino*, no. 13 (1 January 1914): back cover.

62. Heilbrun, *Writing a Woman's Life*, 98; and Kohn Loncarica, Sánchez, and Agüero, "La contribución," 52. Brumberg and Tomes ("Women in the Professions," 281) echo Heilbrun.

63. Slavsky, "Notas"; P. Katz, *Páginas selectas*, 30–31 and 40–41; and Mirelman, *Jewish Buenos Aires*, 171–74. I privilege actresses who crossed from Yiddish to Spanish. The numerous Argentine actresses of Jewish origin deserve an entire book to themselves.

64. Flami file, MCDH; Flami, interview with author, 2000; and Kamenszain, "La importancia de llamarse Golde."

65. Lincovsky, interview with author, 1997.

66. Flami, interview with author, 2000. On the IFT, see Slavsky, "Notas," and IFT, *Boletín Informativo*, 9 (1 September 1938), in Teatro IFT, Box 1031, IWO. Flami is mentioned in four IFT programs in Teatros, Box 72, IWO. Also see *Clarín*, 2 December 1971, unnumbered page, and *La Voz*, 6 February 1985, unnumbered page.

67. *Siete Días*, 12 May 1982, 64; Flami, interview with author, 2000; and *Mujeres argentinas*, 1 April 1947, unnumbered page. Flami appeared in three films after 1986.

68. *Tiempo Argentino*, 3 November 1984, 10; IFT programs, Box 72, IWO; and *Clarín*, 2 December 1971, unnumbered page. On Cipe's father, see Zadoff (*Historia de la educación judía*, 116, note 38, and 298, note 119).

69. *Tiempo Argentino*, 3 November 1984, 10. Cipe's solo shows resemble the social satire and gender consciousness of some U.S. Jewish women performers; see Sochen ("From Sophie Tucker to Barbra Streisand," 68–69).

70. Lincovsky, interview with author, 1997; *Sin Cortes*, June–July 1995, 15.

71. Lincovsky, interview with author, 1997.

72. Ibid.; and *Quebracho*, 1974, directed by Ricardo Wullicher, Filmacción.

73. Lincovsky, interview with author, 1997; Cipe's performances listed in Lincovsky file, MCDH; and *Mundo Israelita*, 27 September 1985, clipping, Lincovsky file, INET.

74. *Claudia* (1974) and *Página 12*, 26 November 1987 (quote), clippings, Lincovsky file, MCDH. Compare to Barbra Streisand's Jewish identity; see Herman ("The Way She *Really* Is," 172).

75. Quote in *Página 12*, 26 November 1987; unidentified clipping, Lincovsky file, MCDH; and *La Voz*, 6 February 1985, unnumbered page.

76. Singerman, *Mis dos vidas*, 11–24; Tiempo, *La vida romántica*, 14–22; Blanco Pazos and Clemente (*Diccionario de actores*, 224–25); and P. Singerman file, MCDH.

77. Information in this and the next paragraph come from Singerman (*Mis dos vidas*, 27–50, 282, and 285–86); Tiempo (*La vida romántica*, 25–68); and *Convicción*, literary supplement, 28 December 1980, 2.

78. Tiempo, *La vida romántica*, 69 and passim; Singerman, *Mis dos vidas*; *Clarín*, 7 July 1985: 17 and 12 April 1992: Section 2, 20; and *A aventura modernista*. I thank Clotilde Lainscek for the last item.

79. Jarvinen, "Colonial Legacies and Common Culture," 14–19; Singerman,

Mis dos vidas, 107; Tiempo, *La vida romántica*, 96–97, 129–30, and 144; *Clarín*, 12 April 1992, Section 2, 20; and Mascato Rey, "Valle-Inclán y Berta Singerman."

80. *A aventura modernista*.

81. Quote in *La Razón*, 14 November 1984, unnumbered page. Also Gaveta 407B, Disco 1847, Faz A-B, and Disco 10632, Faz A ("Pericón Nacional"); Sobre 787, Disco 1452-A; Inventario 8120, recitals of Alberti and Darío, Depto. Documentos de Cine, Audio y Video, AGN.

82. Tiempo, *La vida romántica*, 92; and *Clarín*, 7 July 1985: 16 (quote) and 12 April 1992: Section 2, 20. On her activism, see chapter 7. Singerman illustrated how according to Carol Simpson Stern and Bruce Henderson, quoted in Schechner (*Performance Studies*, 16), performances "affirm individual and cultural values."

83. Neruda quoted in *La Razón*, 14 November 1984, unnumbered page; Foppa, *Diccionario teatral*, 632; *Lyra*, nos. 174–76 (1959): unnumbered pages (quote).

84. Quote in Fux, interview with author, 2000. Information on Fux comes from this interview, Fux (*Danza* and *La formación del danzaterapeuta*), and *La Nacíon*, 28 August 1999, Sections 4 and 5.

85. On this theater, see its website (http://www.teatrodelpueblo.org.ar, accessed 4 May 2009), Saítta ("Entre la cultura y la política," 414–16 and 419–20), and Edelman (*Banderas*, 28–29).

86. Jewish modern dancers in the United States before 1945 were linked to the left; see Foulkes ("Angels 'Rewolt'!," 208 and 210–11).

87. Another modern dance pioneer was the German Jewish refugee Renate Schottelius; see Weinstein, Nasatsky, and Gover de Nasatsky (*Trayectorias musicales judeo-argentinas*, 205–6).

88. Fux, *Danza*, 17.

89. All information on Crilla comes from Crilla (*La palabra en acción*, especially 7–10). On her films, see Blanco Pazos and Clemente, *Diccionario de actores*, 69. On the Freie Deutsche Bühne, see Rojer (*Exile in Argentina*, 137 and 139–43).

90. The Hebraica became known for its avant-garde theater; Mónica Szurmuk, personal communication.

91. Crilla, *La palabra en acción*, 8–9, 11, 28, 134, 154, and 157. Although "method acting" usually refers to Lee Strasberg's adaptation of Stanislavsky's ideas, Crilla used the term to refer to the latter's style. See Schechner (*Performance Studies*, 148–52).

92. Horvath, *Memorias y recuerdos de Blackie*, 22–30; *Tierra de promesas*, 318–19; *Clarín*, 3 September 1992, Espectáculos, 2. I thank Fanny Mandelbaum for all the clippings on Efron.

93. Horvath, *Memorias y recuerdos de Blackie*, 29, 31, 33, and 35.

94. Horvath (*Memorias y recuerdos de Blackie*, 38 and 39 (quote); quote in *Clarín*, 3 September 1992, Espectáculos, 2; *La Maga*, clipping; from Fanny Mandelbaum, and Will Guzmán, personal communication. On Jewish women tango singers, see Judkowski (*El tango*, especially 58–60).

95. "Un servicio a la comunidad," Blackie file, IWO; *La Maga*, 3 May 1995, 17; and Horvath, *Memorias y recuerdos de Blackie*, 36 and 38–41.

96. This paragraph relies on the taped conversations published as Efron's memoir: Horvath (*Memorias y recuerdos de Blackie*, 34, 41–49, and 51–55). The University Archives and Columbiana Library at Columbia University confirmed David Efron's student status but could not find his sister in the records, nor could the registrar's office. The Tuskegee Archives; George Herzog's papers at the Indiana University Archives of Traditional Music; the Tuskegee student newspaper; and the papers of the Tuskegee musicologist William Dawson, in the Emory University Archives, contained no information on Blackie. The Herzog and Tuskegee records have gaps, however, and the Dawson papers consist largely of music. I should note that Efron was known for her honesty. I thank Maceo Dailey, Will Guzmán, and John Moore for their assistance in this search.

97. Horvath, *Memorias y recuerdos de Blackie*, 55; also 44, 54, and 58–59.

98. Ibid., 89–99; Blackie with Nat King Cole in "Noticiero Panamericano" no. 988, Tambor 897, Legajo 1086, Depto. Documentos de Cine, Audio y Video, AGN; *La Maga*, 17 October 1991, 13; "Las herederas de Eva," clipping, from Fanny Mandelbaum.

99. *La Maga*, clipping, from Fanny Mandelbaum; *Clarín*, 3 September 1992, Espectáculos, 2; Horvath, *Memorias y recuerdos de Blackie*, 96; and Fanny Mandelbaum, personal communication.

100. "Instituto Zimra," flier, n.d., 31/225, IWO; Fanny Mandelbaum, personal communication.

FOUR *Prostitutes*

Epigraph sources: Cohen, Jewish Association, *Report 1913*, 39 (Jewish Association publications are located in LL); Noschim, "Trata de blancas. Informe 1934–1935," Sociedad Israelita de Protección a Niñas y Mujeres, "Ezras Noschim," CAHJP-INV 4349.

1. Arthur R. Moro, quoted in Jewish International Conference, *Official Report . . . 1910*, 30.

2. Similar beliefs about prostitutes were common in the United States, according to Feldman ("Prostitution," 194–96) and Friedman-Kasaba (*Memories of Migration*, 140–41).

3. Jewish Association, *Report . . . for 1905*, 24–25.

4. Guy, *Sex and Danger*; Glickman, *The Jewish White Slave Trade*; Mirelman, *Jewish Buenos Aires*, 197–220, and "The Jewish Community Versus Crime"; Vincent, *Bodies and Souls*; Bra, *La organización negra*; and Korn et al., *Los huéspedes del 20*, 84–90. Anti-Semitism mars Rivanera Carlés's *Los judíos*.

5. This view was also common in other countries; see Orum ("The Women of the Open Door," 92).

6. Gilfoyle, "Prostitutes in History," 137. Guy (*Sex and Danger*) and Glickman (*The Jewish White Slave Trade*) contain information on the Jewish women.

7. Anonymous letter to Halphon, Mar. 1927, Folder 1927, CAHJP-INV 4349. Shilo (*Princess or Prisoner?*, 198) argues that concerns over the city's image led Jews to cover up and repress Jewish prostitution in Jerusalem in the 1800s. I thank CAHJP for allowing me to read the INV 4349 files, which at the time were uncatalogued.

8. Many primary sources discuss pimps but do not cover male prostitution.

9. League of Nations, Traffic in Women and Children Committee, "Enquiry into Measures of Rehabilitation of Adult Prostitutes," 76, C.T.F.E. 679, Part III, 25 Mar. 1936, File: Rehabilitation, League of Nation Reports, 3/5, Box III, 4/NVA, FL; and Hyam, *Empire and Sexuality*, 146.

10. Lipman, *A Century of Social Service*, 247–55; and Jewish Association, *Report . . . for 1905*, 30, and *Report 1930*, 31. Jewish women's groups performed similar work in New York; see Rogow (*Gone to Another Meeting*, 140) and Feldman ("Prostitution," 200–4).

11. *Mundo Israelita* 24 June 1939, 8; Sociedad Israelita, *Obra social*, 5–6 and 15; letter 15 Nov. 1926, Folder 1926, and " . . . Ezras Noschim . . . 1931," Folder 1932, CAHJP-INV 4349; and Jewish Association, *Report 1918*, 22.

12. Gilfoyle, "Prostitutes in History," 139–40.

13. Alpersohn, *Colonia Mauricio*, 9–13, 15, and 17; and Insausti ("Hotel de Inmigrantes").

14. Alpersohn, *Colonia Mauricio*, 58, 85, and 87; Cociovitch, *Génesis de Moisés Ville*, 95; and Sigwald Carioli, *Colonia Mauricio*, 64–65.

15. Jewish International Conference, *Official Report . . . 1910*, 33; Argentina, Dirección Nacional de Estadística y Censos, *Censo general . . . 1909*, 1:17, and 88–93; and Guy, *Sex and Danger*, 34.

16. File Policía, 19 Aug. 1930, CAHJP-INV 4349. The statistic of 5 percent comes from the municipal census of 1936: Argentina, Municipalidad de Buenos Aires (*Cuarto censo*, 3:300).

17. The same happened in Brazil; see Orum ("The Women of the Open Door," 93). Statistics cited are from the *Buenos Aires Herald*, 24 June 1930, 1. Also see Guy (*Sex and Danger*, 46), Bristow (*Prostitution and Prejudice*, 142), and María Gabriela Mizraje, personal communication.

18. Guy, *Sex and Danger*, 117 and 131–32.

19. "Encuesta sobre . . . la prostitución . . . 1935–36"; Ganopol, 3 Jan. 1955; both in CAHJP-INV 4349.

20. Jewish Association, *Report 1913*, 39. On Jewish participation in prostitution elsewhere, see Bristow (*Prostitution and Prejudice*, 21, 62–64, 162, 284, and 289), Rosen (*The Lost Sisterhood*, 140), and Friedman-Kasaba (*Memories of Migration*, 142–43).

21. Scarsi, "Tratantes, prostitutas," 13–15; Alsogaray, *Trilogía de la trata de blan-*

cas, 128; Gilfoyle, *City of Eros*, 73; Rivanera Carlés, *Los judíos*, 5; and Guy, *Sex and Danger*, 28–30.

22. "Encuesta sobre . . . la prostitución . . . 1935–36," CAHJP-INV 4349. Also see Cases 581, 590–591, 593, 595, 597, 599, 605–606, 608–610, 612, 615, 620–622, 624, 1935, Vs. 67, and Folder 1936. Rivanera Carlés (*Los judíos*, 5) claims there was a disproportionate number of Jewish *porteras*, the women who guarded and attended prostitutes, in 1875, and this imbalance may have continued.

23. Gilfoyle, "Prostitutes in History," 124, note 24.

24. Among many sources for this practice, see Bra (*La organización negra*, 140) and Vincent (*Bodies and Souls*, 39–41). Novels based on research made these claims; see Stanchina (*Tanka Charowa*, 60) and N. J. Jozami, *Memorias íntimas de Cosia Zeilón* (Buenos Aires: n. p., 1930), cited in Korn et al. (*Los huéspedes del 20*, 84–85). On *kesubahs*, see Jewish International Conference (*Official Report . . . 1910*, 110).

25. Jewish Association, *Report 1911*, 52–53.

26. Jewish Association, *Report 1906*, 27. Other examples are in Jewish Association (*Report 1923 and 1924*, 26–27).

27. Jewish Association, *Report 1913*, 33–34.

28. Jewish Association, *Report 1926*, 35; and Kushnir, *Baile de máscaras*, 64–65.

29. 30 July 1924, 4–5, Box 111, 4NVA, FL; Langsner, 5 Jan. 1931, CIJ, Box 112, 4/IBS, FL.

30. Jewish Association, *Report 1912*, 58–59, *Report 1910*, 41–42, and *Report 1928*, 32.

31. Hyam, *Empire and Sexuality*, 146. Kushnir (*Baile de máscaras*, 51, 140–41, and 144) finds Jewish prostitute families in Brazil.

32. File 1934, CAHJP-INV 4349.

33. Jewish Association, *Report 1923 and 1924*, 20. According to Quaglia ("Corrupción y prostitución infantil," 213–20), Argentine women in general entered prostitution through parents, employers, or neighborhood contacts.

34. Yagupsky, interview, 1984, AP.

35. Jewish International Conference, *Official Report . . . 1927*, 11–12.

36. Jewish Association, *Report 1933 to 1934*, 29.

37. Schalom, *La polaca*, 31, 52–59, 96, and 323–24. Liberman's brother-in-law had died by the 1930 case, but her sister-in-law, Elke Farber de Milbroth, appears in lists of Zwi Migdal members; see *Gaceta del Foro*, 1 November 1930, 3, and Bra (*La organización negra*, 215). On differing versions of Liberman's life, see Glickman (*The Jewish White Slave Trade*), Alsogaray (*Trilogía de la trata de blancas*, 175–87), and Vincent (*Bodies and Souls*, 169–98).

38. File 1928, A.R. and P.J., CAHJP-INV 4349; also see 329–35 V. 62; Gilfoyle, *City of Eros*, 289; and Rosen, *The Lost Sisterhood*, 127–28. In this and the next chapter, I leave out names or use only first names to maintain confidentiality.

39. File "Trata de Blancas 1934 al . . . 1935," CAHJP-INV 4349. On other cases involving husbands, see Jewish Association (*Report 1929*, 22); File 1929, CAHJP-INV 4349; and S. Itzigsohn et al., *Integración*, 206.

40. 936–33 Vs. 32, CAHJP-INV 4349.

41. File Policía, 27 Feb. 1929, CAHJP-INV 4349.

42. File "Trata de Blancas. . . . 1934 al . . . 1935," CAHJP-INV 4349.

43. Ibid.; "Memoria de la Ezras Noschim 1936," 3–7, Folder 1936, CAHJP-INV 4349.

44. Friedman-Kasaba, *Memories of Migration*, 141–42 and 147.

45. File "Trata de Blancas . . . 1934 al . . . 1935," CAHJP-INV 4349. Ezras Noschim files concentrate on women who insisted they were compelled to be prostitutes, girls seen in suspicious company, and police cases. They contain less documentation of women who clearly decided to enter prostitution and were satisfied with that occupation. The group may have handled fewer such cases or refused to accept this interpretation of women's motives.

46. On husbands and lovers, see Pereira ("Prostitutes and the Law"). Mario, the emblematic character in Stanchina (*Tanka Charowa*), generally kept his distance from his lover's sex work. Bayón ("Las locas en Buenos Aires," 238) discusses obligatory maternity.

47. Langsner, 5 Jan. 1931, CIJ, Box 112, 4/IBS, FL. Also see Gilfoyle (*City of Eros*, 287 and 289).

48. "Memoria de la 'Ezras Noschim' 1936," 7–8, Box 291, IWO.

49. Ibid., 17–19.

50. Rosen (*The Lost Sisterhood*, 113) describes a continuum of violent enslavement at one end, casual prostitution at the other, and "varying amounts of choice and coercion" in the middle, the first representing only a minority of cases (133). Corbin (*Women for Hire*, 285) claims white slavery was rare.

51. Stanchina, *Tanka Charowa*, 60.

52. Quote in Stanchina, *Tanka Charowa*, 60; File 1934, CAHJP-INV 4349; and Alsogaray, *Trilogía de la trata de blancas*, 142. The fictional Cosia Zeilón in Jozami's novel, described by Korn et al. (*Los huéspedes del 20*, 87–88), began as a "white slave." Also see Vincent (*Bodies and Souls*, 123) and Bristow (*Prostitution and Prejudice*, 143 and 311).

53. *Gaceta del Foro*, 1 November 1930, 3–4 and 16; Jam, 15 Mar. 1912, File IB: Argentine National Committee, Box 112, 4/IBS, FL.

54. Jewish Association (*Report 1913*, 3, and *Report 1923 and 1924*, 26–27).

55. *The Standard*, 6 and 22 May 1930, unnumbered page; Korn et al., *Los huéspedes del 20*, 89; and Bra, *La organización negra*, 72, 90–91, and 156.

56. *Buenos Aires Herald*, 31 May 1930, unnumbered page.

57. *La Nación*, 28 January 1931, 1 and 5; and File "Trata de Blancas 1934 al . . . 1935," CAHJP-INV 4349. Some women who had not been prostitutes managed such pensions and apartment buildings; see Jewish Association (*Report 1932*, 30).

58. File "Trata de Blancas 1934 al . . . 1935," CAHJP-INV 4349.

59. The best source on Liberman is Glickman (*The Jewish White Slave Trade*). Also see Jewish Association (*Report 1930*, 30–35); *Gaceta del Foro*, 1 November 1930, 5; Alsogaray, *Trilogía de la trata de blancas*; and Bra, *La organización negra*.

60. Schalom, *La polaca*, 281; and 329–34 Vs. 52, and File "Trata de Blancas 1934 al . . . 1935," CAHJP-INV 4349.

61. Langsner, 29 Jan. 1931, CIJ, Box 112, 4/IBS, FL; and Jewish Association, *Report 1913*, 31–33. In a context of debt peonage, Guatemalan prostitutes were more indebted than those in Argentina; see McCreery ("'This Life of Misery and Shame,'" 341–42 and 348–49).

62. Guy, *Sex and Danger*, 110.

63. Stanchina, *Tanka Charowa*, 56, 68, 71 (quote), 77, 79–83, 96–97, and 104; and Gilfoyle, "Prostitutes in History," 125.

64. Quote in File 1915, 5 Apr. 1915, CAHJP-INV 4349. Also see Stanchina (*Tanka Charowa*, 68, 71, 96, and 106–7) and Kushnir (*Baile de máscaras*, 105).

65. Stanchina (*Tanka Charowa*, 56, 65–66, and 144) inspired these reflections.

66. Ibid., 99, 134–35, and 137; and Jewish Association, *Report 1913*, 31, and *Report 1926*, 35.

67. Shilo, *Princess or Prisoner?*, 201; Yagupsky, interview, 1984, AP; Stanchina, *Tanka Charowa*, 67; Bristow, *Prostitution and Prejudice*, 144; and Vincent, *Bodies and Souls*, 79–81. Ten of twenty-five Argentine Jewish prostitutes studied in 1936 were illiterate; see League of Nations, "Enquiry," File: Rehabilitation 3/5, Box 111, 4/NVA, FL. Also see Bliss (*Compromised Positions*, 198–99).

68. Jewish Association, *Report 1913*, 31; Dávila and Orozco, "Bataclanas y vedettes," 16; and Stanchina, *Tanka Charowa*, 65 and 124.

69. "Memoria . . . 1936," 21, Box 291, IWO.

70. Zak, interview, 1985, AP; Kushnir, *Baile de máscaras*, 146 and 155; and McCreery, "'This Life of Misery and Shame,'" 350–51.

71. Feierstein, *Historia*, 280–81; and Bra, *La organización negra*, 145–64 and 213–17. Also see *La Nación*, 28 January 1931, 1; *La Razón*, 24 December 1930, 1; *Gaceta del Foro*, 1 November 1930, 3–6; and *The Standard*, 21 May 1930, unnumbered page. In contrast, Jewish prostitutes joined and helped lead such groups in Brazil; see Kushnir (*Baile de máscaras*).

72. This is seen in numerous Ezras Noschim cases and Stanchina (*Tanka Charowa*, 60–61 and 135).

73. Pereira ("Prostitutes and the Law," 283–84) found that prostitutes emphasized their victimization to win court cases.

74. *Gaceta del Foro*, 1 November 1930, 5; Glickman, *The Jewish White Slave Trade*, 55; Bra, *La organización negra*, 144–45 and 175; Stanchina, *Tanka Charowa*, 66, 106–8, 115, and 132; and Pereira, "Prostitutes and the Law," 284–85.

75. Bra, *La organización negra*, 123 and 130–31.

76. This is suggested by Stanchina (*Tanka Charowa*, 132).

77. Jewish Association, *Report 1930*, 33; and *Gaceta del Foro*, 1 November 1930, 5. Stanchina (*Tanka Charowa*, 111) attributes pimps' attacks on prostitutes who left them to jealousy and income loss.

78. "Memoria . . . 1936," 11–12, Box 291, IWO. Also see Lighton Robinson, 26 Mar. 1928, Co1: Argentine. Work at Port of Buenos Aires, Box 112, 4/IBS, FL; and Stanchina (*Tanka Charowa*, 60–62).

79. "Memoria . . . 1936," 12–13, Box 291, IWO. Also see 23 Nov. 1931, CAHJP-INV 4349; National Council . . . Moral Welfare Committee, 19 Feb. 1936, File S 135 B: League of Nations, Rehabilitation, Box 111, 4/NVA, FL; Gilfoyle ("Prostitutes in History," 128); McCreery ("'This Life of Misery and Shame,'" 348); and Marks ("Jewish Women," 9–10).

80. Stanchina, *Tanka Charowa*, 76, 82–83, and 111–12. Jozami's novel discussed in Korn et al. (*Los huéspedes del 20*, 87).

81. See Liberman's photos and correspondence in Schalom (*La polaca*, between 176 and 177). Also see Glickman (*The Jewish White Slave Trade*, 55).

82. Photos in "Trata de blancas" box, IWO; and Schalom (*La polaca*, between 176 and 177). I thank Elena Berflein for showing me the photographs. Also see Stanchina (*Tanka Charowa*, especially 72) and Hyam (*Empire and Sexuality*, 146). Kushnir (*Baile de máscaras*) describes mutual aid among Brazilian Jewish prostitutes. While Bliss (*Compromised Positions*, 44–46 and 119) finds lesbianism among Mexican prostitutes, I cannot document it.

83. P. Katz, *Páginas selectas*, 30; Pereira, "Prostitutes and the Law"; Korn et al., *Los huéspedes del* 20, 89; and Stanchina, *Tanka Charowa*, 89 and 133.

FIVE *Family and Sexuality*

Epigraph sources: Levy, *Crónica de una familia sefaradí*, 67; Zak, interview, 1985, AP.

1. Zak interview, 1985, AP.

2. My thoughts on Jews and respectability draw upon Prell (*Fighting to Become Americans*, 26; also 10 (quote); Guy (*Sex and Danger*, especially 18–23, 34–35, 118–19, 126, and 129); Tananbaum ("Philanthropy and Identity," 951); Marks ("Jewish Women"); and Margaret Power, personal communication. Foote ("Race, Gender and Citizenship") argues similarly for black Costa Ricans. On women's honor, see Caulfield (*In Defense of Honor*) and "Gender and Sexuality in Latin America."

W. French ("Prostitutes and Guardian Angels," 537) found that prostitutes were the "dominant symbol of lower-class cultural and moral degeneracy" in Porfirian Mexico.

3. Deutsch, "Los nacionalistas." On liberals and Jews before 1930, see Avni (*Argentina and the Jews*, 16–20, 22–25, 29–30, and 91).

4. See the related argument in Guy ("'White Slavery'").

5. File 1279–33, Vs. 46, and Folder 1952, CAHJP-INV 4349; and Jewish Association, *Report 1934 to 1935*, 32. Ezras Noschim was Ashkenazi, as were most of its cases—including, unless otherwise noted, those discussed here. This reflected the Mediterranean and Central European Jews' minority status, and the pride and cultural differences that may have kept them from seeking the organization's services.

6. Friedman-Kasaba, *Memories of Migration*, 149 and 151; Burstein, "Translating Immigrant Women," 15–29; and W. French, "Prostitutes and Guardian Angels," 538–39. James (*Doña María's Story*, 255–70) and Guy (*Sex and Danger*) show that many Argentines associated prostitution and licentious sexuality with women's work outside the home. According to Nouzeilles ("An Imaginary Plague," 59), doctors blamed assertive female sexuality on modernity.

7. Cosse, "Cultura y sexualidad"; Barrancos, "Moral sexual" and "Historia"; Felitti, "El placer de elegir"; and Nari, "Las prácticas anticonceptivas." I found no information on abortion or contraception.

8. Jewish Association, *Report 1913*, 40; R. L. de Glucksmann, 27 Nov. 1926, Folder 1926, CAHJP-INV 4349; Eissler, interview with author, 2000; Smolensky and Vigevani Jarach, *Tantas voces*, 66; and Schwarcz, *Y a pesar de todo*, 41.

9. Teubal, *Consejos a la mujer*, 23, 26–27; and quotes in Levy, *Crónica de una familia sefaradí*, 67, 77, and 84. For Mediterranean Jews, family honor went beyond sexual purity; see Gutkowski (*Erase una vez*, 316).

10. Yadid de Chami, interview with author, 1998.

11. Farja, interview with author, 2000.

12. Emanuel, interview, 1988, AP. Stolen (*The Decency of Inequality*, 57 and 59) describes Italo-Argentine chaperones.

13. Kohen, *El color de la nostalgia*, 51 and 55–56; *Colonia Mauricio*, 69–70; Jurkowicz de Eichbaum, *Cuando*, 157, 159; and Pascaner, interview with author, 1997. These practices resembled those of the broader society; see Barrancos ("Moral sexual," 210).

14. Nissensohn de Stilerman, interview, 1991, AP.

15. Soprotimis, Libro de Actas, esp. 3 Sept. 1923, CAHJP-HM2/1424a; Sommer, interview with author, 2000; *Mundo Israelita*, 8 June 1923, 4; statistics in Sociedad de Damas, *Memoria y balance*, 1930, 29 and 31. On a Jewish organization with similar goals in New York in the early 1900s, see Sinkoff ("Educating for 'Proper' Jewish Womanhood," 589 and 596).

16. Sociedad de Damas Israelitas de Beneficencia, Libro de Actas, 24 Sept. 1945, 75, MTL; *Mundo Israelita*, 24 September 1927: 2 and 24 September 1932: 1. The same was true of U.S. Jewish girls' orphanages; see Friedman ("Founders," 35–36).

17. *Tribuna Hebrea*, 15 November 1931: 18, and 15 August 1932: 20 (quote).

18. Zanders de Silber, interview, 1986, AP.

19. Kohen, *El color de la nostalgia*, 56–57; Yadid de Chami, interview with author, 1998; *Tiempo Argentino*, 3 November 1984, 10; and Barrancos, "Moral sexual," 212. Klapper (*Jewish Girls*, 226), finds similar ignorance among U.S. Jewish girls.

20. Poch and Turjanski de Gold, *Orígenes y trascendencia*, 121–22; anonymous interview, with author, 1998; and *Tiempo Argentino,* 3 November 1984, 10.

21. Mayo, interview with author, 2000; see Galante de Franco, interview with author, 1997, for another example.

22. Levy, *Crónica de una familia sefaradí*, 60 and 65–66; and Emanuel, interview, 1988, AP. The young couple may have married at a later date.

23. Ropp, *Un colono judío*, 40; Garfunkel, *Narro mi vida*, 93–94 and 337–39; Grimberg and Trumper, interview, 1989, AP; and Schvartz de Pitasni, interview, with author, 1998 (quote). On Jewish marriage customs in Europe and Palestine, see Freeze (*Jewish Marriage*, 11–72), M. Kaplan (*The Making of the Jewish Middle Class*, 85–116), and Shilo (*Princess or Prisoner?*, 35–68).

24. Alpersohn, *Colonia Mauricio*, 110–11; N. Rapoport, *Desde lejos hasta ayer*, 53; *Mundo Israelita*, 6 January 1940: 2, and 1 June 1940: 2; and Tolcachier, "Continuidad o ruptura," 50, note 28. Stolen (*The Decency of Inequality*, 180) finds Italo-Argentine matchmakers in the early 1900s; Joselit (*The Wonders of America*, 12) discovers Jewish marriage brokers in New York in 1938.

25. Kohen, *El color de la nostalgia*, 115, 121, and 126–27; and N. Rapoport, *Desde lejos hasta ayer*, 58. While marriage brokers operated in the Mediterranean region—see Gutkowski (*Erase una vez*, 169, 316, and 422) and Shilo (*Princess or Prisoner?*, 41–42)—I have not found any of these backgrounds in Argentina. Biale ("Love, Marriage") finds romance in Jewish arranged marriages in the 1700s and 1800s.

26. 534–34 Vs. 55, CAHJP-INV 4349. For a case with a happier ending, see Jurkowicz de Eichbaum, *Cuando*, 85.

27. M. Kaplan, *The Making of the Jewish Middle Class*, 86; Caplan (1989), Ehrenfeld (1996), and Maladietzsky (1989), interviews, AP; and Sommer, interview with author, 2000.

28. *Tribuna Hebrea*, 5 October 1929, unnumbered page; and *Mundo Israelita*, 8 June 1940, 2.

29. *Juventud* 2, no. 17 (1 November 1912): 9–10; and *Israel*, 4 March 1921, 1 and 4. On changing marital patterns among immigrants in New York, see Ewen (*Immigrant Women*, 226–29).

30. Cohen de Isaharoff, interview with author, 1997.

31. Poch and Turjanski de Gold, *Orígenes y trascendencia*, 118–19 and 138.

32. 388 C. 129, 1144–37 V. 100, 368–39 V. 118, CAHJP-INV 4349; Cociovitch, *Génesis de Moisés Ville*, 147; N. Rapoport, *Desde lejos hasta ayer*, 58; Deere and León de Leal, "Liberalism," 653–54; and Dora Barrancos, Adriana Brodsky, Donna Guy, Robin Judd, Marion Kaplan, and Muriel Nazzari, personal communications. However, Zimerman de Faingold (*Memorias*, 30) notes that her colonist father provided a dowry in the late 1910s.

Dowries in twentieth-century Argentina have not been studied. Like the Mediterranean Jews, Italo-Argentines had trousseaus; see Stolen (*The Decency of In-*

equality, 57). On dowries and trousseaus among Jews in the Mediterranean, see Gutkowski (*Erase una vez*, 56, 62, 127–28, 193, 196–98, 273, 315, 320, 368, and 477) and Shilo (*Princess or Prisoner?*, 50–54). On Europe, see M. Kaplan (*The Making of the Jewish Middle Class*, 87–88, 93–98, and 99–101) and Freeze (*Jewish Marriage*). In the 1920s dowries died out in Germany and, according to Prell (*Fighting to Become Americans*, 101–2), among U.S. Ashkenazim.

33. Ambasch de Staravolsky (1998), Cohen de Isaharoff (1997), Yadid de Chami (1998), Mayo (2000), Tawil de Ini (1998), and Salón de Esperanza (2000), interviews with author; *Israel*, 13 and 20 April 1934, 5; Kohen, *El color de la nostalgia*, 51–52; and Bensignor, interview, 1992, AP. Epstein ("Los judeo-marroquíes," 125), however, finds that in the early years, Moroccan brides averaged 20.5 years old. Brothers sometimes also married in order of age, according to Bercovich de Zlotnitsky, interview with author, 1997.

34. Quote in 163–41, 127, CAHJP-INV 4349; Silvia Hansman, personal communication; M. Kaplan, *The Making of the Jewish Middle Class*, 92–93; and Freeze, *Jewish Marriage*, 24.

35. Gutkowski, *Rescate de la herencia cultural*, 85; and Farja, interview with author, 2000.

36. Farja (2000) and Frank (2000), interviews with author; Smolensky and Vigevani Jarach, *Tantas voces*, 82; Knopoff (n.d.), Tarica (n.d.), and Koval Magrán (1989), interviews, AP.

37. Elnecavé, *Crisol de vivencias judías*, 29; Smilg, interview with author, 2000; Jurkowicz de Eichbaum, *Cuando*, 161, 163; and Edelman, *Banderas*, 24. Other examples are in Ruetter, interview with author, 2000; Knopoff, interview, n.d., AP; and Schvartz de Pelasni, interview with author, 1997. Klapper (*Jewish Girls*, 221) describes how young U.S. Jews met in literary societies and clubs.

38. Prell, *Fighting to Become Americans*, 59–60; Corbin, *Women for Hire*; Barrancos, "Moral sexual"; and Hunefeldt, *Liberalism in the Bedroom*.

39. Heilbrun, *Writing a Woman's Life*, 21; and *Israel*, 24 September 1920, 34.

40. Nissensohn de Stilerman, interview, 1991, AP. Both became Zionist leaders; see chapter 8.

41. Guelman de Belmes, interview with author, 1997.

42. Yadid de Chami, interview with author, 1998.

43. Cohen de Isaharoff, interview with author, 1997.

44. *Israel*, 24 September 1920, 35–36.

45. I. Katz, *De raíces y sitios*, 236 and 269–70.

46. Yadid de Chami, interview with author, 1998.

47. Shilo, *Princess or Prisoner?*, 50.

48. *Israel*, 13 August 1920: unnumbered page; Appointment book 1931, entry no. 30, 29 April 1931, and 577–32 Vs. 16, CAHJP-INV 4349; Levy, *Crónica de una familia sefaradí*, 85, 89, and 91; Gutkowski, *Rescate de la herencia cultural*, 213; and Ford, *The Girls*, 66–67.

49. *Mundo Israelita*, 25 March 1933, 1. This is the only information I found on lesbianism, imagined or real.

50. Folder 1936, planilla 1935; 17 Sept. 1953, Sociedad to HIAS; Ezras Noschim, *Obra social*, 15; 321–32 Vs.9, all in CAHJP-INV 4349.

51. Galante de Franco, interview with author, 1997.

52. Yadid de Chami, interview with author, 1998.

53. Ibid.

54. Bensignor, interview, 1992, AP; Rebhun, *The Heart Is Unknown Country*, 211; Shilo, *Princess or Prisoner?*, 147; and numerous interviews with men in AP.

55. Hassid (1998) and Elnecavé (1997), interviews with author; Edelman, *Banderas*, 31–34; Bortnik de Duchovny, *Recuerdos*. Also see Guelman de Belmes (1997), Ruetter (2000), and Furman (1997), interviews with author.

56. "Memoria . . . 1936," 35–38, Box 291, IWO. U.S. middle-class reformers in the early 1900s associated "youthful female sexual behaviors" with prostitution; see Friedman-Kasaba (*Memories of Migration*, 149).

57. 290–38 V. 103, CAHJP-INV 4349.

58. "Memoria . . . 1936," 9–10, Box 291, IWO. Caulfield (*In Defense of Honor*) describes how elites and plebeians utilized common notions about gender and honor to support their differing interests.

59. 245–42 V. 127, CAHJP-INV 4349.

60. Ezras Noschim, Libro de Actas, 1930–1949, 28 June 1944, 344; 181–34 Vs. 50; 306–34 V. 51, CAHJP-INV 4349; Gílenberg, interview with author, 1997; S. Itzigsohn et al., *Integración*, 256; and Grunfeld, *Memorias de un anarquista*, 45. Many Argentine couples sought Uruguayan divorces, although Argentina did not recognize them, and a few couples made use of a law that permitted divorce if the couple had been separated for ten years and did not want to reunite; see Lavrin (*Women*, 236–42).

61. 336 Carpeta 128 and 370–39 V. 118, 464–37 V. 92, 186–37 V. 89, 36–38 V. 101, CAHJP-INV 4349. Compare to Klubock (*Contested Communities*, 208–15), Stern (*The Secret History of Gender*), Rebhun (*The Heart Is Unknown Country*), and Stolen (*The Decency of Inequality*, 190–91 and 196–99). Shilo (*Princess or Prisoner?*, 82–83) does not find deep intimacy among Jewish couples in Jerusalem.

62. Asociación Filantrópica Argentina, 7 Oct. 1941, #1070, file 1, AJJDCA.

63. 306–34 V. 51, CAHJP-INV 4349.

64. 934–38 V. 111, CAHJP-INV 4349.

65. Plinie Katz cited in Schers, "Inmigrantes y política," 78; and "Memoria . . . 1936," 7–8, CAHJP-INV 4349. Such stories abounded among U.S. Jews; see Friedman ("'Send Me My Husband,'" 4).

66. Singerman, *Mis dos vidas*, 307. See 800–37 V. 96, CAHJP-INV 4349, for an adulterous woman who felt no guilt.

67. Bargman, "Un ámbito," 55. Susana Sigwald de Carioli, director of a local archive, finds many so-called abductions in the history of Carlos Casares. On such

behavior among non-Jews, see Slatta (*The Gauchos*, 59) and Chasteen ("Trouble Between Men and Women," 126–27).

68. Gerchunoff, *The Jewish Gauchos*, 61–64. He also suggests another *rapto* (38).

69. Yagupsky, interview, 1984, AP.

70. José Winderman, "Breve historia de la Colonia Mauricio," AHAM.

71. *Noticias Gráficas*, 24 April 1934, unnumbered page; *La Prensa*, 25 April 1934; and 173–34 Vs. 50, CAHJP-INV 4349. For other cases of Jewish girls who ran off with non-Jews, see 630–32 Vs. 18, and Policía File, 19 Sept. 1930, CAHJP-INV 4349.

72. File 1934, 191–34 Vs. 50, and "Trata de Blancas Informe 1934 al . . . 1935," CAHJP-INV 4349; also see Tinsman, *Partners in Conflict*, 77.

73. Folder 1927, 4 April 1927, CAHJP-INV 4349. Also see Folder 1179–53, VA. 43, Trata de Blancas box, IWO; and Corbin (*Women for Hire*, 290 and 298).

74. Chirom, *Pequeña familia*, 18–19. For a similar story set among Sephardim, see Brodsky ("The Contours of Identity," 285–86).

75. Schallman, interview, 1991, AP.

76. Dora Alpersohn, "La tragedia del Acantilado," *Juventud*, July 1914, 33–37.

77. Blomberg, "La vuelta de Sonia." Norton ("Un casamiento en el gran mundo") relates the story of a doomed marriage between a Jewish man and non-Jewish woman. Popular theater, however, lauded intermarriage between Jewish women and Catholic men to promote assimilation; see Castro ("The Sainete Porteño").

78. Faingold de Villagra (1997) and Salón de Esperanza (2000), interviews with author.

79. Eissler, interview with author, 2000.

80. Tolcachier, "Continuidad o ruptura," 51–53; Lifchitz de Hamburgo, interview with author, 1997; and Viviana Gorbato, "Apuntes de una viajera," in *Colonia Mauricio*, 73–75.

81. Mirelman, *Jewish Buenos Aires*, 102–3; Green, *Jewish Workers*, 212. Epstein, "Los judeo-marroquíes," 116 and 127; Schwarcz, *Y a pesar de todo*, 229; and *Tribuna Hebrea* 1, no. 4 (November 20, 1929): unnumbered page.

82. Mirelman, *Jewish Buenos Aires*, 104–9; and Zemer, "The Rabbinic Ban."

83. Schmeltz and Dellapergola, "The Demography of Latin American Jewry," 79–80; and Geldstein, "Matrimonios mixtos," 228. Of the couples Geldstein (228 and 230) studied in Salta in 1986, 19 percent of those who were forty or older were mixed. The intermarriage rate among U.S. Jews in the 1940s was only 3 percent; see Klapper (*Jewish Girls*, 220). On other immigrant groups and intermarriage, see Baily ("Marriage Patterns"), Szuchman ("The Limits of the Melting Pot"), Freundlich de Seefeld ("La integración de extranjeros"), Moya (*Cousins and Strangers*, 329–30), Stolen (*The Decency of Inequality*, 162–63); and Míguez ("Marriage," 186).

84. Cociovitch, *Génesis de Moisés Ville*, 146–47; and Levy, *Crónica de una familia sefaradí*, 66 and 91.

85. Yagupsky, interview, 1984, AP. Also see Bargman, "Un ámbito," 53; Epstein,

"Los judeo-marroquíes," 127; *Israel,* 30 April 1918, 325; and Brodsky, "The Contours of Identity," 306–8. Shilo (*Princess or Prisoner?*, 45–49) discusses intercommunal marriages in Jerusalem.

86. Soriano, interview with author, 2000.

87. *Israel*, 9 September 1921: 13 and 30 December 1921: 5.

88. Alpersohn, *Colonia Mauricio*, 236–43, quote on 236; Y. Levin, "Posturas genéricas," 57; and Sichel (1996) and Yagupsky (1984), interviews, AP.

89. Folder 1938, 4 Dec. 1938, CAHJP-INV 4349.

90. On this incident, see *El Diario,* 17 July 1925: 1 and 18 July 1925: 5; Cohen, 20 October 1925, Folder 1925, Box 16, and Copiador (1924–28), 15 June and 10 August 1925, CAHJP-INV 4349; *Mundo Israelita*, 20 June 1925, 1; and *Israel*, 24 July 1925, 14. I thank Adela Harispuru for *El Diario.* On hysteria and sexuality, see Nouzeilles ("An Imaginary Plague," 59).

91. Y. Levin, "Posturas genéricas," 58; and 136–41 Vs. 127, CAHJP-INV 4349.

92. 362–37 V. 91, Box 291, IWO.

93. "Trata de Blancas. Informe 1934 . . . 1935," CAHJP-INV 4349.

94. 986–33, Vs. 35, CAHJP-INV 4349. On domestic violence, see Freeze (*Jewish Marriage*, 173–77) and Shilo (*Princess or Prisoner?*, 85–89). U.S. Jewish philanthropies also tried to salvage troubled marriages; see Friedman ("'Send Me My Husband'").

95. 75–40 V. 121, CAHJP-INV 4349.

96. 69–40 V. 120; 561–34 Vs. 55, CAHJP-INV 4349. Also see 790–36 V. 82; 438/43 129, and Exp. 805, Carp. 132; 536 C. 130.

97. Liniado, *Recuerdos imborrables*, 25, 34, 42, 47–48, and 53–55. Desertion also afflicted Jews elsewhere; see Friedman ("'Send Me My Husband'"), Freeze (*Jewish Marriage*, 232–35), and Shilo (*Princess or Prisoner?*, 190–97).

98. Shilo, *Princess or Prisoner?*, 190–97.

99. 682–37, V. 94, CAHJP-INV 4349; Donna Guy, personal communication.

100. 63–37 Vs. 101, CAHJP-INV 4349.

101. 388 C. 129, CAHJP-INV 4349; and Freeze, *Jewish Marriage*, 181–82.

102. 154–34 Vs. 49, CAHJP-INV 4349.

103. In contrast, the feminist-led Jüdischer Frauenbund did; see M. Kaplan (*The Making of the Jewish Middle Class*, 214).

104. Guy, *Sex and Danger*, 19–20; S. Itzigsohn et al., *Integración*, 207; and Zak, interview, 1985, AP.

SIX *Leftists and Union Members through the 1930s*

Epigraph sources: Kanutsky, interview, 1985–86, AP; Absatz, *El Obrero Textil*, no. 22 (June 1938), 6.

1. Ellen DuBois in "Considering," 151, helped inspire these thoughts.

2. Olcott, *Revolutionary Women*, 72, 91.

3. On these activities, see Suriano (*Anarquistas*), Barrancos (*Anarquismo, Educación*, and *La escena iluminada*), and Camarero and Herrera (*El Partido Socialista en Argentina*).

4. Shepherd, *A Price below Rubies*; and Glenn, *Daughters of the Shtetl*, 179. An exception was Margherita Sarfatti, Benito Mussolini's former mistress, who lived in Buenos Aires and Montevideo in the 1940s, but her fascism had cooled and she was no longer politically active; see Cannistraro and Sullivan (*Il Duce's Other Woman*, 529–45).

5. Exceptions include Bellucci ("Anarquismo y feminismo"), Clementi (*María Rosa Oliver*), Lobato ("Mujeres en la fábrica"), Navarro ("Hidden, Silent, and Anonymous"), and Tuccio ("La mujer obrera argentina").

6. Among many works, see Moya ("Italians"), Suriano (*Anarquistas*), Barrancos (*Anarquismo*), Rock (*Politics in Argentina*), and Molyneux, "No God."

7. Moya, "The Positive Side of Stereotypes."

8. *La Protesta*, 22 July 1932: 12 and 12 August 1930: 3; Moya, "The Positive Side of Stereotypes," 30–31 and 34–35; and Feierstein, *Historia*, 185–86.

9. Dubovsky and Grunfeld, interviews with author, both 2000.

10. Information on Chanovsky comes from Benjamín Dubovsky (interview with author, 2000); Dubovsky, "Los compañeros que conocí: I," *El Libertario*, 47 (December 1999): 8; "Los compañeros que conocí: II," *El Libertario*, no. 48 (April–May 2000): 5; and Bellucci ("Anarquismo y feminismo," 67–68).

11. This library is mentioned in *La Revuelta* (first half November 1919): unnumbered page.

12. The FACA, founded in 1935, was renamed the FLA in 1955; see Pérez. Anarchism after 1930 is largely unexplored; see the firsthand account by Grunfeld (*Memorias de un anarquista*).

13. Grunfeld and Dubovsky, interviews with author, both 2000; Sara Dubovsky, *Nuestra Tribuna*, 1 May 1924: 4; Bellucci, "Anarquismo y feminismo"; and Rouco Buela, *Historia de un ideal vivido*, 62.

14. Dubovsky and Grunfeld, interviews with author, both 2000; L. Milstein, interview, 1986, AP; Dubovsky, "Los compañeros que conocí: III," *El Libertario*, no. 49 (August–September 2000): 6; *Nuestra Tribuna*, 15 December 1922: 3, 1 January 1923: 4, 15 July 1923: 4, and 1 November 1924: 4; and *La Protesta*, 24 September 1932, 4. On anarchist festivities, see Suriano (*Anarquistas*), Evans ("Setting the Stage for Struggle"), and Castro ("Workers, Strikes").

15. *Boletín de la Liga de Educación Racionalista*, 25 January 1915: 7, and March 1915: 1–2 and 5; and *La Escuela Popular*, 15 September 1913: 14–17, 15 October 1913: 2 and 22. Also see Barrancos (*Anarquismo*, 222–25) and Suriano (*Anarquistas*, 245–48).

16. This and the preceding paragraph draw on N. Bursuk (interview with author, 2000, and "Recuerdos del anarquismo"); Schoijet (*Páginas para la historia*,

29, photo after 32, and 117–18); S. Itzigsohn et al., *Integración*, 29–30, 32, 42–3, 70; and Bursuk de Scher, interview, n.d., AP. On Jazanovich, see Rawin, interview with author, 2000; P. Katz (*Páginas selectas*, 29–30); and Schers ("Inmigrantes y política," 83–86).

17. N. Bursuk, interview with author, 2000, and "Recuerdos del anarquismo"; and S. Itzigsohn, et al, *Integración*, 43–4, 71.

18. Bursuk de Scher interview, n.d., AP; N. Bursuk, interview with author, 2000; S. Itzigsohn, et al, *Integración*, 72; and *La* FORA, June 1934, 4.

19. Myerhoff, *Remembered Lives*, 233–35.

20. Rawin, interview with author, 2000; Koifman, "La 'Asociación Racionalista Judía' "; Pelacoff, "Judíos, anarquistas, argentinos"; and "La Asociación Racionalista Judía y el anarquismo en Argentina," MS, Archivo de los Compañeros. The archive also has Racionalista publications in Spanish. Also see *La Antorcha*, 12 January 1923, 4; *La Protesta*, 19 October 1932: 8 and 10 December 1932: 1; and Barrancos (*Anarquismo*, 225–27). The Racionalista was not directly related to the Liga de Educación Racionalista.

21. S. Milstein, Rawin, and N. Bursuk, interviews with author, all 2000; L. Milstein and Chalcoff, interviews, both 1986, AP; Pelacoff, "Judíos, anarquistas, argentinos"; and Koifman, "La 'Asociación Racionalista Judía.' "

22. Laubstein, *Bund*, especially 169–207; Frydman interviews, with author 2000, and 1998, AP; and Schers, "Inmigrantes y política," 79. The Workmen's Circle of the U.S., a Jewish Socialist group with a large female membership, had no Argentine equivalent; see McCune ("Creating a Place for Women").

23. Reflecting their importance and the party's legality, there is more literature on female Socialists than on women of other affiliations. See, for example, Lavrin (*Women* and "Alicia Moreau de Justo"), Carlson (*¡Feminismo!*), Barrancos (*Inclusión/Exclusión* and "Socialismo y sufragio femenino"), Feijóo ("Gabriela Coni" and *Las feministas*), Guy ("Emilio and Gabriela Coni"), Henault (*Alicia Moreau de Justo*), Iñigo Carrera ("Perfiles"), and Ferro (*Las socialistas*).

24. Two fundamental studies are Walter (*The Socialist Party of Argentina*) and Camarero and Herrera (*El Partido Socialista en Argentina*).

25. On the Chertkoffs and Gucovsky, I rely on *La Vanguardia*, 12 July 1928, 2 and 4; Iñigo Carrera ("Perfiles" and personal communications); and Rocca ("Juan B. Justo"). Also see *Fray Mocho*, August 9, 1912, unnumbered page; *Juventud* 6, no. 49 (July 1916): 21; *Fenia Chertcoff*; Cuello, *Ejemplo noble*; *Acción Socialista* 6, no. 1 (14 June 1928); Ferro, *Las socialistas*; and Escliar, *Mujeres en la literatura*, 54–63. In the literature, the family name sometimes appears as Chertcoff and sometimes as Chertkoff.

26. On Adela and Mariana, see *Juventud* 2, no. 15 (1 September 1912): 16; *La Vanguardia*, 8 October 1904: 3, 20–21 May 1912: 2, 11–12 August 1927: 5, and 24 May 1933: 1; Ferro, *Las socialistas*, 35; Rocca, "Juan B. Justo," 110–11; and articles and letters in Caja Justo, AIC. After Mariana's death, Justo married Alicia Moreau.

27. *La Vanguardia*, 14 November 1909: 1 (quote), 13–14 May 1912: 1, 12 July 1928: 2, and 4 June 1934: 3; "Rocca, Juan B. Justo," 108; Chertcoff de Repetto, "El movimiento social femenino," 141–45; Cuello, *Ejemplo noble*, 52–53; Lavrin, *Women*, 258 and 261; and Carlson, *¡Feminismo!*, 142. *La Vanguardia* covered many CSF events. Socialism refers to the Argentine party, socialism to the general ideology. The Sociedad de Beneficencia, which oversaw women's welfare institutions, had long lobbied officials; see Guy (*Performing Charity*). Yet these women exerted influence as members of the elite, while Socialist women were middle- and lower-class.

28. *Fenia Chertcoff*, 8 and 82–83; Cuello, *Acción femenina*, 17 and 19, and *Ejemplo noble*, 42–43 and 162; Chertcoff de Repetto, "El movimiento social femenino," 142–44; Rocca, "Juan B. Justo," 108; Lavrin, *Women*, 261–63; and Navarro, "Hidden, Silent, and Anonymous," 170–72.

29. *Unión y Labor* 1, no. 10 (21 July 1910): 19 (quote), 20; and Primer Congreso, *Historia*, 11. On the congress, see Lavrin (*Women*, 29–32) and Carlson (*¡Feminismo!*, 139–52).

30. *Humanidad Nueva* (1916): 70.

31. *Humanidad Nueva* (1918): 1–3; and Primer Congreso, *Historia*, 426.

32. *Fenia Chertcoff*, 8, 100 (quote), and 122; Chertkoff quoted in Rocca, "Juan B. Justo," 108; Justo quoted in Camarero and Herrera, *El Partido Socialista en Argentina*, 13; *La Vanguardia*, 12 July 1928, 2; Cuello, *Ejemplo noble*, 54; and Barrancos, *La escena iluminada*, especially 41 and 226–27, and *Educación*, 21–34. Morgade ("La docencia," 98–104) discusses the importance of Socialist teachers.

33. *Acción Socialista* 6, no. 1 (14 June 1928): 49 and 119; Barrancos, *Educación*, 42–49 and 56–74; *La Vanguardia*, 12 July 1928, 2; and Omar de Lucía, "Los socialistas y la infancia," 51.

34. Nicolás Iñigo Carrera, personal communication; *Nuestra Causa* 3, no. 24 (June 1921): 281; *La Vanguardia*, 12 July 1928: 2, and 31 December 1904: 2; Ferro, *Las socialistas*, 29; *Vida Femenina* 2, no. 21 (15 April 1935): 19; Cuello, *Ejemplo noble*, 53 and 58; and Omar de Lucía, "Los socialistas y la infancia," 50.

35. *La Vanguardia*, 28 July 1929, 6; *Acción Socialista* 1, no. 7 (1 January 1924): 102–4; and 6, no. 1 (14 June 1928): 49; *Fenia Chertcoff*, 42–44, 86–87, 94, 96, and 126–33; and Barrancos, "Socialistas." The recreos lasted into the 1940s.

36. Repetto, *Mi paso por la agricultura*, 13, 41–46, and 51–69; *Acción Socialista* 6, no. 1 (14 June 1928): 27 and 49; Rocca, "Juan B. Justo," 120 and 129; and *Fenia Chertcoff*, 61.

37. *La Vanguardia*, 12 July 1928: 2, and 4 June 1934: 3; and *Acción Socialista* 6, no. 1 (14 June 1928): 49. Fenia was also an artist; see *Acción Socialista* (ibid., 185–86) and Casa del Pueblo (*Exposición*).

38. Di Carlo, "Mujeres de actuación destacada"; "Liga Pro Alfabetismo de Adultos," in Folder 45, and *La Razón*, 1930, clipping, Folder 46, Box 14, Frances R. Grant papers, MC 671, RUL; Rocca, "Juan B. Justo," 129–30; *La Vanguardia*, 13–14 May 1912: 1, 5 December 1927: 2, 6 May 1928: 1, 21 August 1928: 1, 26 August 1929:

3, 15 December 1928: 4, 28 July 1929: 6, 2–3 January 1930: 3, and 13 September 1932: 1; and *Unión y Labor* 1, no. 12 (September 21, 1910): 27. Also see Sosa de Newton (*Diccionario biógrafico*, 207), Weinstein and Gover de Nasatsky (*Escritores judeo-argentinos*, 1:305–6); and Gucovsky (*Tierra adentro*).

39. Quote in Di Carlo, "Mujeres de actuación destacada," unnumbered page. See Gucovsky's commentaries on music in *Anuario Socialista* (1928), 116–20; *Mundo Israelita*, 25 August 1923, 2; and *La Vanguardia*, 10 April 1927, 1. On literature, see Gucovsky, *La Vanguardia*, 16 October 1921: 7–8, 25 September 1927: 7, 15 April 1927: 1, 25 August 1928: 1–2, and 1 May 1929: 1. *La Vanguardia* reported on her lectures, from 1907 to 1932.

40. *La Vanguardia*, 3 July 1927: 1, and 9 March 1928: 1.

41. *La Vanguardia*, 27 December 1928: 1, 31 March 1929: literary supplement, 3 (quote), 21 April 1929: 2, 1 May 1929: 2, and 13 November 1930: 1–2 (quote). On the tour, see the *New York Times*, 16 January 1929: 8, 19 January 1929: 5, 25 January 1929: 9, and 2 February 1929: 14; and "Argentine Educators."

42. Rosa Perla Resnick, personal communication; *Humanidad Nueva* (1911): 529–31, (May–June 1919): 115–22 and 130–32; *La Vanguardia,* 21 January 1909: 2, and 22 March 1909: 1; *Nuestra Causa* 1, no. 8 (10 December 1919): 190–91, no. 12 (10 April 1920): 285–86; *Nuestra Causa* 2, no. 19 (November 1920): unnumbered page, no. 22 (April 1921): 231–33; *Nuestra Causa* 3, no. 23 (May 1921): 265–67, no. 24 (June 1921): unnumbered page, and no. 28 (October 1921): 417–18; *Anuario "La Razón"* (1922): 130; and Barrancos, *Inclusión/Exclusión*, 66, and *La escena iluminada*, 45. On Socialists and women's suffrage, see Lavrin (*Women*), Carlson (*¡Feminismo!*), Barrancos (*Inclusión/Exclusión*), and Hollander ("Women in the Political Economy of Argentina," 177–249).

43. *Nuestra Causa* 3, no. 23 (May 1921): 265 and 267, no. 24 (June 1921): 277–80; and *Libertad* (1 June 1928): unnumbered page. I thank Mónica Szurmuk for *Libertad*.

44. *La Vanguardia*, 21 July 1909, 2. Also see her series in *Vida Femenina* (beginning 1, no. 4, 12 November 1933, 28–29). She first wrote for *La Vanguardia* under a pen name.

45. *La Vanguardia*, 16 August 1932, 8 (quote); *Vida Femenina* 1, no. 9 (April 1934): 22, no. 11 (June 1934): 18–20, *Vida Femenina* 2, no. 13 (August 1934): 26–27 (quote), and no. 14 (September 1934): 20–22; and *Federación*, March 1935, 9, cited in Arnaiz and Chomnalez, *Mujeres que trabajan*, 39–40.

46. *La Vanguardia*, 27 February 1933, 8.

47. *La Vanguardia*, 13 February 1933: 10, and 23 February 1934: 12 (quote).

48. *La Vanguardia*, 1 May 1932, 24.

49. On this party, see *Avance* (various issues, 1937–38) and Quijada (*Aires de república*, 73).

50. *La Vanguardia,* 23 May 1903: 3, 2 June 1930: 1, 13 August 1930: 2, 15 November 1932: 9, 19 April 1934: 6, 1 June 1934: 10, and 12 February 1946: 9; Tarshish de

Wainstein (2001) and Itzcovich (2000), interviews with author; *Boletín del Partido Socialista*, September–October 1935, 14; *El Alba*, 20 October 1931: 3 and 1 November 1932: 2; *Israel*, 17 June 1921, 9; *Nuestra Causa* 2, no. 19 (November 1920): unnumbered page), and no. 22 (April 1921): 233–34; Biblioteca Obrera, *Memoria*, 16–17; and Barrancos, "Los niños proselitistas," 15–16.

51. Cohen de Isaharoff (1997) and Abourachit (1998), interviews with author; and Sergio Eisen, "Rebeca Levy de Estambul a la Boca," *El Diario*, 11 April 1995, 6.

52. *La Vanguardia*, 5 March 1930: 1, 23 February 1934: 12, 30 April 1934: 9, 9 February 1936: 3, 3 May 1936: 10, 16 March 1938: 3, 19 March 1938: 5, and 23 March 1938: 2; and *Tiempo Argentino*, 26 May 1986, 4 (quote).

53. Cernadas, Pittaluga, and Tarcus, "La historiografía"; Camarero, *A la conquista de la clase obrera*; and Schenkolewski-Kroll, "El Partido Comunista."

54. Camarero, *A la conquista de la clase obrera*, 300–301.

55. Teper, interview, 1986, AP; Corbière, "Los archivos," 21–22; and *La Internacional*, 3 February 1924: 4, 19 July 1924: 8, 17 January 1925: 7, and 21 March 1925: 4.

56. *La Internacional*, 9–10 January 1922: 3–4, 14 January 1922: 3, and 7 November 1924: 4.

57. Romo to Droz, 4 Feb. 1926; Codovilla to Stirner, n.d.; Romo to Comité Ejecutivo, Comintern, n.d.; Romo to Presidium, Comintern, 27 Sept. 1926, all in Vol. 15, Legajo 4, 1924–1928, 3363, Fondo Partido Comunista, AGN; and Corbière, "Los archivos," 15 and 22.

58. Baumkoler, *La lucha es vida*, 19–23; López, "Informe de organización del C.L.A.," n.d., vol. 17; *Boletín de Información* 1, no. 1 (1927): 13, Vol. 20, Legajo 5, 1927–1935, 3364, Fondo Partido Comunista, AGN; *El Alba*, 30 April 1922: 1, 14 May 1922: 1, and 6 March 1923: 2; Lerner, interview, 1986, AP; Svarch, "'El comunista sobre el tejado'"; Schenkolewski-Kroll, "Los judíos"; and Mateu, "La integración de los grupos idiomáticos," especially 5–6. Argentine Communists called themselves "progressives."

59. Gílenberg, interview with author, 1997; S. Itzigsohn, et al., *Integración*, 256; Partido Comunista Argentino, Comité Central, Bureau Político, acta no. 22, 1928, 1–2, Vol. 21, Legajo 5, 3364, Fondo Partido Comunista, AGN; "Manifiesto," Dec. 1935, Box 1070, IWO; Schenkolewski-Kroll, "Los judíos," 6–12; *La Internacional* 25 April 1925: 6, and 31 May 1925: 2; *La Luz*, 25 May 1934, 226; and P. Katz, *Páginas selectas*, 110. On Procor in Moisesville, see *El Alba*, 16 February 1926: 1, 31 December 1929: 2, 21 January 1930: 3, 11 February 1930: 1, 18 February 1930: 2, 20 May 1930: 2, and 21 April 1931: 2. Also see Dekel-Chen (*Farming the Red Land*) and R. Weinberg (*Stalin's Forgotten Zion*, especially 50–51 and 56).

60. *¡Alerta!*, 23 June 1937: 1 and 3; Lerner, interview, 1986, AP; Zadoff, *Historia de la educación judía*, 60 and 161–63; Rivanera Carlés, *Las escuelas comunistas en Argentina*; Lvovich, *Nacionalismo*, 456–58; and Visacovsky, "El discurso pedagógico."

61. IFT, *Boletín informativo*, and flyer 1938, Box 1031; IFT programs, Box 72; all in IWO; and *Di Idische Froi*, nos. 22–23 (August–September 1956): 1–2.

62. Camarero, *A la conquista de la clase obrera*; J. Horowitz, "El movimiento," 262; Iñigo Carrera, *La estrategia*, especially 234–51; and Tamarin, *The Argentine Labor Movement*, especially 129–69 and 206–7.

63. Morgade, interview with author, 2000; *El Alba*, 22 April 1930: 2, 6 June 1933: 4, 13 June 1933: 1, 20 June 1933: 1, 17 July 1934: 2, and 14 July 1936: 2; Sanjurjo, "Rosa Ziperovich," 18–19; Rajschmir, "Rosa Ziperovich"; and *Rosario/6* (16 November 1995). On delayed salaries, see Dreier (*Five Months in the Argentine*, 120–21) and Spalding ("Education in Argentina," 52). On an important early teachers' strike, see Crespí ("La huelga docente"). Olcott (*Revolutionary Women*, 96–97, 106, and passim) discusses Mexican women teachers' Communist activism.

64. Kanutsky (1985–86), Chiaskelevitz (n.d.), Rozenfarb (1986), I. Novodvorsky (1986), and Zak (1985), interviews, AP; Mina Ruetter, personal communication; Kessler-Harris, "Organizing the Unorganizable," 103; Navarro, "Hidden, Silent, and Anonymous," 183; Tuccio, "La mujer obrera argentina," 37; and S. Itzigsohn, et al., *Integración*, 188. Glenn (*Daughters of the Shtetl*, 171–72 and passim) discusses Jewish women's militancy in U.S. garment unions.

65. Kanutsky, interviews, AP (1985–86) and with Ruetter (1980); *La Vanguardia*, 3 June–2 July 1929; *La Internacional*, 8 June 1929: 4 and 15 June 1929: 3; and Tuccio, "La mujer obrera argentina," 67.

66. Kanutsky and Lewintal, interviews, both 1985–86, AP; *El Obrero de la Confección*, 1 December 1934, 1–2; *La Vanguardia*, September–November 1934; Liberman, *La unidad*, 18–19; and Tuccio, "La mujer obrera argentina," 71.

67. *El Obrero de la Confección*, 1 December 1934: 1 and October 1935: 4; *F.O.V.*, no. 6 (July 1936): 3–4; *El Obrero del Vestido*, no. 10 (September 1941): 8; *La Vanguardia*, 18 July 1936: 4 and 23 July 1936: 4; Kanutsky and Lewintal, interviews, both 1985–86, AP; and Liberman, *La unidad*, 49–52.

68. Furman, interview with author, 1997; Lewintal (1985–86) and Rozenfarb (1986), interviews, AP; *El Obrero de la Confección*, October 1935, 8; *El Obrero Sastre*, nos. 49–50 (June–July 1935): 8; *F.O.V.*, no. 4 (May 1936): 1, no. 6 (July 1936): 1, no. 9 (April 1938): 4 and 6, and no. 11 (December 1938): 2. On another Communist garment activist, Cecilia Kamenetsky, see *F.O.V.*, no. 6 (July 1936): 3). On Celia Schatz, a Communist and member of the F.O.V. board, see Liberman (*La unidad*, 27, 28); *El Obrero de la Confección*, no. 3 (October 1935): 4; *F.O.V.*, no. 6 (July 1936): 1, no. 8 (May 1937): 2, and no. 11 (December 1938): 9; and *El Obrero del Vestido*, no. 10 (November 1945): 8.

69. *El Obrero Textil*, no. 11 (May 1936): 11; J. Horowitz, *Argentine Unions*, 50–55, 67, 92–95, and 117–19; and Chiaskelevitz (n.d.) and Zak (1985), interviews, AP.

70. Absatz, interview, 1986, AP; *El Obrero Textil*, no. 9 (March 1935): 4, no. 12 (October 1936): 5, no. 16 (June 1937): 16, and no. 23 (July 1938): 4; Tuccio, "La mu-

jer obrera argentina," 84–85 and 94; Di Tella, "La Unión," 209; and J. Horowitz, *Argentine Unions*, 95.

71. *El Obrero Textil*, no. 11 (May 1936): 11, no. 16 (June 1937): 6 (quote), and no. 41 (May 1941): 4.

72. Flora Absatz, *El Obrero Textil*, no. 22 (June 1938): 6.

73. Di Tella, "La Unión," 174, note 9, and 186–87; Navarro, "Hidden, Silent, and Anonymous," 188–89; *El Obrero Textil*, no. 52 (April 30, 1942): unnumbered page, and no. 67 (September 1945): 2; and Joel Horowitz, personal communication.

74. *El Obrero Textil*, no. 31 (January 1940): 4.

SEVEN *Contesting Anti-Semitism, Fascism, and Peronism*

Epigraph sources: Drucaroff, in Comisión Femenina Israelita de Solidaridad, *Nuestros talleres*, 30; Agrupación de Intelectuales, Artistas, Periodistas, y Escritores, *Unidad*, 1, no. 1 (January 1936), 1.

1. According to Bell ("The Jews and Perón," 35), in the 1930s and 1940s, Jews fought anti-Semitism defensively instead of asserting "a positive ideal of Argentine-Jewish ethnicity." I argue that Jewish women activists constructed positive and progressive Argentine Jewish identities.

2. Bisso, *Acción Argentina* and *El Antifascismo argentino*; Cane, " 'Unity for the Defense of Culture' "; and Deutsch, "Changing the Landscape," 63–67.

3. Seibel, *Crónicas*, 123–24, 141, 147, 155, 182, and 197–99; P. Katz, *Páginas selectas*, 70–72; Carulla, *Al filo del medio siglo*, 159; and *Israel*, 16 February 1919, 791. Also see Lvovich (*Nacionalismo*, 133–86, especially 160–65), Deutsch (*Counterrevolution*, 34–37 and 73–79), and Lewin (*Cómo fue la inmigración judía*, 171).

4. Fairman, *Mate y sámovar*, 64–65.

5. Levy, *Crónica de una familia sefaradí*, 79–80.

6. *Israel*, 15 January 1919: supplement, 1 February 1919: 758 and 764–65, and 1 March 1919: 821; and Deutsch, *Counterrevolution*, 78–79.

7. Deutsch, *Counterrevolution*, especially 129–34; Caterina, *La Liga Patriótica Argentina*, 136–44; Merener (1987) and Kipen (1989), interviews, AP; P. Katz, *Páginas selectas*, 74–75; and Lewin, *Cómo fue la inmigración judía*, 173. On Jewish Liguistas, see *Vida Nuestra* 3, no. 1 (July 1919): unnumbered page; and *Israel*, 18 July 1919: 1276, 25 July 1919: 1323, 8 August 1919: 1341, and 4 March 1921: 8.

8. Solberg, *Immigration and Nationalism*, especially 20.

9. "La inmigración después de la guerra," especially 36–37, 54, 84, and 141; and Lvovich, *Nacionalismo*, 212–23.

10. Deutsch, *Las derechas*, 193–247; Zanatta, *Del estado*; and Lvovich, *Nacionalismo*. Nacionalistas and their sympathizers also were prejudiced against Asians and Arabs; see Schneider ("Inmigrantes europeos," 168).

11. Deutsch, "Los nacionalistas"; Federico Finchelstein, personal communication; Seibel, *Crónicas*, 241; Ben-Dror, *Católicos, nazis y judíos*, 78 and 111; Lvovich, *Nacionalismo*, 411, 417, and 502; and Rivanera Carlés, *Los judíos*. Nazis tended to see Jewish women as sexually unrestrained; see M. Kaplan (*Between Dignity and Despair*, 80). Gilman (*Love*, 65–90) describes how observers at the beginning of the twentieth century constructed European Jewish women as destructive sexual creatures.

12. Congreso Nacional, *Diario . . . Senadores*, 3:156. I thank Jorge Nállim for calling my attention to this material.

13. *Israel*, 26 October 1934, 3; *El Alba*, 29 June 1937, 2; *Mundo Israelita*, 24 September 1932: 3 and 8 June 1935: 5; *Argentina Libre*, 29 August 1946, 6; *Reconstruir por el Socialismo y la Libertad* (2nd half of June 1956: 1; Senkman, *La identidad judía*, 220–21 and 230; Lvovich, *Nacionalismo*, 312–71 and 443–66; and Deutsch, *Las derechas*, 225–31.

14. Itzcovich, interview with author, 2000; *¡En Guardia!* 3, no. 11 (15 April 1936): 2; *Alerta* (February–March 1942): 1 and 4. Chapter 2 mentioned additional instances.

15. Braslavsky (2000) and Guelman de Belmes (1997), interviews with author; and Mirelman, *Jewish Buenos Aires*, 47.

16. Magrán (1988) and Camín de Efron (1989), interviews, AP; *Israel*, 26 May 1933: 7, 9 June 1933: 8, and 22 June 1934: 3–4; Senkman, "Identidades colectivas," 424; Miguel Kipen, letter to *El Pueblo*, undated, Miguel Kipen archive, MHRC; *Tribuna Hebrea*, 16 May 1941, 1; and Lvovich, *Nacionalismo*, 321, and personal communication.

17. *La Vanguardia*, 17 March 1929: literary supplement, vii; 13 November 1930: 1–2; also see 1 May 1929: 1.

18. *La Vanguardia*, 2 August 1932, 12. Also see "Conferencia . . . por la Paz . . . ," Argentina Collective Box, Peace Collection, Swarthmore College; Gucovsky, 1 Oct. 1931, Folder 45, and *La Vanguardia*, 9 Nov. 1931, clipping, Folder 46, Box 14, Grant papers, RUL; *Mundo Argentino*, 25 April 1928, 11; and Lavrin ("Alicia Moreau de Justo," 188).

19. Letters in Folder 45, and *La Razón*, 11 Aug. 1931, clipping, Folder 46, Box 14, Grant papers, RUL; Nicolás Iñigo Carrera, personal communication; *La Vanguardia*, 29 August 1932: 2, 12 September 1932: 1, 13 September 1932: 1, and 16 September 1932: 2; *La Nación*, 20 August 1932: 5, and 21 August 1932: 7. I thank Asunción Lavrin and Mariela Rubinzal for this material. On the rally, see Deutsch (*Las derechas*, 208–9) and Lvovich (*Nacionalismo*, 389–90). A Gucovsky story appeared in a Socialist publication after her departure; it is reprinted in Ferro (*Las socialistas*, 67–68).

20. Clipping, sobre F-M, Caja Escritores Judeo Argentinos, CMT; Di Carlo, "Mujeres de actuación destacada"; *El Mercurio*, 12 November 1932, unnumbered page; *La Vanguardia*, 20 September 1932, unnumbered page; Barrancos, *Inclusión/*

Exclusión, 115–21; Lavrin, *Women*, 277–79 and 298; and Carlson, *¡Feminismo!*, 171–74. I thank Asunción Lavrin for the material in *La Vanguardia*.

21. *Vida Femenina* 3, no. 35 (15 June 1936): 40–42; Filer, interview with author, 1999; and Magrán, interview, 1988, AP. Also see Scheiner in *La Vanguardia,* 13 February 1933: 10, 23 February 1933: 12, 6 May 1934: 5, and 8 May 1934: 5.

22. *La Luz*, 19 August 1935: 370, 27 September 1935: 473, and 14 October 1938: 551–52; *Mundo Israelita*, 1 June 1935, 7; *El Alba*, 22 November 1938, 1; Avni, *Argentina and the Jews*, 131, 139, and 147; and P. Katz, *Páginas selectas*, 117–20.

23. *Informativo ACI*, Sept. 1941, Box 1028 / 13, and Box 266, "Antisemitismo," IWO; Ruetter, interview with author, 2000; Schenkolewski-Kroll, "El Partido Comunista," 103; and Lvovich, *Nacionalismo*, 322.

24. *Mundo Israelita*, 10 December 1938, 1 and 5; and *El Alba*, 30 July 1935: 1 (quote), and 24 September 1935: 1.

25. *Alerta*, February–March 1941, 5; and *La Luz*, 9 December 1938: 642 and 5 December 1941: 714–15.

26. *Unidad* 1, no. 1 (January 1936): 1 (quote), 2, no. 2 (September 1937): unnumbered page; *Nueva Gaceta*, no. 19 (October 1942): 10, and no. 21 (January 1943): 4; Cane, "'Unity for the Defense of Culture'"; and James Cane and Jorge Nállim, personal communications. Some leftist writers, however, criticized nineteenth-century liberals as reactionaries who feared the masses; see Cattaruzza ("Descifrando pasados" 437–40).

27. Ethel Kurlat, *Nueva Gaceta*, no. 11 (December 1941): 4. On Kurlat, see Sosa de Newton (*Diccionario biógrafico*, 237), and Weinstein and Gover de Nasatsky, 1:412.

28. Serafina Warshaver, in *Contra-fascismo* 1, no. 2 (August–September 1936): 22–25 and 31; Weinstein and Gover de Nasatsky, 2: 343–5.

29. *El Alba,* 18 June 1935: 1, 10 September 1935: 2, and 25 August 1936: 2; *Mundo Israelita,* 10 September 1938, 6; and Myerhoff, *Remembered Lives*. On reformist liberalism, see Nállim ("Conflictive Legitimacies").

30. Smolensky and Vigevani Jarach, *Tantas voces*, 300–301; also see 179 and 296.

31. Edelman, *Banderas*, 28; *Filantropía*, no. 64 (April–May 1999): 11; Rojer, *Exile in Argentina*, 130–43; Mansilla, "Breve historia del Teatro del Pueblo"; and Saítta, "Entre la cultura y la política," 414–16.

32. Braslavsky, interview with author, 2000; Rosa Scheiner, *Contra-fascismo* 1, no. 2 (August–September 1936): 27–28; Bisso, "¿Batir al naziperonismo?," 49–59; and Quijada, *Aires de república*, especially 133–37.

33. On the affinity between German Jewish and Spanish refugees, see Schwarzstein ("Entre *Franco y Perón*").

34. *C.I.A.P.E.*, 1, no. 1 (June 1937): 1–5; and Comisión Israelita de Ayuda al Pueblo Español, "Manifiesto a la Colectiridad," n.d., Box 1070, IWO.

35. *C.I.A.P.E.*, 1, no. 1 (June 1937): 1–2; CIAPE donation booklet, Box 1070, IWO;

Ayuda al Pueblo Español, 21 June 1941, 7; *Tribuna Hebrea*, 20 August 1938, 3; Edelman, *Banderas*, 71–73; Schenkolewski-Kroll, "El Partido Comunista," 101–2; Poch and Turjanski de Gold, *Orígenes y trascendencia*, 123; *Mundo Israelita*, 27 March 1937, 6; and *El Alba*, 18 May 1937: 1 and 31 January 1939: 1. On general aid efforts, see Edelman (*Banderas*, 43–49), Schwarzstein (*Entre Franco y Perón*, 102–8), Quijada (*Aires de república*, 135–68), and Trifone and Svarzman (*La repercusión*, 83–84).

36. Wasserman (1998), Tarshish de Wainstein (2001), and Ruetter (2000), interviews with author.

37. Statistics in Quijada, *Aires de república*, 232; Levenson, *Ejemplo de una mujer*, 10 and 12–14; Baumkoler, *La lucha es vida*, 27–50; Trumper, interview with author, 1998; Trifone and Svarzman, *La repercusión*, 85–87; and Edelman, *Banderas*, 52–70.

38. Tarcus, "Historia de una pasión revolucionaria"; and Felman, *Mi guerra de España*.

39. *Clarín*, 7 July 1985: 16 and 12 April 1992: second section, 20 (quote); *Tribuna Hebrea*, 15 February 1939, unnumbered page.

40. *El Alba*, 28 March 1939, 1; Wasserman (1998) and Bursuk (2000), interviews with author; Oliver, *Mi fe es el hombre*, 11; and Falcoff, "Argentina," 319–20. The Bursuks and other Jewish farmers mobilized with colonists demanding higher prices for cotton. See *La Vanguardia*, 10–31 May, 10 June, 21 June, 9 July, 26 August, 27 October, 17 December, all 1936; and *La Protesta*, June 1936, 1.

41. Bisso, *Acción Argentina*, especially 83, 88, 122, 171, 210, and 343–46. I am grateful to Andrés Bisso for providing a list of prominent AA women, which revealed very few who might have been of Jewish origin.

42. On these and other groups, see *Principios*, 5 October 1946: 16, 15 May 1947: 21–22, and 15 June 1947: 15; *Mundo Israelita*, 30 November 1940: 10 and 23 December 1944: 2; *Israel*, 10 October 1941: 21 and 29 May 1942: 4; *Tribuna Hebrea*, 26 September 1941, 6; *La Luz*, 5 December 1941: 712–13, 23 January 1942: 42, and 4 April 1947: 168; Comité Central Pro-Socorro, *Memoria y balance* 1941–1942; and Junta de Ayuda Judía, *Memoria y balance*. Bisso (*Acción Argentina*, 113–14) finds that AA opposed Nazi anti-Semitism yet did not pressure the government to admit Jewish refugees.

43. Comisión Femenina Israelita de Solidaridad, *Nuestros talleres*, 31. On these and other groups, see #1071, Files 1–2, AJJDCA; Mina Ruetter, personal communication; *La Hora*, 27 May 1942: 5, 18 October 1942: 5, and 21 May 1943: 5; and Edelman (*Banderas*, 81–82). Also see Comité de Taller para Vestir . . . , flyer, n.d.; Comité Israelita con la Unión Soviética . . . , flyer, n.d.; Comité Industrial y Obrero Textil de Villa Lynch, *Boletín*, no. 2 (n.d.); all in Box 1070, IWO; *Solidaridad* (no. 3, October 1942, 2, and no. 4, May 1943, 7, 9, and 10); Comisión Femenina Israelita, *Mujeres en la ayuda*; *La Hora*, 27 May 1942: 5, 18 October 1942: 5, and 21 May 1943: 5; and Edelman (*Banderas*, 81–82).

44. Comisión Femenina Israelita de Solidaridad, *Nuestros talleres*, 28–29 (quote); and *Mujeres en la ayuda (1941–1942)*, 22.

45. Delila Saslavsky in *La voz argentina*, 13; and Drucaroff in Comisión Femenina Israelita de Solidaridad, *Nuestros talleres*, 30.

46. Bisso ("¿Batir al naziperonismo?") emphasizes the fragility of Argentine antifascists' claims on democracy.

47. Oliver, *Mi fe es el hombre*, 41–43; Oliver, interview, 1971, Proyecto de Historia Oral; *La Hora*, 22 August 1941, 4; Goldsmith, n.d. 1940, #1069, File 2, AJJDCA; Lavrin, *Women*, 282–83; and Carlson, *¡Feminismo!*, 177. Although the Spanish aid effort was larger than the pro-Allied one, it is not clear if its main women's group, CAMHE, was larger than the Junta. Edelman (*Banderas*, 46) writes that CAMHE had 150 branches but does not give a membership figure.

48. Scheiner, in *La Hora*, 13 September 1941, 4; and *Crítica*, 14 September 1941, 4.

49. Junta de la Victoria, *Ayuda*; Oliver, *Mi fe es el hombre*, 43–44; *La Hora*, 28 August 1941: 4, 14 September 1941: 5, 27 September 1941: 5, 5 October 1941: 4, 25 October 1941: 7, 28 October 1941: 7, 15 April 1942: 1, 15 December 1941: 5, 16 December 1941: 5, and 27 December 1942: 5.

50. *Revista ICUF*, nos. *101–102* (October–November 1951): 50–54; *Mujeres en la Ayuda (1941–1942)*, 11–16 and 47–64; Clementi, *María Rosa Oliver*, 143; and Braslavsky, interview with author, 2000.

51. Langer, *From Vienna to Managua*, 95–96; Halperin (2000), Monín (1997), Rapaport (1998), and Braslavsky (2000), interviews, with author; *La Hora*, 30 November 1941: 5, 8 May 1942: 5, and 11 December 1942: 5; Comisión Femenina Israelita, *Mujeres en la Ayuda*, 63.

52. Statistics in Junta de la Victoria to President Ramírez, 30 June 1943, CeDInCI. Also see *Mujeres en la Ayuda (1941–1942)*, 14, 20, and 23; *La Hora*, 28 September 1941: 10, 24 April 1942: 8, 22 May 1942: 8, 3 June 1942: 5, 7 June 1942: 5, and 7 April 1943: 5; and Edelman, *Banderas*, 86.

53. *La Hora*, 28 September 1941: 10 and 8 May 1943: 6; Monín (1997) and Halperin (2000), interviews with author; Plotkin, *Mañana es San Perón*, 187; and Deutsch, "Changing the Landscape," 64.

54. *La Hora*, 15 April 1942: 1, 7 May 1942: 5, 27 October 1942: 5, and 29 November 1942: 7; Federico Finchelstein and Jorge Nállim, personal communications. AA also tried to attract Catholics; see Bisso (*Acción Argentina*, 198–204). On *Orden Cristiano*, see Finchelstein and Lvovich ("L'Holocauste et l'Eglise argentine"), Ben-Dror (*Católicos, nazis y judíos*, 264–71), Caimari (*Perón y la iglesia católica*, 80–85), and Zanatta (*Del estado*, 282 and 285). A complex figure, Silveyra de Oyuela was related to a Nacionalista publicist and supported Franco; see Memorandum, 18 Feb. 1942, 835.00/1177, United States, Department of State.

55. Peso figure in Junta de la Victoria to President Ramírez, 30 June 1943, CeDInCI. Also see Edelman (*Banderas*, 86); Oliver, interview, 1971, Proyecto de Historia Oral; *La Hora*, 28 May 1941: 9, 11 April 1942: 5, 29 May 1942: 5, 25 November 1942: 5, 10 December 1942: 5, 11 December 1942: 5, 9 May 1943: 6, and 10 May 1943: 3.

56. *La Hora,* 5 December, 1943: 5 and 21 May 1943: 5; *Mujeres en la ayuda (1941–1942),* 32 (quote) and 40; and Singerman, *Mis dos vidas*, 114.

57. For this and the next paragraph, see Isa Kremer collection, IWO, esp. Box 1117/4, 53 (quote); and *Isa Kremer: The People's Diva* (2000, directed by Nina Baker Feinberg and Ted Schillinger).

58. Junta de la Victoria, *Estatutos; Mujeres en la Ayuda (1941–1942),* 50; Junta de la Victoria to President Ramírez, 30 June 1943, CEDINCI; *La Hora,* 28 September 1941: 9, 14 April 1942: 5, 15 April 1942: 5, 9 April 1943: 5, 12 April 1943: 5, 16 April 1943: 5, 4 May 1943: 5, 5 May 1943: 5, 19 May 1943: 3, and 21 May 1943: 5; Bisso, *Acción Argentina;* and Bianchi and Sanchís, *El partido peronista femenino,* 2:32–36. On the first convention, see Bisso (*El antifascismo argentino*, 162–68).

59. *La Hora,* 1 September 1942: 5, and 3 January 1943: 5; and Deutsch, *Las derechas*, 238. Nacionalistas also targeted AA; see Bisso (*Acción Argentina*, 169–71).

60. *New York Times*, 24 November 1943; clipping, Folder 52, Box 18, Grant papers, RUL; Duggan, 26 June 1943, 835.00/1575; Duggan, 10 July 1943, 835.00/1647; Armour, 15 July 1943, 835.00/1645; Armour, 22 July 1943, 835.00/1665; Hoover, 2 Aug. 1943, 835.00/1709; U.S. Department of State, National Achieves, Schlieper to Secretary General of the FONC, Capital, letter, 12 July 1943, CEDINCI; Junta de la Victoria to President Ramírez, 30 June 1943, CEDINCI; Oliver, interview, 1971, Proyecto de Historia Oral; Braslavsky, interview with author, 2000; *La Hora,* 24 April 1942: 8, 10 December 1942: 6, 19 December 1942: 5, 27 December 1942: 5, 28 December 1942: 6, 31 December 1942: 5, 10 January 1943: 7, 11 February 1943: 5, 21 March 1943: 6, and 10 May 1943: 3.

61. *Monitor de la educación común*, especially no. 855 (March 1944): 83 (quote), no. 857 (May 1944): supplement, 21, and no. 858 (June 1944): supplement, 72 (quote), 72–74; Lightman, 14 June 1944, letter 204, #1070, File 2, Lightman, n.d., letter 234 and attachment, #1070, File 3, Levy, 8 Aug. 1944, #1070, File 3, all in AJJDCA; Munges, "Academic Freedom under Perón," 278–79; Almaráz, Corchon, and Zemborain, *¡Aquí FUBA!*; Senkman, "El 4 de junio," especially 70–72; and Ben-Dror, *Católicos, nazis y judíos*, 138–43.

62. Traub, report, April 1945, CZA/F49/3; Blejer, interview, 1985, AP; Furman de Bendersky, interview with author, 1997; and Senkman, "Identidades colectivas," 424–25.

63. Kipen and Furman de Bendersky, interviews with author, both 1997; *Atalaya*, 4 September 1944: 7, 5 September 1944: 8, and 6 September 1944: 1 and 8; *La Acción*, 28 November 1944: 7 and 19 December 1944: 5; Confidential report, Oct. 1944, 835.00/6–1848, U.S. Dept. of State, National Archives; *Monitor de la Educación Común*, nos. 867–868 (March–April 1945): 74; and Lvovich, *Nacionalismo*, 537–38. I thank Daniel Lvovich for *Atalaya* and *La Acción* and Raanan Rein for the Department of State material.

64. Lvovich, *Nacionalismo*, 538, and "Peronismo y antisemitismo."

65. Edelman, *Banderas*, 89; Singerman, *Mis dos vidas*, 112–15; *Clarín*, 7 July 1985,

16; Wasserman (1998) and Halperin (2000), interviews with author; Traub, report, Apr. 1945, CZA/49/3; and Romero, *A History of Argentina*, 95.

66. Lincovsky, interview with author, 1997; Almaráz Corchon, and Zemborain, *¡Aquí FUBA!*; and Romero, *A History of Argentina*, 95–98.

67. Tarshish de Wainstein, interview with author, 2001; and Bisso, *Acción Argentina*, 314.

68. *Socorro Rojo*, no. 6 (10 June 1932): 5 and 7, and no. 9 (November 1933): 2 and 8; Socorro Rojo Internacional, *Bajo el terror de Justo*, 28–29 and 42; *La Internacional*, 5 October 1933, 1.

69. Activist statistic in Edelman, *Banderas*, 88; and *Derechos del Hombre* (May 1945), mimeo, 2–6, Folder 13, Box 38, Grant papers, RUL; Legajo 15, Expediente 17414, Legajo 20, Expediente 24032, Legajo 26, Expediente 56427, 1944, Fondo Ministerio del Interior, AGN.

70. *Tribuna*, 28 April 1955: 12 and 21 October 1955: 1; and *Nuestras Mujeres*, no. 54 (November 1954): 10, and no. 56 (February 1955): 10. Also see Liga Argentina por los Derechos del Hombre, "Torturas a los detenidos antifascistas . . . ," mimeo, 1945, 4, 6, Folder 13, Box 38, Grant papers, RUL. *Tribuna*'s claim foreshadows Jewish prisoners' experiences from 1976 to 1983.

71. Corbière, "Los archivos," 19–20; and *El Alba*, 30 July 1935: 1, 7 January 1936: 1, and 16 June 1936: 1.

72. *Mundo Israelita*, 25 December 1937, 3.

73. *Derechos del Hombre* 1, no. 1 (June 1938); Liga Argentina por los Derechos del Hombre, invitation, Dec. 1941, Box 1176, IWO; *La Hora*, 11 July 1942: 5, 15 July 1942: 6, 17 January 1943: 6, 22 May 1943: 1 and 5, 13 November 1945: 5, 19 November 1945: 5, 1 December 1945: 1, 12 December 1945: 6, and 16 December 1945: 5; and *Mundo Israelita*, 17 June 1939, 8.

74. *La Nación*, 20 July 1936: 8, 21 July 1936: 9 (quote), 22 July 1936: 10, and 23 July 1936: 9; *La Vanguardia*, 20 July 1936: 8, and 22 July 1936: 7; Edelman, *Banderas*, 27–28; Ruetter, interview with author, 2000; and James Cane, personal communication.

75. *Avanzada* 1, no. 7 (July 1941): unnumbered page; and *La Hora*, 18 September 1941: 5, 5 December 1942: 6, and 6 December 1942: 6. On Andrea's political evolution, see Caimari (*Perón y la iglesia católica*, 86–90).

76. *Derechos del Hombre* 1, no. 1, 2nda. época (November 1945): 2; *Antinazi*, 6 June 1946, 6; and *La Hora*, 22 November 1945: 6 and 24 January 1946: 5. In the 1950s, the Comisión's name changed to the Grupo Ethel y Julius Rosenberg.

77. Quote in *Socorro Rojo*, 1 May 1932, 7; and Gílenberg, interview with author, 1997.

78. Items in previous note; *Derechos del Hombre* 1, no. 1, 2nda. época (November 1945): 8; and Edelman, *Banderas*, 25.

79. Edelman, *Banderas*, 25; Baumkoler, *La lucha es vida*, 26; Rapaport (1998), Gílenberg (1997), and Ruetter (2000), interviews with author; Raquel, interview

with Rapaport, 1994; and *Antinazi*, 6 June 1946, 6. The other prominent solidarity worker was Carolina Molessini.

80. Gílenberg, interview with author, 1997; Liberman, *La unidad*, 49. On fear, see Tuccio ("La mujer obrera argentina," 99–104).

81. Among many works on this subject, see Girbal-Blacha (*Estado*), Senkman ("The Transformation of Collective Identities"), Guy ("Parents Before the Tribunals," 188–89), Plotkin (*Mañana es San Perón*), Elena ("What the People Want"), James (*Doña María's Story*), and Deutsch ("Gender," 271–82). On Social Catholicism, see Deutsch (*Counterrevolution*, 51–59 and passim, and "The Catholic Church").

82. Daniel Lvovich and Raanan Rein, personal communications. Press reports on the OIA did not mention women's names. I found not a single Peronist among women interviewees or authors of memoirs. Dos Santos (*Las mujeres peronistas*) and Bianchi and Sanchís (*El partido peronista femenino*) name only a few who could have been of Jewish origin.

83. On Jewish-Peronist relations, see especially Rein (*Argentina, Israel, and the Jews*), as well as Delegación de Asociaciones Israelitas Argentinas (*Perón y el pueblo judío*), Bell ("In the Name of the Community"), Senkman ("El peronismo" and "Etnicidad"), J. Itzigsohn (*Una experiencia judía contemporánea*, 21), and Lvovich ("Peronismo y antisemitismo"). Ross ("Justicia social") questions the extent to which Perón improved popular well-being.

84. Furman, interview with author, 1997; Rozenfarb (1986) and Garberis (n.d.), interviews, AP; and Liberman, *La unidad*, 55.

85. *El Obrero Textil*, no. 67 (September 1945): 7; *La Hora*, 26 January 1946, 6; J. Horowitz, *Argentine Unions*, 207–12; and Di Tella, "La Unión," 204–8.

86. Almaráz, Corchon, and Zemborain, *¡Aquí FUBA!*, 129; Sanjurjo, "Rosa Ziperovich," 19–20 (quote on 20); *El Litoral*, 16 January 1995, unnumbered page.

87. Ruetter (2000) and Gertel (1998), interviews with author; Senkman, "The Transformation of Collective Identities," 137–38; and Bell, "The Jews and Perón," 99.

88. Singerman, *Mis dos vidas*, 116; and *Isa Kremer: The People's Diva* (2000, directed by Nina Baker Feinberg and Ted Schillinger).

89. García Sebastiani, "The Other Side of Peronist Argentina"; and Romero, *A History of Argentina*, 113.

90. Filer, interview with author, 1999.

91. Freidkes, "25 años"; *Vocero del ICUF* 1, no. 1 (May 1966): unnumbered page; Zalel, interview, 1985, AP; Ruetter, interview with author, 2000; Kanutsky, interviews, 1985–86, AP; *Comentarios y Opiniones* 5, no. 3 (December 1999–January 2000): 9–13; Zadoff, *Historia de la educación judía*, 272–73; Svarch, "'El comunista sobre el tejado'"; and Bacci, "Las políticas culturales."

92. Ruetter, interview with author, 2000; and Kanutsky, interviews, 1985–86, AP. Also see Kogan, in *Revista ICUF* (nos. 101–2, October–November 1951, 50–54).

93. Kogan and Lerner, interviews, both 1986, AP; S. Novodvorsky, interview, 1985, AP; FIJIA [Federación de Instituciones Juveniles Israelitas Argentinas], flyer, 1017/17, and "Resoluciones Fundamentales del Congreso Extraordinario de FIJIA," pamphlet, 1948, 1017/13, IWO; *Di Idische Froi*, no. 9 (April-May 1953): 10 (quote); Ruetter, interview with author, 2000.

94. Statistics in Comisión Israelita to Secretario del Comité de la Capital, 21 July 1956, Legajo 26, Comité Central, Partido Comunista Argentino archive (PCA); *Revista ICUF*, nos. 101–2 (October–November 1951): 50–54; *Vocero del ICUF*, 1966; *Di Idische Froi*, no. 10 (June–July 1953): 7 and 9, no. 12 (November–December 1953): 10, no. 16 (November–December 1954): 9, no. 18 (June–October 1955): 15, no. 25 (June–August 1957): 10, no. 27 (August–September 1958): 11, no. 28 (October–December 1958): 5, and 13, no. 29 (January–June 1959): 25, and nos. 34–35 (September–October 1960): 35–36; Mina Ruetter, personal communication; Kanutsky, interview, 1985–86, AP; and Lerner, interview, 1986, AP.

95. Mina Ruetter, personal communication; *Revista ICUF*, nos. 101–2 (October–November 1951): 50–54; Comisión Israelita, 21 July 1956, PCA; and Visacovsky, "*Di idishe froi.*"

96. *Revista ICUF*, nos. 101–2 (October–November 1951): 50–54; *Di Idische Froi*, no. 20–21 (March–June 1956): 1, no. 25 (June–August 1957): 1–2 and 10, and no. 26 (March–May 1958): 3 and 11; and Bell, "Bitter Conquest."

97. Grushka and Ruetter, interviews with author, both 2000; and Rein, *Argentina, Israel, and the Jews*, 63.

98. Leike Kogan, *Di Idische Froi*, no. 25 (June–August 1957): 1; Freidkes, "25 años," 32; Gílenberg, interview with author, 1997; Kanutsky, interviews, 1985–86, AP, and Ruetter 1980 interview; Bell, "The Jews and Perón," 278–81; and M. Rapaport, "Argentina and the Soviet Union," especially 251–53, 263–64, and 267–71.

99. Kanutsky, 1985–86, AP; Ruetter, interview with author, 2000; numbers in Comisión Israelita, 21 July 1956, PCA.

100. ICUF, "Por una . . . cultura judía popular y laica," 1953, Box 153, IWO; *Mundo Israelita*, 6 December 1952: 2, 20 December 1952: 2, 10 January 1953: 2, 14 February 1953: 5, 7 March 1953: 4, and 21 March 1953: 3; Zadoff, *Historia de la educación judía*, 405 and 411–13; Comisión Israelita, 21 July 1956, PCA; "Algunas conclusiones . . . para su labor . . . en . . . la colectividad judía," n.d., and Comisión Israelita to Secretario del Comité de la Capital, 30 July 1956, Legajo 26, PCA; Lerner, interview, 1986, AP; and Bell, "Bitter Conquest."

101. Bacci, "Las políticas culturales."

102. Since Peronism represented a new pact of rule and means of engagement with the masses, I use the word "state."

103. Warshaver in "A los escritores argentinos," Oct. 1952, Legajo 13, PCA; *Mujeres Argentinas*, 1 June 1947: unnumbered page, 1 October 1947: unnumbered page, 15 November 1947: unnumbered page, 15 February 1948: 10, and 1 April 1948: 3 and 10; *Nuestras Mujeres*, no. 4 (April 1, 1948): 6 and no. 12 (November 3, 1948): 3;

Diament, *Testimonios*, 223; Braslavsky, interview with author, 2000, and personal communication; and Girbal-Blacha, "Poder y cultura."

104. *II ° Congreso* (Aug. 12, 1946), 14, Legajo 5, PCA; *Mujeres Argentinas*, 9 August 1946, 7; Braslavsky and Ruetter, interviews with author, both 2000; and Victorio Codovilla, "A las camaradas . . . ," Mar. 1952, Legajo 13, PCA. On the postwar Junta and its context, see Walter ("Right," 106–7), Edelman (*Banderas*, 94–95), Rein (*The Franco-Perón Alliance* , 150–52 and 286, note 39), and *La Hora,* especially November 1945 and April 1946).

105. Edelman, *Banderas*, 99–100, 102–4, and 110; Grushka, interview with author, 2007; *¿Qué es la U.M.A.?*, 1961, UMA folder, Legajo 28, PCA; "Raíces en el pueblo"; *Nuestras Mujeres*, nos. 52–54, July, September, and November 1954.

106. Woscoboinik de Levin, interview with author, 1998; and Edelman, *Banderas*, 31. Also see Baumkoler (*La lucha es vida*, 60).

107. Gílenberg (1997) and Ruetter (2000), interviews with author; Kanutsky, interviews, 1985–86, AP; and Baumkoler, *La lucha es vida*, 55.

108. Deutsch, "Changing the Landscape," 61–62 and 66–67; Halperín-Donghi, *Argentina en el callejón*; and Bisso, *Acción Argentina*.

EIGHT *Philanthropies and Zionism*

Epigraphs: Maldavsky, 1998, interview with author; *OSFA*, no. 64 (May–June 1945), 1.

1. Among other works, see M. Kaplan (*The Making of the Jewish Middle Class*, 194 and 199–202), Tananbaum ("Philanthropy and Identity," 937), Gutkowski (*Erase una vez*, 55, 156–57, 205, and 410–11), Benbassa and Rodrigue (*Sephardi Jewry*, 22, 25, 31, and 82), Goitein (*The Community*, 91–143), Farine ("Charity and Study Societies," no. 1, 27–28; and no. 2, 169 and 173), and Shilo (*Princess or Prisoner?*, 129–41).

2. On women and the practical, see McCune ("Social Workers," 137–38) and Stolen (*The Decency of Inequality*, 206).

3. An important exception is Shilo (*Princess or Prisoner?*).

4. I study women's groups only, except for the mixed-sex Departamento de Juventud del Centro Sionista Sefaradí. On non-Jewish immigrant women's beneficence, see Urquiza ("Las suecas de 'Verdandi' "), Guy (*Performing Charity*), Moya (*Cousins and Strangers*, 284–85), Schneider (*Futures Lost*, 182–84), and Bestene ("Formas de asociacionismo," 120).

5. Moya, *Cousins and Strangers*, 302; and Schneider, *Futures Lost*, 183.

6. Lázaro Schallman, "Las primeras agrupaciones de mujeres judías en la Argentina," *OSFA*, no. 306 (December 1972): 37; Cullen to Goldschmid, 3-6-1892, Jewish Colonization Association, Papers, 297 (1), CAHJP; *Mundo Israelita,* 29 May 1923): 4; Guy, "Women's Organizations"; Lerner, "La historia del Asilo Argentino"; and Feierstein, *Historia*, 56–59 and 74. A few Moroccans belonged to the CIRA, but

none apparently to the Sociedad. The composition of the reconstituted Sociedad shows that no neat line separated Western European Jewish women philanthropists and Eastern European recipients, as opposed to the situation in the United States. On the United States, see Baum, Hyman, and Michel (*The Jewish Woman in America*, 179–85).

7. *Israel,* 23 and 30 September 1927, unnumbered page; and *Presencia sefaradí en la Argentina*, 56.

8. Literat-Golombek, *Moisés Ville*, 43–44; Schallman, "Las primeras," 37; and *El Alba,* 1 January 1923, 7.

9. The statistics were compiled from the Argentine Jewish press. Also see Sociedad, *1937 JKG 1942*, 18; *Filantropía*, no. 583 (November–December 1987): 16; and Brodsky, "The Contours of Identity," 224–27.

10. Guy, *Performing Charity*; Mead, "Beneficent Maternalism" and "Oligarchs, Doctors, and Nuns"; Little, "Society"; and Carlson, *¡Feminismo!*, 49–57.

11. Comité de Damas/WIZO, Libro de Actas, July 8, 1925–Oct. 11, 1926, OSFA; *OSFA*, no. 71 (October 1946): 1; *Tribuna Hebrea*, 5 October 1929, unnumbered page; and *Mundo Israelita,* 7 December 1940, 2. I distinguish between the Argentine OSFA and the global WIZO.

12. Consejo de Mujeres Israelitas (hereafter CMI), Libro de Actas 1: 19 Oct. 1937, 5 Nov. 1937, 11 Aug. 1938, 26 May 1941, 11 June 1941, Libro de Actas 2: 29 June 1953, 50, CAMI.

13. CMI, Libro de Actas 1: 19 Oct. 1937, 26 Nov. 1937, 19 Apr. 1939, 6 Sept. 1939, 8 Nov. 1939, CAMI; *Mundo Israelita,* 24 June 1939, 8 and 12; Rogow, *Gone to Another Meeting*; and Las, *Jewish Women in a Changing World*.

14. Sociedad de Damas, Libro de Actas, "Memoria," 1, AIB.

15. *Israel,* March 1918: 280, and 22 November 1929: 20; Sociedad de Basavilbaso, Libro de Actas, 20 Jan. 1924, 23 Aug. 1924, AIB; Comisión Damas de Beneficencia Pro Inmigrantes (Sociedad) Domínguez, SS I 1.6 No. 02, and Sociedad de Damas Auxiliares al Hospital Clara, Libro de Actas, 10 Jan. 1928, 5 Jan. 1929, 29 Jan. 1929, SSJ A.1 Acta 3, MHRC; Sociedad de Damas Ezrah, Libro de Actas, 11 Aug. 1929, 10 Nov. 1929, 10 Jan. 1930, 10 Aug. 1930, AHAM. Also see Verbitsky (*Rivera*, 141), Blumenfeld (*Historia de la comunidad israelita*, 135–38), and Movimiento de Ex-Colonos Residentes en la Capital (*Pioneros*, 139 and 141–42).

16. *Reseña 1918–19*, 13, *1922–23*, 23, *1923–24*, 14 and 23, *1924–25*, 10 and 22, *1925–26*, 24–26; *Mundo Israelita,* 19 September 1925: 1 and 5, and 5 December 1925: 1; and *La Luz,* 11 October 1933, 580.

17. Sociedad Ezrah, Libro de Actas, 18 Aug. 1929, AHAM; Rogow, *Gone to Another Meeting*, 156; Brodsky, "The Contours of Identity," 56–57; Tolcachier, "Asociaciones israelitas," 468–69, 472, 476, and 488.

18. *OSFA*, no. 103 (September 1949): unnumbered page (quote); McCune, "Social Workers," especially 138, 142–43, and 151; and Berkowitz, "Transcending 'Tzimmes and Sweetness.'"

19. *Revista WIZO*, no. 31 (July 1938): 16, nos. 32–33 (August–September 1938): 3 (quote) and 15, no. 39 (June 1939): 11–12 and 14, no. 45 (March 1940): 9, and no. 49 (June 1941): 3; *OSFA*, no. 153 (February–March 1954): 19–20; and "Festival Infantil . . . 1941"; "Festival Infantil . . . 1942"; "Young WIZO . . . Primera Gran Tertulia," n.d.; "Young WIZO Menorah . . . 1937"; "Plan de trabajo de la Young WIZO," n.d.; Box 149, IWO.

20. *El Alba,* 22 January 1924: 1, 15 April 1924: 1 (quote), and 18 May 1937: 1.

21. *Tribuna Hebrea,* 5 October 1929, unnumbered page.

22. *Juventud*, no. 43 (May 1915): 5–8. Moya (*Cousins and Strangers*, 284) discusses the classism of the Patronato Español, founded by a Spanish-born woman. U.S. Jewish socialists regarded the NCJW similarly; see McCune ("*'The Whole Wide World,'*" 117). Weiner ("Jewish Women," 25) finds that Appalachian Jewish ladies' aid societies resembled Christian groups.

23. On non-Jewish societies, see Urquiza ("Las suecas de 'Verdandi'"), Ciafardo ("La práctica benéfica," 394–97), Rodríguez ("Ante las demandas sociales," 126), and Recalde (*Beneficencia*). Also see Sociedad de . . . Damas Israelitas Carlos Casares, Libro de Actas, Estatutos and 20 Dec. 1931, AHAM; Sociedad de Basavilbaso, "Memoria," 4, AIB; *Israel,* 19 June 1925: 18, 14 August 1925: 21, and 22 November 1929: 20; *Sulem* 1, no. 10 (May 1934): 84.

24. Quote in Ciafardo, "La práctica benéfica," 397; Mayo, interview with author, 2000; *Israel,* 3 February 1933: 20, 28 April 1933: 16, and 25 August 1933: 20; Saidman, "Colectividad judía de Posadas"; and Brodsky, "Becoming 'Argentine.'"

25. "Informe . . . 'WIZO,'" 1929–31, Box 149, IWO; *Revista WIZO*, nos. 32–33 (August–September 1938): 4; and "Argentine (1946–1948)," CZA/F49/5. McCune ("*'The Whole Wide World,'*" 154), found that the NCJW and Hadassah mostly excluded poor and leftist women.

26. See chapter 2. Jacob Marcus, cited in Kirshenblatt-Gimblett ("Kitchen Judaism," 96), made the same point for the United States.

27. *Revista WIZO*, nos. 34–35 (November–December 1938): 5 (quote). The Jewish press and the groups' records detail their money-raising activities. Also see Sociedad de Damas Israelitas, Sub-Comité Domínguez, Libro de Actas 1932-1937, and receipts, in Archivo Rosa Gabis, IWO; *Reseña (1923–24*, 19); Sociedad y Asilo, *Memoria y balance*, esp. 1931, 18–19; CMI, Libro de Actas 1: 13 Dec. 1939, 25 Mar. 1942, Libro de Actas 2: 15 Sept. 1952, 22, CAMI; Consejo de Mujeres Israelitas de la Argentina (*Almanaque-Agenda*); Cincuentenario, n.p.); and Guy ("Women's Organizations," 78).

28. "Informe de la Organización Femenina Sionista . . . 1929–1931," n.p., Box 149, IWO; WIZO Moisés Ville, Libro de Actas 1928–1939, CZA, M336/2; Buenos Aires, 27 Nov. 1936, CZA/F49/1; General Secretariat, 4 Feb. 1944, CZA/F49/2; Sieff, 31 May 1945, CZA/F49/3; WIZO Argentine, 4 May 1954, CZA/F49/15; Comité Ejecutivo, "Guía," 1954, CZA/F49/17. Some women who did not belong to OSFA also had blue collection boxes in their homes.

29. WIZO Moisés Ville, Libro de Actas, 17 July 1929, CZA; Nijensohn, 23 July 1952, CZA/F49/12; Mibashan, 26 July 1941, #1070, File 1, AJJDCA; *Israel,* 22 November 1929, 20; *Mundo Israelita,* 16 March 1935, 3; and Sociedad de Carlos Casares, Libro de Actas, 10 Feb. 1932, AHAM.

30. Sociedad de Basavilbaso, Libro de Actas, 28 Oct. 1923, 14 Dec. 1925, 28 Jan. 1926, 7 Feb. 1926, "Memoria," 5–10, AIB. Financially dishonest members also hurt some organizations. See CMI, Libro de Actas 2: 5 Dec. 1951, 23 Mar. 1953, 22 June 1953, 28 May 1954, CAMI; Sociedad Pro-Maternidad, Libro de Actas, 2 Feb. 1930, AHAM.

31. *Israel,* 8 May 1925, 19.

32. E. H. and Cohn, interviews with author, both 2000; *Filantropía,* no. 588 (September–October 1988): 21–23, no. 589 (November–December 1988): 23, no. 592 (June–July 1989): 24, and no. 623 (April–May 1995): 16–17; and Borchard, 26 May 1940, #1069, file 2, AJJDCA.

33. Pablo Chami and Steve Hyland, personal communications; Benbassa, "Education for Jewish Girls in the East," 163–64; *Presencia sefaradí en la Argentina,* 56 and 67–68; *Israel,* 22 July 1921: 16, 21 and 28 September 1923: 3, 7 July 1933: 16, and 15 October 1937: 4; and *La Luz,* 26 May 1933: 244, 16 September 1936: 425, 6 November 1936: 478, 23 April 1937: 165, and 3 September 1937: 388.

34. Sociedad de Damas Israelitas de Beneficencia [Buenos Aires], Libro de Actas, 25 June 1945, 24 Sept. 1945, 23 Sept. 1946, MTL; *Mundo Israelita,* 29 May 1923: 4 (quote), 8 June 1923: 7, 1 September 1923: 3, 14 June 1924: 2, 19 September 1925: 5, 6 December 1925: 1, and 16 September 1933: 1; and Guy, "Women's Organizations," 81–83, and "Gendering Child Labor in Argentina," 5–6.

35. *Mundo Israelita,* 5 April 1924: 5 and 14 June 1924: 2; Sociedad [Buenos Aires], Libro de Actas, 24 Sept. 45, MTL; *La Luz,* 11 October 1933, 580; and Guy, "Women's Organizations," 82. This preoccupation with girls' religious education also shows that Jews had absorbed the local norm of female spirituality. U.S. Jewish girls' orphanages trained girls for marriage but placed them as servants; see Friedman ("Founders").

36. *OSFA,* no. 65 (October 1945): 5.

37. Sociedad y Asilo, *Memoria y balance, 1936–37,* 45 (statistic), 50, 81–84; *1937–1938,* 11–12; *1939–1940,* 38; *Israel,* March 1918, 280; *La Luz,* 28 June 1938: 38, and 22 March 1940: 142; and *Principios,* nos. 146–47 (October 1937): 25, and nos. 168–69 (September 1938): 117.

38. CMI, Libro de Actas 1: 19 Oct. 1937, 5 Nov. 1937, 26 Nov. 1937, 11 Aug. 1938, 13 Dec. 1939, 29 May 1940, 29 Oct. 1940, 21 Nov. 1941, 11 Aug. 1943, and Libro de Actas 2: 6 June 1956, 3 June 1957, 4 Nov. 1957, CAMI; CMI de la Argentina, flier, n.d. (quote), Box 149, IWO; Comedores Populares Israelitas Argentinas, pamphlet, 1115/1, IWO; E. H., interview with author, 2000.

39. *La Luz,* 13 March 1931, 3; and *Israel,* 1 and 8 October 1926: unnumbered page, 19 November 1926: 9, 22 July 1927: 7, 18 November 1927: 7, 25 November 1927: 8,

16 and 23 December 1927: 8, 31 May 1935: 15, 8 May 1936: 9, and 5 November 1948: 14–15. Also see Brodsky ("The Contours of Identity," 172–74).

40. *Israel,* 24 and 31 May 1929, 21; *Mundo Israelita,* 11 November 1933: 2, and 18 November 1933: 2; *La Luz,* 3 September 1937, 388; and Gerchunoff, 16 June 1937, CZA/F49/1.

41. Wind, interview with author, 2000; *La Luz,* 28 May 1937, 220–21; *OSFA*, nos. 174–75 (December 1955–January 1956): 4; Mibashan, 1 Apr. 1938 (quote), CZA/F49/1; Unknown, 20 Apr. 1947, CZA/F49/3; Nissensohn, 11 Mar. 1955, CZA/F49/18.

42. Traub, April 1945, CZA/F49/3; Gerchunoff, 5 Apr. 1948, CZA/F49/4, Nissensohn, 16 Mar. 1955, CZA/F49/18; *La Luz,* 13 April 1945, 190; *OSFA*, no. 105 (November 1949): unnumbered page; *Vivencias*, no. 24 (November 1996): 9; and Cohen de Isaharoff, interview with author, 1997.

43. Camji, interview with author, 2001; A. Kaplan, *Memoria de un médico,* 53; *Israel,* 30 August 1940, 15; and *Mundo Israelita,* 28 June 1941, 6.

44. Departamento de Juventud del Centro Sionista Sefaradí, "Programa . . . 1945," and *Actas*, 22 Nov. 1944, 9 Jan. 1945 (I thank Margalit Bejarano for this material); Camji, interview with author, 2001; *Israel,* 11 February 1944: 13, 10 March 1944: 14, 28 April 1944: 12–13 (quote), 25 May 1945: 11, and 16 and 24 April 1948: 20–21; *Mundo Israelita,* 22 April 1944, 12; Deutsch, "Changing the Landscape," 59; and Brodsky, "The Contours of Identity," 185–89.

45. Departamento del Keren Kayemeth Leisroel del Centro Sionista Sefaradí, Comisión de Señoritas, *Actas*, 21 Dec. 1944, 21 Mar. 1945, 14 June 1945 (I thank Margalit Bejarano for this material); *Israel,* 19 January 1945, 18.

46. Camji (2001), Tawil de Ini (1998), and Elnecavé (1997), interviews with author; *Israel,* 16 June 1944: 20, 25 October 1946: 9–10, and 31 May 1948: 8; Departamento de Juventud, *Actas*, 28 Nov. 1944; *La Luz,* 6 September 1946: 439, and 11 October 1946: 514.

47. *OSFA*, nos. 74–75 (March–April 1947): 24, no. 99 (May 1949): unnumbered page, no. 100 (June 1949): unnumbered page, no. 145 (April 1953): unnumbered page, nos. 164–65 (February–March 1955): 5, no. 166 (April 1955): 5, no. 168 (June 1955): 5, and no. 171 (September 1955): 5; *La Luz,* 26 November 1954, 164; and *Mundo Israelita,* 26 November 1955, 6.

48. Elnecavé, interviews with author (1997) and AP (1992); Elnecavé, *Crisol de vivencias judías*, 66–86.

49. Wind, 6 Sept. 1946, CZA/F49/3; "Argentine (1946–1948)," CZA/F49/5; Nissensohn, 5 Nov. 1953, CZA/F49/14; Kohn, 27 Jan. 1954, CZA/F49/15; Grinberg, 21 July 1955, CZA/F49/19; *OSFA*, no. 69 (August 1946): 1 and 16, no. 82 (November 1947): 32, no. 83 (December 1947): 31, no. 112 (June 1950): unnumbered page, no. 117 (November 1950): 53–54, and no. 155 (May 1954): 19–20; Wind, interview with author, 2000, and brief written descriptions of his mother that he provided; and Schwarcz, *Y a pesar de todo*, 151.

50. Cohen de Isaharoff, interview with author, 1997; Moise and Hadida, interview, HUJ, 1988; *La Luz,* 11 October 1946: 520, and 31 December 1947: 603; *Israel,* 16 August 1946: 15, 8 November 1946: 10, 7 February 1947: 18, 19 June 1947: 14, and 16 January 1948: 16; and Brodsky, "The Contours of Identity," 180–81.

51. "Argentine (1946–1948)," CZA/F49/5.

52. Tawil de Ini, interview with author, 1998; *La Luz,* 21 May 1948: 207 and 28 September 1951: 530; and *Israel,* 31 May 1948: 6–7, 25 June 1948: 18, 6 May 1949: 13, 17 June 1949: 18, 15 June 1951: 31, 2 May 1952: 9, and 4 December 1953: 21.

53. *D.E.S.A.*, 7 June 1952, 4, 28 Nov. 1952, 6; and *Mundo Israelita,* 1 May 1954, 3.

54. Nissensohn, 9 May 1951, 16 Apr. 1951, CZA/F49/10; Jagufsky, 15 Jan. 1952, CZA/F49/11; Nissensohn, 24 Sept. 1952, CZA/F49/12; Nissensohn, 5 Feb. 1953, Federation, 25 Nov. 1953, CZA/F49/13; Hauser-Zeissler, 16 Feb. 1953, Mallah, 23 Mar. 1954, CZA/F49/15.

55. *Revista WIZO*, no. 56 (March–April 1943): 3 and 8.

56. Sociedad Pro-Maternidad, Libro de Actas, 11 Aug. 1929, 18 Aug. 1929, 10 Nov. 1929, 10 Jan. 1930, 26 Nov. 1932, AHAM; Sigwald Carioli, *Colonia Mauricio*; and *Colonia Mauricio*.

57. Sociedad de Carlos Casares, Libro de Actas, 25 Jan. 1944, AHAM; *La Luz,* 28 January 1944, 37; *International Council of Jewish Women Newsletter,* October 1956, unnumbered page; and Maldavsky, interview with author, 1998. For another example, see CMI, Libro de Actas 1: 16 Feb. 1939, 22 Mar. 1939, CAMI. By meeting non-Jews through social work, CAMI resembled earlier German Jewish women's groups; see M. Kaplan (*The Making of the Jewish Middle Class*, 206).

58. Sociedad de Damas Israelitas de Beneficencia, *Mundo Israelita,* 5 April 1924, 5; and CMI de Argentina, "Origen . . . ," 1939, 2, Box 149, IWO. Korelitz ("'A Magnificent Piece of Work'") describes how the NCJW's inculcation of U.S. ideals of womanhood represented Americanization.

59. *El Alba,* 27 January 1925: 1, 10 February 1925: 1, 19 February 1929: 4, 2 June 1931: 1, 30 August 1932: 1, and 6 September 1932: 1; Sociedad de Basavilbaso, Libro de Actas, 28 Oct. 1923, 7 Feb. 1926, AIB; Cohen de Isaharoff, interview with author, 1997; and Forment, *Civic Selfhood*, 299 and passim. Work and distance hurt the Swedish women's society in Misiones; see Urquiza ("Las suecas de 'Verdandi'").

60. Comunidad Israelita Sefaradí (CIS), Libro de Actas, 14 Oct. 1942, 8 Dec. 1942, CAHJP-HM2/1422c-d; Tawil de Ini, interview with author, 1998; *Israel,* 24 March 1922: 9, 22 September 1922: 16, and 21 and 28 September 1923: 3; and Brodsky, "The Contours of Identity," 225–27. Similarly, NCJW members became Americanized through charity; see Rogow (*Gone to Another Meeting*).

61. Sociedad [Buenos Aires], Libro de Actas, 24 Sept. 1945, 23 Sept. 1946, MTL; and *Filantropía*, no. 621 (November–December 1994): 8–9 and 24, and no. 647 (March–April 2000): 18.

62. Hortensia de Ambram in *OSFA*, no. 62 (February 1945): 10.

63. Rebeca B. de Topel, "Argentina y judía," *Principios*, 20 September 1948, 23.

64. Pascaner, interview with author, 1997; Lesser and Rein, "New Approaches"; and Brodsky, "The Contours of Identity," 220–21.

65. Polak (1997) and Wind (2000), interviews with author.

66. *Mundo Israelita,* 8 March 1924: 4, 5 April 1924: 5 (statistics), and 9 June 1928: 1; *Reseña (1923–24,* 19). *Reseña* (*1924–26*) and Sociedad y Asilo, *Memoria y balance, 1927–54,* also include funding information. See Sociedad de Basavilbaso, "Memoria," AIB, on its government subsidy.

67. Diputado Colom in Argentina, Congreso Nacional, Congreso Nacional, *Diario de Sesiones de la Cámara de Diputados,* 3 (1949), 2185; Guy, "La 'verdadera historia'"; Navarro, *Evita,* 225–31; and Plotkin, *Mañana es San Perón,* 137–64.

68. Sociedad [Buenos Aires], Libro de Actas, 23 Sept. 1946, 14 July 1947; Sociedad y Asilo, *Memoria y balance, 1943–54.*

69. Argentina, Congreso Nacional, *Diario de Sesiones de la Cámara de Diputados,* 3: (1949), 2,184–2,199, especially 2,193; and Donna Guy, personal communication.

70. Haim Avni, Raanan Rein, and Silvia Schenkolewski-Kroll, personal communications; Avni, *Argentina and the Jews,* 177–95; Rein, *Argentina, Israel, and the Jews,* 53–59; *La Congregación,* no. 50 (1950): 13; and G. Lerner, "La historia," 61–64.

71. Anonymous, 2000, interview with author; Consejo, *Almanaque-Agenda,* 1950-1951, 88; CMI, Libro de Actas 2: 10 June, 19 June, 30 June, 8 Sept., 22 Sept. 1952, 22 Jan. 1953, CAMI; Ganopol, 1 Dec. 1939, folder 1939, 31 Dec. 1953, folder 1953, 15 Jan. 1954, folder 1954, EN, CAHJP-INV; and *Mundo Israelita,* 2 September 1950: 3. CMI records for 1945–50 are missing. On Jewish and non-Jewish fear, see Wohl, 26 July 1953, #881-1093, AJJDCA; and Benegas Lynch and Krauze (*En defensa de los más necesitados,* 137 and 140).

72. Resnick, interview with author, 2006; CMI, Libro de Actas 2: 25 Apr., 8 Aug., 22 Aug., 10 Oct., 14 Dec. 1955, 17 Jan., 23 Feb., 5 Apr., 2 July 1956, CAMI; *International Council of Jewish Women Newsletter,* May 1956: unnumbered page, and October 1956: unnumbered page; 2 July 1948, 26 Aug. 1949, ICJW History 1912–1951 folder, and 6–7 May 1952, ICJW 1949–1952 folder, CAHJP O-IL/8, file 310, INV 6842; *La Congregación,* no. 29 (September 18, 1949): 9 and no. 65 (August 26, 1953): 9; Consejo, *Almanaque-Agenda,* 1946–1947, 2, and 1948–1949, 135; Las, *Jewish Women in a Changing World,* 48 and 165; and Favelukes de Kohan, *Desafío a los años.*

73. Favelukes de Kohan was ICJW vice president from 1960 to 1963, and Dr. Rosa de Herczeg was president from 1972 to 1978. See *International Council of Jewish Women Newsletter,* Winter 1992, 4; and Consejo Argentino de Mujeres Israelitas, *Cincuentenario 1937–1987.*

74. Sujoy and Yankelevich de Kreimer, interview with author, 2000; *International Council of Jewish Women Newsletter,* June 1959, 3–4; Romero, *A History of Argentina,* 104.

75. *Filantropía,* no. 593 (August 1989): 31; Chair, Palestine WIZO Publicity, 29 Apr. 1948, and Malenky, n.d., CZA/F49/5; Gerchunoff, 1 Dec. 1950, CZA/F49/9.

76. Maldavsky, interview with author, 1998; Rein, *Argentina, Israel, and the Jews*, 94 and 97; Nissensohn, 19 Sept. 1949, CZA/F49/7; Nissensohn, 21 Jan. 1950, and Secretary, 30 Jan. 1950, 7 Feb. 1950, CZA/F49/8; Lightman, 18 Nov. 1949, #881-1093, AJJDCA.

77. Rein, *Argentina, Israel, and the Jews*, 79, 92, and 103–5; Pascaner (1997), Wind (2000), and Maldavsky (1998), interviews with author; *La Luz,* 20 April 1951, 183; Nissensohn, 10 May 1950, CZA/F49/8; Klompers, 2 June 1950, and WIZO Executive, 20 July 1950, CZA/F49/9; Nissensohn, 2 Mar. 1951, 29 May 1951, CZA/F49/10; Hauser, 7 Apr. 1952, CZA/F49/11; Nissensohn, 11 Sept., 12 Sept., 12 Nov., 26 Nov., Kaufman, 18 Dec. 1952, CZA/F49/12; Nissensohn, 27 Aug. 1953, CZA/F49/14; Nissensohn, 16 Mar. 1954, CZA/F49/15; Nissensohn, 2 Sept. 1954, CZA/F49/16; Hauser Zeissler, 23 Dec. 1954, CZA/F49/17. The Argentine government may have paid shipping costs for OSFA, as it did for other cargoes sent to Israel, according to Raanan Rein, personal communication.

78. Guelman de Belmes, interview with author, 1997; *D.E.S.A.*, 7 June 1952, 4; *Israel,* 2 May 1952: 9, and 4 December 1953: 21. According to Bell ("The Jews and Perón," 258), the government made similar arrangements with the United Campaign.

79. *OSFA*, no. 138 (August 1952): 1. On homage see, for example, CMI, Libro de Actas 2: 4 Aug. 1952, AHAM; Sociedad de Carlos Casares, Libro de Actas, 31 Aug. 1952, CAMI; Sociedad y Asilo, *Memoria y balance, 1952*, 3.

80. Elena, "What the People Want," especially 87–88, and 101; Bell, "The Jews and Perón," 276, 283, and 306; and Senkman, "The Transformation of Collective Identities," 141–42. Whether the Peróns permitted other immigrant groups to send substantial aid to their homelands deserves study. Schneider (*Futures Lost*, 273) suggests that Italians did so.

81. Sociedad Pro-Maternidad, 10 Aug. 1930 (quote), AHAM; *Revista WIZO*, no. 50 (August 1941): 3; *OSFA*, no. 64 (May–June 1945): 1.

82. *Revista WIZO*, no. 49 (June 1941): 3 (quote); *OSFA*, no. 63 (April 1945): 1, no. 64 (May–June 1945): 1 (quote), and no. 185 (November 1956): 4; Elnecavé, *Crisol de vivencias judías*, 66–67, and interview with author, 1997; and Pascaner, interview with author, 1997.

83. Quotes in *Revista WIZO*, no. 49 (June 1941): 3, and no. 51 (November 1941): 27; and *Mundo Israelita,* 18 January 1941, 7.

84. *Revista WIZO*, no. 31 (July 1938): 17–18; *Vanguardia Juvenil*, no. 18 (October 1944): 8; and McCune, "Social Workers," 159–60. On Zionist women's sponsorship of agricultural schools, see Hakim ("Creating the Pioneer Jewish Woman Farmer").

85. *Boletín Mensual del Consejo de Mujeres Israelitas*, no. 6 (May 1949): unnumbered page; CMI, Libro de Actas 2: 10 June 1952 (quote), CAMI; and Wenger, "Jewish Women and Voluntarism," 25.

86. Sujoy and Yankelevich de Kreimer, interview with author, 2000; Grove, 15 June 1953, CZA/F49/13; Nissensohn, 3 Dec. 1954, CZA/F49/17 (figures). The training of Hospital Italiano volunteers began around the same time as that of Jewish volunteers, however. so CADMI's activity was not unique.

87. *International Council of Jewish Women Newsletter,* March 1965, 3.

88. Pascaner, interview with author, 1997 (quote); *OSFA*, no. 167 (May 1955): 4 (quote); and *Vivencias*, no. 24 (November 1996): 15.

89. Polak (1997), Pascaner (1997), and Maldavsky (1998), interviews with author; Nissensohn de Stilerman, interview, 1991, AP; *OSFA*, no. 63 (April 1945): 5, and no. 170 (August 1955): 6; Klompers, 23 Dec. 1947, CZA/F49/3; Chair, 1 Jan. 1948, CZA/F49/4; *Mundo Israelita,* 11 July 1942, 12; *Vivencias*, no. 24 (November 1996): 15. The Gerchunoffs may have left Socialism because of what they perceived as Juan B. Justo's anti-Semitism; see *Mundo Israelita,* 29 November 1924: 1, and 17 January 1925: 1; Juan B. Justo in Sebreli, *La cuestión judía*, 86–90; and Metz ("Juan B. Justo and the Jews"). Justo, however, criticized all religions and ethnic separatism.

Gerchunoff shared her feminism with German Jewish women philanthropists; see M. Kaplan (*The Jewish Feminist Movement in Germany*). On her continuing support for women's suffrage, see CMI, Libro de Actas 1: 25 Nov. 1942, CAMI.

90. Pascaner and Polak, interviews with author, both 1997.

91. Sief, 27 November 1951, CZA/F49/10 (quote); Alman, 8 Aug. 1945, CZA/F49/3; *OSFA*, no. 62 (February 1945): 12, and no. 171 (September 1955): 4; and Polak, interview with author, 1997.

92. Fundraising Chair, 16 Jan. 1948, CZA/F49/4; Pascaner, interview with author, 1997; Elnecavé, *Crisol de vivencias judías*, 77–86; and *Revista WIZO*, nos. 32–33 (August–September 1938): 4, 7, and 9–10.

93. Camji, interview with author, 2001; *Hanoar Hasefaradí*, nos. 1–17 and 19–23, 1948–50). I thank Adriana Brodsky for this periodical.

94. See, for example, *Israel,* 24 March 1922: 9. Intellectual activities seemed more important for the Swedish Sociedad Verdandi; see Urquiza ("Las suecas de 'Verdandi'").

95. CMI, Libro de Actas 2: 22 Sept. 1952, CAMI; Consejo, *Almanaque-Agenda*, 1946–1947, 2–3; *Mundo Israelita,* 1 September 1945: 10, 15 September 1945: 33, 15 June 1946: 15, 7 September 1946: 9, and 7 June 1947: 1; and Smiley, 29 Jan. 1942, and General Secretary, 4 Feb. 1944, CZA/F49/2. U.S. Jewish women's groups also encouraged intellectual pursuits; see Greenberg ("Savannah's Jewish Women," 770–71), Toll ("A Quiet Revolution," 16–18), and Wenger ("Jewish Women of the Club," 316).

96. *Mundo Israelita,* 11 November 1933: 2, 8 February 1941: 7, and 22 February 1941: 2. Hortensia de Ambram, the health administrator Fanny Banett de Wachs, and the German-born author Erna de Schlesinger also addressed Jewish women's groups.

97. Filer, interview with author, 1999; *Mundo Israelita,* 21 December 1946: 6, and 31 December 1949: 4; *Boletín . . . de Pioneras Argentina*, n.d., Box 149, IWO; and

Avanzada Judía, no. 3 (May 1947): 18, no. 10 (20 July 1948): 15, no. 14 (December 1948): 14–15, no. 17 (5 July 1949): 6, and no. 20 (5 September 1949): 6. Schliapnik also participated in the reorganization of CMI; see CMI, Libro de Actas 2: 14 Dec. 1955, 2 Feb. 1956, 29 May 1956, CAMI.

98. Elnecavé, *Crisol de vivencias judías*, 83–86, and interview with author, 1997; *Revista WIZO*, nos. 34–35 (November–December 1938): 3 (quote); Cohen de Isaharoff, interview with author, 1997; Sujoy and Yankelevich de Kreimer, interview with author, 2000 (quote).

99. *Israel,* 21 and 28 September 1923, 3; CIS, Libro de Actas, 4 July 1943, 19 Sept. 1943, 19 June 1945, CAHJP-HM 2/1422c-d; *Mundo Israelita,* 22 December 1928: 2, and 29 December 1928: 1. Jewish women's groups elsewhere depended on men; see Shilo (*Princess or Prisoner?*, 132 and 139), Greenberg ("Savannah's Jewish Women," 762–63), and Toll ("A Quiet Revolution," 11).

100. Sociedad de Damas Auxiliares al Hospital Clara, Libro de Actas, 10 Jan. 1928, 16 Jan. 1928, 24 Jan. 1928, MHRC; López de Borche, *Cooperativismo y cultura,* 76–77 and 117.

101. *Mundo Israelita,* 20 December 1930, 1.

102. Sociedad de Basavilbaso, Libro de Actas, 20 Jan. 1924, 1 Aug. 1926, 2 Sept. 1926, AIB.

103. Sociedad de Basavilbaso, Libro de Actas, 5–7 Sept., 16 Oct. 1926, AIB. Urquiza ("Las suecas de 'Verdandi' ") reported a similar conflict between a Swedish women's group and a male one.

104. Mibashan, 19 Jan. 1942, CZA/F49/2; Alman, 10 Feb. 1948, CZA/F49/4; Nissensohn, 1 Aug. 1949, CZA/F49/7. Hadassah fought similar battles; see McCune ("Social Workers," 156–58) and Antler (*The Journey Home*, 108).

105. Women's International Zionist Organization, *WIZO in the British Empire and Latin America*, 3; *Mundo Israelita,* 4 July 1936, 1 (quote); Gold, 19 Aug. and 1 Sept. 1948, CZA/F49/5. Nor did male Zionists sufficiently recognize Hadassah, the largest U.S. Zionist group, according to Antler, *Journey*, 108. In Jerusalem, Jewish men denigrated women's philanthropic work; see Shilo (*Princess or Prisoner?*, 142).

106. *OSFA*, no. 135 (May 1952): 2, and no. 137 (July 1952): inside cover; "Argentine (1946–1948)," CZA/F49/5; CMI, Libro de Actas 2: 19 Aug. 1957, CAMI; *La Luz,* 28 April 1950: 206, and 13 October 1950: 503; *Mundo Israelita,* 10 June 1950, 6.

107. *Mundo Israelita,* 22 February 1941, 2. Moya (*Cousins and Strangers*, especially 288–89) notes that Spanish groups also marginalized women.

108. Sociedad de Carlos Casares, Libro de Actas, 31 Dec. 1940, 15 Feb. 1941, 28 Dec. 1950, 26 Aug. 1951, 15 Sept. 1954, AHAM, described one society's closure. Rosa Gabis was another veteran activist who left Villa Domínguez for the capital. See Sociedad de Damas . . . y Asilo, Villa Domínguez, Libro de Actas, 14 Jan. 1935, Archivo Gabis, IWO.

109. OSFA officers described in Alman, 10 Feb. 1948, CZA/F49/4; members with

the Dr. prefix in CMI, Libro de Actas, by the 1950s, CAMI; Sujoy and Yankelevich de Kreimer, interview with author, 2000; *Tribuna Hebrea*, 8 November 1941, 1; Traub, April 1945, CZA/F49/3; Gold, 19 Aug. and 1 Sept. 1948, CZA/F49/5; and Tolcachier, "Asociaciones israelitas," 477. Lack of turnover was a characteristic of both male and female groups. Grove, 12 May 1955, CZA/F49/17, noted that WIZO affiliates in general tended not to attract younger women. McCune ("'*The Whole Wide World,*'" 115) finds that older women retained control of U.S. Jewish women's groups.

Conclusion

1. "Canto a la Colonización Judía."

2. Chamosa, "Indigenous or Criollo."

3. "Considering the State of U.S. Women's History" (151–52) helped me frame this paragraph.

4. Forment, *Civic Selfhood and Public Life in Mexico and Peru*.

5. Olcott (*Revolutionary Women in Postrevolutionary Mexico*) shows this for Mexico.

6. "Considering the State of U.S. Women's History," 150.

7. See Nállim ("Conflictive Legitimacies," "The Crisis of Liberalism," and "Del antifascismo al antiperonismo").

8. Bisso (*Acción Argentina*, *El antifascismo argentino*, and "¿Batir al naziperonismo?") and Jeanne Delaney's current research on twentieth-century nationalism facilitates this understanding.

BIBLIOGRAPHY

ARCHIVES

Argentina (in Buenos Aires, unless otherwise stated)

Archivo de los Compañeros, Biblioteca Popular José J. Ingenieros
Archivo del Fondo Comunal, Villa Domínguez
Archivo General de la Nación (AGN)
Archivo General de la Nación, Departamento Documentos Fotográficos (AGN-D)
Archivo Histórico Antonio Maya (AHAM), Carlos Casares
Archivo Iñigo Carrera (AIC)
Asociación Filantrópica Israelita (AFI)
Asociación Israelita de Basavilbaso (AIB), Basavilbaso
Consejo Argentino de Mujeres Israelitas (CAMI)
Centro de Documentación e Información sobre Judaísmo Argentino Marc Turkow, Asociación Mutual Israelita Argentina (CMT)
Centro de Investigación de la Cultura de las Izquierdas (CeDInCI)
Instituto Científico Judío (IWO)
Instituto Nacional de Estudios del Teatro (INET)
Museo del Cine Ducrós Hicken (MCDH)
Museo del Templo Libertad (MTL)
Museo Histórico Comunal y de la Colonización Judía Rabino Aaron Halevi Goldman (MHC), Moisesville
Museo Histórico Regional de Las Colonias (MHRC), Villa Domínguez
Organización Sionista Femenina Argentina (OSFA)
Partido Comunista Argentino (PCA)
Seminario de Maestros Hebreos Iosef Draznin, Moisesville
Sociedad Argentina de Escritores (SADE)
Unión de Mujeres Argentinas

Brazil

Arquivo Edgardo Leuenroth, IFCH / UNICAMP, Campinas

Israel

Aviezer Yellin Archive of Jewish Education in Israel and the Diaspora (AYAJE), Central Library, Tel Aviv University

Central Archive for the History of the Jewish People (CAHJP), Jerusalem
Central Library, Tel Aviv University, Tel Aviv
Central Zionist Archive (CZA), Jerusalem
Museum of the Diaspora, Tel Aviv

Netherlands
International Instituut voor Sociales Geschiedenis (IISG), Amsterdam

United Kingdom
Fawcett Library, London Guildhall University (FL), London
London Library (LL), London

United States
American Jewish Joint Distribution Committee Archives (AJJDCA), New York
New York Public Library, New York
Rutgers University Libraries (RUL), Special Collections and University Archives, New Brunswick, N.J.

INTERVIEWS

With Author (interviews in Buenos Aires, unless otherwise noted)
Abourachit, Esther. 1998.
Adida de Bentata, Luna H., Alegría Levi de Benahin, Lea Benahin de Fresco, Matilde Hadida, and Esther Benmaman. 2000.
Ambasch de Staravolsky, Berta. 1998, Moisesville.
Anonymous, 1997.
———, 1998.
———, 2000.
Barbouth de Abadi, Simone. 2000.
Bercovich de Zlotnitsky, Dora. 1997, Villa Domínguez.
Besedovsky de Farber, Rosa. 1997.
Braslavsky, Berta Perelstein de [Perlstein, Berta]. 2000.
Bursuk, Nelia. 2000.
Camji, Julieta. 2001, phone, Israel.
Cohen de Isaharoff, Judith. 1997.
Cohn, Gabriel. 2000.
Cusien, Rosa de. 2000.
Dubovsky, Benjamín. 2000.
E. H. [name withheld by request]. 2000.
Eissler, Marie. 2000.
Elnecavé, Bruria. 1997.
Faingold de Villagra, Rosita. 1997.

Farja, Lidia. 2000.
Filer, Malva. 1999, New York.
Flami, Golde. 2000.
Frank, Irma. 2000, San Miguel.
Frydman, Melej. 2000.
Furman, Esther. 1997, San Isidro.
Furman de Bendersky, Luisa. 1997, Villa Domínguez.
Fux, María. 2000.
Galante de Franco, Rebeca. 1997.
Gartenstein-Faigenblat, Lena. 2000.
Gertel, Clara. 1998.
Gílenberg, Teresa. 1997.
Glombovsky de Edelman, Laura. 2000, Posadas.
Grunfeld, José. 2000.
Grushka, Angel. 2000.
Guelman de Belmes, Luisa. 1997.
Gutman de Landman, Sofía. 2000.
Haboba, Liliana. 1998, La Plata.
Halperin, Ida. 2000, phone, United States.
Hassid de Treves, Catherine. 1998.
Hirsch, Horacio. 2002, Rio de Janeiro.
Itzcovich, Mabel. 2000.
Kantasovich, Sandra. 1998, La Plata.
Kipen, Olga. 1997, Basavilbaso.
Kohen, Natalia. 2000.
Levi, Julia. 2000.
Lifchitz de Hamburgo, Ana. 1997, Carlos Casares.
Lincovsky, Cipe. 1997.
Maldavsky, Adela de. 1998.
Mayo, Luna de. 2000.
Milstein, Sara. 2000.
Monín, Ana. 1997, San Isidro.
Morgade, Graciela. 2000.
Pascaner, Rosa. 1997.
Polak, Amalia de. 1997.
Rapaport, Rosa. 1998.
Rawin, Gregorio. 2000.
Resnick, Rosa Perla. 2006, New York.
Rollansky, Esther. 2000.
Ruetter, Mina. 2000.
Sacerdote de Lustig, Eugenia. 2000.
Salón de Esperanza, Sara. 2000.

Salzman de Glombovsky, Ana. 2000, Posadas.
Schvartz de Pitasni, Dora. 1997, Basavilbaso.
Simsolo, Victoria. 2002.
Smilg, José and Ilse. 2000.
Sommer, Ruth de. 2000.
Soriano, Regina. 2000.
Sujoy, Elena de, and Raquel Yankelevich de Kreimer. 2000.
Sulkin, Sara. 2001, Tel Aviv.
Tarshish de Wainstein, Paloma. 2001, Tel Aviv.
Tawil de Ini, Chola. 1998.
Trumper, Frida. 1998, Moisesville.
Wasserman, Perla. 1998.
Wind, Peter. 2000.
Wolf, Tea. 1998, Moisesville.
Woscoboinik de Levin, Rosa. 1998.
Yadid de Chami, Matilde. 1998.

Archivo de la Palabra (AP), Centro Marc Turkow
Absatz, Flora. No. 1, 1986.
Ballhorn, Pedro y Señora. No. 118, 1989.
Benchik, Moisés. No. 80, n.d.
Bensignor, Lidia. No. 183, 1992.
Blejer, David. No. 5, 1985.
Blutrajt, Samuel. No. 6, 1986.
Brummer, Hermán and Blanca. No. 155, 1972.
Bursuk de Scher, Tamara. No. 104, n.d.
Camín de Efron, María. No. 96, 1989.
Caplan, Dora. No. 81, 1989.
Chalcoff, Higinio. No. 9, 1986.
Chiaskelevitz, José. No. 11, n.d.
Cohen de Isaharoff, Judith. No. 182, 1992.
Efrón de Boianovsky, Rebeca. No. 111, 1989.
Ehrenfeld, Kurt. No. 324, 1996.
Eidman de Tkach, Sofía. No. 145, n.d.
Elnecavé, Bruria. No. 184, 1992.
Emanuel, David, Marcos, and Rafael. Nos. 138–39, 1988.
Frydman, Melej. No. 338, 1998.
Fuks, Carlota. No. 323, n.d.
Garberis, Jacobo. No. 20, n.d.
Grimberg, Rebeca, and Jacinta Trumper. No. 108, 1989.
Isaharoff, Judith. No. 182, 1992.
Kaller de Gutman, Frida. No. 93, 1989.

Kanutsky, Guitl. No. 32, 1985–86.
Kipen, Olga. No. 74, 1989.
Knopoff, Malka de. No. 119, n.d.
Kogan, Leike. No. 37, 1986.
Koval Magrán, Celia. No. 84, 1989.
Kreimberg, Dr. Edith. No. 172, 1991.
Lerner, Gregorio. No. 41, 1986.
Lewintal, Simón. No. 42, 1985–86.
Magrán, Salomón. No. 72, 1988.
Makoff de Sevi, Iona. No. 121, 1989.
Maladietzky, Julia. No. 98, 1989.
Merener, Davíd. No. 92, 1987.
Milstein, Lázaro. No. 48, 1986.
Neumark, Martín, and Señora. No. 322, n.d.
Nissensohn de Stilerman, Susan. No. 175, 1991.
Notvovich, Lipe. No. 116, 1989.
Novodvorsky, Israel. No. 52, 1986.
Novodvorsky, Sara. No. 53, 1985.
Ojberg de Aisicovich, Juana. No. 112, 1989.
Reiser, Samuel. No. 162, n.d.
Riegner, Loni. No. 325, 1997.
Rosenthal de Garber, Ana. No. 142, 1989.
Rozenfarb, David. No. 57, 1986.
Salomón de Susman, Flora. No. 76, 1989.
Sauer, Jenny de. No. 321, 1997.
Schallman, Lila. No. 174, 1991.
Sichel, Lote, and Heinz Sichel. No. 326, 1996.
Speckman de Klein, Adela. No. 110, n.d.
Tarica, José. No. 137, n.d.
Teper, José. No. 65, 1986.
Voloshin de Lisnofsky, Eva. No. 97, 1989.
Waisman, Rita. No. 106, n.d.
Yagupsky, Máximo. No. 68, 1984.
Zak, Benito. No. 59, 1985.
Zalel, Blitz. No. 69, 1985.
Zanders de Silber, Edith. No. 70, 1986.

Institute of Contemporary Judaism, Department of Oral History, Hebrew University of Jerusalem (HUJ)
Gutman, Frida. No. 3146, 1990–91.
Itzigsohn, José. No. 112, 1977.
Moise, Ninette, and Alicia Hadida. No. 171, 1988.

Other Interviews
Gesel, Dominich. Interview with Mina Ruetter, n.d. Ruetter psersonal papers.
Kanutsky, Guitl. Interview with Mina Ruetter, 1980. Ruetter personal papers.
Oliver, María Rosa. Interview, 1971. Proyecto de Historia Oral del Instituto de Historia Torcuato di Tella, Universidad Torcuato di Tella, Buenos Aires.
Raquel. Interview with Rosa Rapaport, 1994. [Rapaport wished to keep Raquel's last name confidential.]

PERIODICALS (IN BUENOS AIRES, UNLESS OTHERWISE NOTED)

La Acción, Paraná, 1944 and 1946
Acción Socialista, 1923–28
El Alba, Moisesville, 1922–41
¡Alerta!, 1935, 1937, 1938, and 1940–42
Antinazi, 1940 and 1946–47
La Antorcha, 1923
Anuario "La Razón," 1922
Anuario Socialista, 1928
Argentina Libre, 1940 and 1946
Atalaya, Gualeguay, 1944
Avance, 1937–38
Avanzada, 1941 and 1943
Avanzada Judía, 1947–49
Ayuda al Pueblo Español: Órgano del Movimiento Argentino de Solidaridad con el Pueblo Español, 1941
Boletín de la Liga de Educación Racionalista, 1915
Boletín del Partido Socialista, 1935
Boletín Mensual del Consejo de Mujeres Israelitas, 1948–49
Buenos Aires Herald, 1930
El Campo, Villa Domínguez, 1927–31
C.I.A.P.E. [Órgano de la Comisión Israelita de Ayuda al Pueblo Español], 1937
Clarín, 1971, 1985, 1992, and 1993
Claudia, 1974
El Colono Cooperador, 1972
Comentarios y Opiniones, 1999–2000
La Congregación, 1943–57
Contra-fascismo, 1936
Convicción, 1980
Crítica, 1941
Crónica, Villaguay, 1981
Democracia, 1993
Derechos del Hombre, 1938 and 1945

D.E.S.A. [Delegación de Entidades Sefaradíes Argentinas], 1952
El Diario, 1925 and 1995
¡En Guardia! Contra la Xenofobia y el Antisemitismo, 1936
La Escuela Popular, 1913
Filantropía, 1981–2000
Fin de Semana, 1984
Flash, 1984
La FORA [Federación Obrera Regional Argentina], Rosario, 1934
F.O.V. [Federación Obrera del Vestido], 1936–39
Fray Mocho, 1912
Gaceta del Foro, 1930
Hanoar Hasefaradí, 1948–50
El Heraldo, Concordia, 1994
La Hora, 1941–43 and 1945–46
Humanidad Nueva, 1911, 1916, and 1918–19
Di Idische Froi, 1953–60
La Internacional, 1917–19, 1922–25, 1929, 1931, and 1933
International Council of Jewish Women Newsletter, Jerusalem, 1956, 1959, and 1992
Israel, 1918–55
El Israelita Argentino, 1913 and 1914
Jewish Chronicle, London, 1894, 1898, 1903, 1905, 1946–56
Juventud, 1912–17
Juventud, Carlos Casares, 1925–26
Libertad, 1928
El Libertario, 1999–2000
El Litoral, Santa Fe, 1995
La Luz, 1931–55
Lyra, 1959
La Maga, 1991 and 1995
El Mercurio, Santiago, Chile, 1932
Monitor de la Educación Común, 1910 and 1944–45
Mujeres Argentinas, 1946–48
Mundo Argentino, 1928
Mundo Israelita, 1923–55 and 1985
La Nación, 1931, 1936, and 1999
New York Times, 1929 and 1943
Noticias Gráficas, 1932 and 1934
Nuestra Causa, 1919–21
Nuestras Mujeres, 1947–55
Nuestra Tribuna, Necochea, 1922–25
Nueva Gaceta, 1941–43
El Obrero de la Confección, 1934–35 and 1938

El Obrero del Vestido, 1941 and 1943–46
El Obrero Sastre, 1935
El Obrero Textil, 1933–45
OSFA [Organización Sionista Femenina Argentina], 1943–57, 1976, and 1996
Página 12, 1987
La Prensa, 1934
Principios, Paraná, 1937–38 and 1945–48
La Protesta, 1930, 1932, and 1936
La Razón, 1930 and 1984
Reconstruir por el Socialismo y la Libertad, 1956
Revista ICUF [Idischer Cultur Farband], 1951
Revista WIZO [Women's International Zionist Organization], 1938–43
La Revuelta, Santa Fe, 1919
Rosario/6, 1995
Sarmiento, Carlos Casares, 1936–37
SHA [Sociedad Hebraica Argentina], 1949
Siete Días, 1982
Sin Cortes, 1995
Socorro Rojo, 1932–35
Solidaridad, 1942–43
The Standard, 1930
Sulem, 1934
Tiempo Argentino, 1984 and 1986
Tribuna, 1954–55
Tribuna Hebrea, 1929, 1930–32, 1934, 1938–39, and 1940–43
Unidad, 1936–43
Unión y Labor, 1909–13
La Vanguardia, 1903–12 and 1921–39
Vanguardia Juvenil, Dror, 1944
Vida Femenina, 1933–37 and 1939–43
Vida Nuestra, 1919
Vivencias, 1996
Vocero del ICUF [Idischer Cultur Farband], 1966
La Voz, 1985

OTHER PRINT SOURCES

Abeijón, Carlos, and Jorge Santos Lafauci. *La mujer antes y después de Eva Perón*. Buenos Aires: Cuarto Mundo, 1975.

Adler, Eliyanna R. "Jewish Girls as Agents of Social Change in Tsarist Russia." Paper presented at the Berkshire Conference, Scripps College, 2005.

Allegrone, Norma. *La mujer y el poder en las organizaciones profesionales*. Buenos Aires: FUNDAI, 2000.

Almaráz, Roberto, Manuel Corchon, and Rómulo Zemborain. *¡Aquí FUBA! Las luchas estudiantiles en tiempos de Perón (1943–1955)*. Buenos Aires: Planeta, 2001.

Alpersohn, Marcos. *Colonia Mauricio: Memorias de un colono judío*. Translated by Eliahu Toker. Carlos Casares, Argentina: Archivo Centro Cultural José Ingenieros, n.d.

Alsogaray, Julio. *Trilogía de la trata de blancas (rufianes, policía, municipalidad)*. Buenos Aires: L. J. Rosso, 1933.

Anderson, Benedict. *Imagined Communities: Reflections on the Origin and Spread of Nationalism*. Rev. ed. New York: Verso, 1991.

Andrews, George Reid. *The Afro-Argentines of Buenos Aires, 1800–1900*. Madison: University of Wisconsin Press, 1980.

Antler, Joyce. *The Journey Home: How Jewish Women Shaped Modern America*. New York: Schocken, 1997.

Anzaldúa, Gloria. *Borderlands/La Frontera: The New Mestiza*. 2nd ed. San Francisco: Aunt Lute Books, 1999.

Applebaum, Nancy P., Anne S. Macpherson, and Karin Alejandra Rosemblatt, eds. *Race and Nation in Modern Latin America*. Chapel Hill: University of North Carolina Press, 2003.

Arcuschin, María. *De Ucrania a Basavilbaso*. Buenos Aires: Marymar, 1986.

Argentina. Buenos Aires, Dirección General de Estadística Municipal. *Censo general de población, edificación, comercio e industrias de la ciudad de Buenos Aires . . . 1909*. 3 vols. Buenos Aires: Compañía Sudamericana de Billetes del Banco, 1910.

Argentina. Comisión Directiva del Censo. *Segundo censo de la República Argentina*. 3 vols. Buenos Aires: Taller Tipográfico de la Penitenciaria Nacional, 1898.

Argentina. Comisión Nacional del Censo. *Tercer censo nacional*. 10 vols. Buenos Aires: L. J. Rosso, 1916.

Argentina. Congreso Nacional. *Diario de Sesiones de la Cámara de Diputados*, 1936 and 1949. Buenos Aires.

———. Congreso Nacional. *Diario de Sesiones de la Cámara de Senadores*, 1936. Buenos Aires.

Argentina. Dirección Nacional de Estadística y Censos. *Censo nacional de población 1960*. Buenos Aires: Dirección Nacional de Estadística y Censos, 1960.

Argentina. Municipalidad de la Ciudad de Buenos Aires. *Cuarto censo general 1936*. 4 vols. Buenos Aires: Guillermo Kraft, 1939.

Argentina. Presidencia de la Nación, Ministerio de Asuntos Técnicos. *Cuarto censo general de la nación*. 3 vols. Buenos Aires: Guillermo Kraft, 1952.

"Argentine Educators Look at the United States." *Pan American Union Bulletin* 63 (1929): 340–52.

Arnaiz, María del Carmen, and Patricia Chomnalez. *Mujeres que trabajan (1930–1940)*. Buenos Aires: Centro Editor de América Latina, 1992.

A aventura modernista de Berta Singerman: Uma voz argentina no Brasil. São Paulo: Museu Lasar Segall, 2003.

Avni, Haim. *Argentina and the Jews: A History of Jewish Immigration*. Translated by Gila Brand. Tuscaloosa: University of Alabama Press, 1991.

———, and Leonardo Senkman. *Del campo al campo: Colonos de Argentina en Israel*. Buenos Aires: Milá, 1993.

Bacci, Claudia. "Las políticas culturales del progresismo judío argentino: La revista *Aporte* y el ICUF en la década de 1950." *Políticas de la Memoria*, no. 5 (summer 2004–2005): 159–68.

Baily, Samuel L. *Immigrants in the Lands of Promise: Italians in Buenos Aires and New York City, 1870–1914*. Ithaca, N.Y.: Cornell University Press, 1999.

———. "Marriage Patterns and Immigrant Assimilation in Buenos Aires, 1882–1923." *Hispanic American Historical Review* 60, no. 1 (February 1980): 32–48.

———, and Eduardo José Míquez, eds. *Mass Migration to Modern Latin America*. Wilmington, Del.: Scholarly Resources, 2003.

Ballent, Anahi, and Adrián Gorelik. "País urbano o país rural: La modernización territorial y su crisis." In *Crisis económica, avance del estado e incertidumbre política (1930–1943)*, vol. 7 of *Nueva historia argentina*, edited by Alejandro Cattaruzza, 143–200. Buenos Aires: Sudamericana, 2001.

Banner, Lois W. *American Beauty*. Chicago, Ill.: University of Chicago Press, 1983.

Bargman, Daniel Fernando. "Un ámbito para las relaciones interétnicas: Las colonias agrícolas judías en Argentina." *Revista de Antropología*, no. 11 (1992): 50–58.

Barrancos, Dora. *Anarquismo, educación y costumbres en la Argentina de principios de siglo*. Buenos Aires: Contrapunto, 1990.

———. *Educación, cultura, y trabajadores (1890–1930)*. Buenos Aires: Centro Editor de América Latina, 1991.

———. *La escena iluminada: Ciencias para trabajadores (1899–1930)*. Buenos Aires: Plus Ultra, 1996.

———. "Historia, historiografía y género. Notas para la memoria de sus vínculos en la Argentina." Unpublished manuscript.

———. *Inclusión/Exclusión: Historia con mujeres*. Buenos Aires: Fondo de Cultura Económica, 2002.

———. "Moral sexual, sexualidad y mujeres trabajadoras en el período de entreguerras." In *La Argentina entre multitudes y soledades: De los años treinta a la actualidad*, vol. 3 of *Historia de la vida privada en la Argentina*, edited by Fernando Devoto and Marta Madero, 199–225. Buenos Aires: Taurus, 1999.

———. "Los niños proselitistas de las vanguardias obreras." Documento de Trabajo no. 24. CEIL, May 1987, Buenos Aires.

———. "Socialismo y sufragio femenino: Notas para su historia (1890–1947)." In *El Partido Socialista en Argentina: Sociedad, política e ideas a través de un siglo*, edited by Hernán Camarero and Carlos Miguel Herrera, 159–83. Buenos Aires: Prometeo, 2005.

———. "Socialistas y la suplementación de la escuela pública: la Asociación de Bibliotecas y Recreos Infantiles (1913–1930)." In *Mujeres en la educación: Género y docencia en Argentina: 1870–1930*, edited by Graciela Morgade, 130–50. Buenos Aires: Miño y Dávila, 1997.

Baum, Charlotte, Paula Hyman, and Sonya Michel. *The Jewish Woman in America*. New York: New American Library, 1977.

Baumkoler, Berta. *La lucha es vida*. Buenos Aires: Carlos A. Firpo, 2000.

Bayón, Silvia S. "Las locas en Buenos Aires: Una representación social de la locura en la mujer en las primeras décadas del siglo XX." In *La política social antes de la política social (Caridad, beneficencia y política social en Buenos Aires, siglos XVII a XX)*, edited by José Luis Moreno, 225–86. Buenos Aires: Trama/Prometeo, 2000.

Beezley, William, William French, and Cheryl E. Martin, eds. *Rituals of Rule, Rituals of Resistance: Public Celebrations and Popular Culture in Mexico*. Wilmington, Del.: Scholarly Resources, 1994.

Bell, Lawrence D. "Bitter Conquest: Zionists against Progressive Jews and the Making of Post-War Jewish Politics in Argentina, 1946–1955." *Jewish History* 17 (2003): 285–308.

———. "In the Name of the Community: Populism, Ethnicity, and Politics among the Jews of Argentina under Perón, 1946–1955." *Hispanic American Historical Review* 86, no. 1 (February 2006): 93–122.

———. "The Jews and Perón: Communal Politics and National Identity in Peronist Argentina, 1946–1955." Ph.D. diss., Ohio State University, 2002.

Bellucci, Mabel. "Anarquismo y feminismo: El movimiento de mujeres anarquistas con sus logros y desafíos hacia principios de siglo." *Todo Es Historia*, no. 321 (April 1994): 58–70.

———. "Sarmiento y los feminismos de su época." In *Mujeres en la educación: Género y docencia en Argentina: 1870–1930*, edited by Graciela Morgade, 31–66. Buenos Aires: Miño y Dávila, 1997.

Benarós, León. "Rosa Pavlovsky: Una médica rusa que cruzó el océano a pedido de Sarmiento." *Todo Es Historia*, no. 241 (June 1987): 58–59.

Benbassa, Esther. "Education for Jewish Girls in the East: A Portrait of the Galata School in Istanbul, 1879–1912." *Studies in Contemporary Jewry* 9 (1993): 163–73.

———, and Aron Rodrigue. *Sephardi Jewry: A History of the Judeo-Spanish Community, 14th–20th Centuries*. Berkeley: University of California Press, 2000.

Ben-Dror, Graciela. *Católicos, nazis y judíos: La iglesia argentina en los tiempos del Tercer Reich*. Buenos Aires: Lumiere, 2003.

Benegas Lynch (h.), Alberto, and Martín Krauze. *En defensa de los más necesitados*. Buenos Aires: Atlántida, 1998.

Berkowitz, Michael. "Transcending 'Tzimmes and Sweetness': Recovering the History of Zionist Women in Central and Western Europe, 1897–1933." *Active Voices: Women in Jewish Culture*, edited by Maurie Sacks, 43–62. Urbana: University of Illinois Press, 1995.

Bertoni, Lilia Ana. "De Turquía a Buenos Aires: Una colectividad nueva a fines del siglo XX." *Estudios Migratorios Latinoamericanos*, no. 26 (April 1994): 67–94.

———. *Patriotas, cosmopolitas y nacionalistas: La construcción de la nacionalidad argentina a fines del siglo XIX*. Buenos Aires: Fondo de Cultura Económica, 2001.

Besse, Susan K. "Defining a 'National Type': Brazilian Beauty Contests in the 1920s." *Estudios Interdisciplinarios de América Latina y el Caribe* 16, no. 1 (January–June 2005): 95–117.

Bestene, Jorge O. "Formas de asociacionismo entre los sirio-libaneses en Buenos Aires (1900–1950)." In *Asociacionismo, trabajo e identidad étnica: Los italianos en América Latina en una perspectiva comparada*, edited by Fernando J. Devoto and Eduardo J. Míguez, 115–33. Buenos Aires: CEMLA, CSER, IEHS, 1992.

Biale, David. "Love, Marriage, and the Modernization of the Jews." In *Approaches to Modern Judaism*, edited by Marc Lee Raphael, 1–17. Chico, Calif.: Scholars Press, 1983.

———, Michael Galchinsky, and Susannah Heschel. "Introduction: The Dialectic of Jewish Enlightenment." In *Insider/Outsider: American Jews and Multiculturalism*, edited by David Biale, Michael Galchinsky, and Susannah Heschel, 1–13. Berkeley: University of California Press, 1998.

Bianchi, Susana, and Norma Sanchís. *El partido peronista femenino*. 2 vols. Buenos Aires: Centro Editor de América Latina, 1988.

Biblioteca Obrera Juan B. Justo. *Memoria del XXXVIII ejercicio correspondiente al año 1935*. Buenos Aires: Casa del Pueblo, 1936.

Bisso, Andrés. *Acción Argentina: Un antifascismo nacional en tiempos de guerra mundial*. Buenos Aires: Prometeo, 2005.

———, ed. *El antifascismo argentino*. Buenos Aires: Buenos Libros, 2007.

———. "¿Batir al naziperonismo? El desarrollo de la apelación antifascista argentina y su recepción en la práctica política de la Unión Democrática." Tesis de licenciatura, Universidad Nacional de la Plata, 2000.

Blancos Pazos, Roberto, and Raúl Clemente. *Diccionario de actores de cine argentino, 1933–1994*. Buenoes Aires: Corregidor, 1999.

Blank, Boris. *La mujer judía en la ciudad de Córdoba a comienzos del siglo XX*. Córdoba, Argentina: Junta Provincial de Historia de Córdoba, 1994.

Bliss, Katherine Elaine. *Compromised Positions: Prostitution, Public Health, and Gender Politics in Revolutionary Mexico City*. University Park: Pennsylvania State University Press, 2001.

Blomberg, Héctor Pedro. "La vuelta de Sonia." *La novela semanal* 10, no. 444 (17 May 1926): 3–14.

Blumenfeld, Israel. *Historia de la comunidad israelita de Tucumán*. Tucumán, Argentina: Sociedad Unión Israelita Tucumana, 1971.

Bortnik de Duchovny, Dora. *Recuerdos de una maestra de campaña*. San Isidro, Argentina: Instituto Dr. Juan S. Fernández, 1980.

Botana, Natalio R. *El orden conservador: La política argentina entre 1880 y 1916*. Buenos Aires: Sudamericana, 1977.

Boulgourdjian, Nélida, and Diana L. Epstein. "Armenios y judíos en el Once, 1910–1950." In *Encuentro y alteridad: Vida y cultura judía en América Latina*, edited by Judit Bokser Liwerant and Alicia Gojman de Backal, 163–81. Mexico City: Universidad Autónoma de México, 1999.

Boxer, Marilyn Jacoby. *When Women Ask the Questions: Creating Women's Studies in America*. Baltimore, Md.: Johns Hopkins University Press, 1998.

Bra, Gerardo. *La organización negra: La increíble historia de la Zwi Migdal*. Buenos Aires: Corregidor, 1999.

Brauner Rodgers, Susana. "La comunidad judía alepina en Buenos Aires: De la ortodoxia religiosa a la apertura y de la apertura a la ortodoxia religiosa (1930–1953)." *Estudios Interdisciplinarios de América Latina y el Caribe* 11, no. 1 (January–June 2000): 45–64.

Bristow, Edward J. *Prostitution and Prejudice: The Jewish Fight against White Slavery, 1870–1939*. Oxford: Clarendon Press of Oxford University Press, 1982.

Brodsky, Adriana. "Becoming 'Argentine': Sephardic Jewish Women and the Zionist Project." Paper presented at the annual meeting of the American Historical Association, Washington, D.C., 2004.

———. "The Contours of Identity: Sephardic Jews and the Constructions of Jewish Communities in Argentina, 1880 to the Present." Ph.D. diss., Duke University, 2004.

Brumberg, Joan Jacobs, and Nancy Tomes. "Women in the Professions: A Research Agenda for American Historians." *Reviews in American History* 10 (June 1982): 275–95.

Brumberg, Stephen F. *Going to America, Going to School: The Jewish Immigrant Public School Encounter in Turn-of-the-Century New York City*. New York: Praeger, 1986.

Buchrucker, Cristián. *Nacionalismo y peronismo: La Argentina en la crisis ideológica mundial (1927–1955)*. Buenos Aires: Sudamericana, 1987.

Burstein, Janet. "Translating Immigrant Women: Surfacing the Manifold Self." In *Talking Back: Images of Jewish Women in American Popular Culture*, edited by Joyce Antler, 15–29. Hanover, N.H.: Brandeis University Press, 1998.

Bursuk, Nelia. "Recuerdos del anarquismo." *Autopiano* (1996): unnumbered page.

Bushnell, David. *Reform and Reaction in the Platine Provinces, 1810–1852*. Gainesville: University of Florida Press, 1983.

Caimari, Lila. *Perón y la iglesia católica: Religión, estado y sociedad en la Argentina (1943–1955)*. Buenos Aires: Ariel, 1995.

Calof, Rachel. *Rachel Calof's Story: Jewish Homesteader on the Northern Plains*. Edited by J. Sanford Rikoon. Translated by Jacob Calof and Molly Shaw. Bloomington: Indiana University Press, 1995.

Camarero, Hernán. *A la conquista de la clase obrera: Los comunistas y el mundo del trabajo en la Argentina, 1920–1935*. Buenos Aires: Siglo Vientiuno, 2007.

———, and Carlos Miguel Herrera, eds. *El Partido Socialista en Argentina: Sociedad, política e ideas a través de un siglo*. Buenos Aires: Prometeo, 2005.

Cane, James. "'Unity for the Defense of Culture': The AIAPE and the Cultural Politics of Argentine Antifascism, 1935–1943." *Hispanic American Historical Review* 77, no. 3 (August 1997): 443–82.

Cannistraro, Philip V., and Brian R. Sullivan. *Il Duce's Other Woman: The Untold Story of Margherita Sarfatti, Benito Mussolini's Italian Mistress, and How She Helped Him Come to Power*. New York: Morrow, 1993.

Capizzano de Capalbo, Beatriz, and Matilde Larisgoitia de González Canda. *La mujer en la educación preescolar argentina*. Buenos Aires: Latina, 1982.

Carlson, Marifran. *¡Feminismo! The Women's Movement in Argentina from Its Beginnings to Eva Perón*. Chicago, Ill.: Academy Chicago, 1988.

Carulla, Juan A. *Al filo del medio siglo*. Paraná, Argentina: Llanura, 1951.

Casa del Pueblo. *Exposición Fenia Chertcoff de Repetto*. Buenos Aires: La Vanguardia, 1928.

Castro, Donald S. "The Sainete Porteño, 1890–1935: The Image of Jews in the Argentine Popular Theater." *Studies in Latin American Popular Culture* 21 (2002): 29–57.

———. "Workers, Strikes, and Labor Unrest as Themes in the Popular Theatre of Buenos Aires (1890–1920)." Manuscript.

Caterina, Luis María. *La Liga Patriótica Argentina: Ungrupo de presión frente a las convulsiones sociales de la década del '20*. Buenos Aires: Corregidor, 1995.

Cattaruzza, Alejandro. "Descifrando pasados: Debates y representaciones de la historia nacional." In *Crisis económica, avance del estado e incertidumbre política (1930–1943)*, vol. 7 of *Nueva historia argentina*, edited by Alejandro Cattaruzza, 429–76. Buenos Aires: Sudamericana, 2001.

Caulfield, Sueann. *In Defense of Honor: Sexual Morality, Modernity, and Nation in Early Twentieth-Century Brazil*. Chapel Hill: University of North Carolina Press, 2000.

Cernadas, Jorge, Roberto Pittaluga, and Horacio Tarcus. "La historiografía sobre el Partido Comunista de la Argentina: Un estado de la cuestión." *El Rodaballo* 4, no. 8 (fall/winter 1998): 31–40.

Chamosa, Oscar. "Indigenous or Criollo: The Myth of White Argentina in Tucuman's Calchaquí Valley." *Hispanic American Historical Review* 88, no. 1 (February 2008): 71–106.

Chasteen, John Charles. "Trouble between Men and Women: Machismo on Nineteenth-Century *Estancias*." In *The Middle Period in Latin America: Values and Attitudes in the 17th–19th Centuries*, edited by Mark D. Szuchman, 123–40. Boulder, Colo.: Lynne Rienner, 1989.

Chertcoff de Repetto, Fenia. "El movimiento social femenino en la República Argentina." *Almanaque de Trabajo para el Año 1918*, 141–45.

Chirom, Perla. *Pequeña familia, pequeña historia*. Buenos Aires: Milá, 1991.

Chromoy, Etel. *Un barco azul y blanco*. Buenos Aires: Milá, 2006.

Ciafardo, Eduardo O. "La práctica benéfica y el control de los sectores populares de la ciudad de Buenos Aires, 1890–1910." *Revista de Indias*, no. 54 (May–August 1994): 383–408.

Clementi, Hebe. *María Rosa Oliver*. Buenos Aires: Planeta, 1992.

Clifford, James. *The Predicament of Culture: 20th Century Ethnography, Literature, and Art*. Cambridge: Harvard University Press, 1988.

Cociovitch, Noé. *Génesis de Moisés Ville*. Translated by Iaacov Lerman. Buenos Aires: Milá, 1987.

Colonia Mauricio: 100 años. Buenos Aires: Shalom, 1991.

Comisión Femenina Israelita. *Mujeres en la ayuda a las democracias*. Buenos Aires: n.p., n.d.

Comisión Femenina Israelita de Solidaridad. *Nuestros talleres en plena labor*. Buenos Aires: n.p., n.d.

Comité Central Pro-Socorro a las Víctimas de la Guerra y Refugiados. *Memoria y balance 1941–1942*. Buenos Aires: n.p., 1942.

Consejo Argentino de Mujeres Israelitas (CAMI). *Cincuentenario 1937–1987*. Buenos Aires: n.p., 1987.

Consejo de Mujeres Israelitas de la Argentina. *Almanaque-Agenda*. Buenos Aires: n.p., 1941–53.

"Considering the State of U.S. Women's History." *Journal of Women's History* 15, no. 1 (spring 2003): 145–63.

Corbière, Emilio J. "Los archivos secretos del PC Argentino: La internacional comunista en la Argentina (1919–1943)." *Todo Es Historia*, no. 372 (July 1998): 8–23.

Corbin, Alain. *Women for Hire: Prostitution and Sexuality in France after 1850*. Translated by Alan Sheridan. Cambridge: Harvard University Press, 1990.

Cosse, Isabel. "Cultura y sexualidad en la Argentina de los sesenta: Usos y resignificaciones de la experiencia transnacional." *Estudios Interdisciplinarios de América Latina y el Caribe* 17, no. 1 (January–June 2006): 39–60.

Crespí, Graciela. "La huelga docente de 1919 en Mendoza." In *Mujeres en la educación: Género y docencia en Argentina: 1870–1930*, edited by Graciela Morgade, 51–174. Buenos Aires: Miño y Dávila, 1997.

Crilla, Hedy. *La palabra en acción*. Edited by Cora Roca. Buenos Aires: Instituto Nacional del Teatro, 1998.

Criscenti, Joseph T., ed. *Sarmiento and His Argentina*. Boulder, Colo.: Lynne Rienner, 1993.

Cuello, Nicolás. *Acción femenina*. Buenos Aires: n.p., 1939.

———. *Ejemplo noble de una mujer*. Buenos Aires: n.p., 1936.

Dávila, Valeria, and Andrea Orozco. "Bataclanas y vedettes en la noche porteña." *Todo Es Historia*, no. 384 (July 1999): 6–36.

Deere, Carmen Diana, and Magdalena León de Leal. *Empowering Women: Land and Property Rights in Latin America*. Pittsburgh: University of Pittsburgh Press, 2001.

———. "Liberalism and Married Women's Property Rights in Nineteenth-Century Latin America." *Hispanic American Historical Review* 85, no. 4 (November 2005): 627–78.

Dekel-Chen, Jonathan L. *Farming the Red Land: Jewish Agricultural Colonization and Local Soviet Power, 1924–1941*. New Haven, Conn.: Yale University Press, 2005.

Delaney, Jeanne. "Imagining *El Ser Argentino*: Cultural Nationalism and Romantic Concepts of National Identity in Early Twentieth-Century Argentina." *Journal of Latin American Studies* 34, no. 3 (August 2002): 625–58.

Delegación de Asociaciones Israelitas Argentinas. *Perón y el pueblo judío*. Buenos Aires: Micrográfica, 1974.

Departamento de Juventud del Centro Sionista Sefaradí. *Actas*. 1944–1945.

———. "Programa de Acción, Año 1945."

Departamento del Keren Kayemeth Leisroel del Centro Sionista Sefaradí. Comisión de Señoritas. *Actas*. 1944–1945.

Deutsch, Sandra McGee. "The Catholic Church, Work, and Womanhood in Argentina, 1890–1930." *Gender and History* 3 (autumn 1991): 304–25.

———. "Changing the Landscape: The Study of Argentine Jewish Women and New Historical Vistas." *Jewish History* 18, no. 1 (2004): 49–73.

———. *Counterrevolution in Argentina, 1900–1932: The Argentine Patriotic League*. Lincoln: University of Nebraska Press, 1986.

———. *Las derechas: The Extreme Right in Argentina, Brazil, and Chile, 1890–1939*. Stanford, Calif.: Stanford University Press, 1999.

———. "Gender and Sociopolitical Change in Twentieth-Century Latin America." *Hispanic American Historical Review* 71, no. 2 (May 1991): 259–306.

———. "Los nacionalistas y la sexualidad, 1919–1940." *Reflejos*, no. 10 (2001–2): 193–212.

———. "The Visible and Invisible Liga Patriótica Argentina, 1919–1928: Gender Roles and the Right Wing." *Hispanic American Historical Review* 64, no. 2 (May 1984): 233–58.

———. "What Difference Does Gender Make? The Extreme Right in the ABC Countries in the Era of Fascism." *Estudios Interdisciplinarios de América Latina y el Caribe* 8, no. 2 (July–December 1997), 5–21.

———. "Women: The Forgotten Half of Argentine Jewish History." *Shofar* 15, no. 3 (spring 1997): 49–65.

Devoto, Fernando, and Marta Madero, eds. *Historia de la vida privada en la Argentina*; vol. 3 of *La Argentina entre multitudes y soledades. De los años treinta a la actualidad*. Buenos Aires: Taurus, 1999.

Di Carlo, Adelia. "Mujeres de actuación destacada: Doña Victoria Gucovsky." *Caras y Caretas*, no. 1795 (February 25, 1933): unnumbered page.

Di Tella, Torcuato. "La Unión Obrera Textil 1930–1945." In *Sindicalistas como los de antes*, edited by Torcuato Di Tella, 169–214. Buenos Aires: Biblos, 1993.

Diament, Ana, ed. *Testimonios para la experiencia de enseñar: Berta P. de Braslavsky—Maestra, profesora, militante, humanista*. Buenos Aires: Universidad de Buenos Aires, n.d.

Diner, Hasia R. *Hungering for America: Italian, Irish and Jewish Foodways in the Age of Migration*. Cambridge: Harvard University Press, 2001.

Dios de Martina, Ángeles de. *Mujeres inmigrantes: historias de vida*. Buenos Aires: Dunken, 2001.

Dore, Elizabeth, and Maxine Molyneux, eds. *Hidden Histories of Gender and the State in Latin America*. Durham, N.C.: Duke University Press, 2000.

Dos Santos, Estela. *Las mujeres peronistas*. Buenos Aires: Centro Editor de América Latina, 1983.

Dreier, Katherine S. *Five Months in the Argentine from a Woman's Point of View*. New York: Frederic Fairchild Sherman, 1920.

Dubovsky, Benjamín. "Los compañeros que conocí (I-III)." *El Libertario*, part I, no. 47 (December 1999/January 2000), 8; part II, no. 48 (April–May 2000), 5; and part III, no. 49 (August–September 2000), 6.

Dworkin, Susan. *Miss America 1945: Bess Myerson and the Year That Changed Our Lives*. New York: Newmarket, 1987.

Edelman, Fanny. *Banderas, Pasiones, Camaradas*. Buenos Aires: Dirple, 1996.

"La educación argentina desde la reforma Saavedra-Lamas hasta el fin de la década infame." In *Historia de la educación argentina*, edited by Adriana Puiggrós, vol. 3, 15–97. Buenos Aires: Galerna, 1992.

El educador Pablo A. Pizzurno: Recopilación de trabajos—Medio siglo de acción cultural en la enseñanza secundaria, normal y primaria. Buenos Aires: Establecimiento Gráfico Argentino, 1934.

Efron, Jedidia. "La obra escolar en las colonias judías." In *La colonización judía*, edited by Leonardo Senkman, 71–79. Buenos Aires: Centro Editor de América Latina, 1984.

Eisen, Sergio. "Rebeca Levy de Estambul a la Boca." *Diario*, 11 April 1995, 6.

Elena, Eduardo. "What the People Want: State Planning and Political Participation in Peronist Argentina, 1946–1955." *Journal of Latin American Studies* 37, no. 1 (February 2005): 81–108.

Elkin, Judith Laikin. *The Jews of Latin America*. Rev. ed. New York: Holmes and Meier, 1998.

———. "Latin American Jewry Today." In *American Jewish Yearbook 85* (1984), 3–50. Philadelphia: Jewish Publication Society of America, 1984.

Elnecavé, Bruria. *Crisol de vivencias judías*. Buenos Aires: La Luz, 1994.

Epstein, Diana L. "Aspectos generales de la inmigración judeo-marroquí a la Argentina. 1875–1930." *Temas de Africa y Asia, 2: Africanos y mediorientales en América (Siglos XVIII-XX)* (1993): 151–70.

———. "Los judeo-marroquíes en Buenos Aires: Pautas matrimoniales 1875–1910." *Estudios Interdisciplinarios de América Latina y el Caribe* 6, no. 1 (1995): 113–33.

———. "Maestros marroquíes: Estrategia educativa e integración, 1892–1920." *Anuario IEHS* 12 (1997): 347–69.

Escliar, Myriam. *Mujeres en la literatura y la vida judeoargentina*. Buenos Aires: Milá, 1996.

Escudé, Carlos. *El fracaso del proyecto argentino: Educación e ideología*. Buenos Aires: Tesis, 1990.

Evans, Judith. "Setting the Stage for Struggle: Popular Theater in Buenos Aires, 1890–1914." *Radical History Review* 21 (fall 1979): 49–61.

Ewen, Elizabeth. *Immigrant Women in the Land of Dollars: Life and Culture on the Lower East Side, 1890–1925*. New York: Monthly Review Press, 1985.

Fairman, Silvia C. de. *Mate y sámovar*. Buenos Aires: Lumen, 2000.

Falcoff, Mark. "Argentina." In *The Spanish Civil War 1936–1939: American Hemispheric Perspectives*, edited by Mark Falcoff and Frederick B. Pike, 291–348. Lincoln: University of Nebraska Press, 1982.

Farine, Avigdor. "Charity and Study Societies in Europe of the Sixteenth–Eighteenth Centuries." *Jewish Quarterly Review* 64, no. 1 (1973): 16–47 and no. 2 (1974): 164–75.

Farnsworth-Alvear, Ann. *Dulcinea in the Factory: Myths, Morals, Men, and Women in Colombia's Industrial Experiment, 1905–1960*. Durham, N.C.: Duke University Press, 2000.

Favelukes de Kohan, Felisa. *Desafío a los años*. Buenos Aires: Macagno, Landa y Cía., 1970.

Feierstein, Ricardo. *Historia de los judíos argentinos*. Buenos Aires: Ameghino, 1999.

Feijóo, María del Carmen. *Las feministas*. Buenos Aires: Centro Editor de América Latina, 1980.

———. "Gabriela Coni y la lucha feminista." *Todo Es Historia*, no. 175 (1981).

Feldman, Egal. "Prostitution, the Alien Woman and the Progressive Imagination, 1910–1915." *American Quarterly* 19, no. 2 (summer 1967): 192–206.

Felitti, Karina. "El placer de elegir: Anticoncepción y liberación sexual en la década del sesenta." In *Historia de las mujeres en la Argentina: Siglo XX*, edited by Fernanda Gil Lozano, Valeria Pita, and María Gabriela Ini, 155–71. Buenos Aires: Taurus, 2000.

Felman, Mika. *Mi guerra de España*. Barcelona: Plaza and Janes, 1976.

Fenia Chertcoff. Buenos Aires: n.p., n.d.

Ferreras, Norberto O. "La cuestión de la alimentación obrera en Buenos Aires y Río de Janeiro entre 1930 y 1945." *Estudos Ibero-Americanos* 24, no. 2 (December 1998): 93–111.

———. "Evolución de los principales consumos obreros en Buenos Aires, 1880–1920." *Ciclos* no. 22 (2001): 157–80.

Ferris, Marcie Cohen. "'From the Recipe File of Luba Cohen': A Study of Southern Jewish Foodways and Cultural Identity." In *American Jewish Women's History: A Reader*, edited by Pamela S. Nadell, 256–80. New York: New York University Press, 2003.

Ferro, Lucía. *Las socialistas que hicieron futuro*. Buenos Aires: Agencia Periodística CID-Diario del Viajero, 1996.

Finchelstein, Federico. *Fascismo, liturgia e imaginario: El mito del general Uriburu y la argentina nacionalista*. Buenos Aires: Fondo de Cultura Económica, 2002.

Finchelstein, Federico, and Daniel Lvovich. "L'Holocauste et l'Eglise argentine: Perceptions et Réactions." *Bulletin Trimestriel de la Fondation Auschwitz*, nos. 76–77 (2002): 9–30.

Foote, Nicola. "Race, Gender and Citizenship: Black West Indian Women in Costa Rica, c. 1920–1940." *Bulletin of Latin American Research* 23, no. 2 (2004): 198–212.

Foppa, Tito Livio. *Diccionario teatral del Río de la Plata*. Buenos Aires: Argentores, 1961.

Ford, Carole Bell. *The Girls: Jewish Women of Brownsville, Brooklyn, 1940–1995*. Albany: State University of New York Press, 2000.

Forment, Carlos A. *Civic Selfhood and Public Life in Mexico and Peru*, vol. 1 of *Democracy in Latin America 1760–1900*. Chicago, Ill.: University of Chicago Press, 2003.

Foulkes, Julia L. "Angels 'Rewolt'! Jewish Women in Modern Dance in the 1930s." In *American Jewish Women's History: A Reader*, edited by Pamela S. Nadell, 201–17. New York: New York University Press, 2003.

Freeze, ChaeRan Y. *Jewish Marriage and Divorce in Imperial Russia*. Hanover, N.H.: Brandeis University Press, 2002.

Freidenberg, Judith Noemí. *Memorias de Villa Clara*. Buenos Aires: Antropofagia, 2005.

Freidkes, José. "25 años de lucha en defensa de la cultura popular judía en la Argentina." *Aporte*, no. 10 (November–December 1955): 31–32.

French, John D., and Daniel James. *The Gendered World of Latin American Women Workers: From Household and Factory to the Union Hall and Ballot Box*. Durham, N.C.: Duke University Press, 1997.

———, eds. "Oral History, Identity Formation, and Working-Class Mobilization." In *The Gendered World of Latin American Women Workers: From Household and Factory to the Union Hall and Ballot Box*, edited by John D. French and Daniel James, 297–313. Durham, N.C.: Duke University Press, 1997.

———. "Squaring the Circle: Women's Factory Labor, Gender Ideology, and Necessity." In *The Gendered World of Latin American Women Workers: From Household and Factory to the Union Hall and Ballot Box*, edited by John D. French and Daniel James, 1–30. Durham, N.C.: Duke University Press, 1997.

French, William E. "Prostitutes and Guardian Angels: Women, Work, and the Family in Porfirian Mexico." *Hispanic American Historical Review* 72, no. 4 (November 1992): 529–54.

Freundlich de Seefeld, Ruth. "La integración de extranjeros en Buenos Aires: Según sus pautas matrimoniales: ¿pluralismo cultural o crisol de razas? (1860–1923)." *Estudios Migratorios Latinoamericanos* 1–2 (1986): 203–31.

Frid de Silberstein, Carina L. "Immigrants and Female Work in Argentina: Questioning Gender Stereotypes and Constructing Images—The Case of the Italians, 1879–1900." In *Mass Migration to Modern Latin America*, edited by Samuel L. Baily and Eduardo José Míguez, 195–218. Wilmington, Del.: Scholarly Resources, 2003.

Fridman, Roberto. "La familia Fridman." *Toldot*, no. 12 (August 2000): 20–21.

Friedman, Reena Sigman. "Founders, Teachers, Mothers and Wards: Women's Roles in American Jewish Orphanages, 1850–1925." *Shofar* 15, no. 2 (winter 1997): 21–42.

———. "'Send Me My Husband Who Is in New York City': Husband Desertion in the American Jewish Immigrant Community, 1900–1926." *Jewish Social Studies* 44, no. 1 (winter 1982): 1–18.

Friedman-Kasaba, Kathie. *Memories of Migration: Gender, Ethnicity, and Work in the Lives of Jewish and Italian Women in New York, 1870–1924*. Albany: State University of New York Press, 1996.

Fux, María. *Danza: experiencia de vida*. Buenos Aires: Paidós, 1981.

———. *La formación del danzaterapeuta: Vivencias con la danzaterapia*. 2nd ed. Barcelona: Gedisa, 1997.

Gandolfo, Romolo. "Del Alto Molise al centro de Buenos Aires: Las mujeres agnonesas y la primera emigración transatlántica (1870–1900)." *Estudios Migratorios Latino-americanos*, no. 20 (1992): 71–99.

García Sebastiani, Marcela. "The Other Side of Peronist Argentina: Radicals and Socialists in the Political Opposition to Perón (1946–1955)." *Journal of Latin American Studies* 35, no. 2 (May 2003): 311–39.

Garfunkel, Boris. *Narro mi vida*. Buenos Aires: Optimus, 1960.

Geldstein, Rosa N. "Matrimonios mixtos en la población judía de Salta: Un análisis sociodemográfico." *Estudios Migratorios Latinoamericanos* 9 (August 1988): 217–37.

"Gender and Sexuality in Latin America." Special issue. *Hispanic American Historical Review* 81, no. 3–4 (August–November 2001).

Gerchunoff, Alberto. *The Jewish Gauchos of the Pampas*. Translated by Prudencio de Pereda. Albuquerque: University of New Mexico Press, 1998. Originally published as *Los gauchos judíos* (La Plata: Joaquin Sesé, 1910).

Gilfoyle, Timothy J. *City of Eros: New York City, Prostitution, and the Commercialization of Sex, 1790–1920*. New York: Norton, 1992.

———. "Prostitutes in History: From Parables of Pornography to Metaphors of Modernity." *American Historical Review* 104, no. 1 (February 1999): 117–41.

Gilman, Sander L. Introduction. In *Jewries at the Frontier: Accommodation, Identity, Conflict*, edited by Sander L. Gilman and Milton Shain, 1–25. Urbana: University of Illinois Press, 1999.

———. *Jewish Frontiers: Essays on Bodies, Histories, and Identities*. New York: Palgrave Macmillan, 2003.

———. *Love + Marriage = Death and Other Essays Representing Difference*. Stanford, Calif.: Stanford University Press, 1998.

Girbal-Blacha, Noemí M., ed. *Estado, sociedad y economía en la Argentina (1930–1997)*. Bernal, Argentina: Universidad Nacional de Quilmes, 2001.

———. "Poder y cultura en la Argentina peronista (1946–1955)." *Investigaciones y Ensayos*, no. 50 (2000): 191–228.

Glenn, Susan A. *Daughters of the Shtetl: Life and Labor in the Immigrant Generation*. Ithaca, N.Y.: Cornell University Press, 1990.

Glickman, Nora. *The Jewish White Slave Trade and the Untold Story of Raquel Liberman*. New York: Garland, 1999.

Glombovsky, Moisés I. *Los gringos: Su historia, sus historias*. Buenos Aires: Del Carril, 1985.

Gluck, Sherna Berger, and Daphne Patai. *Women's Words: The Feminist Practice of Oral History*. New York: Routledge, 1991.

Goitein, S. D. *The Community*, vol. 2 of *A Mediterranean Society: The Jewish Communities of the Arab World as Portrayed in the Documents of the Cairo Geniza*. Berkeley: University of California Press, 1971.

González Leandri, Ricardo. "La nueva identidad de los sectores populares." In *Crisis económica, avance del estado e incertidumbre política (1930–1943)*, vol. 7 of *Nueva historia argentina*, edited by Alejandro Cattaruzza, 201–38. Buenos Aires: Sudamericana, 2001.

Gorbato, Viviana. "Apuntes de una viajera." In *Colonia Mauricio: 100 años*, 60–81. Buenos Aires: Shalom, 1991.

Graziani-Levy, Robert. *Wanderings and Wonderments of a Sephardic Jew*. Edited by Moshe Lazar. Culver City, Calif.: Labyrinthos, 1991.

Green, Nancy L., ed. *Jewish Workers in the Modern Diaspora*. Berkeley: University of California Press, 1998.

Greenberg, Mark I. "Savannah's Jewish Women and the Shaping of Ethnic and Gender Identity, 1830–1900." *Georgia Historical Quarterly* 82, no. 4 (winter 1998): 751–74.

Grimson, Alejandro. "Ethnic (In)Visibility in Neoliberal Argentina." *NACLA Report on the Americas* 38, no. 4 (January–February 2005): 25–29.

Grunfeld, José. *Memorias de un anarquista*. Buenos Aires: Grupo Editor Latinoamericano, 2000.

Guber, Rosana. "Identidad cultural y tradición en el folklore." *Coloquio* 4, no. 9 (spring–summer 1982–83), 67–85.

Gucovsky, Victoria. *Tierra adentro*. Buenos Aires: Agencia General de Librería y Publicaciones, 1921.

Guerin-Gonzales, Camille. *Mexican Workers and American Dreams: Immigration, Repatriation, and California Farm Labor, 1900–1939*. New Brunswick, N.J.: Rutgers University Press, 1996.

Guía anual israelita de los países latinoamericanos. Buenos Aires: Gráficos, 1947.

Gutiérrez, Leandro H., and Luis Alberto Romero. *Sectores populares, cultura y política: Buenos Aires en la entreguerra*. Buenos Aires: Sudamericana, 1995.

Gutiérrez, Talía Violeta. "La educación del colono pampeano en épocas de conflicto: Entre la defensa de sus intereses y el control social, 1910–1922." *Estudios Interdisciplinarios de América Latina y el Caribe* 16, no. 2 (July–December 2005): 85–110.

Gutkowski, Hélène. *Erase una vez . . . sefarad: Los sefaradíes del Mediterráneo—Su historia, Su cultura 1880–1950, Testimonios*. Buenos Aires: Lumen, 1999.

———. *Rescate de la herencia cultural: Vidas . . . en las colonias*. Buenos Aires: Contexto, 1991.

Guy, Donna J. "The Economics of Womanhood in Arizona, 1880–1912." In *On Their Own: Widows and Widowhood in the American Southwest, 1848–1939*, edited by Arlene Scadron, 195–223. Urbana: University of Illinois Press, 1988.

———. "Emilio and Gabriela Coni, Reformers: Public Health and Working Women." In *The Human Tradition in Latin America: The Nineteenth Century*, edited by Judith Ewell and William Beezley, 233–48. Wilmington, Del.: Scholarly Resources, 1989.

———. "Gendering Child Labor in Argentina." Unpublished manuscript.

———. "Parents Before the Tribunals: The Legal Construction of Patriarchy in Argentina." In *Hidden Histories of Gender and the State in Latin America*, edited by Elizabeth Dore and Maxine Molyneux, 172–93. Durham, N.C.: Duke University Press, 2000.

———. *Sex and Danger in Buenos Aires: Prostitution, Family, and Nation in Argentina*. Lincoln: University of Nebraska Press, 1991.

———. "La 'verdadera historia' de la Sociedad de Beneficencia." In *La política social antes de la política social (Caridad, beneficencia y política social en Buenos*

Aires, siglos XVII a XX), edited by José Luis Moreno, 321–41. Buenos Aires: Trama / Prometeo, 2000.

———. "'White Slavery,' Citizenship and Nationality in Argentina." In *Nationalisms and Sexualities*, edited by Andrew Parker, Mary Russo, Doris Sommer, and Patricia Yaeger, 201–17. New York: Routledge, 1992.

———. *Women Build the Welfare State: Performing Charity and Creating Rights in Argentina, 1880–1955*. Durham, N.C.: Duke University Press, 2009.

———. "Women, Peonage, and Industrialization: Argentina, 1810–1914." *Latin American Research Review* 16, no. 3 (1981): 65–89.

———. "Women's Organizations and Jewish Orphanages in Buenos Aires, 1918–1955." *Jewish History* 18, no. 1 (2004): 75–93.

Hakim, Esther Carmel. "Creating the Pioneer Jewish Woman Farmer: A Russian, German, English, and American Project 1911–1929." Paper presented at the Berkshire Conference, Scripps College, 2005.

Hall, Stuart. "Ethnicity: Identity and Difference." *Radical America* 23, no. 4 (January 1991): 9–20.

Halperín-Donghi, Tulio. *Argentina en el callejón*. Buenos Aires: Espasa Calpe / Ariel, 1995.

———. "¿Para qué la inmigración? Ideología y política inmigratoria y aceleración del proceso modernizador: El caso argentino (1810–1914)." *Jahrbuch für Geschichte von Staat, Wirtschaft und Gesellschaft Lateinamerikas* 13 (1976): 437–89.

———, Iván Jaksic, Gwen Kirkpatrick, and Francine Masiello. *Sarmiento: Author of a Nation*. Berkeley: University of California Press, 1994.

Hecker de Uchitel, Julia. *Vivencias*. N.p., n.d.

Heilbrun, Carolyn G. *Writing a Woman's Life*. New York: Ballantine, 1988.

Henault, Mirta. *Alicia Moreau de Justo*. Buenos Aires: Centro Editor de América Latina, 1983.

Herman, Felicia. "The Way She *Really* Is: Images of Jews and Women in the Films of Barbra Streisand." In *Talking Back: Images of Jewish Women in American Popular Culture*, edited by Joyce Antler, 171–90. Hanover, N.H.: Brandeis University Press, 1998.

Hollander, Nancy Caro. "Women in the Political Economy of Argentina." Ph.D. diss., University of California at Los Angeles, 1974.

Horowitz, Irving Louis. "The Jewish Community of Buenos Aires." *Jewish Social Studies* 24 (October 1962): 195–222.

Horowitz, Joel. *Argentine Unions, the State and the Rise of Perón, 1930–1945*. Berkeley: University of California Press, 1990.

———. "El movimiento obrero." In *Nueva Historia Argentina*, vol. 7 of *Crisis económica, avance del estado e incertidumbre política (1930–1943)*, edited by Alejandro Cettaruzzi, 239–82. Buenos Aires: Sudamericana, 2001.

Horvath, Ricardo, ed. *Memorias y recuerdos de Blackie*. Buenos Aires: Palermo, 1979.

Hunefeldt, Christine. *Liberalism in the Bedroom: Quarreling Spouses in Nineteenth-Century Lima*. University Park: Pennsylvania State University Press, 2000.

Hunt, Lynn. "The Objects of History: A Reply to Philip Stewart." *Journal of Modern History* 66 (September 1994): 539–46.

Hyam, Ronald. *Empire and Sexuality: The British Experience*. Manchester, England: Manchester University Press, 1990.

Hyman, Paula E. *Gender and Assimilation in Modern Jewish History: The Roles and Representation of Women*. Seattle: University of Washington Press, 1995.

Icaza, Jorge. *Huasipungo, novela*. Quito: Romero, 1937.

Iñigo Carrera, Nicolás. *La estrategia de la clase obrera 1936*. Buenos Aires: La Rosa Blindada, 2000.

———. "Perfiles: Fenia Chertkoff." Printout.

In Memoriam: Sara Fischer Szusterowicz (1907–1997). Tel Aviv: n.p., 1997.

"La inmigración después de la guerra." *Boletín Mensual del Museo Social Argentino*, nos. 85–90 (January–June 1919).

Insausti, Magdalena. "Hotel de Inmigrantes: Un proyecto colossal para la gran Argentina." *Todo Es Historia*, no. 398 (September 2000): 6–31.

Itzigsohn, José A. "La atención médica en las colonias agrícolas de la Argentina." In *Judaica Latinoamericana: Estudios histórico-sociales*, vol. 2, edited by Amilat, 17–26. Jerusalem: Universitaria Magnes and Universitaria Hebrea, 1993.

———. *Una experiencia judía contemporánea*. Buenos Aires: Paidós, 1969.

Itzigsohn, Sara, et al. *Integración y marginalidid: Historias de vidas de immigrantes judías en la Argentina*. Buenos Aires: Editorial Pardes, 1965.

Ivereigh, Austen. *Catholicism and Politics in Argentina, 1810–1960*. New York: St. Martin's, 1995.

Jacobson, Matthew Frye. *Whiteness of a Different Color: European Immigrants and the Alchemy of Race*. Cambridge: Harvard University Press, 1999.

Jaher, Frederic Cople. *The Jews and the Nation: Revolution, Emancipation, State Formation, and the Liberal Paradigm in America and France*. Princeton, N.J.: Princeton University Press, 2002.

James, Daniel. *Doña María's Story: Life, History, Memory, and Political Identity*. Durham, N.C.: Duke University Press, 2000.

———. "Tales Told Out on the Borderlands: Doña María's Story, Oral History, and Issues of Gender." In *The Gendered World of Latin American Women Workers: From Household and Factory to the Union Hall and Ballot Box*, edited by John D. French and Daniel James, 31–52. Durham, N.C.: Duke University Press, 1997.

Jarvinen, Lisa. "Colonial Legacies and Common Culture: Fox Film's Spanish Department, 1932–1935." Unpublished paper, 2006.

Jewish Association for the Protection of Girls and Women. *Report of the Secretary on His Visit to South America 1913*. London: Women's Printing Society, 1913.

———. *Reports, 1905–35*. London: Women's Printing Society, 1905–35.
Jewish Colonization Association. *Rapport de L'Administration Centrale au Conseil D'Administration pour l'année 1898*. Paris: R. Veneziani, 1899.
Jewish International Conference on the Suppression of the Traffic in Girls and Women. *Official Report of the Jewish International Conference on the Suppression of the Traffic in Girls and Women . . . 1910*. London: Wertheimer, Lea, 1910.
———. *Official Report of the Jewish International Conference on the Suppression of the Traffic in Girls and Women . . . 1927*. London: Women's Printing Society, 1927.
Johnson, Benjamin. "Engendering Nation and Race in the Borderlands." *Latin American Research Review* 37, no. 1 (2002): 259–71.
Joselit, Jenna Weissman. *The Wonders of America: Reinventing Jewish Culture, 1880–1950*. New York: Hill and Wang, 1994.
Joseph, Gilbert, and Daniel Nugent, eds. *Everyday Forms of State Formation: Revolution and the Negotiation of Rule in Modern Mexico*. Durham, N.C.: Duke University Press, 1994.
Judkowski, José. *El tango: Una historia con judíos*. Buenos Aires: IWO, 1998.
Junta de Ayuda Judía a las Víctimas de la Guerra. *Memoria y balance*. Buenos Aires: n.p., 1945.
Junta de la Victoria. *Ayuda de las mujeres argentinas a los países que luchan contra el nazismo*. Buenos Aires: n.p., 1941.
———. *Estatutos*. Buenos Aires: n.p., n.d.
Jurkowicz de Eichbaum, Marta E. *Cuando las mujeres hacen memoria: Testimonios de historia oral de la inmigración judía en la Argentina*. Buenos Aires: Grupo Editor Latinoamericano, 1999.
Kamenszain, Tamara. "Los barrios judíos: Flores—Un ghetto entre arboles frutales." *Plural* (October 1979): 23–27.
———. "Los barrios judíos: Una pequeña metropolis llamada el Once." *Plural* (November 1979): 11–14.
———. "Los barrios judíos: Villa Crespo—Vida cotidiana y alienación." *Plural* (May 1979): 24–29.
———. "La importancia de llamarse Golde: Retrato de una gran actriz." *Plural* (November 1978): 20–23.
Kaplan, Alberto D. *Memoria de un médico*. Buenos Aires: Grupo Editor Latinoamericano, 1993.
Kaplan, Marion A. "As Germans and as Jews in Imperial Germany." In *Jewish Daily Life in Germany, 1618–1945*, edited by Marion A. Kaplan, 173–270. New York: Oxford, 2005.
———. *Between Dignity and Despair: Jewish Life in Nazi Germany*. New York: Oxford University Press, 1998.
———. *The Jewish Feminist Movement in Germany: The Campaigns of the Frauenbund, 1904–1938*. Westport, Conn.: Greenwood, 1979.

———. *The Making of the Jewish Middle Class: Women, Family, and Identity in Imperial Germany*. New York: Oxford University Press, 1991.

———. "Tradition and Transition: Jewish Women in Imperial Germany." In *Jewish Women in Historical Perspective*, edited by Judith R. Baskin, 202–21. Detroit, Mich.: Wayne State University Press, 1991.

Kaplan, Temma. *Taking Back the Streets: Women, Youth, and Direct Democracy*. Berkeley: University of California Press, 2004.

Katz, Ilse Esther. *De raíces y sitios*. Buenos Aires: Botella al Mar, 1988.

Katz, Pinie. *Páginas selectas*. Translated by Mina Fridman Ruetter. Buenos Aires: ICUF, 1980.

Kaufman, Ilse, and Helena Pardo. *Un viaje hacia la vida: La historia de Ilse Kaufman*. Unpublished manuscript, 2000.

Kertzer, David I., and Peter Laslett, eds. *Aging in the Past: Demography, Society, and Old Age*. Berkeley: University of California Press, 1995.

Kessler-Harris, Alice. "Organizing the Unorganizable: Three Jewish Women and Their Union." In *American Jewish Women's History: A Reader*, edited by Pamela S. Nadell, 100–15. New York: New York University Press, 2003.

Kinzer, Nora Scott. "Women Professionals in Buenos Aires." In *Female and Male in Latin America: Essays*, edited by Ann Pescatello, 159–90. Pittsburgh, Pa.: University of Pittsburgh Press, 1973.

Kirkendall, Andrew. *Classmates: Male Student Culture and the Making of a Political Class in Nineteenth-Century Brazil*. Lincoln: University of Nebraska Press, 2002.

Kirshenblatt-Gimblett, Barbara. "Kitchen Judaism." In *Getting Comfortable in New York: The American Jewish Home, 1880–1950*, edited by Susan L. Braunstein and Jenna Weissman Joselit, 75–105. New York: Jewish Museum, 1990.

Klapper, Melissa R. *Jewish Girls Coming of Age in America, 1860–1920*. New York: New York University Press, 2005.

Klubock, Thomas Miller. *Contested Communities: Class, Gender, and Politics in Chile's El Teniente Copper Mine, 1904–1951*. Durham, N.C.: Duke University Press, 1998.

Knaphais, Moises, and Wolf Bresler. *Album de oro judeo-argentino*. Buenos Aires: Graf Stylos, 1973.

Kohen, Natalia. *El color de la nostalgia: Casi una autobiografía*. Buenos Aires: El Ateneo, 1998.

Kohn Loncarica, Alfredo G., and Norma Sánchez. "La mujer en la medicina argentina: Las médicas de la primera década del siglo XX." *Saber y Tiempo* 2 (July–December 1996): 113–38.

———. "La mujer en la medicina argentina: Las médicas de la segunda década del siglo XX." *Saber y Tiempo* 9 (January–June 2000): 89–107.

Kohn Loncarica, Alfredo G., Norma Sánchez, and Abel Luis Agüero. "La contribución de las primeras médicas argentinas a la enseñanza universitaria." *Anales de la Sociedad Científica Argentina* 228, no. 2 (1998), 39–58.

Koifman, Moishe. "La 'Asociación Racionalista Judía.'" *Di Presse*, December 1982, unnumbered page. Translated by Gregorio Rawin.

Korelitz, Seth. "'A Magnificent Piece of Work': The Americanization Work of the National Council of Jewish Women." *American Jewish History* 83, no. 2 (June 1995): 177–203.

Korn, Francis, et al. *Los huéspedes del 20*. Buenos Aires: Sudamericana, 1974.

Kowalska, Marta. "La emigración judía de Polonia a la Argentina en los años 1918–1939." *Estudios Latinoamericanos* (Warsaw) 12 (1989): 249–72.

Kushnir, Beatriz. *Baile de máscaras: Mulheres judías e prostituição—As polacas e suas asociações de ajuda mutual*. Rio de Janeiro: Imago, 1996.

Langer, Marie, with Enrique Guinsberg and Jaime del Palacio. *From Vienna to Managua: Journey of a Psychoanalyst*. Translated by Margaret Hooks. London: Free Association Books, 1989.

Las, Nelly. *Jewish Women in a Changing World: A History of the International Council of Jewish Women 1899–1995*. Translated by Stephanie Nakache. Jerusalem: Avraham Harman Institute of Contemporary Jewry, Hebrew University, 1996.

Laskier, Michael M. "Aspects of the Activities of the Alliance Israélite Universelle in the Jewish Communities of the Middle East and North Africa: 1860–1918." *Modern Judaism* 3, no. 2 (May 1983): 147–71.

Laubstein, Israel. *Bund: Historia del movimiento obrero judío*. Buenos Aires: Acervo Cultural, 1997.

Lavrin, Asunción. "Alicia Moreau de Justo: Feminismo y política, 1911–1945." In *Mujer y familia en América Latina, siglos XVII-XX*, edited by Susana Menéndez and Barbara Potthast, 175–200. Málaga, Spain: AHILA, Algazara, 1996.

———. *Women, Feminism, and Social Change in Argentina, Chile, and Uruguay, 1890–1940*. Lincoln: University of Nebraska Press, 1995.

Lerner, Gloria Rut. "La historia del Asilo Argentino de Huérfanas Israelitas." Tesis de licenciatura. Universidad Nacional de Luján, 2002.

Lesser, Jeffrey. "In Search of Home Abroad: German Jews in Brazil, 1933–45." In *The Heimat Abroad: The Boundaries of Germanness*, edited by Krista O'Donnell, Renate Bridenthal, and Nancy Reagin, 167–83. Ann Arbor: University of Michigan Press, 2005.

———. *Negotiating National Identity: Immigrants, Minorities, and the Struggle for Ethnicity in Brazil*. Durham, N.C.: Duke University Press, 1999.

Lesser, Jeffrey, and Raanan Rein, "New Approaches to Ethnicity and Diaspora in Twentieth-Century Latin America." In *Rethinking Jewish-Latin Americans*, edited by Jeffrey Lesser and Raanan Rein, 23–40. Albuquerque: University of New Mexico Press, 2008.

Levenson, Raquel. *Ejemplo de una mujer revolucionaria argentina*. Buenos Aires: Frente Unico, 1972.

Levin, Elena. *Historias de una emigración (1933–1939): Alemanes judíos en la Argentina*. Buenos Aires: Manrique Zago, 1991.

Levin, Yehuda. "Posturas genéricas en las colonias de la Jewish Colonization Association (JCA) en la Argentina a principios del siglo XX." *Judaica Latinoamericana: Estudios históricos, sociales y literarios*, edited by Amilat, 49–67. Jerusalem: Universitaria Magnes and Universitaria Hebrea, 2005.

Levins Morales, Aurora. *Medicine Stories: History, Culture, and the Politics of Integrity*. Cambridge, Mass.: South End, 1998.

Levinsky, Roxana. *Herencias de la inmigración judía en la Argentina: Cincuenta figuras de la creación intelectual*. Buenos Aires: Prometeo, 2005.

Levy, Estela. *Crónica de una familia sefaradí*. Buenos Aires: Carcos, 1983.

Lewin, Boleslao. *Cómo fue la inmigración judía a la Argentina*. Buenos Aires: Plus Ultra, 1971.

Liberman, Julio. *La unidad, organización y lucha de los trabajadores del vestido*. Buenos Aires: Centro de Estudios, 1980.

Lieberman, José. *Los judíos en la Argentina*. Buenos Aires: Libra, 1966.

Liniado, Argentino S. *Recuerdos imborrables*. Buenos Aires: Milá, 1994.

Lipman, V. D. *A Century of Social Service 1859–1959: The Jewish Board of Guardians*. London: Routledge and Kegan Paul, 1959.

Literat-Golombek, Lea. *Moisés Ville: Crónica de un shtetl argentino*. Jerusalem: La Semana, 1982.

Little, Cynthia Jeffress. "The Society of Beneficence in Buenos Aires, 1823–1900." Ph.D. diss., Temple University, 1980.

Lobato, Mirta Zaida, ed. *Cuando las mujeres reinaban: Belleza, virtud y poder en la Argentina del siglo XX*. Buenos Aires: Biblos, 2005.

———. "Mujeres en la fábrica: El caso de las obreras del frigorífico Armour, 1915–1969." In *Historia y género*, edited by Dora Barrancos, 65–97. Buenos Aires: Centro Editor de América Latina, 1993.

———. *La vida en las fábricas: Trabajo, protesta y política en una comunidad obrera, Berisso (1904–1970)*. Buenos Aires: Prometeo / Entrepasados, 2001.

———. "Women Workers in the 'Cathedrals of Corned Beef': Structure and Subjectivity in the Argentine Meatpacking Industry." In *The Gendered World of Latin American Women Workers: From Household and Factory to the Union Hall and Ballot Box*, edited by John D. French and Daniel James, 53–71. Durham, N.C.: Duke University Press, 1997.

Lockhart, Darrell B. "Is There a Text in This Gefilte Fish? Reading and Eating with Ana María Shua." In *El río de los sueños: Aproximaciones críticas a la obra de Ana María Shua*, edited by Rhonda Dahl Buchanan, 103–16. Washington, D.C.: Organization of American States, 2001.

López, Rick Anthony. "The India Bonita Contest of 1921 and the Ethnicization of Mexican National Culture." *Hispanic American Historical Review* 82, no. 2 (May 2002): 291–328.

López de Borche, Celia Gladys. *Cooperativismo y cultura: Historia de Villa Domínguez*. 2nd ed. Concepción del Uruguay, Argentina: El Pensador, 1985.

Luiggi, Alice Houston. *65 Valiants*. Gainesville: University of Florida Press, 1965.

Lvovich, Daniel. *Nacionalismo y antisemitismo en la Argentina*. Buenos Aires: Javier Vergara, 2003.

———. "Peronismo y antisemitismo: Historia, memorias, mitos." Unpublished manuscript.

Lynch, John. *Massacre in the Pampas, 1872: Britain and Argentina in the Age of Migration*. Norman: University of Oklahoma Press, 1998.

Mactas, Rebeca. *Los judíos de Las Acacias (cuentos de la vida campesina)*. Buenos Aires: n.p., 1936.

Maldavsky, Adela de. "Raíces." *Kol Hilel Boletín Semanal*, no. 154 (19 October 1996), unnumbered page.

Mansilla, Camila. "Breve historia del Teatro del Pueblo." http://teatrodelpueblo.org.ar (accessed 8 May 2009).

Markowitz, Ruth Jacknow. *My Daughter, the Teacher: Jewish Teachers in the New York City Schools*. New Brunswick, N.J.: Rutgers University Press, 1993.

Marks, Lara. "Jewish Women and Jewish Prostitution in the East End of London." *The Jewish Quarterly* 34 (1987): 6–10.

Martínez, Oscar J. *Border People: Life and Society in the U.S.-Mexico Borderlands*. Tucson: University of Arizona Press, 1994.

Mascato Rey, Rosario. "Valle-Inclán y Berta Singerman: La renovación del arte escénico." *Anales de la literatura española contemporánea* 27, no. 3 (2002): 73–93.

Mateu, Cristina. "La integración de los grupos idiomáticos en la cultura obrera argentina, a través de la política del Partido Comunista en la década del '20." Paper presented at the Congreso de las Colectividades, Instituto de Desarrollo Económico y Social (IDES), Buenos Aires, 2000.

Mazo, Gabriel del, ed. *La reforma universitaria y la universidad latinoamericana*. Corrientes, Argentina: Universidad Nacional del Nordeste, 1957.

McCreery, David. "'This Life of Misery and Shame': Female Prostitution in Guatemala City, 1880–1920." *Journal of Latin American Studies* 18, no. 2 (1986): 333–53.

McCune, Mary. "Creating a Place for Women in a Socialist Brotherhood: Class and Gender Politics in the Workmen's Circle, 1892–1930." *Feminist Studies* 28, no. 3 (2002): 585–610.

———. "Social Workers in the *Muskeljudentum*: 'Hadassah Ladies,' 'Manly Men' and the Significance of Gender in the American Zionist Movement, 1912–1928." *American Jewish History* 86, no. 2 (June 1998): 135–65.

———. *"The Whole Wide World, Without Limits": International Relief, Gender Politics, and American Jewish Women, 1893–1930*. Detroit, Mich.: Wayne State University Press, 2005.

Mead, Karen. "Beneficent Maternalism: Argentine Motherhood in Comparative Perspective, 1880–1920." *Journal of Women's History* 12, no. 3 (Fall 2000): 120–45.

———. "Oligarchs, Doctors, and Nuns: Public Health and Beneficence in Buenos Aires, 1880–1914." Ph.D. diss., University of California at Santa Barbara, 1994..

Mernissi, Fatima. *Dreams of Trespass: Tales of a Harem Girlhood*. Reading, Mass.: Addison-Wesley, 1994.

Metz, Allan. "Juan B. Justo and the Jews: The Prejudice of an Argentine Socialist." *Ethnic Groups* 9, no. 2 (1991): 119–34.

Míguez, Eduardo José. "Marriage, Household, and Integration in Mass Migration to Argentina: The Case of Tandil." In *Mass Migration to Modern Latin America*, edited by Samuel L. Baily and Eduardo José Míguez, 167–94. Wilmington, Del.: Scholarly Resources, 2003.

Mirelman, Victor A. *Jewish Buenos Aires, 1890–1930: In Search of An Identity*. Detroit, Mich.: Wayne State University Press, 1990.

———. "The Jewish Community Versus Crime: The Case of White Slavery in Buenos Aires." *Jewish Social Studies* 46, no. 2 (spring 1984): 145–68.

———. "Sephardic Immigration to Argentina Prior to the Nazi Period." In *The Jewish Presence in Latin America*, edited by Judith Laikin Elkin and Gilbert W. Merkx, 13–32. Boston, Mass.: Allen and Unwin, 1987.

Molyneux, Maxine. "No God, No Boss, No Husband: Anarchist Feminism in Nineteenth-Century Argentina." *Latin American Perspectives* 13, no. 1 (winter 1986): 119–45.

———. "Twentieth-Century State Formation in Latin America." In *Hidden Histories of Gender and the State in Latin America*, edited by Elizabeth Dore and Maxine Molyneux, 33–81. Durham, N.C.: Duke University Press, 2000.

Moreno, José Luis, ed. *La política social antes de la política social (Caridad, beneficencia y política social en Buenos Aires, siglos XVII a XX)*. Buenos Aires: Trama/Prometeo, 2000.

Morgade, Graciela. "La docencia para las mujeres: Una alternativa contradictoria en el camino hacia los saberes 'legítimos.'" In *Mujeres en la educación: Género y docencia en Argentina: 1870–1930*, edited by Graciela Morgade, 67–114. Buenos Aires: Miño y Dávila, 1997.

———, ed. *Mujeres en la educación: Género y docencia en Argentina: 1870–1930*. Buenos Aires: Miño y Dávila, 1997.

Morris, Katherine, ed. *Odyssey of Exile: Jewish Women Flee the Nazis for Brazil*. Detroit, Mich.: Wayne State University Press, 1990.

Movimiento de Ex-Colonos Residentes en la Capital. *Pioneros (en homenaje al cincuentenario de Rivera "Barón Hirsch")*. Buenos Aires: Columbia, 1957.

Moya, José C. "A Continent of Immigrants: Postcolonial Shifts in the Western Hemisphere." *Hispanic American Historical Review* 86, no. 1 (February 2006): 1–28.

———. *Cousins and Strangers: Spanish Immigrants in Buenos Aires, 1850–1930*. Berkeley: University of California Press, 1998.

———. "Italians in Buenos Aires' Anarchist Movement: Gender, Ideology, and Women's Participation." In *Women, Gender, and Transnational Lives: Italian Workers of the World*, edited by Donna Gabaccia and Franca Iacovetta. Toronto: Toronto University Press, 2002.

———. "The Positive Side of Stereotypes: Jewish Anarchists in Early-Twentieth-Century Buenos Aires." *Jewish History* 18, no. 1 (2004): 19–48.

Mujeres en la Ayuda (1941–1942). Buenos Aires: n.p., 1942.

Munges, William L. "Academic Freedom under Perón." *Antioch Review* (summer 1947): 275–90.

Myerhoff, Barbara. *Remembered Lives: The Work of Storytelling, Ritual, and Growing Older*. Ann Arbor: University of Michigan Press, 1992.

Nadell, Pamela S., ed. *American Jewish Women's History: A Reader*. New York: New York University Press, 2003.

Nállim, Jorge. "Conflictive Legitimacies: Argentine Liberalism(s), 1930s/1940s." Paper presented at the annual meeting of the Latin American Studies Association, Dallas, Texas, 2001.

———. "The Crisis of Liberalism in Argentina, 1930–1946." Ph.D. diss., University of Pittsburgh, 2002.

———. "Del antifascismo al antiperonismo: *Argentina Libre*, *Antinazi*, y el surgimiento del antiperonismo político e intelectual." In *Fascismo y antifascismo: Peronismo y antiperonismo—Conflictos políticos e ideológicos en la Argentina (1930–1955)*, edited by Marcela García Sebastiani, 77–105. Madrid: Iberoamericana, 2006.

Nardo de Aguirre, Violeta. "Canto a la Colonización Judía." In *75 aniversario de la colonización judía en la República Argentina y fundación de Moisesville*. N.p.: Ariel, 1964.

Nari, Marcela. "Las prácticas anticonceptivas, la disminución de la natalidad y el debate médico." In *Política, médicos y enfermedades: Lecturas de historia de la salud en la Argentina*, edited by Mirta Zaida Lobato, 151–89. Buenos Aires: Biblos/UNMP, 1996.

Navarro, Marysa. *Evita*. Buenos Aires: Corregidor, 1981.

———. "Hidden, Silent, and Anonymous: Women Workers in the Argentine Trade Union Movement." In *The World of Women's Trade Unionism: Comparative Historical Essays*, edited by Norbert C. Soldon, 167–86. Westport, Conn.: Greenwood, 1985.

Newton, Ronald C. "The Evanescent Community: Italian Jewish Refugees in Argentina, 1938–1947." Paper presented at the annual meeting of the American Historical Association, Seattle, Wash., 1998.

———. *The Nazi Menace in Argentina, 1931–1947*. Stanford, Calif.: Stanford University Press, 1992.

Norman, Theodore. *An Outstretched Arm: A History of the Jewish Colonization Association*. London: Routledge and Kegan Paul, 1985.

Norton, Elisa [Enrique García Velloso]. "Un casamiento en el gran mundo." *La novela semanal* 2, no. 15 (15 February 1918): unnumbered page.

Nouzeilles, Gabriela. "An Imaginary Plague in Turn-of-the-Century Buenos Aires: Hysteria, Discipline, and Languages of the Body." In *Disease in the History of Modern Latin America: From Malaria to AIDS*, edited by Diego Armus, 51–75. Durham, N.C.: Duke University Press, 2003.

Oficina Nacional de la Mujer. *Evolución de la mujer en las profesiones liberales en Argentina (1900–1965)*. 2nd ed. Buenos Aires: Oficina Nacional de la Mujer, 1970.

Ogilvie, Sheilagh. "How Does Social Capital Affect Women? Guilds and Communities in Early Modern Germany." *American Historical Review* 109, no. 2 (April 2004): 325–59.

Olcott, Jocelyn. *Revolutionary Women in Postrevolutionary Mexico*. Durham, N.C.: Duke University Press, 2005.

Oliver, María Rosa. *Mi fe es el hombre*. Buenos Aires: Carlos Lohlé, 1981.

Omar de Lucía, Daniel. "Los socialistas y la infancia." *Todo Es Historia*, no. 355 (February 1997): 44–55.

Orum, Thomas T. "The Women of the Open Door: Jews in the Belle Epoque Amazonian Demimonde, 1890–1920." *Shofar* 19, no. 3 (spring 2001): 86–99.

Owensby, Brian P. *Intimate Ironies: Modernity and the Making of Middle-Class Lives in Brazil*. Stanford, Calif.: Stanford University Press, 1999.

Palmer, Steven, and Gladys Rojas Chaves. "Educating Señorita: Teacher Training, Social Mobility, and the Birth of Costa Rican Feminism, 1885–1925." *Hispanic American Historical Review* 78, no. 1 (February 1998): 45–82.

Parush, Iris. *Reading Jewish Women: Marginality and Modernization in Nineteenth-Century Eastern European Jewish Society*. Translated by Saadya Sternberg. Waltham, Mass.: Brandeis University Press, 2004.

Payá, Carlos Manuel, and Eduardo José Cárdenas. *El primer nacionalismo argentino en Manuel Gálvez y Ricardo Rojas*. Buenos Aires: A. Peña Lillo, 1978.

Pelacoff, Javier. "Judíos, anarquistas, argentinos." *Raíces*, no. 5 (summer 1993): 44–45.

Pereira, Cristiana Schettini. "Prostitutes and the Law: The Uses of Court Cases over Pandering in Rio de Janeiro at the Beginning of the Twentieth Century." In *Honor, Status, and the Law in Modern Latin America*, edited by Sueann Caulfield, Sarah C. Chambers, and Laura Putnam, 273–94. Durham, N.C.: Duke University Press, 2005.

Perelstein, Berta. *Positivismo y antipositivismo en la Argentina*. Buenos Aires: Procyon, 1952.

Pérez, Pablo M. "El movimiento anarquista y los orígenes de la Federación Libertaria Argentina." In *Catálogo de publicaciones políticas, sociales y culturales anarquistas, 1890–1945*, edited by Pablo M Pérez. Buenos Aires: Editorial Reconstruir, 2002.

Perruelo, Nicolás. "Sara Satanowsky, 1892–1971." *Actas de las VI Jornadas de Historia del Pensamiento Científico Argentino* (1992): 167–79.

"Los pesares de la infancia de Tea." *El Litoral* (Santa Fe), "De raíces y abuelos" section. N.d., n.p.

Plotkin, Mariano Ben. *Freud in the Pampas: The Emergence and Development of a Psychoanalytic Culture in Argentina*. Stanford, Calif.: Stanford University Press, 2001.

———. *Mañana es San Perón: A Cultural History of Perón's Argentina*. Translated by Keith Zahniser. Wilmington, Del.: Scholarly Resources, 2003.

Poch, Susana, and Miriam Turjanski de Gold. *Orígenes y trascendencia: Historia de una familia*. Buenos Aires: Granica, 1998.

Prell, Riv-Ellen. *Fighting to Become Americans: Assimilation and the Trouble between Jewish Women and Jewish Men*. Boston, Mass.: Beacon, 1999.

Presencia sefaradí en la Argentina. Buenos Aires: Centro Educativo Sefaradí, 1992.

Primer Congreso Femenino Internacional de la República Argentina. *Historia, actas y trabajos*. Buenos Aires: A. Ceppe, 1911.

Puiggrós, Adriana, ed. *Historia de la educación argentina*, vol. 3: *Escuela, democracia y orden (1916–1943)*. Buenos Aires: Galerna, 1992.

Putnam, Robert D. "Bowling Alone: America's Declining Social Capital." *Journal of Democracy* 6, no. 1 (January 1995): 65–78.

Quaglia, María Dolores. "Corrupción y prostitución infantil en Buenos Aires (1870–1904): Una aproximación al tema." In *La política social antes de la política social (Caridad, beneficencia y política social en Buenos Aires, siglos XVII a XX)*, edited by José Luis Moreno, 205–23. Buenos Aires: Trama / Prometeo, 2000.

Quijada, Mónica. *Aires de república, aires de cruzada: La guerra civil española en Argentina*. Barcelona: SENDAI, 1991.

———, Carmen Bernard, and Arnd Schneider. *Homogeneidad y nación, con un estudio de caso: Argentina, siglos XIX y XX*. Madrid: Consejo Superior de Investigaciones Científicas, 2000.

"Raíces en el pueblo y unión para la lucha: El nacimiento y los primeros pasos de la Unión de Mujeres de la Argentina." Unpublished manuscript. Unión de Mujeres Argentinas, Buenos Aires.

Raíces que dieron alas. Buenos Aires: A. Weiss, 1993.

Rajschmir, Cinthia. "Rosa Ziperovich . . . con 81 años hace camino al andar." Newspaper clipping, n.d.

Rapaport, Mario. "Argentina and the Soviet Union: History of Political and Commercial Relations (1917–1955)." *Hispanic American Historical Review* 66, no. 2 (May 1986): 239–86.

Rapoport, Nicolás. *Desde lejos hasta ayer*. Buenos Aires: Zlotopiow Hermanos, 1957.

Rebhun, L. A. *The Heart Is Unknown Country: Love in the Changing Economy of Northeast Brazil*. Stanford, Calif.: Stanford University Press, 1999.

Recalde, Héctor. *Beneficencia, asistencialismo estatal, y previsión social*. 2 vols. Buenos Aires: Centro Editor de América Latina, 1991.

Rein, Raanan. *Argentina, Israel, and the Jews: Perón, the Eichman Capture and After*. Translated by Martha Grenzeback. Bethesda: University Press of Maryland, 2003.

———. *The Franco-Perón Alliance: Relations between Spain and Argentina 1946–1955*. Translated by Martha Grenzeback. Pittsburgh: University of Pittsburgh Press, 1993.

———. "Nationalism, Education, and Identity: Argentine Jews and Catholic Religious Instruction, 1943–1955." In *Memory, Oblivion, and Jewish Culture in Latin America*, edited by Marjorie Agosín, 163–75. Austin: University of Texas Press, 2005.

———. "Together yet Apart: Israel and Argentine Jews." *Latin American Jewish Studies* 24, no. 1–2 (summer 2004): 1–7.

Repetto, Nicolás. *Mi paso por la agricultura*. Buenos Aires: Santiago Rueda, 1959.

Rescate de la herencia cultural. Buenos Aires: Sociedad Hebraica Argentina, 1982.

Reseña sobre la marcha de la Sociedad de Socorros de Damas Israelitas, 1918–1926. Buenos Aires: n.p., 1919–27.

Riegner, Kurt Julio. "Un proyecto migratorio judeo-alemán cincuenta años después: El 'Grupo Riegner' en la Argentina (1938/88)." *Coloquio*, no. 19 (1988): 123–73.

Rippberger, Susan J., and Kathleen A. Staudt. *Pledging Allegiance: Learning Nationalism at the El Paso-Juárez Border*. New York: Routledge, 2003.

Rivanera Carlés, Federico. *Las escuelas comunistas en Argentina: Documentación secuestrada por la policía*. Buenos Aires: Artes Gráficas, 1986.

———. *Los judíos y la trata de blancas en Argentina*. Buenos Aires: Artes Gráficas, 1986.

Rocca, Carlos José. "Juan B. Justo y su entorno." Unpublished manuscript. Archivo Iñigo Carrera, Buenos Aires.

Rock, David. *Authoritarian Argentina: The Nationalist Movement, Its History and Its Impact*. Berkeley: University of California Press, 1993.

———. "Intellectual Precursors of Conservative Nationalism in Argentina, 1900–27." *Hispanic American Historical Review* 67, no. 2 (May 1987): 271–300.

———. *Politics in Argentina: The Rise and Fall of Radicalism, 1890–1930*. Cambridge: Cambridge University Press, 1975.

Rodrigue, Aron. *Images of Sephardic and Eastern Jewries in Transition: The Teachers of the Alliance Israélite Universelle, 1860–1939*. Seattle: University of Washington Press, 1993.

Rodríguez, Ana María T. "Ante las demandas sociales, las mujeres responden: La beneficencia en el territorio pampeano en la primera mitad del siglo XX." In *Mujeres y estado en la Argentina: Educación, salud, y beneficencia*, edited by María Herminia B. Di Liscia and José Maristany, 125–36. Buenos Aires: Biblos, 1997.

Roediger, David R. *Working toward Whiteness: How America's Immigrants Became White—The Strange Journey from Ellis Island to the Suburbs*. New York: Basic Books, 2005.

Rogow, Faith. *Gone to Another Meeting: The National Council of Jewish Women, 1893–1993*. Tuscaloosa: University of Alabama Press, 1993.

Rojer, Olga Elaine. *Exile in Argentina, 1933–1945: A Historical and Literary Introduction*. New York: Peter Wang, 1989.

Romero, Luis Alberto. *A History of Argentina in the Twentieth Century*. Translated by James P. Brennan. University Park: Pennsylvania State University Press, 2002.

Ropp, Tuba Teresa. *Un colono judío en la Argentina*. Buenos Aires: IWO, 1971.

Rose, Sonya O. "Gender History / Women's History: Is Feminist Scholarship Losing Its Critical Edge?" *Journal of Women's History* 5, no. 1 (spring 1993): 89–101.

Rosen, Ruth. *The Lost Sisterhood: Prostitution in America, 1900–1918*. Baltimore, Md.: Johns Hopkins University Press, 1982.

Rosenwaike, Ira. "The Jewish Population of Argentina: Census and Estimate, 1887–1947." *Jewish Social Studies* 22 (October 1960): 195–214.

Ross, Peter. "Justicia social: Una evaluación de los logros del peronismo clásico." *Anuario IEHS* 8 (1993): 105–24.

Rotker, Susana. *Captive Women: Oblivion and Memory in Argentina*. Translated by Jennifer French. Minneapolis: University of Minnesota Press, 2002.

Rouco Buela, Juana. *Historia de un ideal vivido por una mujer*. Buenos Aires: Julio Kaufman, 1964.

Ruggiero, Kristin. "Gringo and Creole: Foreign and Native Values in a Rural Argentine Community." *Journal of Interamerican Studies and World Affairs* 24, no. 2 (May 1982): 163–82.

Sábato, Hilda. *The Many and the Few: Political Participation in Republican Buenos Aires*. Stanford, Calif.: Stanford University Press, 2001.

Sacerdote de Lustig, Eugenia. *De los alpes al Río de la Plata: Recuerdos para mis nietos*. Buenos Aires: Leviatán, 2005.

Saidman, Sheila Nadia. "Colectividad judía de Posadas." Tesis de licenciatura, Universidad Nacional de Misiones, 1999.

Saítta, Sylvia. "Entre la cultura y la política: Los escritores de izquierda." In *Crisis económica, avance del estado e incertidumbre política (1930–1943)*, vol. 7 of *Nueva historia argentina*, edited by Alejandro Cattaruzza, 383–428. Buenos Aires: Sudamericana, 2001.

Salomón, Mónica Liliana. "Las escuelas judías de Entre Ríos (1908–1912)." *Todo Es Historia*, no. 332 (March 1995): 30–39.

Sampedro, Carmen. *Madres e hijas: Historias de mujeres inmigrantes*. Buenos Aires: Planeta, 2000.

Sánchez, George. *Becoming Mexican American: Ethnicity, Culture, and Identity in Chicano Los Angeles, 1900–1945*. Berkeley: University of California Press, 1993.

Sanjurjo, Liliana Olga. "Rosa Ziperovich: Una lección de vida." In *Rosario: Historias de aquí a la vuelta*. Rosario, Argentina: Ediciones de Aquí a la Vuelta, n.d.

Sarlo, Beatriz. *La máquina cultural: Maestras, traductores y vanguardistas*. Buenos Aires: Ariel, 1998.

Sarna, Jonathan D. "A Great Awakening: A Transformation That Shaped Twentieth-Century American Judaism." In *American Jewish Women's History: A Reader*, edited by Pamela S. Nadell, 43–63. New York: New York University Press, 2003.

Sartori, Jennifer. "'The Most Beautiful Jewish Innovation of the Century': Girls' Initiation Religieuse in Nineteenth-Century France." Paper presented at the Berkshire Conference, Scripps College, 2005.

Scadron, Arlene, ed. *On Their Own: Widows and Widowhood in the American Southwest, 1848–1939*. Urbana: University of Illinois Press, 1988.

Scalabrini Ortiz, Raúl. *Historia de los ferrocarriles argentinos*. Buenos Aires: Reconquista, 1940.

Scarsi, José Luis. "Tratantes, prostitutas y rufianes en 1870." *Todo Es Historia*, no. 342 (January 1996): 9–17.

Schallman, Lázaro. *Pela Szechter: La cantante que sobrevivió al Holocausto*. Buenos Aires: Pelagia, 1977.

Schalom, Myrtha. *La polaca: Inmigración, rufianes y esclavos a comienzos del siglo XX*. Buenos Aires: Grupo Editorial Norma, 2003.

Schapira, Lucy. *Argentina, mi arbol*. Tucumán, Argentina: Gutenberg, 1990.

Schechner, Richard. *Performance Studies: An Introduction*. New York: Routledge, 2002.

Schenkolewski-Kroll, Silvia. "Los judíos comunistas de Argentina de grupo idiomático a la emigración a Birobidjan (1920–1937), en los archivos de Moscú." Paper presented at the meeting of the Latin American Jewish Studies Association, Princeton, N.J., 1999.

———. "El Partido Comunista de la Argentina ante Moscú: Deberes y realidades, 1930–1941." *Estudios Interdisciplinarios de América Latina y el Caribe* 10, no. 2 (July–December 1999): 91–107.

Schers, David. "Inmigrantes y política: Los primeros pasos del Partido Sionista Socialista Poalei Sión en la Argentina, 1910–1916." *Estudios Interdisciplinarios de América Latina y el Caribe* 3, no. 2 (July–December 1992): 75–88.

Schiller, Nina Glick, Linda Basch, and Cristina Blanc-Szanton. "Towards a Definition of Transnationalism." In *Towards a Transnational Perspective on Migration: Race, Class, Ethnicity and Nationalism Reconsidered*, edited by Nina Glick Schiller, Linda Basch, and Cristina Blanc-Szanton, ix–xiv. New York: New York Academy of Science, 1992.

Schloff, Linda Mack. "'We Dug More Rocks': Women and Work." In *American Jewish Women's History: A Reader*, edited by Pamela S. Nadell, 91–99. New York: New York University Press, 2003.

Schmeltz, U. O., and Sergio Dellapergola. "The Demography of Latin American Jewry." *American Jewish Yearbook* 85 (1985): 51–104.

Schneider, Arnd. *Futures Lost: Nostalgia and Identity Among Italian Immigrants in Argentina*. Bern: Peter Lang, 2000.

———. "Inmigrantes europeos y de otros orígenes." In *Homogeneidad y nación, con un estudio de caso: Argentina, siglos XIX y XX*, by Mónica Quijada, Carmen Bernard, and Arnd Schneider, 141–78. Madrid: Consejo Superior de Investigaciones Científicas, 2000.

———. "La política de la resistencia y la adaptación: Una comparación entre inmigrantes italianos judíos y otros exiliados italianos en Argentina a partir de 1938." In *Encuentro y alteridad: Vida y cultura judía en América Latina*, edited by Judit Bokser Liwerant and Alicia Gojman de Backal, 306–24. Mexico City: Universidad Autónoma de México, 1999.

Schoijet, Ezequiel. *Páginas para la historia de la colonia Narcis Leven (en adhesión a su cincuentenario)*. Buenos Aires: n.p., 1961.

Schwarcz, Alfredo José. *Y a pesar de todo . . . los judíos de habla alemana en la Argentina*. 2nd ed. Buenos Aires: Grupo Editor Latinoamericano, 1991.

Schwarzstein, Dora. *Entre Franco y Perón: Memoria e identidad del exilio republicano español en Argentina*. Barcelona: Crítica, 2001.

———. "Entre la tierra perdida y la tierra prestada: refugiados judíos y españoles en la Argentina." In *La Argentina entre multitudes y soledades: De los años treinta a la actualidad*, vol. 3 of *Historia de la vida privada en la Argentina*, edited by Fernando Devoto and Marta Madero, 111–40. Buenos Aires: Taurus, 1999.

Scott, Joan Wallach. *Gender and the Politics of History*. New York: Columbia University Press, 1988.

Sebreli, Juan José, ed. *La cuestión judía en la Argentina*. Buenos Aires: Tiempo Contemporáneo, 1968.

Seibel, Beatriz. *Crónicas de la semana trágica de enero de 1919*. Buenos Aires: Corregidor, 1999.

Sel, José Manuel del. "La cirujana Sara Satanowsky: Recuerdos biográficos y anecdotario." *Actas de las VI Jornadas de Historia del Pensamiento Científico Argentino* (1992): 184–92.

Senkman, Leonardo. "El 4 de junio de 1943 y los judíos." *Todo Es Historia*, no. 193 (June 1983): 67–78.

———. "Etnicidad e inmigración durante el primer peronismo." *Estudios Interdisciplinarios de América Latina y el Caribe* 3, no. 2 (July–December 1991): 3–38.

———. *La identidad judía en la literatura argentina*. Buenos Aires: Pardes, 1983.

———. "Identidades colectivas de los colonos judíos en el campo y la ciudad entrerrianos." In *Encuentro y alteridad: Vida y cultura judía en América Latina*, edited by Judit Bokser Liwerant and Alicia Gojman de Backal, 405–37. Mexico City: Universidad Autónoma de México, 1999.

———. "Nacionalismo e inmigración: La cuestión étnica en las elites liberales e intelectuales argentinos: 1919–1940." *Estudios Interdisciplinarios de América Latina y el Caribe* 1, no. 1 (January–June 1990): 83–105.

———. "El peronismo visto desde la legación israelí en Buenos Aires: Sus relaciones con la OIA (1949–1954)." In *Judaica Latinoamericana: Estudios histórico-sociales*, 2, edited by Amilat, 115–36. Jerusalem: Universitaria Magnes and Universitaria Hebrea, 1993.

———. "The Transformation of Collective Identities: Immigrant Communities under the Populist Regimes of Vargas and Perón." In *Constructing Collective Identities and Shaping Public Spheres: Latin American Paths*, edited by Luis Roniger and Mario Sznajder, 123–47. Brighton, England: Sussex Academic Press, 1998.

Shepherd, Naomi. *A Price below Rubies: Jewish Women as Rebels and Radicals*. London: Weidenfeld and Nicolson, 1993.

Shijman, Osías. *Colonización judía en la Argentina*. Buenos Aires: German Artes Gráficas, 1980.

Shilo, Margaret. *Princess or Prisoner? Jewish Women in Jerusalem, 1840–1914*. Translated by David Louvish. Waltham, Mass.: Brandeis University Press, 2005.

Shumway, Nicolás. *The Invention of Argentina*. Berkeley: University of California Press, 1991.

Sigwald Carioli, Susana B. *Colonia Mauricio: Génesis y desarrollo de un ideal*. 2nd ed. Carlos Casares, Argentina: Editora del Archivo, 1991.

———. "¿Fueron antiargentinas los escuelas judías de Colonie Mauricio?" In *Colonie Mauricio: 100 años*, 118–30. Buenos Aires: Shalom, 1991.

Singerman, Berta. *Mis dos vidas*. Buenos Aires: Tres Tiempos, 1981.

Sinkoff, Nancy B. "Educating for 'Proper' Jewish Womanhood: A Case Study in Domesticity and Vocational Training, 1897–1926." *American Jewish History* 77, no. 4 (June 1988): 572–99.

Slatta, Richard W. *The Gauchos and the Vanishing Frontier*. Lincoln: University of Nebraska Press, 1983.

Slavsky, Leonor. "Notas para una etnografía del teatro idisch en la Argentina." Unpublished manuscript, 2001.

Smolensky, Eleonora María. "Una mujer italo argentina: Un relato de vida." In *Los relatos de vida: El retorno a lo biográfico*, edited by Magdalena Chiricó, 128–41. Buenos Aires: Centro Editor de América Latina, 1992.

Smolensky, Eleonora María, and Vera Vigevani Jarach. *Tantas voces, una historia: Italianos judíos en la Argentina, 1938–1948*. Buenos Aires: Tema Grupo Editorial, 1999.

Sochen, June. "From Sophie Tucker to Barbra Streisand: Jewish Women Entertainers as Reformers." In *Talking Back: Images of Jewish Women in American Popular Culture*, edited by Joyce Antler, 68–84. Hanover, N.H.: Brandeis University Press, 1998.

Sociedad de Damas Israelitas de Beneficencia y Asilo Argentino de Huérfanas Israelitas. *Memoria y balance*. 1927–54. Buenos Aires: n.p.

Sociedad Hebraica Argentina. *Memoria y balance mayo 1926–octubre 1927*. Buenos Aires: Sociedad Hebraica Argentina, 1928.

———, Club 65. *Vidas: Rescate de la herencia cultural*. Buenos Aires: Pardes, n.d.

Sociedad Israelita de Protección a Niñas y Mujeres "Ezras Noschim." *Obra social de la institución*. Buenos Aires: n.p., 1936.

Sociedad Kadima. *Boletín del 25 aniversario, 1909–mayo–1934*. Moisesville: Sociedad Kadima, 1934.

Socorro Rojo Internacional. *Bajo el terror de Justo*. Buenos Aires: Socorro Rojo, 1934.

Sofer, Eugene F. *From Pale to Pampa: A Social History of the Jews of Buenos Aires*. New York: Holmes and Meier, 1982.

Solberg, Carl. *Immigration and Nationalism: Argentina and Chile, 1890–1914*. Austin: University of Texas Press, 1970.

Sosa de Newton, Lily, ed. *Diccionario biógrafico de mujeres argentinas*. 2nd ed. Buenos Aires: Plus Ultra, 1980.

Spalding, Hobart A., Jr. "Education in Argentina, 1890–1914: The Limits of Oligarchical Reform." *Journal of Interdisciplinary History* 3, no. 1 (summer 1972): 31–61.

Spektorowski, Alberto. *The Origins of Argentina's Revolution of the Right*. Notre Dame, Ind.: University of Notre Dame Press, 2003.

Spitzer, Leo. *Hotel Bolivia: The Culture of Memory in a Refuge from Nazism*. New York: Hill and Wang, 1998.

Stanchina, Lorenzo. *Tanka Charowa*. 2nd ed. Buenos Aires: Eudeba, 1999.

Staudt, Kathleen, and David Spener, "The View from the Frontier: Theoretical Perspectives Undisciplined." In *The U.S.-Mexico Border: Transcending Divisions, Contesting Identities*, edited by David Spener and Kathleen Staudt, 1–33. Boulder, Colo.: Lynne Rienner, 1998.

Stephen, Lynn. *Transborder Lives: Indigenous Oaxacans in Mexico, California, and Oregon*. Durham, N.C.: Duke University Press, 2007.

Stern, Steve. *The Secret History of Gender: Women, Men, and Power in Late Colonial Mexico*. Chapel Hill: University of North Carolina Press, 1995.

Stolen, Kristi Anne. *The Decency of Inequality: Gender, Power, and Social Change on the Argentine Prairie*. Oslo: Scandinavian University Press, 1996.

Suriano, Juan. *Anarquistas: Cultura y política libertaria en Buenos Aires, 1890–1910*. Buenos Aires: Manantial, 2001.

Svarch, Ariel. "'El comunista sobre el tejado': Historia de la militancia comunista en la calle judía (Buenos Aires, 1920–1950)." Tesis de licenciatura, Universidad Torcuato di Tella, 2005.

Syrquin, Moshe. "The Economic Structure of Jews in Argentina and Other Latin American Countries." *Jewish Social Studies* 47, no. 2 (spring 1985): 115–34.

Szuchman, Mark D. "The Limits of the Melting Pot in Urban Argentina: Marriage and Integration in Córdoba, 1869–1909." *Hispanic American Historical Review* 57, no. 1 (February 1997): 24–50.

Szurmuk, Mónica. "At Home in the Pampas: Alberto Gerchunoff's Jewish Gauchos." In *Jews at Home: The Domestication of Identity*, edited by Simon Bronner. Oxford: Littman, 2010.

Tamarin, David. *The Argentine Labor Movement, 1930–1945: A Study in the Origins of Peronism*. Albuquerque: University of New Mexico Press, 1985.

Tananbaum, Susan L. "Philanthropy and Identity: Gender and Ethnicity in London." *Journal of Social History* 30, no. 4 (summer 1997): 937–61.

Tarcus, Horacio. "Historia de una pasión revolucionaria: Hipólito Etchebehere y Mika Felman, de la reforma universitaria a la guerra civil española." *El Rodaballo* 6, no. 11–12 (spring / summer 2000): 39–51.

Terracini, Lore. "Una inmigración muy particular: 1938, los universitarios italianos en la Argentina." *Anuario IEHS* 4 (1989): 335–69.

Teubal, Nissim. *Consejos a la mujer*. Buenos Aires: n.p., 1958.

Tiempo, César [Israel Zeitlin]. *La vida romántica y pintoresca de Berta Singerman*. Buenos Aires: Sopena Argentina, 1941.

Tierra de promesas: 100 años de colonización judía en Entre Ríos. Colonia Clara, San Antonio y Lucienville. N.p.: Nuestra Memoria, 1995.

Tinsman, Heidi. "Good Wives and Unfaithful Men: Gender Negotiations and Sexual Conflicts in the Chilean Agrarian Reform, 1964–1973." *Hispanic American Historical Review* 81, no. 3–4 (August–November 2001), 587–619.

———. *Partners in Conflict: The Politics of Gender, Sexuality, and Labor in the Chilean Agrarian Reform, 1950–1973*. Durham, N.C.: Duke University Press, 2002.

Tolcachier, Fabina Sabina. "Asociaciones israelitas en el partido de Villarino." *Studi Emigrazione/Etudes Migrations* 31 (September 1994): 461–93.

———. "Continuidad o ruptura de identidades étnicas: El comportamiento matrimonial de los israelitas en el partido de Villarino (1905–1934)." *Estudios Migratorios Latinoamericanos*, no. 20 (1992): 37–69.

———. "Movilidad socio-ocupacional de los israelitas en el partido de Villarino, 1905–1950." *Estudios Migratorios Latinoamericanos*, no. 31 (1995): 633–71.

Toll, William. "A Quiet Revolution: Jewish Women's Clubs and the Widening Female Sphere, 1870–1920." *American Jewish Archives* 41, no. 1 (spring / summer 1989): 7–26.

Topp, Michael Miller. *Those without Country: The Political Culture of Italian American Syndicalists*. Minneapolis: University of Minnesota Press, 2001.

Torre, Juan Carlos, ed. *Los años peronistas (1943–1955)*. Vol. 8 of *Nueva historia argentina*. Buenos Aires: Sudamericana, 2002.

Trifone, Victor, and Gustavo Svarzman. *La repercusión de la guerra civil española en la Argentina (1936–1939)*. Buenos Aires: Centro Editor de América Latina, 1993.

Tuccio, Liliana Cristina. "La mujer obrera argentina y su participación en las organizaciones sindicales entre 1930 y 1943." Tesis de licenciatura, Universidad de Buenos Aires, 2002.

Tyrell, Ian. "American Exceptionalism in an Age of Intellectual History." *American Historical Review* 96, no. 4 (October 1991): 1031–55.

Ufford, Jack Twiss Quarles van, and Joep Merkx. "Ich Hab' Noch einen Koffer in Berlin: German-Jewish Identity in Argentina, 1933–1985." *Jewish Social Studies* 50, nos. 1–2 (1992): 99–110.

United States. Department of State. Records of the Department of State Relating to the Internal Affairs of Argentina, 1940–1944, M1322.

Urquiza, Emilia Yolanda. "Las suecas de 'Verdandi': Una comunidad femenina." Unpublished manuscript.

Vaughan, Mary Kay. *Cultural Politics in Revolution: Teachers, Peasants, and Schools in Mexico, 1930–1940*. Tucson: University of Arizona Press, 1997.

Veccia, Theresa R. " 'My Duty as a Woman': Gender Ideology, Work, and Working-Class Women's Lives in São Paulo, Brazil, 1900–1950." In *The Gendered World of Latin American Women Workers: From Household and Factory to the Union Hall and Ballot Box*, edited by John D. French and Daniel James, 100–146. Durham, N.C.: Duke University Press, 1997.

Verbitsky, Gregorio. *Rivera: Afán de medio siglo*. Buenos Aires: Julio Kaufman, 1955.

Vila, Pablo. *Crossing Borders, Reinforcing Borders: Social Categories, Metaphors, and Narrative Identities on the U.S.-Mexico Border*. Austin: University of Texas Press, 2000.

Vincent, Isabel. *Bodies and Souls: The Tragic Plight of Three Jewish Women Forced into Prostitution in the Americas*. New York: HarperCollins, 2005.

Visacovsky, Nerina. "*Di idische froi*: Imágenes de la mujer judeo progresista argentina durante el peronismo." Unpublished manuscript.

———. "El discurso pedagógico de la izquierda judía en Argentina, 1940–1975." Tesis de doctorado, Universidad de Buenos Aires, 2010.

La voz argentina contra la barbarie. Buenos Aires: n.p., 1942.

Walter, Richard J. *Politics and Urban Growth in Buenos Aires, 1910–1942*. Cambridge: Cambridge University Press, 1993.

———. "The Right and Peronists, 1943–1955." In *The Argentine Right: Its History and Intellectual Origins, 1910 to the Present*, edited by Sandra McGee Deutsch and Ronald H. Dolkart, 99–118. Wilmington, Del.: Scholarly Resources, 1993.

———. *The Socialist Party of Argentina: 1890–1930*. Austin: University of Texas Press, 1977.

———. *Student Politics in Argentina: The University Reform and Its Effects, 1918–1964*. New York: Basic Books, 1968.

Weill, George. "The Alliance Israélite Universelle and the Emancipation of Jewish Communities in the Mediterranean." *Journal of Jewish Sociology* 24, no. 2 (December 1982): 117–34.

Weill, Simón. *Estudios sobre las comunidades judía y francesa en Argentina: Los escritos de Simón Weill*. Compiled by Alberto Kleiner. Buenos Aires: Polígono, 1983.

Weinberg, Robert. *Stalin's Forgotten Zion: Birobidzhan and the Making of a Soviet Jewish Homeland—An Illustrated History, 1928–1996*. Berkeley: University of California Press, 1998.

Weinberg, Sydney Stahl. "Longing to Learn: The Education of Jewish Immigrant Women in New York City, 1900–1934." *Journal of American Ethnic History* 8 (spring 1989): 108–26.

Weiner, Deborah. "Jewish Women in the Central Appalachian Coal Fields, 1890–1960: From Breadwinners to Community Builders." *American Jewish Archives* 52, nos. 1–2 (2000): 10–33.

Weinstein, Ana E., and Miryam E. Gover de Nasatsky, eds. *Escritores judeo-argentinos: Bibliografía 1900–1987*. 2 vols. Buenos Aires: Milá, 1994.

Weinstein, Ana E., Roberto Nasatsky, and Miryam E. Gover de Nasatsky, eds. *Trayectorias musicales judeo-argentinas*. Buenos Aires: Milá, 1998.

Weisbrot, Robert. *The Jews of Argentina: From the Inquisition to Perón*. Philadelphia, Pa.: Jewish Publication Society of America, 1979.

Wenger, Beth S. "Budgets, Boycotts, and Babies: Jewish Women in the Great Depression." In *American Jewish Women's History: A Reader*, edited by Pamela S. Nadell, 185–200. New York: New York University Press, 2003.

———. "Jewish Women and Voluntarism: Beyond the Myth of Enablers." *American Jewish History* 79, no. 1 (autumn 1989): 16–36.

———. "Jewish Women of the Club: The Changing Public Role of Atlanta's Jewish Women (1970–1930)." *American Jewish History* 76, no. 3 (March 1987): 311–33.

Winocur, Perlina. *Desarrollo, alimentación y salud del niño: Algunos aspectos de la medicina preventiva en el medio escolar*. Buenos Aires: El Ateneo, 1948.

Wolff, Martha, and Myrtha Schalom. *Judíos y argentinos, judíos argentinos*. Buenos Aires: Manrique Zago, 1988.

Women's International Zionist Organization (WIZO). "WIZO in the British Empire and Latin America: 1939–1946." Mimeo paper. London, 1946.

Yannoulas, Silvia. "Maestras de antaño: ¿mujeres tradicionales? Brasil y Argentina (1870–1930)." In *Mujeres en la educación: Género y docencia en Argentina: 1870–1930*, edited by Graciela Morgade, 175–91. Buenos Aires: Miño y Dávila, 1997.

Zadoff, Efraim. *Historia de la educación judía en Buenos Aires (1935–1957)*. Buenos Aires: Milá, 1994.

Zanatta, Loris. *Del estado liberal a la nación católica: Iglesia y ejército en los orígenes del peronismo, 1930–1943*. Bernal, Argentina: Universidad Nacional de Quilmes, 1996.

———. *Perón y el mito de la nación católica: Iglesia y ejército en los orígenes del peronismo, 1943–1946*. Buenos Aires: Sudamericana, 1999.

Zemer, Moshe. "The Rabbinic Ban on Conversion in Argentina." *Judaism* 37 (winter 1988): 84–96.

Zimerman de Faingold, Raquel. *Memorias*. Buenos Aires: n.p., 1987.

Ziperovich, Rosa W. de. "Memoria de una educadora: Experiencias alternativas en la provincia de Santa Fe durante los últimos años de la década del 10, la del 20 y primeros años de 1930." In *Historia de la educación argentina*, Vol. 3, *Escuela, democracia y orden (1916–1943)*, edited by Adriana Puiggrós, 161–256. Buenos Aires: Galerna, 1992.

INDEX

Page numbers in *italics* refer to illustrations.

AA (Acción Argentina), 183
ABRI (Asociación Bibliotecas y Recreos Infantiles), 157
Absatz, Flora, 52, 148, 169, 170, 196, 241
Acción Antiracista Entrerriana, 178, 179
Acción Argentina (AA), 183
Active School movement, 76, 79–80
Adler, María, 216–17
Adler, Raquel, 61–62
Adultery, 137–38
Agrupación Comunista Israelita, 165
Agrupación de Intelectuales, Artistas, Periodistas, y Escritores (AIAPE), 172, 179–80
Aguirre, Violeta Nardo de, 13, 35, 40, 236
AIAPE (Agrupación de Intelectuales, Artistas, Periodistas, y Escritores), 172, 179–80
AIU (Alliance Israélite Universelle), 16, 21, 59
AJIA (Asociación Juventud Israelita Argentina), 61, 79
Albernini, Cariolano, 80
Alberti, Rafael, 96
Aleijem, Scholem, 94
Aleppine Jews, 45–46, 64
Algarrobos Cemetery, *109*
Alianak, Paulina, 73, 75–76
Alliance Israélite Universelle (AIU), 16, 21, 59
Almanaque Agenda, 230
Alpersohn, Marcos, 13, 142
Alsogaray, Julio, 115, 116
Alvear, Marcelo T. de, 75, 222
Alvear, Regina Pacini, 222
Amaral, Tarsila do, 96
Ambram, Hortensia de, 216, 221
Amigas Sefaradíes de la Histadrut, 219
Anarchists, 150–54, 246
Anderson, Marian, 102
Andrade, Osvaldo de, 96
Antifascism, 5, 69; Communism and, 179–89; equality and, 187; groups, 178, 240, 243; help for Allies and, 183–89; liberalism and, 203, 246; Socialism and, 177
Anti-Marxism, 195
Anti-Semitism: antifascism and, 240; beauty pageants and, 69; campaigns against, 11; Catholicism and, 82; Communism and, 99, 165; DAIA and, 199, 208; extreme, 43, 57; impressions of, 9, 10; intermarriage and, 140; Italy and, 70; Jewish women and, 5; laws, 43; Lincovsky and, 94; Nacionalismo and, 173–77, 189–90, 203, 209, 239; national origin and, 239; otherness and, 35; Peronism and, 241; politics and, 86–87, 104; prevalence of, 14; in professions, 74–81, 89–91, 94, 231; rural, 36, 41; Schliapnik and, 231; Soviet, 99;

Anti-Semitism (*cont.*)
Spanish Civil War and, 182–83, 188; spread of, 37, 239; transnational, 172
AOT (Asociación Obrera Textil), 196
APA (Asociación Psicoanalítica Argentina), 87
Appointment with the Stars (television program), 102
Arab Voice (radio program), *66*
Argentinidad, 12, 23, 38–39, 175, 206, 221
Ashkenazi Hebrew Radio Matinee (radio program), 63
Ashkenazim, 3; actresses, 92; in agricultural colonies, 13, 32; criollos and, 35; education and, 28, 77; as gauchos, 37; inclusion and, 61–62, 171, 240; leftist movements and, 148–49; marginalization by, 239; marriage customs, 128, 130, 141–42; midwifery and, 19–20; on moral behavior, 146; nationalism of, 38; preservation of culture, 31; prostitution and, 109–10, 120, 121, 122; Sephardim and, 67–68, 142, 245; teaching by, 83–84; transnationalism and, 148; women's roles, 19, 32
Asilo Argentino de Huérfanas Israelitas, 57, 206, *213*, 232
Aslán, Hélène R. de, 107, 123, 224
Asociación Bibliotecas y Recreos Infantiles (ABRI), 157
Asociación Juventud Cultural Sionista, 61
Asociación Juventud Israelita Argentina (AJIA), 61, 79
Asociación Mutual Israelita Argentina, 200
Asociación Obrera Textil (AOT), 196
Asociación Psicoanalítica Argentina (APA), 87
Asociación Racionalista Judía, 153–54
Ateneo Estudiantil Israelita, 61
Ateneo Juventud Hebraica Sefaradí, 60. *See also* Sociedad Hebraica Argentina
Ateneo Juventud Israelita of Rosario, 61
Attach, Regina, 50, 64, 125
Avukah, 217

Balkan Jews, 24
Baumkoler, Berta, 182, 195
Beauty contests, 68–69, 126, 239–40, 274 n. 90
Beneficent societies: charity balls of, 210–11, 217; dues of, 211, 212; functions of, 208–10; fundraising by, 212–14; Jewish identity and, 206; respectability and, 209, 240–41; rhetoric of, 227–28; rise of, 206–8; state and, 220–23
Benzaquen, Vida Malatón de, 21
Benzión, Ida de, 207, 216
Benzión, Uriel, 207
Berlatsky, Anita, 126
Bermann, Gregorio, 187
Biblioteca Popular Barón Hirsch, 28
Biblioteca Popular Domingo F. Sarmiento, 28
Blackie (Paloma "Blackie" Efron), 101–3, 104, 187, 240, 244
Boletín Mensual (periodical), 230
Bordabehere, Enzo, 179
Bordellos, 45, 106, 109–10, 117, 119, 120, 122
Borders: bordellos, prostitution and, 106; communal, 43, 44, 45, 60, 62–64, 79, 80, 83, 87; cultural, 13, 14, 244; gender and, 1, 10, 20, 74, 163, 237; Jewish women and, 4–5, 10, 42, 147; margins and, 5; meanings of, 236–38; national identity and, 1; prostitution and, 106, 120–21; rural areas and, 34–36; schools and, 23, 29; skills and, 4, 32, 41, 54, 71, 74, 79, 81, 103, 237; transnationalism and, 5; urban areas and, 43–48. *See also* Boundaries
Borlenghi, Angel, 196

Boundaries: communal, 32, 41, 61, 148–49, 206; cultural, 32–33, 216, 236–37; ethnic, 214; marriage and, 137–38, 147; metaphorical and physical, 4; national, 5, 94, 173, 246; private and professional, 121; Zionism and, 12. *See also* Borders
Braslavsky, Berta Perelstein de, 75, 76, 77–79, 80, 180, 185, 189, 201, 227, 240; *Positivismo y antipositivismo en la Argentina*, 81
Buenos Aires: affluent neighborhoods, 47; Bajo neighborhood, 44; Barracas neighborhood, 45; Boca neighborhood, 45; borders and, 43–48, 62–70; commercial sex in, 108; *conventillo*, 49; cultural activities in, 60–62, 66–67, 129; education and literacy in, 56–60; Flores neighborhood, 45–46; identities and, 62–70; immigration to, 43–44; literacy rates in, 254–55; Once neighborhood, 45, 48; organizations in, 60–62; polio epidemic in, 85–86; population statistics on, 44, 251–52; porteños in, 43–44, 46, 69, 143; poverty in, 49–50, 71; settlement in, 43–48; Villa Crespo neighborhood, 46, 51; Villa Lynch neighborhood, 46–47, 51; work and marginalization in, 48–55; workforce statistics on, 253–54
Bunge, Augusto, 193
Bursuk, Berish, 152–53
Bursuk, Bruje, 152
Bursuk, Meier, 152–53
Bursuk, Nelia, 152
Bursuk, Yosl, 152

CADMI, CAMI (Consejo Argentino de Mujeres Israelitas / Consejo de Mujeres Israelitas de la Argentina), 208, 220, 224–25, 226, 234
Camji, José, 217
Camji, Julieta, 217, 228
Campo, El (periodical), 17, 18
Castillo, Ramón, 189, 198
Catholics: anti-Semitism and, 35–36, 57–58; Argentine identity and, 70, 189, 242–43; divorce and, 136; dowries and, 130; education and, 81–83, 189, 196, 239, 243; imitation of, 12, 38, 66, 129, 211, 215; intermarriage and, 128, 155; Jewish conversion and, 11, 25, 36, 137, 176; Jewish outreach to, 237; Jewish sexuality and, 11, 123–26; junta and, 185–89; liberalism and, 247; as mentors, 240; Nacionalismo and, 175, 239, 242; nationalism and, 74, 189; orphans and, 215, 235; prejudice of, 35–36, 57–58; prostitution and, 108; publications by, 187; race and, 189; school interventions and, 81; sexual fraternization with, 135–42, 143, 146, 237
CCRA (Comité contra el Racismo y el Antisemitismo), 178
Centro de Documentación e Información sobre Judaísmo Argentino "Marc Turkow," 8
Centro de Estudiantes Santo Tomás de Aquino, 80
Centro Juventud Israelita Argentina, 61
Centro Recreativo Israelita, 62
Centro Sionista N. Sovolov, 63
Centro Sionista Sefaradí, 217
Centro Socialista Femenino (CSF), 155–56
Chami, Esther Gedalievitch de, 214–15, 216, 228
Chami, Marcos, 132–33
Chami, Mois, 214
Chanovsky, Rosa, 150–51, 166, 237
Chertkoff, Adela, 154–55
Chertkoff, Fenia, 28, 154–58, 166, 237, 242
Chertkoff, Mariana, 154–55

CIAPE (Comisión Israelita de Ayuda al Pueblo Español), 181–82
Cipe, 93–95, 99, 104, 127, 166, 177, 240, 244
Círculo de Maestros, 166–67
Cities and towns: migration to, 13, 40; railroad towns, 15; women's roles in, 18–19
Civita, Cesare, 54–55
Class boundaries: professions and, 74; in schools, 21, 23, 43, 76–77
Club Azul y Blanco, 67
Club Israelita de Flores, 67
Clubs, 29, 43, 46, 61, 62–63, 67, 164–65
Club Social Alianza, 62
CMI (Consejo Argentino de Mujeres Israelitas / Consejo de Mujeres Israelitas de la Argentina), 208, 220, 224–25, 226, 234
Cohabitation, 136–37
Cohen, Samuel, 105, 109, 111, 117
Cohn, Esther, 115
Cole, Nat King, 103
Colmena, La, 23
Comisión de Señoritas del KKL, 218
Comisión Israelita de Ayuda al Pueblo Español (CIAPE), 181–82
Comisión Israelita Femenina, 193
Comité contra el Racismo y el Antisemitismo (CCRA), 178
Comité de Damas del Fondo Nacional, 207
Comité de Damas Israelitas pro Ayuda a los Expulsados de Alemania, 179
Comité Juvenil contra el Fascismo y el Antisemitismo, 179, 180
Communism, Communists: antifascism and, 179–89; anti-Semitism and, 99–100, 165, 178; Ashkenazi women and, 164, 245; discrimination and, 78–80, 87, 91, 135; education and, 60, 80, 84, 176, 198, 246; expulsion of, 239; illegality of, 80, 87, 164, 165, 175; Jewish, 193; labor and, 166–71; liberalism and, 164; Nacionalistas and, 175–76, 243; party of, 163–66, 198–204, 228; Peronism and, 195–98; publications by, 81; repression of, 189–95; Socialism and, 162; spread of, 164–65; stereotyping and, 68; theater and, 92–94; Yiddish primary schools and, 29
Communist Party, 1, 243; antifascism of, 178–79; education and, 60; inclusiveness of, 203–4; Jewish women and, 163–66; Jews' loyalty to, 197; marginalization of, 228; outlawing of, 87, 175; pro-Allies group, 184–85; Socialists and, 163; union strategies of, 196–97, 198–202; Yiddish theater and, 92–93, 163–66
Communist Youth, 78, 94
Community: activism and, 205; Argentine Jewish women and, 3, 44, 62–64, 71; honor and, 124–27, 146
Concordancia, 149, 175
Consejo Argentino de Mujeres Israelitas / Consejo de Mujeres Israelitas de la Argentina, 208, 220, 224–25, 226, 234
Consejo Central de Damas Sefaradíes, 219, 231, 242
Cooperatives: empowering women through, 159–60; rural, 17–18, 19, 154, 238; school, 23, 29, 41, 79, 240
Courtship customs, 132–34, 147
Crilla, Hedy, 100–101, 103, 240
Criollos: cuisine of, 32–33, 38; culture of, 34–35, 39, 221; defined, 16; Jewish women and, 23, 26–27, 34–36, 39, 41; land ownership and, 160; racism toward, 26, 117, 138, 244–45; rapes and, 36, 142, 147

CSF (Centro Socialista Femenino), 155–56
Cuisine: communal borders and, 64; criollo, 32–33, 38; in rural areas, 30–34
Cultural activities: border spaces and, 34–35; in Buenos Aires, 60–62, 66–67, 129; marriage customs and, 129, 131; patriotic celebrations, 37–39; preservation of, 31; in rural areas, 27–30

Dachevsky, Sara, 26, 36
DAIA (Delegación de Asociaciones Israelitas Argentinas), 178, 180, 199, 200, 208
Dali, Salvador, 98
Damascene Jews, 45
Davidovich, Deborah, 19–20, 25
Day of the Race, 190
Debussy, Claude, 98
Delegación de Asociaciones Israelitas Argentinas (DAIA), 178, 180, 199, 200, 208
Democracy, promotion of, 41
Dentistry profession, 89–90
Dick, Celina, 109
Dickmann, Adolfo, 155
Dietary laws, 34
Diner, Hasia, 32
Discrimination: Communism and, 78–80, 87, 91, 135; in community organizations, 233–34; in education, 77, 82, 83; infrequency of, 68, 74; in medical profession, 89, 91; Nacionalismo and, 239; outsiders and, 5; overcoming, 240; perception and, 9; Perón on, 195–96, 199; political, 104; in United States, 102; women's contributions and, 1
Divorce, 136–37, 147, 156, 239, 290 n. 60
Dlugates, Zlate, 195
Draznin, Iosef, 29
Drucaroff, Berta Blejman de, 172, 184
Dubovsky, Adolfo, 150
Dubovsky, Sara, 150–51

Edelman, Bernardo, 131, 135
Edelman, Fanny, 131, 135, 182, 186, 188, 192–93, 201–2
Editorial Abril, 55
Education: for boys, 25; Catholic, 57–58, 81–82, 189; class structure and, 21, 23, 43, 76–77; Communism and, 60, 80, 84, 176, 198, 246; Communist-oriented Yiddish schools, 29; discrimination in, 77, 82, 83; foreign degrees and, 85; for girls, 22, 24–26, 56–57, 59, 238; Hebrew schools, 29, 190, 214–15; Jewish schools, 83–84; liberalism and teaching, 74; male domination in research, 81; nationalism and, 39–40, 75, 189; political change and, 76; power of, 76; prejudice in, 57; primary schools, 59; for prostitutes, 118; rationalist, 152; religious, 81–83; rural, 21–27; school cooperatives, 23, 29, 41, 79, 240; surveillance and, 83; synagogue schools, 59; teacher regulations, 77; transferring to schools, 25–26; universal secular, 6, 22, 24, 40, 242; Villa Crespo school, 57–58; vocational, 60; Yiddish schools, 47, 59, 165–66, 184
Efron, Jedidio, 101
Efron, Paloma "Blackie," 101–3, 104, 187, 240, 244
Ellington, Duke, 102
Elnecavé, Bruria, 42, 67–68, 135, 218, 230, 231–32
Elnecavé, Nissim, 135, 232
Ema the Millionaire (Esther Cohn), 115
Engel, Eta, 186
Entertainment profession, 91–97; jazz and, 98, 101–2; Junta benefits and, 187–88; marginality and, 103; modern

Entertainment profession (*cont.*)
dance and, 73, 99–100, 104; performances and, 30, 166, 187
Equality: anarchism and, 150–51; antifascists and, 187; education and, 75, 152; gender, 148, 227, 231, 242; liberty and, 187; Socialism and, 161
Escuela Libre para Trabajadores, 157
Escuela Yahaduth, 29
Etchebehere, Hipólito, 182
Eva Perón Foundation, 226
Exclusion, 142–46, 241; Jewishness and, 36, 104; Jewish women and, 10, 41, 62, 74, 238–40; male, contesting, 231–34; motives for, 74; Nacionalismo and, 189–91; political, 161–62; prostitutes and, 117; rural women and, 21, 41; Sociedad Hebraica and, 62; in unions, 169–70; Yiddish language and, 239
Ezras Noschim, 105; abuse and, 142–46; arranged marriage and, 129, 134–35; as Ashkenazi, 287 n. 5; CMI and, 208; communal honor and, 124–26, 135–39; mission of, 107; prostitution and, 107–8, 111–13, 116, 119–20, 284 n. 45

FACA (Federación Anarco Comunista Argentina), 151
Family honor, 125, 146, 242
Farrell, Edelmiro, 190
Fascism, 2, 47, 176, 203, 238. *See also* Antifascism
Federación Anarco Comunista Argentina (FACA), 151
Federación Libertaria Argentina (FLA), 151
Federación Obrera del Vestido (FOV), 168
Federación Obrera Nacional del Vestido (FONICA), 196
Federación Obrera Regional Argentina (FORA), 150
Federación Obrera Textil, 168
Felman, Mika, 164, 182
Fischer, Sara, 84, 104
Fitzgerald, Ella, 102
FLA (Federación Libertaria Argentina), 151
Flami, Golde, 92, 104, 166, 187, 244
FONICA (Federación Obrera Nacional del Vestido), 196
FORA (Federación Obrera Regional Argentina), 150
FOV (Federación Obrera del Vestido), 168
Freie Deutsche Bühne, 181
Freie Wort, Dos (periodical), 152
Freud, Sigmund, 87
Frondizi, Arturo, 86
Frondizi, Risieri, 86
Furman, Esther, 42, 52, 53–54, 104, 190
Furman, Luisa, 79
Fux, María, 73, 98–100, 104, 166, 240

Ganopol, Selig, 107, 112, 114, 118, 146
García Lorca, Federico, 96, 99
Gardel, Carlos, 101
Garment industry, 51–52, 167–68
Gartenstein-Faigenblat, Lena, 55
Gauchos, Jewish, 37
Gelpy, Alfred, 107
Gender: acting and, 92–95, 166; barriers and, 61, 79, 203, 219, 238; bias, 86, 233–34; borders and, 1, 10, 20, 74, 163, 237; code, 54; discrimination and, 74, 240; expectations and, 56; Ezras Noschim and, 124; marginalization and, 14, 42–43, 231–34; moral behavior and, 146; norms, 4, 14, 42–43, 147, 149, 206, 238; notions, 43, 74, 103, 189, 237; practices, 146; public debate and, 133; restrictions of, 71, 229, 238–39; roles, 16, 83, 240, 241; schooling and, 22, 28
Genkin, Dora, 169–70, 196

Gerchunoff, Alberto, 37, 176
Gerchunoff, Berta Wainstein de, 161, 226, 229, *230*, 244
German Jews, *18*, 22, 26–27, 31–33, 70
German language, 27, 28, 47, 70
Gertel, Clara, 247
Gilenberg, Teresa, 53, 166, 193–94, 200, 202
Glusberg, Samuel, 96
Gogosch, Beatriz, 176
Goodman, Benny, 102
Graham, Martha, 99
Grierson, Cecilia, 88
Grupo Anaconda, 96
Gucovsky, Gabriel, 154
Gucovsky, Victoria, 154–55, 158–61, 177–78, 240
Gutman, Frida, 37
Gutman, Isaac, 28–29

Halphon, Samuel, 107
Hanoar Hasefaradí (periodical), 230–31
Hashomer Hatzair, 131
Hassid, Catherine, 18–19, 31, 35, 135
Hebrew language, 59, 165
Hebrew Radio Matinee (radio program), 63
Helman, Clara, 185, 188
Hermandad Femenina, 207
Herschkovitz, Fanny Blitz de, 89–90
Herzog, George, 102
Hirsch, Maurice de, 15
Holocaust survivors, 2–3
Homeless children, 49
Homemaking, 48, 53–54, 215
Houssay, Bernardo, 85
Hughes, Langston, 102
Hygiene, 19, 158

IAR (Instituto Argentino de Reeducación), 81
Icaza, Jorge, 80

ICJW (International Council of Jewish Women), 224–25
ICUF (Idischer Cultur Farband), 93, 198–201, 203–4, 237, 243
Identity: charities and, 206; creation of, 3; hybrid, 6, 40–41, 43, 71, 74, 120, 241; Jewishness and, 3, 36, 69; women's construction of, 9
Idische Folks Theater (IFT), 92–93, 99, 166, 181, 182, 198, 200
Idische Froi, Di (periodical), 199
Idischer Cultur Farband (ICUF), 93, 198–201, 203–4, 237, 243
Idische Tzaitung, Di (periodical), 27
IFT (Idische Folks Theater), 92–93, 99, 166, 181, 182, 198, 200
Illiteracy, 21, 118, 122, 271 n. 49; rates, 22, 23, 56, 250, 254–55
Immigration: to Buenos Aires, 43–44, 71–72; Jewish, beginning of, 2, 6; liberals and, 123; prostitution and, 108; to rural areas, 13; whiteness and, 7; women and, 1
Inclusion, 60, 238; Ashkenazi activists and, 61–62, 171, 240; Jewishness and, 43, 71, 239; Jewish women and, 10, 41, 74, 240–41; Peronist, 235, 247; prostitutes and, 122; reputation and, 124; rural women and, 18, 41; Socialism and, 158; teaching and, 75
Indigenous peoples, 7
Insiders. *See* Inclusion
Instituto Argentino de Reeducación (IAR), 81
Instituto Zimra, 103
International Brigade, 87
International Council of Jewish Women (ICJW), 224–25
International Feminine Congress, 156
International Peace Congress (Warsaw, 1955), 99

International Socialists, 163. *See also* Communist Party
Isaharoff, Judith Cohen, 129–30, 133, 163, 217, 219, 221, 228, 232
Israel, Matilde, 65
Israel (periodical), 27, 31
Italian Jews, 63, 69–70
Italian Racial Laws, 85

Jazz, 98, 101–2
JCA (Jewish Colonization Association), 15–17, 21–22, 34, 40, 59, 108, 138, 152, 206, 213–14, 238
Jewish Association for the Protection of Young Girls and Women, 8, 107
Jewish Colonization Association (JCA), 15–17, 21–22, 34, 40, 59, 108, 138, 152, 206, 213–14, 238
Jewish National Fund, 212, 217
Jewishness: amalgamating of, 31; exclusion and, 104; identity and, 3, 9; inclusion and, 43, 71, 239; performance and, 187; submerging, 71
Jewish Sociedad de Protección a los Inmigrantes, 51
Jews: conversion to Catholicism by, 11; immigration by, 2, 6; marginalization by, 174; naming of, 68; population statistics on, 44; porteños, 43–44, 46, 69, 143; segregation of, 47–48, 160, 245; Spanish Civil War and, 181–83; statistics on, 250–55; varied cultures of, 2, 67–68; whiteness and, 7, 36, 41, 43. *See also* Women, Argentine Jewish
Jiménez, Juan Ramón, 96
JKG (Jüdische Kulturgemeinschaft), 62
Johnson, Rosamond, 102
Jolson, Al, 102
Jüdische Kulturgemeinschaft (JKG), 62
Junta de la Victoria, 190, 245; aid to Allies, 187–89; members, 185–86
Justo, Agustín P., 78, 191
Justo, Alicia Moreau de, 161, 220
Justo, Juan B., 155, 157, 158, 316 n. 89
Juventud Libertaria, 153

Kaller, Bela Trumper de, 13, 28
Kaller, Frida, 28–29, 30
Kantor, Ida Bondareff de, 164
Kanutsky, Guitl, 53, 148, 167–68, 170, 196, 198
Katz, Ilse, 17, 133
Kaufman, Carlos, 66
Kaufman, Ilse, 47, 65–66
Kidnapping, ritualized, 138–39
Kipen, Miguel, 19–20
Klein, Melanie, 87
Kogan, Leike, 199–200
Kohan, Felisa Favelukes de, 224–25, 228
Korn, José Salomon, 116
Kremer, Isa, 187–88, 244
Krislavin, Clara, 196
Kuper, Catalina, 193
Kushnir, Beatriz, 111

Labor. *See* Unions and labor; Work
Ladino language, 16, 31
Landownership, 17, 41, 160, 246
Langer, Marie Glas de, 86–87, 186
Leftist movements: anarchists and, 150–54; anti-Semitism and, 172–77; anti-Zionists and, 212; Communists and, 163–66, 198–204; exclusion and, 189–90, 243; fascism and, 172, 177–89, 190–91; gender barriers and, 238–41; human rights and, 191–95; identity and, 3, 65, 93, 246; Idische Folks Theater and, 99; as Jewish heritage, 231; Jewish women and, 5, 80, 147, 148–71; liberalism and, 6, 206, 242; libraries and, 60, 71, 130; Nacionalismo and, 172–77; non-Jewish women and, 246; Peronism and, 7, 195–98; schools and, 47, 59, 157,

165–66; transnational, 5; unions and, 148–49, 166–71
Leonardo da Vinci Society, 63
Lesbianism, 134
Levenson, Raquel, 182
Levin, Emanuel, 91
Levin, Rosa Woscoboinik de, 91, 104, 201
Liberalism: Communism and, 164; Jewish immigrants and, 123; Jewish women and, 6, 41, 74, 146–47, 242; liberty and, 150; Nacionalistas and, 247
Liberman, Julio, 168
Liberman, Raquel, 112, 116–17, 120, 121
Liberty: democracy and, 185; equality and, 187; liberalism and, 150; liberal promise of, 6; in national anthem refrain, 192; personal choice and, 132; sex and, 142; social justice and, 178; sweetness of, 14, 39; Zionism and, 222
Librarianship, 28
Libraries, 27–28, 29, 59, 60
Liceo de Señoritas, 56
Licht, David, 92
Liga Argentina por los Derechos del Hombre, 192–95
Liga de Educación Racionalista, 152
Lincovsky, Cipe, 93–95, 99, 104, 127, 166, 177, 240, 244
Liniado, Elena, 48
Literacy, 24–27; Communists and, 182; illiteracy, 21, 118, 122, 271 n. 49; rates, 22, 23, 56, 250, 254–55; Sociedad Kadima and, 28; training and, 158; voting and, 157

Mactas, Rebeca, 40
Mailbox nights, 29–30
Makoff, Iona, 21
Malajovich, Rebeca de, 187
Malamud, Teresa, 88, 91
Maldavsky, Adela de, 205, 225
Mama Loshn Idish (theatrical work), 94
Marcovich, Cecilia, 180, 185, 201
Marginalization, 8; of blacks, 102; causes of, 14, 43, 71; by charities, 238; Communist, 228; education and, 59, 83; equality and, 148; escape from, 21; fears of, 17; gender and, 14, 42–43, 231–34; by government, 180; ICUF and, 199; intellectual, 10, 41; of Jewish teachers, 83; by Jews, 174, 239; by men, 147, 234; by Nacionalismo, 242–43; Peronism and, 198; politics and, 156; professions and, 103; prostitution and, 106, 110, 117, 119, 121–22; reputation and, 106, 124, 239; sensuality and, 104, 105; by teachers, 23; unions and, 196; voluntary organizations and, 206; work and, 48–55, 56; Yiddish language and, 218
Margins: borders and, 5; center and, 240; dance and, 100; female activists and, 241; as Jewish and female, 1, 74; philanthropy and, 204; poetry and, 98; professionalism and, 104; voluntarism and, 226–27; Zionism and, 204. *See also* Borders
Marriage: abuse and, 144–47; arranged, 127–30; boundaries and, 137–38, 147; courtship customs, 132–34, 147; dowries and, 128, 130, 136; egalitarian, 135; endogamy and intermarriage, 139–42; freedom to choose, 130–32; prostitution and, 110–14
Martínez Guerrero, Ana Rosa Schlieper de, 185, 220
Marxism, 80, 81, 88, 162–63, 164
Maternalism, 162
Matisse, Henri, 98
Maximalism, 173, 174
May 25 celebration, 37–38
Mayo, Luna de, 18, 19, 25, 38, 127, 211

Medical profession, 86–87; discrimination in, 89, 91; female physicians, 20–21, 88–92; foreign degrees and, 85
Meir, Golda, 226
Mesulam, Estela, 56, 67, 128, 174
Mesulam, Rachel, 56, 125
Michellon, Jorge, 169
Midwifery, 19–20, 41, 242
Miss Argentina contest, 68–69
Mistral, Gabriela, 96
Mitre, Bartolomé, 190
Modern dance, 73, 99–100, 104
Monín, Raquel A. de, 186
Montiel, Alberto, 174
Moroccan Jews, 15, 24, 26, 44, 206
Mother Tongue Yiddish (theatrical work), 94
Myerson, Bess, 69, 240

Naamat, 219–20, 221, 231, 242
Nacionalismo, Nacionalistas, 7; anti-Semitism and, 123–24, 173–77, 189–90, 203, 209, 239; Catholicism and, 242–43; fascism and, 203; liberalism and, 247; Peronism and, 190, 196; Spanish Civil War and, 181
Nada más que una mujer (film), 96
National Council of Jewish Women (NCJW), 208, 224, 244
National Directorate of Social Assistance, 223
Nationalism: antifascism and, 177–81; Communist Party and, 198–202; displays of, 37–40; education and, 39–40, 75, 189; essentialist, 40, 174; exclusion and, 189–91; Jewish women and, 7, 12, 24, 37–40, 202–4, 221–22; moral progress and, 151–52; Peronism and, 195–98; political prisoners and, 181–95; right-wing, 7, 94; schools and, 39–40, 75; Spanish Civil War and, 181–83; support for Allies, 183–89; teachers and, 26. *See also* Nacionalismo, Nacionalistas
Nazism: in Argentine schools, 70; escape from, 17; victims of, 187
NCJW (National Council of Jewish Women), 208, 224, 244
Neruda, Pablo, 96, 98
Nery, Ismael, 96
Neumann, Frau, 28
Nissensohn, Isaac, 132
Nissensohn, Sofía Rabinovich de, 25, 132, 228–29
Noble, Julio, 78
Noticias Gráficas (tabloid), 69–70
Nursing profession, 20, 183, 215

OF (Organización Femenina), 199
OIA (Organización Israelita Argentina), 196
Oliver, María Rosa, 185
Oral history, 8–9
Organización Femenina (OF), 199
Organización Israelita Argentina (OIA), 196
Organización Popular contra el Antisemitismo, 178
Organización Sionista Femenina Argentina (OSFA), 205, 207, 209–10, 211, 215, 217, 225, 233, 242
Orphanages, Jewish girls', 57, 126, 129, 134, 206, 215–16, 223–24, 232, 235
OSFA (Organización Sionista Femenina Argentina), 205, 207, 209–10, 211, 215, 217, 225, 233, 242
Ottoman Jews, 15, 50
Outsiders. *See* Exclusion
Oyuela, Eugenia Silveyra de, 187

Paisanas, 30
Parodi, Armando, 85
Partido Demócrata Progresista. *See* Progressive Democratic Party (PDP)

Pascaner, Rosa, 230
Pasco, Sofía Schwartzman de, 115
Passover, 65
Patriarchy, 5, 10, 54, 135
Pavlovsky, Rosa, 88
PDP (Progressive Democratic Party), 77, 179
Peddlers, 15, 27, 44, 45, 46, 50
Perelstein, Berta, 75, 76, 77–79, 80, 180, 185, 189, 201, 227, 240; *Positivismo y antipositivismo en la Argentina*, 81
Performances, 30, 166, 187
Perón, Eva, 82, 195, 243
Perón, Juan: on Argentine Jews, 7, 195–97, 199; on discrimination, 195–96, 199; expulsion of, 86; fascism and, 191, 196; inclusion and exclusion by, 243; Jewish Damas and, 223–24; on pensions, 225; support for, 191; Zionists and, 225–26
Peronism, 227–31; as civic religion, 82; Communist Party and, 87, 198–204; fascism and, 191; inclusiveness, 235, 247; Jews affected by, 7, 195–97, 223–26; marginalization and, 198; Nacionalismo and, 190, 196; nationalism and, 195–98; pensions and, 225; Zionism and, 196, 225–26, 243, 247
Pestalozzi, Johann Heinrich, 84
Philanthropy: borders and, 214–20; Jewish identity and, 206; respectability and, 209, 240–41; state and, 220–23; women's emancipation and, 230; Zionism and, 205–35. *See also* Beneficent societies
Physicians, female, 20–21, 88–92
Picasso, Pablo, 98
Pikelín, Ana, 20
Pizzurno, Pablo, 78
Plaza, Señora de, 25
Plotkin, Mariano, 87
Polio epidemic, 85–86
Political prisoners, female Jewish, 191–95
Porteños, 43–44, 46, 69, 143
Power: gender relations and, 4
Prejudice: by Catholics, 35–36; against Jewish students, 57; against Jewish women, 4, 43
Prell, Riv-Ellen, 123
Presse, Di (periodical), 27
Prisoners, 191–95
Procor, 165
Professions, 5; anti-Semitism in, 74–81, 89–91, 94, 231; boundaries and, 121; margins and, 103–4; as point of connection, 73, 100; support in, 91–92, 231–32; workforce statistics on, 75, 253–54, 255
Progressive Democratic Party (PDP), 77, 179
Prostitution: arranged marriages and, 128, 133, 134; bordellos and, 45, 106, 109–10, 117, 119, 120, 122; borders and, 106, 120–21; community reputation and, 123–27; documentation on, 107–8; earnings in, 115–17; entry into, 110–15; eradication of, 106; exclusion and, 238, 240; fear of, 138, 139, 142, 145; history of, 108–10; Jews and, 105–22, 242; marginalization and, 106, 110, 117, 119, 121–22; marriage and, 110–14; as means of support, 19, 51, 114; novels on, 10; promiscuity and, 146, 175; Sociedad de Damas and, 209; stigma of, 245; studies of, 2, 106; subjugation and, 117–20; transnational sex trade, 5; white slavery and, 105, 107–8, 110–11, 121, 139
Psychoanalysis practice, 87–88
Pugliese, Osvaldo, 194

Quebracho (film), 94
Quiroga, Horacio, 96

Rabinovich, Sofía, 25, 132, 228–29
Race: Catholicism and, 189; identity and, 74; immigrants and, 7; Jews and, 10, 68, 74, 92, 174, 244–45
Racism: toward criollos, 26, 117, 138, 244–45; whiteness and, 43
Radicals, 149
Radio Argentina, 63
Rapto, 138
Raquel, Doña, 44
Ratto, Cora, 185
Ravel, Maurice, 98
Rawson, Elvira, 88
Rawson prison, 194
Reading circles, 27, 199, 200
Real, Juan José, 182
Religion and oppression, 162
Religious holidays, 31, 65
Repetto, Nicolás, 155, 157
Riegner group, 127
Riegner, Loni, 28, 30
Rivadavia, Bernardino, 24
Robberies, 36
Roffo, Angel, 85
Rogalsky, Olga, 20
Roosevelt, Eleanor, 102
Roosevelt, Franklin, 102
Rosa, Juan Manuel de, 179
Rosenberg, Ethel, 199
Rosenberg, Julius, 199
Rosenberg, Taiba Pasternak de, 115
Rouco Buela, Juana, 151
Rovner, Ana, 68–69, 126, 240, 241, 244
Ruetter, Mina, 197, 198
Rural areas: border spaces and, 34–36; cooperatives and, 17–18, 19, 154, 238; cuisine in, 30–34; cultural activities and, 27–30; education and, 21–27; isolation in, 17; migration from, 14, 40; population statistics on, 250; state formation and, 37–40; study of, 13; work and settlement in, 15–21
Sabah, Señora, 21
Sacerdote de Lustig, Eugenia, 85–86, 91, 103, 240
Sajón, Regina, 60, 90
Saleswoman of Harrods, The (film), 96
Salón, Regina Mendes de, 19, 25, 35
Salón, Sara, 35–36
Salzman, Ana, 77, 82
Sánchez Sorondo, Matías, 176
Sánchez Viamonte, Carlos, 193
Sarfatti, Margherita, 293 n. 4
Sarmiento, Domingo Faustino: on criollos, 26; lectures on, 38, 180; on power of education, 76; on secular school system, 24, 40, 76, 242; on women's roles, 6
Saslavsky, Delila, 184, 185, 186, 192
Satanowsky, Paulina, 88–89, 91
Satanowsky, Sara, 88–89, 90, 91, 240
Scalabrini Ortiz, Raúl, 80
Schalom, Myrtha, 112, 116
Scheiner, Rosa, 161–63, 170, 181, 185, 192, 241
Schiffre, 134
Schliapnik, Clara: as antifascist, 91, 178; education and, 23, 28, 30, 61; Junta de la Victoria and, 186; on male privilege, 241; as physician, 20–21; repression of, 197–98; women's emancipation and, 241; Zionism and, 231–34
Schlichter, Hedwig, 100–101, 103, 240
Schlieper, Ana Rosa, 185, 220
Schnitman, Sara, 91, 176
Schvartz, Dora, 18, 25
Segal, Lazar, 96
Segal, Sara, 179, 182
Segregation, 47–48, 160, 245
Seminario de Maestros Hebreos Iosef Draznin, 29, 34
Sensual other, 2, 11, 69, 92, 104, 105, 106, 123–24, 175, 239

Sephardi Hour (radio program), 63
Sephardim, 2; Ashkenazim and, 67–68, 142, 245; criollos and, 35; culture preserved by, 31; education and, 77; marginalization of, 239; marriage customs of, 141–42; Zionism and, 5, 67–68, 216–20, 234, 237, 245
Settlement: rural, 15–21; urban, 43–48. *See also* Immigration
Sexuality: abuse and, 142–47; adultery and, 137–38; Argentine Jewish women and, 123–47; borders and, 147; Jewish, and Catholics, 11; Jewish-gentile, 138–40; lack of teaching on, 127; marriage and, 135; studies of, 2; transgression and, 135
Ship sisters, 64
Sieff, Rebecca, 229
Simsolo, Victoria, 44, 90–91
Singerman, Berta, 62, 95–98, 104, 183, 187, 191, 197, 244
Singerman, Paulina, 187, 197
social Catholicism, 195
Socialism, Socialists: Acción Argentina and, 183; antifascism and, 177; Communism and, 162–63; cooperatives and, 17–18; education and, 60, 61, 95, 152–53; equality and, 161; inclusion and, 158; Jewish women and, 154–63, 246; Peronism and, 197; protection of, 185; publications of, 18, 27; repression and, 173–75, 197; spread of, 246; transnational, 246; unions and, 166–71, 196; women's emancipation and, 241; women's roles and, 164
Socialist Party, 154, 162, 246
Socialist Worker Party, 163
Social justice, 178
Sociedad de Beneficencia, 207–9, 215, 223
Sociedad de Damas Israelitas de Beneficencia, 57, 126, 206, 208, 209, 237; Perón and, 223–24
Sociedad de Protección a los Inmigrantes Israelitas, 126
Sociedad de Socorro Femenina, 207
Sociedad de Socorros de Damas Israelitas, 57
Sociedad Hebraica Argentina, 62, 63, 100
Sociedad Israelita de Protección a Ninas y Mujeres "Ezras Noschim." *See* Ezras Noschim
Sociedad Kadima, 28
Sociedad Pro-Colonización Israelita en Birobidjan, 165
Socorro Rojo Internacional, 192
Solari, Juan Antonio, 78
Soprotimis (Sociedad de Protección a los Inmigrantes Israelitas), 126
Sosa Molina, José Humberto, 190
Soussia, Maestra, 21
Spalding, Hobart, 88
Spanish Civil War (1936–39), 135, 171, 181–83
Spanish language, 16, 26–27, 217
Special Section, 165–66, 168, 191
Stanislavsky, Konstantin, 92, 101
State formation, 5; Jewish women in, 6, 10, 41, 70, 203, 241–43; rural areas and, 37–40
Stereotyping, 68
Stolek, Rubén Enrique, 96
Storni, Alfonsina, 96
Sujoy, Enrique, 90–91
Syrian Jews, 15
Szechter, Pela, 55

Tawil de Ini, Chola, 64, 219
Teaching profession, 74–81; Jewish schools and, 83–84; nationalism and, 26; regulation of, 77
Teatro del Pueblo, 99, 181
Teatro Popular Israelita Argentino (Idische Folks Theater; IFT), 92–93, 99, 166, 181, 182, 198, 200

Templo Libertad, 64, 66
Templo Raquel, El, 44
Textile industry, 51–52, 196
Tomaso, Antonio de, 155
Torre, Jorge de la, 78
Tragic Week, 174–75, 239
Transnationalism, 245–48; Ashkenazim and, 148; borders and, 5; influence of, 1; Jewish women and, 10, 73, 148, 203, 225, 234, 236, 243–44
Trespassing, 67
Turjanski, Miriam, 127
Turkish Jews, 15, 24, 44

Unión Argentina de Mujeres (UAM), 185
Unión Civica Radical (UCR), 149
Unión Democrática, 191
Unión de Mujeres Argentinas (UMA), 201
Unión Obrera Textil (UOT), 168, 196
Unions and labor, 53–54, 156, 166–70
Uriburu, José Félix, 78, 175

Valle Inclan, Ramón del, 96
Vanguardia, La (periodical), 27
Varsovia society, 45, 106, 112, 115–16, 119–20, 122
Vasconcelos, José, 96
Vigilante attacks, 68, 173–74
Villa Devoto prison, 194
Voluntarism, 6, 26, 227, 234, 241–42

Wainstein, Rosa, 173
Wajovsky, Catalina, 143
Wajovsky, Cecilia, 143
Wald, Pinie, 173
Warshaver, Serafina, 180, 201
Wasserman, Perla, 182, 190, 247
Weil, Anny, 216–17
Weinschelbaum, Rosa, 76, 77, 79–80, 91, 104, 166–67, 179, 186, 188, 196, 242, 244
Weintraub, Paulina, 20, 36
Wernecke, Rosa, 79
Whiteness and Jews, 7, 36, 41, 43, 71
White slavery, 105, 107–8, 110–11, 121, 139. *See also* Prostitution
Wind, Lisbeth, 219, 229, 244
Winocur, Perlina, 88–89, 91
Witemberg, Anita, 27–28
WIZO (Women's International Zionist Organization), 207–8, 219, 220, 228
Wladimersky, Rosa, 193
Women, Argentine Jewish: borders and, 4–5, 10, 42, 62–64, 147; communal honor and, 124–27; criollos and, 23, 26–27, 34–36, 39, 41; cultural activities of, 27–31; identity and, 3, 6, 36, 69–70, 74; leftist movements and, 5, 80, 147, 148–71; nationalism and, 7, 12, 24, 37–40, 202–4, 221–22; as political prisoners, 191–95; roles of, 16, 19, 62; as sensual other, 2, 11, 69, 92, 104, 105, 106, 123–24, 175, 239; sexuality and, 123–47; state formation and, 6, 10, 41, 70, 241–43; studies of, 1–2, 3; transnationalism and, 1, 10, 73, 148, 236
Women's International Zionist Organization (WIZO), 207–8, 219, 220, 228
Work: exploitation of women, 52–53; labor statistics on, 55; marginalization and, 48–55, 56; Peronism and, 196; as point of connection, 73, 100; rural settlement and, 15–21; workforce statistics on, 253–54, 255. *See also* Professions; Unions and labor
World Zionist Organization, 207

Xenophobia, 36

Yadid, Farida, 45, 49, 50, 60, 64, 125, 135
Yadid, Matilde, 132–33
Yarcho, Dr., 20

Yiddish language, 23, 27, 55, 94, 150, 165, 189, 218, 239
Yiddish theater, 92–95

Zatzkin, Margarita, 88
Zavalla, Carlos María, 190
Zionism: acceptance of, 240; alternatives to, 202–4; boundaries and, 12; communal borders and, 67; Communism and, 165, 199; Hebrew language and, 198; liberty and, 222; margins and, 204; opposition to, 198; OSFA and, 211; Palestinians and, 227; Peronism and, 196, 225–26, 243, 247; philanthropy and, 206–35; progressive Jews and, 200–201, 238; recruitment and, 216–20, 237–38; schools and, 61, 83–84; Sephardi women and, 5, 67–68, 216–20, 234, 237, 245; transnational, 243; women's emancipation and, 241; women's groups and, 206–8; women's role and, 5, 12, 30, 60, 84, 149, 161, 228–31; world, 244; Yiddish language and, 198
Ziperovich, Rosa Weinschelbaum de, 76, 77, 79–80, 91, 104, 166–67, 179, 186, 188, 196, 242, 244
Zwi Migdal, 45, 106, 112, 115–16, 119–20, 122

Sandra McGee Deutsch is a professor of history
at the University of Texas, El Paso.

Library of Congress Cataloging-in-Publication Data
Deutsch, Sandra McGee
Crossing borders, claiming a nation:
a history of Argentine Jewish women, 1880–1955 /
Sandra McGee Deutsch.
p. cm.
Includes bibliographical references and index.
ISBN 978-0-8223-4657-9 (cloth : alk. paper)
ISBN 978-0-8223-4649-4 (pbk. : alk. paper)
1. Jewish women—Argentina—History—19th century.
2. Jewish women—Argentina—History—20th century.
I. Title.
F3021.J5D48 2010 920.72'0982—dc22
2009048189